New Feminisms in South Asia

T0298756

This book is a study of the resurgence and re-imagination of new feminist discourse on gender and sexuality in South Asia as told through its cinematic, literary, and social media narratives. It brings incisive and expert analyses of emerging disruptive articulations that represent an unprecedented surge of feminist response to the culture of sexual violence in South Asia. Here, scholars across disciplines and international borders chronicle the expressions of a disruptive feminist solidarity in contemporary South Asia. They offer critical investigations of these newly complicated discourses across narrative forms—social media activism against the culture of sexual violence, journalistic and cinematic articulations on queer rights, and feminist literary and film activism against casteism, communalism, and misogyny in Afghanistan, Bangladesh, India, Kashmir, Nepal, Pakistan, Sri Lanka and within the South Asian diaspora.

Sonora Jha is Professor of Journalism and Media Studies at Seattle University, USA.

Alka Kurian is a Senior Lecturer at the University of Washington Bothell, USA.

Routledge Research in Cultural and Media Studies

For a full list of titles in this series, please visit www.routledge.com.

New Feminisms in South Asia

Disrupting the Discourse Through
Social Media, Film, and Literature

Edited by Sonora Jha and Alka Kurian

Routledge
Taylor & Francis Group

LONDON AND NEW YORK

First published 2018
by Routledge

2 Park Square, Milton Park, Abingdon, Oxfordshire OX14 4RN
52 Vanderbilt Avenue, New York, NY 10017

Routledge is an imprint of the Taylor & Francis Group, an informa business

First issued in paperback 2019

Library of Congress Cataloging in Publication Data
CIP data has been applied for.

ISBN: 978-1-138-66893-5 (hbk)
ISBN: 978-0-367-87841-2 (pbk)

Typeset in Sabon
by codeMantra

Contents

List of Contributors

Bidisha Biswas is Professor of Political Science at Western Washington University. She previously served as a policy adviser on South Asia to the United States Department of State. Bidisha has researched, spoken, and published on diaspora and immigration related issues. In 2014, she published a co-authored book, entitled *Indian Immigrant Women and Work: The American Experience.*

Elora Halim Chowdhury is Associate Professor and Chair of the Women's & Gender Studies Department at the University of Massachusetts Boston. Her teaching and research interests include transnational feminisms, human rights film, and gender violence in South Asia. She is the author of *Transnationalism Reversed: Women Organizing Against Gendered Violence in Bangladesh* (SUNY Press, 2011) and *Dissident Friendships: Feminism, Imperialism & Transnational Solidarity* (University of Illinois Press, 2016).

Rahul K. Gairola is Assistant Professor of English and Comparative Literature in the Department of Humanities & Social Sciences (HSS) at the Indian Institute of Technology Roorkee. He is the author of *Homelandings: Postcolonial Diasporas and Transatlantic Belonging (London and New York: Rowman & Littlefield International, September 2016)* and co-editor (with Amritjit Singh and Nalini Iyer) of *Revisiting India's Partition: New Essays on Memory, Culture, & Politics (New Delhi: Orient Blackswan/ Washington, D.C.: Lexington Books, June 2016).* He is currently working on two contracted book projects: the first critically re-thinks shifting meanings of "home" in digital identities and cultures of 21st-century India and its diasporas, while the second examines gender and home economics in recalibrated kinship relations of migrants from rural regions of Garhwal to urban metropoles in northern India.

Amrita Ghosh has a Ph.D. in postcolonial studies, focusing on Partition Literature. She has been a lecturer at Seton Hall University, New Jersey and has just started working as a postdoctoral researcher at Linnaeus University, Sweden, where she works on literature from a conflict zone, in the context of Kashmir.

Nalini Iyer is Professor of English at Seattle University where she teaches postcolonial literatures. Her publications include the following: *Other Tongues: Rethinking the Language Debates in India* (co-edited with Bonnie Zare, Rodopi 2009); *Roots and Reflections: South Asians in the Pacific Northwest* (co-authored with Amy Bhatt, University of Washington Press 2013); and *Revisiting India's Partition: New Essays in Memory, Culture, and Politics* (co-edited with Amritjit Singh and Rahul K. Gairola, Lexington 2016).

Sonora Jha is Professor of Journalism in the Department of Communication and Media at Seattle University. She is the author of the novel Foreign (Random House India, 2013) and a former journalist with The Times of India. Her research is on the intersections of the press, politics and the Internet.

Shahnaz Khan is the author of *Muslim Women: Crafting a North American Identity,* and *Zina, Transnational feminism and the moral regulation of Pakistani Women.* She has published extensively on gender, Islam, Hindi cinema, and transgender issues in Pakistan.

Alka Kurian is a Senior Lecturer at the School of Interdisciplinary Arts, University of Washington Bothell, where she is Faculty Coordinator of the major in "Culture, Literature and the Arts," and is an Affiliate at the South Asia Center, University of Washington Seattle. She is the author of *Narrative of Gendered Dissent: South Asian Cinemas* and is a former co-editor of the peer-reviewed journal Studies in South Asian Film and Media. She is the board president of Tasveer: A South Asian film and art non-profit.

Padmini Ray Murray heads the digital humanities programme at the Srishti Institute of Art, Design and Technology, Bangalore. Her research interests and publications encompass comics and games studies, feminism and feminist protest, book history and publishing studies, as well as the role of cultural specificity in the digital world.

Shoba Sharad Rajgopal is Professor in Asian Feminist Studies, an area she has developed over her tenure at Westfield State University in Massachusetts, where she teaches courses on gender, race, and representation. Her media experience incorporates several years as a broadcast journalist for the Indian TV networks in Bombay, India that include news reports for CNN International.

Rajini Srikanth is Professor of English at the University of Massachusetts Boston. Her publications include the award-winning book *The World Next Door: South Asian American Literature and the Idea of America* (2004), *Constructing the Enemy: Empathy/ Antipathy in US Literature and Law* (2012), and the co-edited *Cambridge History of Asian American Literature* (2015). She teaches courses on and publishes in the areas of literature and human rights, literature and the political imagination, transnationalism and US ethnic studies, South Africa, and Asian American literature.

Shreerekha Pillai Subramanian is Associate Professor of Humanities and Chair of Department of Liberal Arts at University of Houston-Clear Lake. She published her monograph, *Women Writing Violence: The Novel and Radical Feminist Imaginaries* (Sage 2013); her chapters and articles focus on postcolonial literary and film studies. At present, she is working on her next book on carceral imaginaries.

Bonnie Zare is an Associate Professor of Women's and Gender Studies at Virginia Tech. Her research focuses on discourses of identity, feminism and activism in contemporary India and in South Asian women's fiction. Zare's articles have appeared in *Women's Studies International Forum, International Journal of Cultural Studies* and the *Journal of Commonwealth Literature* among others. She is the founder of the Keep Girls in School Project which has been supporting low-income girls in Telangana and Andhra Pradesh since 2008.

Introduction

Alka Kurian and Sonora Jha

This book examines the resurgence and re-imagination of feminist discourse on gender and sexuality in South Asia as expressed through its theoretical, cinematic, literary, and social media narratives. It brings incisive and expert analyses of emerging disruptive articulations that represent an unprecedented surge of feminist response to the culture of sexual violence in South Asia. The overwhelming and continuing protests in the wake of the 2012 gang rape and murder of a young Delhi student and the subsequent BBC film "India's Daughter" have brought conversations on sexuality and freedom in India within the global public sphere. This incident provided a spark to already brimming emotions of profound discontent with the misogynistic Indian culture and politicized the consciousness of men and women who poured into the streets of India speaking rights-bearing language. It disrupted and redirected traditional discourses on gender and normalized conversations on previously taboo subjects of sexuality, and not just sexual violence, across class, caste, regional, and national boundaries. Some of these discontents have found representations in South Asian social media, film, and literature in recent years.

The 2012 incident also generated reflections and conversations in other South Asian countries all of which, despite their differences, share the culture of misogyny and sexual violence. As much as the eight nation-sates of South Asia—Afghanistan, Bangladesh, Bhutan, India, the Maldives, Nepal, Pakistan, and Sri Lanka—share common cultural and political legacies, marred by the specificities of their histories and conflicts, they continue to remain distinct from each other. The internecine conflicts between India and Pakistan, the Indian imperialistic interjection into the Bangladesh war of secession or into the Sri Lankan ethnic strife, its imposition of the 2015 food embargo on Nepal, and it's banning of Pakistani artists from working in Indian cultural industries are some of the ways that disrupt the articulations of the South Asian region as a unit. However, notwithstanding these processes of separation and alienation, what brings these nations together are the intersecting lives and subjectivities of South Asian women that have put a unifying perspective on the self-inflicted cracks within the region's geographies and ideologies, and offers possibilities of imaging how these nation-states do coalesce together (Srila Roy 2012) in ways that are both regressive as well as progressive.

Examples range from the historical mobilization of middle-class colonial femininities in the bourgeois masculinist conception of national difference from the Western empire during anti-colonial movements for national self-determination; women's participation in the anti-colonial movements, the widespread sexual assault on women's bodies during periods of nation-formation, the use of women's heteronormativized identities as yardsticks for qualifying postcolonial cultural difference, the regressive policing and control of women's bodies and sexualities at the hands of regressive patriarchy in the wake of the region's neo-liberalzation, the growing feminist assertion for gender equality and women's rights in response to nationalism, neoliberalism, and religious fundamentalism, and its dismissal by right-wing bourgeois patriarchy as unsettling expressions of cultural inauthencity, elitism, or Western intrusion. Located within these wider commonalities structured around feminine subject positions in the region are other smaller, geo-specific intersections of feminist articulations that were born in response to a variety of structures of power. The 2012 incident was not the first time that rape became the focus of feminist activism in South Asia. However, it took a while for the women's movements in the region to place sexual violence at the forefront of their agenda. While the women's movements in India and Bangladesh arose in response to "nationalism to neo-liberalism," in Sri Lanka and Nepal they stemmed from ethnic conflicts in the countries (Roy 2012: 7), and in Pakistan, Afghanistan, and increasingly India, they grew against the rise of religious fundamentalism.

A useful way to understand the successes and challenges of feminist activism in South Asia against the culture of misogyny and sexual violence would be by looking at the development of women's movements in the region. The first wave of the Indian women's movement is understood to have begun during the nineteenth-century social reform movement with women's organizations battling against both patriarchy and colonialism. The second wave of women's political activism in the post-colonial India of 1950s and 1960s took on a radically different form and method of mobilizing and embodied class and anti-caste struggles. These included tribal landless laborers' movement against feudal oppression, rallies against price rise, black marketeering and corruption, formation of trade unions for women working in the informal sector, and agitation for land by landless peasants. It was in fact the third wave of the Indian women's movement of the late 1970s that was self-consciously feminist at its core. Deliberately sidestepping party affiliation and hierarchies, this "autonomous" women's movement led agitations against dowry oppression and rape (of, for example, Rameeza Bee 1978; Mathura 1980; Suman Rani 1988). However, the anti-rape campaign championed by the IWM was far too sporadic and episodic for it to be transformed into a genuine civil rights issue (Geetha 2016). Further, the gaps and fissures exposed within the IWM in the 1990s nation-wide post-Mandal agitations, shed light on the limitations of the movement owing to its blindness to the sexual politics of caste (Geetha 2017). The 1990s NGO-ization and careerism of the autonomous women's organizations owing to sudden influx of donor funding, along with people's inexplicable detachment from political and civic life, undermined a genuine feminist movement in India after it peaked in 1970s, 1980s, and early 1990s. Further, the arrival of governance feminism, i.e. the incorporation of feminist knowledge within state led to a greater policing and monitoring of citizens, especially of women, viewed by the regressive, neo-liberal state as vulnerable and passive victims. (Kapur 2014; Iyer 2015). Critics wonder whether this ideological chaos and transformation that could potentially break up the IWM:

> ...into separate groups with their own organizational, funder-driven agendas ... [and] our tendency to turn to the law [that invariably reinforces gendered status quo] to deal with every new instance of devaluation and oppression of women in the realm of 'the body' and sexuality is precisely an indication of the lack of a 'strong movement' in this area.
>
> (Menon 2004: 221, 222)

Incapacitated, therefore, by a sexist legal system on the one hand, and by a fragmented and weakened IWM that offered an ambiguous and unsatisfactory direction on everyday street sexual harassment on the other, leadership on this issue came from young, middle-class, non-mainstream cyberfeminists in India who have been mobilizing in ways that signal a departure both in terms of content and method of resistance.

The first wave of the Bangladeshi women's movement (BWM) can be traced back to the movements for self-determination against Britain and then against Pakistan. BWM has fought against gender-based violence and for the rights of women in the economic, political, and legal arenas. Gender relations in the country have suffered owing to the history of collusion between Islam and the country's leadership both under the 1970s and 1980s dictatorships and during the country's democratic phase. However, anti-women and development politics of the 1980s and 1990s Islamist parties provided a unique opportunity for women's organizations and developmental NGOs to mobilize together around "issue-based coalitions and solidarity movements" (Nazneen and Sultan 2012) during the second wave of the BWM. The concerns related to the NGO-ization of the feminist movement in India are also reflected in the rest of South Asia. Critics in Bangladesh deplore the packaging of women's collective concerns into discrete developmental projects that has undermined the autonomous nature of the feminist movement in the country. However, alienating the younger generation feminists who have a "professionalized/monetary approach" to feminist work, would run the risk of undermining the development of a genuine, "solidarity-based" intergenerational movement in Bangladesh that is essential to tackle the challenge to women's rights from "conservative religious political groups" (Nazneen and Sultan 2012: 88).

The Pakistani Women's Movement (PWM) of the 1980s and 1990s is framed by its opposition to military dictatorship, Western imperialism, and religion, or, in other words, in terms of its opposition to "men, money, mullahs and the military" (Zia 2009). The first wave of the PWM concerned itself with national issues such as the military dictatorship whose mission to Islamize the nation led to severe curtailment of women's rights. It focused mostly on campaigning against legal and policy-level challenges. From 1990s onwards, the movement took two specific issues that is, of political representation and gender-based violence (Shaheed 2010: 89). This second wave of the PWM was significantly weakened by misogynistic religious laws, NGO-ization of the women's movement, and co-option of feminism by the Pakistani state and political parties (see my discussion of governance feminism above). The third wave of the PWM can be seen through the rise of an Islamic feminism in Pakistan that is embedded in the politics of peace and the empowerment of women within Islam. It is important to note that this feminism is not a "post-9/11 development" but has resulted from the 1980s' secular feminism incorporating the Islamic feminist arguments without which the former ran the risk of alienating mainstream Pakistani society (Zia 2009).

The Pre-1990s Nepal Women's Movement focused on bringing democracy in the country. The 2000s women's organizations demanded women's economic, legal, and political rights (Tamang 68). In the post-2006 democratic movement, the Maoists party fought for an alternative to the stereotype of Nepali women as helpless and passive victims through eradicating gender inequality, overthrowing feudal Brahminical patriarchy, giving girls equal rights to property, declaring Nepal a secular state, and holding state-sponsored Hindu casteist feudalism responsible for women's oppression. Although women's rights in Nepal have undergone considerable improvement over the past few years, violence against women and impunity for perpetrators continues. Siera Tamang traces this to the society and cultural structures in Nepal that enable sexual violence and impunity and where "cultural coding" of sexual violence is related to notions of honor, purity and chastity (55). While the donor-funded women's NGOs represent a powerful force on women's rights in Nepal, they have come under attack for being part of middle-class mainstream women's movement and for their style of operation that had "depoliticized gender inequality" (Pudasaini 257).

The Sri Lankan Women's Movement (SWM) over the course of the three-decade civil war has focused is energies to seek political resolutions to end the conflict. It used maternal identity to counter state oppression, state-led military occupation, prevent killings and disappearance of male family members during, seek safe environment to raise their sons, lead normal lives with husbands, and uphold traditional family values. In the present-day Sri Lanka however, there are no autonomous feminist movements and one does not hear of feminist peace activists either. Malathi de Alwis (2009) relates this to feminist being exhausted by mobilizing against a plethora of issues: sexual violence, domestic abuse, and militarism. In addition, what's undermined the radical spirit of SWM is its institutionalization and professionalization due to a massive influx of international humanitarian and development aid into the country. While it has brought stability to feminist organizing, it has also diluted feminists' priorities that are more to do with the financial survival of their organizations, meeting project deadlines than feminist activism, and creation of nine-to-five careerist feminists with a shallow feminist perspective (De Alwis 2009)

The new concept and theorization that is holding this book together is an examination of an "expansionist and exploratory" phase of South Asian feminism. While the Delhi rape galvanized almost all of India, it did not happen in a vacuum, and was merely a flashpoint—albeit an important one—in an already burgeoning culture of feminist dissent. The process of neo-liberalization of the country initiated the resurgence of a regressive brand of right wing patriarchal backlash, which has time and again been challenged by an emerging new feminist consciousness in India. The 2009 "Pink Chaddi" Facebook campaign against women's moral policing in India, the publication of Phadke, Khan and Ranade's 2011 ground-breaking book *Why Loiter* on the construction in the country of gendered and classed "unbelongers," and the 2011 "SlutWalk" inspired by the original phenomenon launched in Toronto in the same year, are examples of this defiance against the deeply entrenched sexist culture of discrimination and abuse, as expressed in scholarship, cultural production, social media, and on the streets. While retuning her National Award as a measure of protest against religious intolerance in contemporary India, Arundhati Roy recently pointed out that "... we had plenty of advance notice of what lay in store for us—so I cannot claim to be shocked by what has happened after this government was enthusiastically voted into office with an overwhelming majority" (2015). We regard the Delhi rape incident and the subsequent protests as not shocking at all but a build-up of this long-simmering malcontentment.

Our book focuses on a new emerging theory of feminist discourse in South Asia, one that makes an unprecedented call for a departure from received notions of the victim-blaming rape culture or paternalistic solution from the nation state. During the 2012 protests, women specifically asserted the right to their bodies, freedom without condition, and a wholesale rejection of older discourses of women's protection. Kavita Krishnan's (Secretary of the All India Progressive Women's Association) rallying call, "in the name of our protection, don't take away our freedom," became central to and galvanized the 2012 movement further.

This was, we claim, transformative and signaled a clear departure from earlier movements against sexual violence. It was different for being located outside the "frameworks of harm and injury," for refuting the traditional equating of women with victimhood, and for not exclusively seeking legal reform or protection. The crises since the 1970s and 80s within global capitalism that was responsible for causing neoliberalization of India's economy, forever transformed the country's fragile social order. On the one had it impoverished large sections of the population as a result of economic deregulation, austerity, budget cuts, and transference of land from the poor to the rich, on the other, it also led to an unprecedented growth of middle class job opportunities. While this enabled a large number of women to come into the public/professional sphere, it elicited a massive backlash from the traditional feudal and social order that continued to have regressive and outmoded expectations of gender roles that women find unacceptable. Material and financial independence has changed women's expectations from life in terms of education, careers, marriage, and sexuality, the latter being in many cases delinked from reproduction. Impatient with the anachronistic reality of self-discipline and asexuality, and doing away with the mutually exclusive categories of sexual safety and sexual freedom, the younger generation of Indian feminists assert their right for sexual freedom without condition.

Powerful online feminist conversations on the culture of sexism are taking place in other South Asian countries too. "Girls at Dhabas" is one of the most popular online feminist movements in Pakistan today where women take their individual or group pictures at dhabas (roadside cafes) and post them online with the hashtag #girlrsatdhabas. Launched in 2005 by Sadia Khatri, this web-based campaign constitutes an oppositional discourse on women's forced domestication in Pakistan. It encourages them to reclaim public spaces because, as Khatri says, their "participation in, and access to, public spaces like parks, streets, and rickshaws is crucial to feminism's central concerns, and to any woman's sanity in [cities like] Karachi and Lahore" (website). With women from outside Pakistan - India, Bangladesh and the diaspora - posting their images at dhabas, discussing gender-related issues, and collaborating with other feminists across borders, this campaign has turned truly transnational. Rather than only share experiences of violence and discrimination, this Pakistani campaign offers women opportunities of imagining themselves in liberating postures of occupying public spaces. In addition, its consciousness-raising modality also helps expand their activities by sharing resources, recommending books, and reading feminist manifestoes of other similar campaigns, including *Why Loiter* from whom members borrow the discursive language of loitering the streets of Pakistani cities as they undertake their journey in search of dhabas.

Some of the younger urban middle-class women in Bangladesh feel that the mainstream women's movement in the country is out of touch with issues and debates on street harassment, something that is of urgent concern to the young. Since the 1990s, college and university students took the lead in organizing anti-sexual harassment campaigns, completely independently of the mainstream women's organizations. One of the possible reasons for the alienation between the two camps is that mainstream feminists have:

> ...failed to capitalize on the new modes and forms of mobilizing ... [such as] ...photo exhibitions, film shows, cartoon competitions focusing on corruption ... [and] the Internet, particularly media such as Facebook, and the mobile phone [and sites and blogs that have] become key ways of transmitting messages ad organizing young people, and was effectively used during the recent anti-sexual harassment movement by students at one of the public universities.
>
> (Nazneen and Sultan 2012: 101)

The 2012 Facebook-led Occupy Baluwatar (OB) movement in Nepal sought to end the culture of violence against women and to challenge the related political and legal impunity on this. As part of Nepal's transition period and the Nepal Women's Movement, OB departed from the other forms of organizing using "New faces, new strategies, new rhetoric ... [and] mobilizing "non-political, inexperienced, urban-based middle class young protesters" (Pudasaini 2016: 256). The movement had no leaders to manipulate decision-making process, was detached from donors and hence was seen as pure with "no strings attached," and collaborated with non-mainstream feminist organizations that had played an important role during the transitional period at the end of the People's Movement in 2006.

The themes that animate our book draw on the work of feminist postcolonial theorists, and provide an examination of the splintering of the monolithized figure of the third world woman, whose double colonization tends to get overlooked by dominant postcolonial preoccupations with the politics of race and nation. Informed by Mohanty's suspicion of the "Third World Woman" as an ahistorical, singular, and universalized monolith, this book examines writers, filmmakers, and social media activists' rejection of essentialist identities in favor of postnational hybridity, pluralism, and intersectionality whereby gendered identify formation is hinged simultaneously on differences of class, sexuality, religion, nation, and ideology. All of the chapters in our book challenge women's representation as metonymy for national culture, and portray instead, women's rebellion against their oppression and heteronormative nationalist commodification. But what makes them interestingly distinct is that they do not do so in a manner that allows for any 'aggregation' across the various texts in this book to constitute a singular subaltern woman, a theme that has not been adequately explored in the current literature. This fracturing of the monolithic third world subject is important not merely as a corrective to Western gazes, but for a repositioning of feminist politics within the third world itself. In our book, we use the perspective of postcolonial theory given that it is most valuable when it enables a self-reflexive response to the present conjuncture. In this regard, while acknowledging the significance of the 2012 unprecedented and highly publicized mass protests and debates globally, our book also looks at the tension embraced by a new feminist politics that questions that hierarchy of empathy reserved for the brutalized women from minority communities.

The anthology here takes a unique and important cultural studies perspective to unravel complex interlinked strands of inquiry where social movements and their representations on sexual violence are studied through the lenses of colonialism, nationalism, citizenship, globalization, transnationalism, neo-liberalism, patriarchy, feminism, queer studies, and the human rights discourse. It examines the embedded nature of sexual violence against gendered and queer bodies in South Asia's heteropatriarchal colonial and neo-colonial legacies. The book offers an analysis of the lived reality of globalization in the day-to-day modernity of the region's dual economy. It looks into the insidious structuring of multiple heteronormativities across class, caste, sectarian, and regional divides by neo-liberal right wing nationalist states and also the human rights and feminist discourse within a transnational context. Central to this study is the ways in which social media—unfettered, immediate, current, and authentic—helps mobilize against forces of capitalist, statist, militaristic, and patriarchal misogyny. Also highlighted is the power of representational discourse (in film and literature) in promoting dissent against systemic oppression and bringing about social change.

We borrow Stuart Hall's idea of the "conjectural" to underline the possibilities of transformation through social action and cultural and political change. These transformations are put into place within this particularly significant and historic moment marked by neo-liberal right wing political ascendency, regressive state policies on gender and sexuality, and limitations on freedom of expression, where notions of "authentic" and "pure" identities are mobilized to silence, make invisible, and marginalize voices that do not fit heteronormative definitions of gender and sexuality. In this manner, we regard the anti-rape protests, the heavy-handed state response, and its censoring of public, creative, and mediatized criticism of the culture of sexual violence as indicative of the inevitable social unrest that precedes social, political, and cultural change, intent on unstitching hidden structures of heteronormative power and oppression. Hall's delineation of cultural theory as "the will to truth and … as a set of contested, localized, conjunctural knowledges, which have to be debated in a dialogical way" (Hall 1992: 286), is particularly pertinent here.

Understanding film, literature and social media narratives as socio-cultural products and locating them within their political, ideological, and historical contexts, this book investigates the ways in which these creative and dialogical articulations help unravel and decenter the uncritical and hegemonic grand narratives on South Asian gender and sexuality. It fractures normative approaches to identity formation and offers an intervention against universal, fixed, simple, predictable, and absolutist notions of gender and sexuality in South Asia. It underlines the politics of difference and introspection by centering contingent over ahistorical, universal, or pure identities and gives primacy to voices—queer, caste, raced, and sexual—that had previously been sidestepped. This book therefore examines the significance of the shifting and contingent identity formation of people living in a hybridized and multicultural/religious/ethnic South Asia undergoing socio-economic, cultural, and political transformations.

In this book, scholars across disciplines and international borders study these representations to chronicle the expressions of a disruptive feminist solidarity in contemporary South Asia. They offer critical investigations of these newly complicated discourses across narrative forms—social media activism against the culture of sexual violence, journalistic and cinematic articulations on queer rights, and feminist literary and film activism against casteism, communalism, and misogyny in Afghanistan, Bangladesh, India, Kashmir, Nepal, Pakistan, Sri Lanka and within the South Asian diaspora.

In the theoretical section of the book, Alka Kurian makes the claim that the 2012 anti-rape movement constitutes a critical breakthrough in intersectional feminist activism in India, which has the potential to lay the groundwork for a fourth wave of feminism in the country. First, its focus on everyday street sexual harassment was articulated by rights-bearing young, urban women seeking their fundamental rights to the city, to the freedom of movement, to their bodies, and to pleasure (and not just civil rights). Second, Kurian claims that this feminist discourse was connected to a global vocabulary of rights facilitated, to a large extent, by means of the Internet; and third, the anti-rape movement resonated with resistance movements against other forms of marginalization as these new rights vocabularies of the feminist movement challenged not only the culture of sexism but also classism, casteism, and communalism. Making this link offers a chance of really pushing forward a different agenda that replaces the developmental state with a progressive alliance. Bidisha Biswas's paper provides a critique of third-wave feminism in India—situating the Jyoti Singh protests within the history of Indian feminism, in particular the landmark Mathura rape case of the 1970s that set the stage for public activism leading to policy change. Biswas points out the contradictions within that history and notes the elitist slant to the 2012–2013 protests. She discusses India's experiences with first, second, and third waves of feminism and provides, in particular, a critique of the individualistic focus of third-wave feminism.

Social Media

In her paper that highlights the need for archiving Indian feminist activism on social media, Padmini Ray Murray discusses how this would be one significant way for different communities to own their ontological self-determination, which in turn could be seen as a decolonizing gesture of resistance as well as one which might allow intersectional possibilities that contemporary Indian feminism currently struggles to address. In her chapter on Two Faces of Afghan Women: Oppressed and Exotic, Shahnaz Khan takes issue with the orientalized representations in mainstream Western news magazines of Third World women and juxtaposes their resultant erasure with an elucidation of a powerful homegrown feminist movement in Afghanistan.[1] Expanding on Padmini Ray Murray's discussion of possibilities for intersectionality is Rahul Gairola, who uses the notion of "the fourth screen" formulated by Rajinder Dudrah et al. (2013: 2) to examine how queer and feminist identities are reconfigured on the portable Fourth Screen (the first three screens being the silver screen, television screen, and the computer screen). Gairola does this through a study of the Facebook page of India's oldest gay periodical, Bombay Dost, and its power in facilitating, online, imagined communities of queers that are yet outlawed by the governing statute. Gairola says, "the Fourth Screen in South Asia enables the movement of queer visibility. Here, that visibility and its further electronic disseminations and use of hyperlinks, screen shots, and other digital, multimedia tools re-calibrate witness, testimony, and truth."

Such a recalibration of intersectional feminist expression is also heralded in the case of the WhyLoiter hashtag campaign, which, as Sonora Jha suggests in her paper, exemplifies how cyberfeminist participation reorients the feminist agenda from law and policy change to now simply posit as political action the foregrounding of pleasure in public space as a manner of protest. #Whyloiter navigates, even re-appropriates from traditional media narratives, a protest repertoire in real life (on the streets), and its representation in mediated spaces (on social media). It is precisely this use of social media that troubles previous feminist modalities, offering unprecedented possibilities of articulating unfiltered and uncensored discourse outside of permissible and official mainstream of official language and charting new territory.

Film

In contemporary South Asian cinema, we are seeing a disruption of traditional feminist discourse and a straining, instead, toward conversations that resist the cinematic narratives of the female body as needing protection through the authority of law, moving now toward female agency in opposition to state-dictated religious-ethnic identity, and even a celebration of transnational female solidarity and the urgency of representing queer identities.

In her analysis of the partition-themed Pakistani film Khaamosh Paani (2003), Amrita Ghosh draws our attention to the protagonist Ayesha's final plunge into the silent waters as constituting an agentic revelation that she refuses to be pinned into fossilized religious-ethnic identities and transgresses the boundaries of a statist notion of religious identity. This, along with the last scene of the film in which a younger character, Zubeida, now a single woman working and living alone in Rawalpindi, walks alone assertively on the streets of the city, signals hope for an alternative future for women who are now achieving a nuanced negotiation of agency in Pakistan.

In her chapter on Gender, War, and Resistance, Alka Kurian makes the point that in areas ridden by political conflict, women's narratives tend to mostly go un-reported. Instead, what gets highlighted is their victimization. However, an increasing number of women use art as a tool to resist this narrative of systemic and interlocking structures of oppression. To substantiate her argument, she examines a range of documentary films that form part of women's resistance movement. Set in Kashmir, Sri Lanka, and Nepal, three of South Asia's most troubled spots, these films explore the gendered fallout of a brutal state-led militarized repression.

Shoba Rajgopal critically examines the representation of alternate sexualities in South Asia in both the precolonial and postcolonial eras and the repercussions of queer representation on the body politic of the nation state. She undertakes her analysis by looking at the role of the social media and some of the key Indian films that have dealt with "deviant" sexualities. Sreerekha Subramanian, through her analysis of the 2014 film *Mardaani* problematizes the promise of liberation and discusses the limitations of liberalization that underline the film's premise. "In all this," says Subramanian, "the violated body as well as the protesting body disappear or emerge as one, the body that needs protection through the authority of law." Meanwhile, in documentary cinema, Canadian filmmaker Elisa Paloschi's *Driving With Selvi* presents a different view of female agency through the story of the first female taxi driver in Southern India, who rejects a life as a child bride and strikes out on her own. Rajini Srikanth's essay on the film examines the complex terrain of transnational feminist solidarity that is the backdrop of the film's production, and also addresses the politics of feminist connections between the global North and the global South. This sort of transnational feminist solidarity or friendship is foregrounded in Shameem Akhtar's 1999 film, Itihaash Konna (Daughters of History: 1999), which Elora Chowdhury analyses by deploying a transnational feminist analysis and women of color theories of friendship to further a discussion on solidarity among women. Choudhury explores the theme of friendship among ordinary women who "renounced the privileges of imperialism and allied with victims of their own expansionist cultures." She defines this specific form of dissident solidarity "as a collective journey among women across differences involving personal transformation and political struggle and striving toward solidarity, reciprocity and accountability," which forms the basis for social transformation undertaken by women across cultural borders at the risk of annihilation by class, family, community or the nation.

Literature

Similarly, in the section on literature, our authors draw attention to the emerging expression in recent South Asian literature, of transnational feminist consciousness on the one hand, and feminisms from the margins of Dalit and minority women's experiences on the other.

Similar to Elora Chowdhury and Rajini Srikanth's analyses of transnational feminism represented in film, Nalini Iyer examines this in her reading of Jhumpa Lahiri's 2015 novel, *Lowland*. She analyzes the evolution of South Asian feminism within the South Asian American diaspora and proposes that "the narrative trajectory of the novel focused on two feminist women, a mother and daughter, offers a nuanced perspective on South Asian diasporic women; the impact of family, community, and state(s) on their lives; their evolving feminist views which shape their lives against dominant perceptions of race, class, and culture; and the transnational connectivities in their perception of feminist politics and praxis." Telugu Dalit women writers, meanwhile, are stepping away from genre conventions and revolutionizing form and content, which leads scholar Bonnie Zare, to urge critics to reject the idea of Dalit short stories as mere expressions of anger, and acknowledge the varied experiences being narrated.

Note

1 We realize that Shahnaz Khan's chapter is not about social media, but we have included it in that section because we see iterations of the use of Orientalist imagery of the oppressed Afghan (or other South Asian) women by liberal feminists in the West now on social media. This chapter, then, although it does not discuss social media, provides an excellent context for understanding the appropriation of such imagery today on social media.

Part I
Theoretical Imaginings

1 Decolonizing the Body

Theoretical Imaginings on the Fourth Wave Feminism in India

Alka Kurian

Introduction

This chapter argues that the 2012 anti-rape movement in India launched a new feminist politics that embodied a rights-based discourse of gender - in particular, against everyday, generalized misogyny, and sexual harassment and violence—in a way that had not been seriously taken up by the mainstream Indian Women's Movement. Asserting their right to be treated as equal fellow citizens, the movement saw young women challenging the subordination of their political identity to moral identity, and demanding that the state criminalize sexual harassment, something that it had ignored to do in the sixty-five years of the country's independence. Second, I claim that this feminist discourse was connected to a global vocabulary of rights facilitated, to a large extent, by means of the Internet. Third, this movement—often referred to as India's "Spring"—resonated with other forms of agitations for plurality and inclusivity within the Dalit and Muslim minority communities, educational institutions, and the country's militarized zones. It is my intention here to argue that this rights-based intersectional feminist movement, led by India's youth, created a ripple effect for other struggles to break out. Providing them with the "form, idiom, and languages of protest" (Anurima, 2017 fb post), it inspired a large number of public intellectuals and members of the civic society to lay claim to their "political citizenship" (Rahul Roy, 2017) and assert their constitutional right to shape the future of the country's secularism that they fear is currently under threat by the Hindutva forces of regressive nationalism. The promise of the 2012 feminist movement, therefore, is in this connection, and is a critical breakthrough that has the potential to lay the groundwork for, what I claim, an Indian fourth wave feminism and for wider class-based struggles.

Central to this rights-bearing discourse of gender is a focus on the issues of freedom, choice, and desire i.e. elements, which in the past, were viewed with suspicion by those who were committed to the idea of developmental nationalism. The developmental state was too quick to dismiss these elements that came out of modernity because of its own postcolonial legacies marked by conservative gender binaries. The Indian Women's Movement, in its turn too, had a narrower set of restrictive and protectionist concerns by placing a limit on what women could ask for or do. Moreover, gender in the public sphere was seen by the IWM only through the lens of the developmental state, focusing on employment, wages, education, housing, health, food, etc. It's examination of gender in the private sphere, on the other hand, concerned itself with issues of maternal health, reproduction, female feticide or infanticide, the girl child, child marriage, dowry, domestic abuse, etc. Sexuality was strictly a private matter for the developmental state; it saw its public manifestation only in terms of sexual violence against which women needed to be protected through controlling and disciplining their sexual behavior and policing their access to public places.

The access by means of the Internet to a global vocabulary of rights enabled India's youth to bring gender out of the shadows of this developmental framework. It also challenged the regressive nationalistic register by turning the tide from protection to women's autonomy at home and in public spaces. One can scorn at these changes as an upper-class, elitist, and Western phenomenon, or leave it fragmented. But to do that would amount to saying that the developmental logic is not part of the global conversation. The protectionist zeal of the state and the IWM had failed in eliminating women's sexual vulnerability in public places, especially since the watershed decade of 1990s, that had brought more and more women out into the public space, unleashing a massive backlash from the conservative sections of the society. Feeling betrayed by the state and spurned by the society, young women didn't wait to be rescued by the mainstream IWM and used what resources they had at their disposal. Online campaigns such as "Occupy the Night," "Why Loiter," "Blank Noise," etc., were some of the earliest manifestations of this collective spirit against everyday sexism. The 2012 anti-rape movement became the tipping point that initiated a conversation on the need for a shift from developmental to a new rights-based state where women had absolute right to their sexual bodies and to public spaces. By bringing the discourse of freedom and sexuality into the public realm—in the streets and through social media—and by insisting on the autonomy of women's political identity, this discourse helped the Indian feminist movement to emerge into modernity.

These new rights vocabularies of the feminist movement challenged not only the culture of sexism but also classism, casteism, and communalism. Alongside slogans against sexual violence, during the 2012 movement, could be heard voices against oppression of Muslims, Dalits, and of people in Kashmir and Manipur. This rights-based anti-rape movement gave an occasion, therefore, to people from a diversity of interest groups to express their rage against the neo-colonial repressive state. It brought together those who were not on the same page, had different goals for human rights and social justice, and differed on what they wanted from the movement. By trying to advance the interest of civil society and by working on bringing about social justice, these leaders fulfilled, therefore, the role of social "meddlers" (Brittney Cooper 2017: 62) or of public intellectuals, that Romila Thapar fears, have become an "endangered species" (2015).

Fired by the spirit to bring about a democratic culture by dismantling the existing power structure within the repressive neoliberal state, many of the trailblazers of this 2012 intersectional movement provided leadership for other movements that followed, such as "Justice for Vemula," "Stand with JNU," "#Pinjra Tod," "Chalo Una," "#DalitWomenFight," and "#NotInMyName," and a further intensified movement against AFSPA in Kashmir and Manipur. Making this link offers a chance of really pushing forward a different agenda that replaces the developmental state with a progressive alliance. The vocabulary of women who are laying claim to these rights – to the city, to freedom of movement, to their bodies, and to pleasure (and not just civil rights) – needs to be understood as an opportunity for a larger fourth wave feminist movement.

2012 Anti-Rape Movement

The gruesome rape and murder in Delhi of twenty-three-year-old Jyoti Singh on December 16, 2012 unleashed mass protests across India, reigniting public debates on the pervasiveness of sexual violence in the country, foregrounding for the first-time sexual violence as a political issue in liberal democracy (Ratna Kapur 2014). Singh had gone out to watch a film with a male friend, Awindra Pandey. On their way home in a private bus, Pandey was savagely attacked and Singh was brutally gang raped. Singh succumbed to her horrific injuries thirteen days later. Her death lit a spark to the simmering discontent in the country against a profoundly misogynistic culture—that oppresses women across class, caste, and religious divide at home, in public places and institutions—and turned it into a broad-based, nation-wide, intersectional, anti-rape movement. People in their thousands—the first protests being led by students of the Jawaharlal Nehru University (JNU) that houses a powerful gender sensitization committee on campus—joined in mass demonstrations on the streets of urban India, "mobilized by a sense of outrage, social media tools and word of mouth" (Sen cited in Titzmann 2015: 79) demanding an end to the state's indifference to sexual violence claming that it denies women their right to life. While the political classes agitated for women's safety, and many young men and women cried for death penalty for the perpetrators and safety for women, the Hindu right bemoaned Indian women's sexual corruption through Westernization and blamed the rise of women's mobility and freedom as the root cause of sexual violence.

The 2013 Criminal Law Amendment Act[1] that followed the 2012 Delhi gang rape and murder of Jyoti Singh was a culmination of feminist discussions that had preceded in the years leading up to this. The unprecedented furor across national and international borders elicited by the 2012 incident was not too dissimilar—albeit magnified manifold in scale and number—to other public expressions of outrage against the culture of sexual violence in India: Mathura 1972; Rameeza Bee 1979; Maya Tyagi 1980; Suman Rani 1989; Bhanvari Devi 1992. It replicated previous cases mobilized by people around the need for ending state apathy to sexual violence, for amending rape law, for holding the police accountable, and implementing tougher penalties for sex offenders. While Singh's rape made talking about sex and sexuality in public "respectable" (Dutta and Sircar 2013), it also offered a platform for some to reflect on the paucity of response to other cases of sexual violence, some even more gruesome than Singh's, such as the rape of women at the hands of the Indian army in Kashmir (Essar Batool et al. 2016) and the Northeast, or of Dalit, tribal, and Muslim women. Instead of empathizing with the mood of the people, the state imposed reactive measures to deal with the intensity of the protests in Delhi and tried to disperse the agitating crowds by means of water cannons, batons, tear gas, and curfews. Faced with an increasing national and international pressure, the government set up the Verma Committee to revise the anti-rape law in the country. The discussions afforded by the Verma Committee outlined precisely the "continuum of violence against women" (Geetha xv) whether at home or in public spaces, in cities or in border states, that targeted women with sexual violence in the name of honor, identity, or national protection (Geetha xv).

In this section, I investigate feminist activism in India that was triggered by this incident and which railed against the culture of sexual violence, especially against everyday sexual harassment in the country, where walking the streets becomes a sexually hazardous activity for women and which is normalized as an inevitable part of the culture. It looks at the gaps and erasures within mainstream Indian Women's Movement with the attempt to understanding where within the civic society are conversations being led on this question. In the first instance, I attempt to understand this phenomenon against the background of the deepening intersection of women's lives with sexual violence in India, a reality that has historically been cloaked in silence.

Second, I draw on Mitra-Kahn's (2012) analysis to reflect on the transformations within the IWM from its earlier "non-autobiographical" formation to its present-day incarnation of non-mainstream cyberfeminism. I draw on Mitra-Kahn to gain an insight into the ideological feminism of the postcolonial IWM and the profoundly transformative 1990s neoliberal turn of the country to understand the rise of online feminist activism (2012: 110–11). The rapid transformations taking place in feminist politics in India today locate cyberfeminists in radically new feminist spaces and conversations on feminism itself, who use the democratically accessible Internet as a tool for activism on a wide range of issues. I claim that the passionate engagement of cyberfeminists with the politics of sexual violence, for example the one that we saw during the 2012 protests, challenged the perceived sense of political apathy, conservatism, and consumerism among younger women and helped inject a new life into the IWM whose NGO-zation since the

1990s had blunted its edge (Menon 2004) and weakened and fragmented its feminist politics. Moreover, IWM has historically privileged institutional forms of women's oppression related to sati, widows, dowry, custodial rape, female infanticide/feticide, inflation, environmental degradation, etc. The IWM's focus, therefore, has tended to be on specific forms of gender oppressions that impact mostly socially and economically backward and mostly rural layers of Indian society. Without undermining IWM's significant contribution to these major "issue-specific conceptual frameworks" (Chakravarti et al. cited in Mitra-Kahn 111), the class differentiation between "activists/theorist middle class feminists" and their disenfranchised "objects of activism and inquiry," (Mitra-Kahn 110–111) has created an unbridgeable solidarity gap between their self and the other. The privileged members of the IWM understood the pain of the socio-economically oppressed: it happened elsewhere and to other women, i.e. the laborer, the cleaner, the widow, the destitute or the Dalit. But operating from the comfort of its middle-class home or workplace, this "split subject" (John 1998) of the IWM juggled the privilege of the self and the oppression of the other by inadvertently emulating, what I claim, a homegrown "Feminist-as-Tourist" model (Mohanty 2003), causing in the process alienation between the two and fundamentally damaging the IWM. This hands-off approach of the IWM, argues Kshama Sawant (2017a), stemmed also from the IWM's NGO-ization, a process that "did not happen in isolation," but caught many social and political movements in its fold.

However, with more and more girls from across the class system joining the workforce in contemporary India, and consequently getting out of domestic and into public space, the dominant feminist discourse post-1990s has shifted from the other to the self and the concerns of the erstwhile IWM have become youth concerns. In a situation like this, by neglecting to theorize everyday street sexual harassment[2], considering it to be exclusively a class issue (Phadke 2003)[3] that was far too incidental and sporadic in nature to merit its intervention, the ideological feminism of the postcolonial IWM, with its focus on developmental issues, projected itself as exclusionary and too out of touch with the needs of contemporary feminism. By intervening in the resultant activism gap, the younger cyberfeminists proceeded to operate along, what I claim, a "comparative model," illustrating through their actions powerful "relations of mutuality, co-responsibility and common interests, anchoring the idea of feminist solidarity" (Mohanty 2003: 242). By using the Internet for discussion and activism, and relying on its power to "call out" and challenge the culture of sexism and misogyny, cyberfeminists or the "power users of social networking" (cited in Munro 2013) have lain claim to both the site as well as the content of knowledge production hitherto monopolized by the mainstream IWM.

Indian Feminisms: A Historical Background

It is difficult to understand social movements from the prism of waves: there are no clear definitions and meanings tend to seep from one into another, and the appellations only make sense retrospectively. The first wave of the Indian women's movement is understood to have begun during the nineteenth-century social reform movement with women's organizations battling against both patriarchy and colonialism. The second wave of women's political activism in the post-colonial India of 1950s and 1960s took on a radically different form and method of mobilizing and embodied class and anti-caste struggles. These included tribal landless laborers' movement against feudal oppression, rallies against price rise, black marketeering and corruption, formation of trade unions for women working in the informal sector, and agitation for land by landless peasants. The third wave of the Indian women's movement that grew in late 1970s was self-consciously feminist at its core. Deliberately sidestepping party affiliation and hierarchies, this "autonomous" women's movement led agitations against dowry oppression and custodial rape (for example, Rameeza Bee 1978; Mathura 1980; Suman Rani 1988). However, the anti-rape campaign championed by the IWM was far too sporadic and episodic for it to be transformed into a genuine civil rights issue (Geetha 2016). Further, the gaps and fissures exposed within the IWM in the 1990s nation-wide post-Mandal agitations, shed light on the limitations of the movement owing to its blindness to the sexual politics of caste (Geetha 2017). The 1990s NGO-ization and careerism of the autonomous women's organizations owing to sudden influx of donor funding, along with people's inexplicable detachment from political and civic life, undermined the essence of a genuine feminist movement in India after it peaked in 1970s, 1980s, and early 1990s. Further, the arrival of governance feminism, i.e. the incorporation of feminist knowledge within state, led to a greater policing and monitoring of citizens, especially of women, viewed by the regressive, neo-liberal state as vulnerable and passive victims (Kapur 2014; Iyer 2015). Critics wonder whether this ideological chaos and transformation that could potentially break up the IWM:

> ...into separate groups with their own organizational, funder-driven agendas ... [and] our tendency to turn to the law [that invariably reinforces gendered status quo] to deal with every new instance of devaluation and oppression of women in the realm of 'the body' and sexuality is precisely an indication of the lack of a 'strong movement' in this area.
>
> (Menon 2004: 221, 222)

Incapacitated, therefore, by a sexist legal system on the one hand, and by a fragmented and weakened IWM that offered an ambiguous and unsatisfactory direction on everyday street sexual harassment on the other, leadership on this issue came from young, middle-class, non-mainstream cyberfeminists in India who have been mobilizing in ways that signal a departure both in terms of content and method of resistance.

Shifting Feminist Parameters: Rise of the Fourth Wave Feminism?

The "watershed decade" of 1990s in India was marked by heightened right-wing Hindu radicalism, welfare cut-backs by the state, informalization of labor, steep income decline for the poor, and theft of mineral-rich lands from indigenous people. As a way out of the deepening crisis of global capitalism in 1980s, Western industrial economies began aggressively to target former colonial economies for cheap labor and an expansive consumer base. While these self-serving neo-colonial trade practices led to Indian economy's neoliberalization with a devastating impact on the country's fragile social order, they also had contradictory outcomes. On the one hand Western industries' un-ending demand for cheap labor led to a massive expansion of jobs (mostly exploitative) for women in urban areas, it caused major anxieties for the conservative sections of the society that did not keep pace with a growing number of educated and professionally skilled women whose financial independence opened untold opportunities for them, fundamentally transforming their expectations from the society. It is precisely the intersection between the new and the old order that catapulted a new women's movement boldly challenging traditional mores, and seeking freedom and not protection from the "Indian capitalist-casteist-feudal-landlordist ruling class (Sawant b)" that wishes to preserve the old ways of being.

The post 1990s India was also marked by regressive constructions of the binary right-wing and neo-liberal imaginings of ideal/subversive Indian femininity. On the one hand, women were venerated as normative, traditional, and family oriented, a reflection of the Hindu right's sexual and cultural anxiety faced with the increasing Westernization of certain sections of the Indian society. On the other, they were celebrated as the hypersexualized, educated, and career-oriented new and modern Indian women (Sunder Rajan 1993; Munshi 2004). Commenting on the resultant transformation of the everyday life of people in India in the 1990s and early 2000s, Menon and Nigam (2007) enumerate the phenomenon that helped coming into being of, what they refer to as the "new economies of desire:" the cell phone revolution[4], the radical transformation of the media[5], consumer revolution[6], and the "explosion of sexual desire" (92) among urban men and women[7]. A detailed examination of this resultant cultural revolution is beyond the scope of this chapter. What I am interested in, however, is to look at the ways in which the explosion of sexual desire that Menon and Nigam claim was facilitated in India by the far easier and greater accessibility of the automobile, the cell phone and the Internet, the proliferation of nightclubs, pubs, and multiplexes, the multiplication of dating sites, and the presence of homosexuals in urban public spaces generating an atmosphere that "pulsate(s) with the desire and possibilities of sexual adventure" (2007: 92). Add to this is the phenomenon of unprecedented population mobility that have together liberated urban spaces from traditional mores and conservatism.

As the media began to open up around the turn of the century, the arrival of sexually explicit images into Indian homes from the West and through the cable TV transformed the essence of sexuality in Indian feminist politics so that it's concern with heterosexual violence moved to a "desire going beyond the bounds of heteronormativity" (2007: 93). While the 1970s and 1980s feminist politics railed against "obscenity" in "explicit" Indian films and advertisements, in 1990s, it shifted from its earlier stance and campaigned against the politics of censorship as it replicated the Hindu right's monitoring of sexuality. It clamored, instead, for creating "a space for greater sexual expression on the part of women ... in which women are willing and active agents [to] ... ensure the proliferation of feminist discourses about sexual pleasure and desire" (93–94).

Print and visual media exploded with images of neo-normative Indian femininity that combined modernity, sexiness, and urbanity with middle-class respectability promoting a "virtuous sexual desirability" (Phadke 2005; Menon 2012; Sunder Rajan 1993; Mitra-Kahn, Maitraiyee Chaudhuri 2014) where stalking, however, was normalized as a reflection of her sexual desirability. Despite the IWM's attempts at resistance against misogyny and sexual violence (see below), it offered a dismal response to this "schizophrenic" (Mitra-Kahn 113) discourse on Indian femininity. The presence of this new woman—agentic and sexually confident—both onscreen (in films and advertisements) and off-screen (in colleges, streets, pubs, and offices), faced the backlash of the heteronormative Hindu right, social vigilante groups, and the police, who collectively harass sex workers, hijras, kothis, gays, and lesbians under article 377 of the Indian Constitution[8], police what girls wear to school or what women drink in pubs, and monitor what people watch in cyber-cafes or whether consenting couples dare to hang out in public spaces on Valentine's day. Those that defy normative prescribed gender norms become victims of everyday sexual harassment as a result.

Sexual harassment can be understood as either transient, usually non-contact, acts in public spaces—lewd comments, cat call, flashing, etc.—or as physical molestation involving groping or touching.

> Sexual harassment is neither a clear-cut example of force, nor a simple display of interest. More than a mere reflection of the highly contradictory nature of gendered power relations, sexual

harassment is productive of these relations ... Sexual harassment is a social exchange in which the very meaning and embodiment of gender identity is at stake.

(Laura Ring, cited in Menon 2014: 144)

Sexual harassment constitutes a politically motivated oppression of women whose mere presence in public spaces is perceived by patriarchy as an act of provocation (Baxi 2001) and is not, what many claim, a benign cultural phenomenon. It is further trivialized by the mainstream media as courtship (Rayaprol 2011: 71) or banalized by the patriarchal state law as "eve-teasing"—a playful, amusing, and harmless teasing of 'eves' by men in public spaces (Gangoli 2007: 63). The silence surrounding this public secret (Baxi 2012) of women's sexual targeting on the streets and professional spaces is compounded, therefore, by its cultural and political tolerance. It is moreover promoted by the state's apathy to the flagrant violation of women's physical and sexual integrity whereby they are routinely stripped, paraded naked, burned, or mutilated with acid across regional, caste, ethnic or religious borders. Instead of characterizing acts of aggravated sexual assaults as politically motivated or facilitating victims to seek redressal, the state pathologizes them as acts of sexual deviancy. This dismissal of the enormity of sexual violence by state representatives ends up normalizing a culture where women are commodified and sexual violence is promoted as a strategy of control and discipline. It is further enabled by state-led strategies of women's surveillance, policing, shaming, naming, and humiliation.

The IWM did successfully lead some campaigns against women's harassment: In 1992 the "Crimes against Women" chapter was added in the "Crimes in India" report that enlisted offences that specifically targeted women such as dowry-related abuse, domestic violence, molestation, and eve-teasing. Campaigns on custodial rape (for example, Rameeza Bee 1978; Mathura 1980) and sexual assault of women in the workplace (Bhanvari Devi 1992) led to the 1983 Criminal Law Act and the 1997 Vishakha Guidelines. The debates conducted during these campaigns related to how rape and women's sexualized bodies were understood both by law and the larger Indian society, and how sexual integrity, caste and class hierarchies were central to India's criminal justice system for which the discourse of normative Indian womanhood was paramount. The second wave of the IWM on sexual violence (Kannabiran 137) saw a remarkable shift in defining rape from a "women's rights" issue to a "human rights" one, expanding it to include the rape of children, homosexual bodies, and the broadening of the definition of sexual-intercourse to non-penile-vaginal penetration as well. India's first and only anti-street sexual harassment act was legislated by means of the Delhi Prohibition of Eve Teasing Act, 1988. In addition, Jagori, the Safe Delhi campaign, and the advocacy group on gender safety in public places were established. However, being based on nineteenth century's outmoded notions of women's propriety and modesty, the specific laws dealing with sexual harassment (Section 509 IPC; Section 354 IPC), were "wholly inadequate in defining the experiences of women" (Agnes 1992 cited in Gangoli 63). In addition, most of the legislation that has successfully been put in place deals only with the workplace, for example, the 1997 Vishakha Guidelines (subsequently reinforced through the 2013 Anti-Sexual Harassment of Women at Workplace Act) laying down instructions to employers of public, private, and unorganized sectors on how to protect their women employees. However, while being welcomed by the IWM, the Vishakha judgement did not involve extensive discussions within the movement (Menon 2004: 220). Barring a few cases, policies related to sexual harassment failed in giving justice to victims due to employer apathy or reluctance, misunderstanding of the definition of the term that can often be ambiguous, slippery, and culturally specific, and owing to loopholes that favor perpetrators (Menon 2014, 2013). Further, the National Commission of Women (NCW) did not feel the need to extensively consult with women's groups before tabling in 2004 the draft bill on Sexual Harassment at the Workplace, an omission that could have had "serious and negative implications for working conditions for women all over the country" (Menon 2004: 146). NCW is known to have alienated itself in other situations too. For example, NCM Chairperson Mamta Sharma claimed in 2015 that women were bringing sexual violence upon themselves by dressing irresponsibly and mindlessly aping the West that was corroding Indian culture (Naidu 2015). Because of its inertia and its politics of victim-blaming, NCW does not project itself as a progressive institution working towards ending violence against women, for which critics have called for its review and audit (Patel 2014). Further, the 2010 Bill on the Protection of Women Against Sexual Harassment at Workplace was formulated in a way that criminalized "false and malicious complaints" of sexual harassment. As a result, rather than guaranteeing their safety, it ended up vulnerablizing women filing complaints against powerful people in their place of work (Menon 2012: 126).

The few examples outlined above are a symptom of a deeper malaise in the Indian society a way out of which, suggests Ratna Kapur, could be in "recuperating and theorizing desire and pleasure ... particularly against the backdrop of the rise of the power of the Hindu Right" (cited in Menon 2004: 146). Failure to do so renders even the most well-meaning and democratic of the legislations anti-feminist in a culture where sexuality and its expressions are regarded as Western intrusions intent upon contaminating Indian culture and tradition, and which therefore feels justified in policing women's sexual behavior. A regressive and conservative ideology such as this that dominates all jurisdiction around sexual harassment, can only offer the same old protectionist solution to complaints about sexual harassment, rather than seeing it as a symptom of a misogynistic culture that denies women the right to their bodies, including their sexuality. Since a disregard of this protectionist discourse is met with the threat or reality of sexual violence - the latter being the "most visible aspect of a general climate of misogyny" (Menon 2012: 131), women are raised to practice self-censorship, forever exercising caution with their dress, speech, demeanor, and behavior, living up to the patriarchal expectations of femininity, and fully participating in a discourse that only "good girls" deserve to be rescued and safeguarded by the state. The question that hovers under the skin of women's consciousness is that if men who smoke or drink alcohol are not classed as sexually deviant and if they are not assaulted or penalized for coming home late, why must women be for doing the same as men? Further while men are more vulnerable than women to violent crimes, they are not accused of having brought them on because of their behavior or their sartorial sense and are not expected to "perceive their body, at all times, as a potential crime scene" (Cochrane 428).

The 2012 women's articulation to the specific right to their bodies and freedom was, I claim, transformative, and signaled a clear departure from earlier movements against sexual violence. My analysis is located within the context of a powerful but gradually bourgeoning discourse on freedom within a new, anti-statist and "expansionist and exploratory" (Carole Vance: 1984) shift in the politics of Indian feminism, asserting itself outside the vocabulary of the law, and centered around the question of pleasure that comes with accessing public spaces and reclaiming one's body and sexuality in both private and public. Menon and Nigam (2007) offer an insightful correlation between economic globalization and the assertion of a series of new aspirations that underline a shifting— albeit triumphant—nature of neo-liberal India's lived reality. As a product of the material changes resulting from India's unprecedented 1990s neo-liberal economic growth, many women in urban areas have been choosing their sexual partners, delinking sex with reproduction, and savoring the autonomy of financial independence. Doing away with what they see as outmoded practices of self-discipline and asexuality, and stepping away from the traditional bargain of the mutually exclusive categories of sexual safety and freedom, they seek sexual freedom and the right to be "sexual in more visible and daring ways" (Vance: 1–2).

Amid the deafening calls during the 2012 anti-rape protest grew organically a powerful appeal for freedom—*Bekhauf Azaadi* or Freedom Without Fear—that was, therefore, different. Slogans such as "Don't Tell Me How to Dress, Tell Him How Not to Rape," "Freedom, Not Protection," "Raped woman is a survivor; she is not worse than death," "My Body, My Right," "Not as a Mother, Not as a Sister, I want my Rights as a Human Being," etc. became rallying points for women affirming their right to be adventurous and reckless, assuming no responsibility

for self-protection, shaming the state and the communal moral policing of law-abiding women, defying archaic notions of honor and seeking the basic freedom of choice. The slogans caught the imagination of
thousands of people (many of them first time protesters, without any
previous initiation into the women's movement,[9] holding placards for
the right to freedom—to college, on public transport, from baap (father),
and from khap (village council). Not only did this demand refer to wom-
en's freedom from sexual violence in public spaces but also to freedom
from the moral policing of women within the private spaces of home and
community. Gender sensitization and programs against sexual harassment in college campuses further fueled such demands.

While this national outrage was a powerful representation of this new
feminist consciousness, critics were disappointed that, in the absence of
guidance from a genuine feminist movement in the country, the masses
that congregated willy-nilly were completely rudderless (Roy 2014, 2015;
Tellis 2014). I challenge this accusation by making the claim that ordinary
women during this mass agitation provided a quantum leap in feminist
politics by laying claim to their "political citizenship," as they pushed their
way through the cordons, telling the police to back off as "This is *our* country" (Leslie Udwin, 2015 India's Daughter). These women certainly did not
see themselves as members of the mainstream IWM. While their spontaneous critique of neo-liberal patriarchal sexism and regressive conservatism
is built on the legacy of the critical framework put in place by the IWM, in
the absence of the latter's comprehensive critique of the everyday street sexual harassment, they took the bull by the horn. Trapped by the donor exigencies, if the post 1990s NGO-ized IWM had lost its way and weakened
as a result, then the 2012 movement showed a way towards regaining its
erstwhile autonomy. In their spontaneous mobilization resides the strength
of the civil collectivities that showed that, rather than relying on the IWM
or political parties, they could really push forward their right to freedom by
engaging in what Roy (2017) refers to as the "politics of citizenship."

One of the voices that stood out among the tumultuous masses was
that of Kavita Krishnan, General Secretary of the All India Progressive Women's Association. Buried beneath her bold articulations[10] and
promotion of the slogan of *Bekhauf Azaadi*, was a radical feminist assertion for women's autonomy on their own terms. Krishnan's insistence
on the need to recognize women's right to freedom without conditions
or fear resonates with Carole Vance's central thematic in her seminal
1984 book *Pleasure and Danger: Exploring Female Sexuality*. Inspired
by the articulations framed by socialist feminism on a multiplicity of
views on female sexuality, not only does Vance highlight women's realistic anxieties about masculinist sexual violence in all its forms including pornography, she also investigates "the complex intrapsychic,
interpersonal fears and anxieties, which produce the many irrational-
ities surrounding sexual intimacy that wreak havoc on our movement

and at the same time are cleverly used against us by the right" (Segal 1995). Krishnan's *Bekhauf Azaadi* offers a lens through which to critically reflect on the meaning of women's affirmation of autonomy, choice, sexual agency, and pleasure set against an asymmetrical gendered hierarchy that regulates female sexuality through the twin arsenals of "control and danger." Her impassioned articulations underline women coming to grips with the pleasurable and dangerous Janus-faced reality of being a sexualized feminine, which while allowing untold possibilities of joy that come with freedom, embraces the risk of danger that goes hand in hand with women seeking this pleasure. Buried therefore, within the challenge to the culture of sexual violence against women in India is Krishnan's intention of addressing the "patriarchal structure within which women act," her commitment to liberating female sexual agency and choice from "sexual terror and despair within which women live," as well as debunking the "one-sided dangers of sexuality" (Segal 1995) that proponents of sexual caution underline. Borrowing Vance's theoretical formation of "pleasure and danger," I make the claim that the specific nature of discourse around women's assertion for freedom in 2012 was not so much for sexual freedom (in the literal sense of sexual pleasure or experimentation) but for the simple pleasure of accessing public places, and rejecting legal reform, protection, and the stereotype of victimhood. The 1980s and 1990s women's movements against the blight of domestic battering and sexual abuse sought women's protection primarily through legal reform (Mitra 2012). No doubt, the 2012 mass agitation did lead to the state-sponsored constitution of the Verma Committee charged with making recommendation to India's criminal law on rape and sexual violence. But while the state's solution to the tumultuous situation through legislative change did satisfy some of the agitators, the radical collectivities of the anti-rape movement sought a more fundamental cultural transformation of the society.

Anxious about "the chasm that lies between India Gate (the site for many of these protest marches) and the slum habitat," critics (Sinha 2013) claimed that, as lay people, the protesters represented self-centered and apolitical middle-class masses who were unconcerned with the brutality of sexual violence suffered by minority women. However, given that the anti-rape movement was seen by many as an example of IWM's inadequate response to the culture of everyday sexual violence (Chaudhury 2015), attempts to dismiss the protesters away simply based on parameters, such as class, smack of exclusionary elitism. In her examination of the question of class in post-liberalization India, Maitrayee Chaudhury too cautions against scoffing at a phenomenon simply because it is led by the middle class. Such a positionality would be erroneous, claims the author, especially because as a product of a "colonially-mediated modernity," without emulating either Western bourgeoisie or achieving hegemonic status in independent India, the middle class has historically played an important role in "managing the ruling bloc, which included the bourgeoisie and landed interests … [and continues to play] a critical ideological role" (2014: 173) in the country today. In addition, celebrated by the media, a successful and growing Indian middle class helps the country position itself as a global economic power admired for the sheer scale of its consumer base. Inversely, its centrality at a global level helps the middle-class garner for itself "greater political visibility and power within the state and society" (173).

Without undermining the developmental framework of protectionist politics that had earlier called for legislative amendments against the culture of sexual violence, freedom for reproductive rights, or for the right to income equality, the 2012 anti-rape movement therefore was a forceful and an unequivocal assertion of women's right to pleasure even if it came at the risk of courting danger. I understand this as the feeling of liberation that comes with women recapturing their bodies from patriarchy without squeamishness—in terms both sartorial and sexual, and reclaiming India's streets and open spaces without having to justify their presence in public spaces regardless of the time of the day or night, irrespective of whether they were alone or with men, and notwithstanding the manner of their dress. If women courted danger in exercising this freedom, then their movement held the state and the larger society accountable for ensuring women's right to this pleasure.

Global Millennial Continuum

Rising above the general pessimism on the spate of mainstream feminism in India (Roy, Tillerson) was the powerful work undertaken by cyberfeminists. Born in the aftermath of the neo-liberal turn of India, with a large number of young women entering the workforce, they had long been "agitating" online for women's rights especially on the everyday sexual harassment and violence in the country. Joyti Singh's brutal gang rape became a flashpoint, triggering an outlet for an offline expression of rage that had long been building online on the culture of sexism, moral policing, and sexual profiling. While mainstream media beaming round-the-clock coverage of the rape[11] escalated the protests in the country, it was the discussions on social media that fanned the accumulated rage and frustrations and became an outlet for ordinary people to express their longstanding grievances on the subject. Further, it is my contention that, the powerful digital activism that ensued with blogs, Twitter (e.g. #DelhiGangRape; #Nirbhaya; #StopThisShame), Facebook, and online discussion forums (e.g. kafila.online; Ladies Fingers, Youth Ki Awaz), had the cumulative effect of moving people from online protests to street demonstrations, occupations, and vigils (Titzmann 80–81). As a result, despite the mammoth outpouring of rage in December 2012, it was not the first time that the "public had risen." Rather than a sudden political awakening, I see this movement as "part of a continuum" (Sen 2013) of a "cyberlife of feminist politics in urban India" (Mitra-Kahn 109) that has roots in a cultural revolution that was unleashed by the forces of the free market stemming from the neo-liberal turn of the country discussed above. The digital turn in India was also part of a global trend where people came together via the Internet on contentious political issues around which to organize protests, rallies, occupations, sit-ins, and demonstrations. During the 2011 "Arab Spring" or the "twitter revolution", corporate digital social network systems, such as Facebook and Twitter, played a key role in fomenting anti-establishment revolts. Further, the numbers of women using the Internet as a tool for feminist activism too is on the rise across the world. For example, women in the Middle East use social media to challenge cultural misogyny and religious conservatism in their countries[12]. The American feminist writer Jessica Valenti's blog Feministing.com is the most widely read feminist publication in the world (Solomon 2009). Gopinathan (2017) claims that the use of twitter has helped feminism to grow 300 percent since 2014.

Technology has often played a subversive role in fomenting revolutions: the 1950s Algerian self-determination nationalists seized the radio—a mouth piece of French imperialism—as a tool for anti-colonial activism (Fanon cited in Maeckelberg 284); a variety of "small media" during the 1979 Iranian revolution mounted an oppositional resistance by exploiting the easy accessibility to "pre-existing cultural networks and communicative patterns" (Mohammadi and Mihammadi cited in Maeckelberg 284); a group of lawyers used the medium of YouTube—that promised "voice for the voiceless"—during the 2007 Movement for the Restoration of Democracy in Pakistan. Clearly, the revolution lay not in the technology per se, but in the ways in which social movements manage to suffuse it with newer, oppositional signification or "countercontexts" (284) with the view to bringing about social change. Maeckelberg hails the power of this "technological drama" where lay persons challenge oppressive state by means of usurping the technological infrastructure that was provided by the state for purposes other than revolutionary. It is important, therefore, to underline that the "challenge occurs not through technology [in itself] but through the use of technology in combination with the creation of a social context that expresses different points of view" (282).

Drawing on Bates (cited in Cochrane), I argue that online activism comes naturally to young, urban-based women today who make little divisions between online and offline experiences of their lives and, having grown up with the Internet, relate to it as "just another part of public, social space ... and are campaigning in [this space] where they habitually spend time" (Cochrane 669–79). Providing a steep learning curve for the young, the Internet has radically altered how feminist ideas circulate where members learn them "on the job" rather than in campus classrooms or from women's organizations. The popularity of these campaigns signals an early politicization of young women who refuse to normalize everyday sexual violence on the streets or keep it under wraps due to embarrassment or acquiescence to a normal part of growing up in India. While they may gloss over expressions such as feminism or patriarchy, they speak out against being called chut or gaand (misogynistic expressions in Hindi for vagina and anus) on the streets and then violated for being identified as such. In addition, the Internet facilitates user-based evaluation of events so that if they wish to understand how a sexist or a "homophobic advert affects people, [they] don't have to just read about it in an article, [they] can follow someone who tweets about it, and learn about it from their opinions and their lived experience," (Cochrane 691) unlike in mainstream media that puts heteronormative voices above all else. Cyberfeminism, then is a form of online feminist organizing where women use the web-based technology to openly articulate their concerns, removing the stigma associated with discussing sex and rape (Valenti 2004, feministing.com). If the anti-dowry mobilization in the 1970s involved feminists doing consciousness-raising where women from grassroots levels spoke about and shared their experiences of domestic abuse, then web-based feminism too has initiated a similar consciousness-raising process around the theme of sexual violence with an outreach that is thousand times broader and whose goal it is to underline the pervasiveness of women's oppression, a collective problem that needs to be politically resolved. In the past, women would have talked about these issues in college canteen or in the privacy of homes; now they are blogging about it, learning feminist vocabulary in the process, challenging appellations of "slacktivism" or "Clicktivism." In her exploration of Feminist Activism on Social Media in India, Sujatha (2014) claims that apart from helping organize "individualised mass communication," the Internet also allows users to sidestep state and commercial "gate-keepers and agenda setters" (5). They use the Internet to protest structures of sexual oppression where prior conversation online with different constellations of people helps them strategize before going on the streets.

The news about the Delhi 2012 incident would not have spread as it did nationally and internationally in the absence of the digital technology where an altered temporality with a 24×7 facility of instant uploading of information brought about "paradigmatic changes of creating, delivering, and consuming content ... [providing] instant access to people and institutions across the world" (Chaudhuri 2015: 22). Unlike some of the landmark cases on gender-based violence in the previous decades, during the Delhi incident, a publicity-driven and a technologically savvy interactive media was both the "actor and a central site for representing public outcry" (Chaudhury 27). It resembled the 2011 anti-corruption movement in the country that had led to the formation of the Lokpal Bill, and where in addition to access to knowledge and the vocabulary for articulating dissent, people's interactive participation in the "production, selection, and distribution" (Chaudhury 27) of the media and the latter's convergence[13] set this event apart from all previous ones.

As an easily accessible tool therefore, the web clearly helped in the formation of complex and culturally nuanced online communities of "computer-mediated spaces," where "Internet affordance" enabled them to engage in an "online resisting work" (Massa 2016: 247) against the culture of street sexual harassment. The value of these online spaces maintaining anonymity, minimizing "exposure, participation risk and organizational maintenance cost," and allowing for activists from a spectrum of social formations possibilities to engage with each other despite class, ethnic, regional, and gender barriers, can hardly be overstated (Massa 2016). Contrary to a generalized perception of the Internet as "an impoverished medium devoid of social cues … [alienating us from] our sense of geographic place and community" (254), it has become an enabler of heightened connectivity (with anyone at any time) and interactivity (simulating real world conditions), that has shrunk the barriers of time, space, and power, and democratized relationship formation in the process. As a result, regardless of geographical locations, and by-passing the rituals of personal, face-to-face interactions, users of Facebook, Instagram, or Twitter networks follow each other through the cyberspace of instant status updates, sharing experiences and building social relationships between what I refer to as *communities of mind* to launch movements and organize resistance work against oppression, in ways that reinforces ties between people that may or may not share geographic commonalities. Faced with critics who disparage the exclusiveness of media technology, Maeckelberg points out that while access to social media or the Internet might smack of capitalist and normative elitism, this certainly does not preclude their use for subversive activities. If technology is used in the service of reproducing and centralizing power relations, it can also be used to subvert these processes. On the ease of transference of ideas from online conversation to mass political mobilization on the streets by online communities, the author argues that the secret lay in Internet-based technology to offer unencumbered possibilities for knowledge production as a "counterweight to mainstream media." She refers to online communities as part of a media infrastructure made up of "connections between people and groups and specifically the political values that are created and mobilized by the activists themselves in order to create activist media" (2016: 281).

Cybderfeminist protests in India are articulated through a combination of multimodal online, offline, and hybrid modalities (Massa 248) to queer masculinized gender relations and spaces in ways that promote taking collective accountability. Their strategies range from online sharing of narratives of street abuse as testimonials of resistance; intervening in public spaces through street performances to disrupt the gendered gaze; and maintaining postings on blogs, Facebook, YouTube, and

Twitter accounts of an expanding member base of these campaigns[14]. Examples include the 2001 "Take Back the Night" project on sexual, domestic, and intimate partner violence; the 2005 "Blank Noise Project" on eve-teasing; the 2009 "Pink Chaddi" campaign to fight conservative right-wing misogyny that targets consenting couples hanging out together in public spaces; the 2009 "A Valentine for India" campaign and the 2011 "Besharmi Morcha (SlutWalk)" against the culture of moral policing; the 2011 "Please Mend the Gap" campaign challenging street sexual harassment in urban spaces; the 2011 "Fight-Back" project against gender-based violence; the 2011 'Why Loiter," "Did You Ask For it," and the 2015 "Occupy the Night," campaigns on women's right to public spaces, and the 2016 "#Pinjra Tod" campaign against gender-discriminatory policies and curfews in Indian universities. The extensive web-based political activism that emerged in the process can be understood to be stemming from unique and contradictory situation of modernity and conservatism that the Indian middle-class femininity saw itself caught up in at the turn of the century. The safe/private space offered in this context can hardly be overestimated for women to make sense of and think through these incongruous and incompatible sets of positionalities.

Central to the articulation of this feminist discourse is the use of humor, sarcasm and satire as a provocative tool to ridicule women's cultural and sexual policing makes. This strategy helps women to stay on the task at hand, and underlines anger in a way that is more effective, as it is often the only way to deal with the absurdity of sexism. To understand this dramatically snowballing phenomenon, I draw on Vance's understating of the "tension between sexual danger and sexual pleasure … where sexuality is simultaneously a domain of restriction, repression, and danger as well as a domain of exploration, pleasure, and agency" (1984: 1). I argue that buried within the clamor for freedom is a radicalization of a rights bearing female agency that is simultaneously joyous and anxious as it willingly courts danger while seeking this freedom from widespread regressive and sexist politics in the country. In 2013, Backchod India uploaded a satirical video called "Rape: It's Your Fault," starring Bollywood actress Kalki Koechlin and Juhi Pandu. The video went viral with over 5 million views, and started conversations about the way that rape victims in India are treated in the media and by law enforcement [12]. Humor, with its capacity for wider outreach, and ability to initiate a conversation on difficult topics, helps attract people who would otherwise be deterred by academic and theoretical discourse. Nisha Susan, founder of the Facebook group "Consortium of Pub-going, Loose [sic] and Forward Women," urged women to send pink chaddis (knickers) as a Valentine's Day gift to Sri Ram Sene's leader Pramod Muthalik, who had been threatening violence if young men and women were seen courting on Valentine's day. The playful message behind the gender-neutral term Chaddi - a term of derision and mockery, a "slang for right-wing hardliners," symbolizing the vulgarity of the Sene actions, and sneering at the image of khaki shorts worn by the self-congratulatory Hindu right wing RSS members—quickly spread like wildfire. The campaign swiftly turned into a movement against widespread right-wing moral policing of well-meaning women asserting their right to relax and have fun. Bollywood stars like Deepika Padukone and Kangana Ranaut have also sparked feminist conversations on the larger, national level, given the cache that these stars enjoy across the spectrum of demographics in India.

Digital technology has changed the very nature of political activism; it is different to how one imagined political engagement such as street demonstrations, rallies and protest marches in the past. Going by its increasing popularity, visibility, and global outreach, online feminist activism has reached a "cultural tipping point" (Munro 2013: 2). This new digital age of feminist activism indicates more than a mere "generational" or a "political" transformation. It represents democratized "citizen journalism" (Gerbaudo 2012) and is filling in the gaps that got left out as feminists were focused on developmental priorities of food, housing, health, education, and economic opportunities. This new engagement is performing a shift in the citing and source of knowledge production. Discarding the trope of "women as a monolithic category, at once objects and users of the 'master's tools,'" (Blair et al. 2009: 1) using the Internet, cyberfeminists "interrupt the flow of masculine codes by boldly declaring the intention to mongrelize, hybridize, provoke, and disrupt the male order of things in the Net environment" (Wilding cited in Blair et al. 1–2). Social media helped push forward activism for women, especially for those that came from the marginalized layers of the society or those living in repressive regions in the world facing serious political, cultural, and physical challenges. Social media, therefore, embodies both a technological tool as well as a cultural organism whose meaning undergoes profound transformation based on how it is deliberately changed by the users. Increasingly, women use the Internet for a variety of reasons: a tool for inclusion, an alternative public space, an "intersection between disability and queer issues," or a site for "multiple, coexisting counterpublics," (Sujatha 2014: 6, 7). This intersectional "cyberdemocracy" enable cyberfeminists "to amplify their own voices ... talking about the things that matter to them, unfiltered, in their own voices" (Interview: "Feminism Online: The New Wave," 2017). Unencumbered by the burden of donor deadlines or priorities, mobilized by new global vocabularies of freedom, initiating urgent, autobiographical modes of feminist engagements, cyberfeminists have laid the ground for a rights-based, intersectional, and autonomous fourth wave of feminism in India.

Conclusion

Unlike previous anti-rape movements, the 2012 protests were not limited to or led exclusively by women; rather, they gained nation-wide importance (Chaudhuri and Fitzgerald 2015: 623) with the first mass demonstrations on December 18th being subsequently intensified by other people joining in: ordinary citizens, members of various political parties and minorities—Dalit, Muslim, and queer identified people with individual longstanding political grievances against the state—who led agitations in their own geographical locations as a means to express solidarity to victims of sexual violence. The movement coalesced therefore activists from a range of political persuasions whose goals were different and varied in nature. It explored other forms of marginalization and pondered over questions of nationalism. The quick and reactive character of these campaigns represented the all-encompassing nature of oppression stemming from corruption, Hindu nationalism, demonization of minorities, the Kashmir issue, etc. It advocated for the freedom of all since no one is free until everyone is free.

The vicious attacks since 2015 on the universities across the country, branding radical students' anti-establishment activism as antinational and seditious, was met by a groundswell of rage garnering support from students, scholars, and members of faculty and of trade unions. Their politics was aimed at the state snuffing out critical and independent thought and its narrow hegemonic and dominant anti-minoritarian definition of nationalism where the entity of the other is substitutable by a minority woman, a Muslim, a Dalit, etc. (EPW: February 20, 2016). The 2016 "Stand With JNU" campaign involving protests, formations of human chains, and a long series of lectures delivered on the university's "Freedom Square' on the meaning of nationalism and freedom, stood up for the heterogeneous tradition of educational institutions that fear being decimated by the majoritarian state. Following Rohith Vemula's suicide in February 2016, the "Justice for Rohith" campaign became a nation-wide movement against institutional persecution of Dalit students in Indian universities. A June 2017 public flogging of four Dalit men by cow vigilantes became a turning point in dalit uprising. The "Chalo Una" protests that followed the incident attracted the support of, among others, liberal Hindus who were upset with this state-led politics of terror, and Muslims who were victimized in 2002 Gujarat. The lynching of a young Muslim boy in July 2017 provided the spark to a large number of concerned citizens to speak out against Hindutva-sponsored violence against minority communities. The nation-wide campaign #NotInMyName that emerged in its wake, challenged the idea of citizenship linked to religion or caste, asserting instead a secular democracy that was hard-won by the country's freedom fighters.

The highly neoliberal, modernist, individualist slogan of *Bekhauf Azaadi* during the 2012 anti-rape movement has opened, therefore, a space for addressing what it means to have a holistic feminist movement, and to see the political possibilities of the experience of these women as a way out of the subject-object distinction. I draw on Anu Anurima's claim with reference to the 2017 "#Pinjra Tod" campaign that women of late have been asserting their rights in a different kind of political space where their struggles have expanded from gender-based oppression to a "wider spectrum of issues from labour and caste-based violence … [represented through] feminist radicalism in educational spaces that was created, named, and is constantly being redefined by women. It cannot be folded into, or contained within, other meta narratives, in which women are 'added and stirred'" (2017 fb post).

It would be important to ask the question whether the 2012 anti-rape movement was only for a narrow group of upper class feminists or whether it travelled. I draw on Sawant (2017a) to make the point that while one must not dismiss the significance of this movement simply because it has so far been a middle class, urban phenomenon However, for it to become a truly meaningful movement, the middle class will the need to mature and embrace class-based demands of urban working class, rural and Dalit women, and those that are victims of state-led brutalization in Kashmir, Manipur and Assam. Sawant has faith that this is bound to happen for "history … demonstrates that movements progress from one stage to the next, not reaching full clarity and maturity on day one, but developing through the real-life experience of struggle … The revolutions therefore are not in any way completed, but are learning to go to the next step (workers' struggles, the need for mass strike actions, etc.), and the step after that, and after that, as so on." The examples of abortion rights movement in the US that was led by the middle class and which matured into a fully developed radical struggle once the working class took it up, is a point in case, just as it is in many of the middle eastern countries that were home to the birth of the 2011 Arab Spring.

It would be useful to ask the question what avenues are there, for example, to connect the urban, middle class "Pink Chaddi" campaign to rural-based Gulabi (pink) Gang or low-income, small-town Ekal Nari Shakti Sangathan (Association of Single Strong Women)? Does women's right to the city happen by displacing others or by seeing the connection between their failed rights and the denial of other people's rights? This is our task and we should be asking these questions. Do women leading the "Why Loiter" movement asserting their right to the city also recognize the right for people from Northeast India or from Africa to walk the streets without being called Chinkies or Habshis, and for Dalits to build homes in upper-caste neighborhoods and gain college admission through affirmative action? Would they recognize working class women's right to public places without being harassed? Do members of the "#Pinjra Tod" movement commiserate with diasporic Indian domestic workers trapped in gilded homes in the Middle East? Would those seeking freedom from the Khaps (village council) encourage their domestic helps to share their kitchen utensils? Would it be possible for these young women to mobilize other concerns? Can there be a new vocabulary that is different to their earlier vocabulary of rights which challenged the protectionist developmental state? Is there a way to see if the rights vocabularies of the feminist movement can be linked to questions of class, caste, and religious minorities? If they have put the question of rights to the public, can it become a new vocabulary of protest not only against sexism but also against classism, casteism, and communalism? Can we use this movement to argue for a connection with other movements in the country such as "Justice for Vemula," "Stand with JNU," "#Pinjra Tod," "Chalo Una," "#DalitWomenFight," "#NotInMyName," or the movement against AFSPA in Kashmir and Manipur? If not, what would it take to make this connection?

Acknowledgement

I would like to thank S. Charusheela, Elora Chowdhury, Ayesha Kidwai, Noel O'Sullivan, Liz Philipose, and Kshama Sawant for their very thoughtful comments and suggestions on this chapter.

Notes

1 Passed by the Lok Sabha on March 19, 2013, this act provides for amendment of Indian Penal Code, India Evidence Act, and Code of Criminal Procedure, 1973 on laws related to sexual offence. The Bill received Presidential assent on April 2, 2013 and came into force from April 3, 2013, in light of the protests in the 2012 Delhi gang rape case (Wikipedia).

2 Lobbied by prominent members of the IWM, India's first and only anti-street sexual harassment act was legislated in 1988, called Delhi Prohibition of Eve teasing Act 1988. In addition, there was the establishment of Jagori, the Safe Delhi campaign, and the advocacy group on gender safety in public places.

3 Indian popular culture regularly projects working-class/lower-caste masculinity as the source of sexual harassment of modern, westernized upper-class women. Despite data that proves to the contrary, that women in Indian cities are sexually vulnerable to masculinities from across a range of backgrounds—class, education, and profession.

4 While in the past one had to wait for years—at times decades—one is now able to buy phone connections literally off the shelf.

5 This resulted from the liberation from the hegemonic stranglehold of mainstream music industries such as Bollywood and big gramophone companies facilitated by small-time music producers who flooded the market with cheaply available vernacular, folk, devotional, fusion, and remix music and by the Internet-based music consumers that dispersed music through blogs, YouTube, and websites. Second, it was caused by the undermining of state-licensing monopoly by video-cassette revolution, and cable and satellite TV.

6 Enabled through the flooding of the market with consumer goods and their easy access via bank loans.

7 This can be gleaned from the exponential popularity of Western-produced pornographic films made easily available in video parlors. While these were mostly watched by men, women too watched these in private collective spaces.

8 That criminalizes "sexual acts against the order of nature."

9 See Kavita Krishnan's YouTube statement, December 19, 2012, www. youtube.com/watch?v=pbOhDJFc0Dc, Accessed March 17, 2015, 12:05 p.m.
10 In her talk on "Capitalism, Misogyny, and Sexual Violence," Kavita Krishnan focused on the anti-rape movement that she and her peers organized in the wake of the 2012 Delhi rape incident and the organic coming into being of the "Freedom without Fear" slogan.
11 News media in India were forbidden from covering rape cases until 2008 (Elizabeth Losh 2014).
12 For example the 2011 #Women2Drive campaign in Saudi Arabia; the 2012 #RIPAmina campaign in Morocco; and the 2010 #harassmap and the 2012 #endSH campaigns in Egypt and Lebanon. The 2012 British blog #every-daysexism has reached global popularity.
13 Merging of TV, radio, print media, and the internet.
14 Trishima Mitra-Kahn provides a detailed outline on these online anti-sexist campaigns in her 2015 chapter "Offline issues, online lives? The emerging cyberlife of feminist politics in urban India" in Srila Roy (Ed.) *New South Feminisms: Paradoxes and Possibilities*, (London and New York: Zed Books).

Bibliography

Agnes, Flavia. "Protecting Women against Violence: Review of a Decade of Legislation, 1980–89." *Economic and Political Weekly* 27.17 (1992): WS19–WS33.

Anurima, Anu, facebook post, 2017.

Aline, Sara. "Digital Activism for Women's Rights in the Arab World." http://womeninwar.org/wordpress/wp-content/uploads/2015/08/Beirut/8/Aline%20Sara_Digital%20Activism%20for%20women's%20rights%20in%20the%20Arab%20World.pdf, downloaded 5/20/2017.

Alwis. Malathi De. 2009. "Interrogating the 'Political': Feminist Peace Activism in Sri Lanka," *Feminist* Review, 91. *South Asian Feminisms: Negotiating New Terrains*, 81–93.

Arif, Rauf. Social Movements, YouTube and Political Activism in Authoritarian Countries: A Comparative Analysis of Political Change in Pakistan, Tunisia & Egypt. Dissertation: University of Iowa, 2014.

Baker, Aryn. "Manal Al-Sharif – The World's 100 Most Influential People: 2012." *Time*. 2012.

Barn, Ravinder. 2013. "Social Media and Protest – The Indian Spring?" *The Huffington Post*, 9 January.

Batool, Essar et al. *Do you Remember Kunan Poshpora?: The Story of a Mass Rape (Zuban Series on Sexual Violence and Impunity)*. New Delhi: Zubaan Books, 2016.

Baxi, Pratiksha. 2001. Seminar, 505 www.indiaseminar.com/2001/505/505%20pratiksha%20baxi.htm.

———. 2012. "Rape Culture in India" in kafila.online, December 12, 2017.

Blair, Kristine, Radhika Gajjala, and Christine Tulley. 2009. *Webbing Cyberfeminist Practice: Communities, Pedagogies, and Social Action*, Hampton Press.

Butalia, Urvashi, and Navsharan Singh. "Sexual Violence and Impunity in India." *Out of Print: The Short Story Online*, 26 March 2017, http://outofprint

magazine.co.in/archive/march-2015-issue/urvashi-navsharan_sexual-violence-impunity-in-southasia.html.

Chakravarty, Uma. "Conceptualizing Brahminical Patriarchy," Economic and Political Weekly, April 3, 1993.

———. "Whatever Happened to the Vedic Dasi?" *Recasting Women*. Eds. Kumkum Sangari and Sudesh Vaid. New Delhi: Kali for Women, 1998.

Chakravarti, Uma, Pratiksha Baxi, Suman Bisht, and Janaki Abraham. "Reclaiming Spaces: Gender Spaces on a University Campus." *Constellation of Violence: Feminist Interventions in South Asia*. Eds. Radhika Coomaraswamy and Nimanthi Perera Rajasingham. New Delhi: Women Unlimited, 2008.

Chatterjee, Partha. "The Nationalist resolution of the Women's Question." *Recasting Women*. Eds. Kumkum Sangri and Sudesh Vaid. New Delhi: Kali for Women, 1989.

Chaudhuri, Maitrayee. "What Is New in the New Social Movements? Rethinking Some Old Categories." *Social Movements, Transformative Shifts and Turning Points*. Eds. Savyasaachi Ravi Kumar. New Delhi: Routledge, 2014.

———. "National and Global Media Discourse after the Savage Death of 'Nirbhaya': Instant Access and Unequal Knowledge." *Studying Youth, Media and Gender in Post-Liberalism India: Focus on and Beyond the 'Delhi Gang Rape'*. Eds. Nadja-Christina Schneider and Fritizi-Marie Titzmann. Berlin: Frank & Timme, 2015.

Chaudhuri, Soma, and Sarah Fitzgerald. "Rape Protests in India and the Birth of a New Repertoire." *Social Movement Studies* 14.5 (2015): 622–28.

Crimes in India Report, Crimes Record Bureau, Government of India, 1994, 1995, 1996.

Cochrane, Kira. *All the Rebel Women: The Rise of the Fourth Wave of Feminism*, Audible Studios on Brilliance Audio: MP3 Una Edition, 2017.

Cooper, Brittney C. *Beyond Respectability: The Intellectual Thought of Race Women*, University of Illinois Press, 2017.

Daniels, Jessie. "Rethinking Cyberfeminism(s): Race, Gender, and Embodiment." *Women's Studies Quarterly* 31.1, 2 (2009): 101–24.

"Feminism Online: The New Wave," NDTV, 2017.

Dutta, Debolina and Oishik Sircar. "Indian winter of Discontent: Some Feminist Dilemmas in the Wake of a Rape." *Feminist Studies* 39.1, (2013): 293–306

Gangoli, Geetanjali. *Indian Feminisms: Law, Patriarchies, and Violence in India*. Hampshire: Ashgate, 2007.

Gerbaudo, Paulo. *Tweets and the Streets: Social Media and Contemporary Activism*. London and New York: Pluto Press, 2013.

Ghosh, Shohini. "The Troubled Existence of Sex and Sexuality: Feminists Engage with Censorship." *Image Journeys: Audio-Visual Media and Cultural Change in India*. Eds. Christiane Brosius and Melissa Butcher. New Delhi: Sage, 1999.

———. "From the Frying Pan to the Fire: Dismantled Myths and Deviant Behaviour." *Researching Indian Women*. Ed. Vijaya Ramaswamy. Delhi: Manohar, 2003.

Gopinathan, Sharanya. "Happy 10th Birthday, Hashtag! Feminism has loved you well," *The Ladies Finger*. September 6 (2017)

Guha, Pallavi. "Hashtagging But Not Trending: The Success and Failure of the News Media to Engage with Online Feminist Activism in India." *Feminist Media Studies* 15.1 (2015).

Iyer, Shruti. "Taking a Break from the State: Indian Feminists in the Legal Reform Process." *Journal of International Women's Studies* 17.2 (2015).

Jad, I. 2004. "The NGO-zation of Arab Women's Movement." *IDS Bulletin* 35.4 (2004): 34–42.

John, Mary. Discrepant Dislocations: Feminism, Theory and Postcolonial Histories. Berkley: U of California P, 1996.

Kannabiran, Kalpana. "Feminist Deliberative Politics in India." *Women's Movements in the Global Era: The Power of Local Feminisms*. Ed. Amrita Basu. Boulder, CO: Westview Press, 2010.

Kapur, Ratna. "A Love Song to our Mongrel Selves: Hybridity, Sexuality and the Law." *Social and Legal Studies* 8.3 (1993).

———. "Pink Chaddis and SlutWalk Couture: The Postcolonial Politics of Feminism Lite." *Feminist Legal Studies* 20.1 (2012): 1–20.

———. "Gender, Sovereignty and the Rise of a Sexual Security Regime in International law and Postcolonial India." *Melbourne Journal of International Law* 14.2 (2014): 1–30.

Kapur, Ratna, and Shomona Khanna, "Memorandum on the Reform of Laws relating to Sexual Offences." Center for Legal Research, Delhi, 1996.

Kumar, Radha. 1993. *The History of Doing*, New Delhi: Kali for Women.

———. "From Chipko to Sati: The Contemporary Indian Women's Movement." *Gender Politics in India*. Ed. Nivedita Menon. New Delhi: Oxford University Press, 1999.

Mani, Lata. "Contentious Traditions: The Debate in Sati in Colonial India." *Recasting Women*. Eds. Kumkum Sangri and Sudesh Vaid. New Delhi: Kali for Women, 1989.

Mayaram, Shail. "New Modes of Violence: The Backlash against Women in the Panchayat System." *The Violence of Development: The Politics of Identity, Gender, and Social Inequality in India*. Ed. Karin Kapadia. New Delhi: Kali for Women, 2002.

Mehta, Kalpana. "Women's Movements in India". 2008. www.india-seminar. com/2008/583/583_kalpana_mehta.htm.

Menon, Nivedita, ed. *Gender Politics in India*. New Delhi: Oxford University Press, 1999.

———. *Recovering Subversion: Feminist Politics beyond the Law*. New Delhi: Permanent Black, 2004.

Menon, Nivedita, and Aditya Nigam. *Power and contestation: India Since 1989*. London and New York: Zed Books, 2007.

Menon, Nivedita, *Seeing Like a Feminist*. New Delhi: Zubaan, 2012.

Mitra-Kahn, Trishima. "Offline issues, Online Lives? The Emerging Cyberlife of Feminist Politics in Urban India." *New South Feminisms: Paradoxes and Possibilities*. Ed. Srila Roy. London and New York: Zed Books, 2015.

Mohanty, Chandra Talpade. *Feminism without Borders: Decolonizing Theory, Practicing Solidarity*. Durham, NC and London: Duke U P, 2003.

Monro, Ealasaid. "Feminism: A Fourth Wave?" *Political Insight* 4.2 (2013): 22–25. www.psa.ac.uk/insight-plus/feminism-fourth-wave.

Mumtaz, Khawar. "Advocacy for an End to Poverty, Inequality, and Insecurity: Feminist Social Movements in Pakistan." *Gender and Development* 13.3 (2005): 63–69.

Munshi, Shoma. "A Perfect 10 – 'Modern and Indian': Representation of the Body in Beauty Pagents and the Visual Media in Contemporary India." *Confronting the Body*. Eds. James H. Mills and Satadru Sen. London: Anthem, 2004.

Nadja-Christina, Schneider, and Fritzi Titzmann. *Studying Youth, Media and Gender in Post-Liberalization India: Focus on and beyond the 'Delhi Gang Rape'*. Berlin: Frank & Timm GmbH, 2014.

Naidu, Shiv. "What Can the Opposition Do if Someone Drags You and Rapes You? Says BJP Lawmaker," *The Citizen*, October 18, 2015.

Nandy, Ashish. *The Intimate Enemy*. New Delhi: Oxford University Press, 1983.

Nazneen, Sohela, and Maheen Sultan. "Contemporary Feminist Politics in Bangladesh: Taking the Bull by the Horn." *New South Asian Feminisms: Paradoxes and Possibilities*. Ed. Srila Roy. London: Zed Books, 2012.

Omvedt, Gail. *We Shall Smash This Prison*. London: Zed Books, 1980.

Patel, Vibhuti. "Campaigns against Rape by Women's Movement in India." *DEP* 24 (2014).

Phadke, Shilpa. "Thirty Years on: Women's Studies reflects on the Women's Movement". *Economic and Political Weekly* 38.43 (2003): 4567–76.

Phadke, Shilpa, Sameera Khan, and Shilpa Ranada. *Why Loiter: Women & Risk on Mumbai Streets*. The Citizen. October 18, 2011.

Pudasaini, Surabhi. "Reflections on Occupy Baluwatar." *A Difficult Transition: The Nepal Papers*. Eds. Mandira Sharma and Seira Tamang. New Delhi: Zubaan, 2016.

Rayaprol, Aparna. "Teaching Gender in Indian Universities: Reflections on Feminist Pedagogy." *Sociological Bulletin* 60.1 (2011): 65–78.

Ring, Laura. "Sexual Harassment and the Production of Gender." *Differences: A Journal of Feminist Cultural Studies* 6.1 (1994): 129–67.

Roberts, Tangwen. "Online Feminist Community and the Rippling of a Fourth Wave." *MA Dissertation*, University of York, 2014.

Roy, Kumkum. "Where Women are Worshipped, There the Gods Rejoice." *Women and the Hindu Right*. Eds. Urvashi Butalia and Tanika Sarkar. New Delhi: Kali for Women, 1995.

Roy, Rahul. Interview. 2017.

Roy, Sandeep. "How Protests Against SC Ruling on Sec 377 Revealed a New India." *Firstpost* 16 December 2013.

Sarkar, Tanika. "The Woman as Communal Subject." *Economic and Political Review*, August 31, 1991. P 2057.

Sassen, Saskia. "Towards a Sociology of Information Technology." *Current Sociology* 50.3 (2002): 365–88.

Sawant, Kshama. "Role of Neoliberal Transformation of India's Economy and the New Women's Movements," Unpublished Manuscript. 2017a.

———. "The New Anti-Rape Movement Compared to the Erstwhile Women's Movements in India, and the Question of Class in Relation to Women's Oppression," Unpublished Manuscript. 2017b.

Shahid, Farida. "The Women's Movement in Pakistan: Challenges and Achievements." *Women's Movement in the Global Era: The Power of Local Feminisms*. Ed. Amrita Basu. Westview Press, 2010.

Sharma, Mandira, and Dhiraj Pokhrel. "Impunity for Conflict-Related Sexual Violence in Nepal." *A Difficult Transition: The Nepal Papers*. Eds. Mandira Sharma and Seira Tamang. New Delhi: Zubaan, 2016.

Shehrbano-Zia, Afiya. "The Reinvention of Feminism in Pakistan." *Feminist Review*, 91. *South Asian Feminisms: Negotiating New Terrains*, 2009: 29–46.

Sen, Ronojoy. "The Delhi Rape Protests: Observations on Middle Class Activism in India." *ISAS Brief* 266, Edited by the Institute of South Asian Studies, National University of Singapore, 2013.

Sinha, Prachi. "Run with Gender, Hunt with Class." *Economic and Political Weekly* January 26, 2013.

Solomon, Deborah. "Fourth Wave Feminism." *The New York Times Magazine* November 13, 2009.

Subramanian, Sujatha. "From the Street to the Web: Feminist Activism on Social Media." 2014.

Sunder Rajan, Rajeswari. *Real and Imagined Women: Gender, Culture and Post-Colonialism*. London: Routledge, 1993.

———. *The Scandal of the State: Women, Law and Citizenship in India*. Durham, NC and London: Duke U P/Permanent Black, 2003.

Tellis, Ashley. "Wanted a New Feminist Movement in India." *sify*. 2012. January 2017. www.sify.com/news/wanted-a-new-feminist-movement-in-india-news-columns-mm5lMlgcabfsi.html.

Thapar, Romila. *The Public Intellectual In India*. New Delhi: Aleph Book Company, 2015.

Vance, Carol. *Pleasure and Danger: Exploring Female Sexuality*. Boston and London: Routledge and Kegan Paul, 1984.

Wilding, Faith, and Maria Fernandez. "Feminism, Difference, and Global Capital." *Next Cyberfeminist International*. Eds. C. Sollfrank and Old Boys Network. Hamburg: Hem & Co, 1999.

2 From Mathura to Jyoti

Mapping Public Protests and Anti-Rape Laws in India

Bidisha Biswas

Introduction

The December 2012 gang rape and murder of a student in Delhi led to unprecedented mass street protests across India. As a direct result of the public outcry, the government of India, not usually known for its rapid responses, made significant legislative changes with regard to sexual violence. The international media labeled the 2012 rape case as one that marked a remarkable shift in the Indian public's perceptions and activism in the area of gender violence. In fact, the 2012 protests should be situated within a larger political history of feminism, sustained campaigns against gendered violence, and resulting legislative change. In particular, the Mathura rape case of 1970s set the stage for public activism leading to policy change. This was the first case in independent India that led to a significant and public questioning of rape legislation in the country. The Mathura campaign and its aftermath helped create the foundation for the 2012–2013 protests. This chapter will situate the Delhi protests in its historical context and describe the longer trajectory of popular mobilization in India with regard to state policy towards sexual violence.

Mathura: A Legal Awakening

The Mathura verdict of 1979 was among the earliest flashpoint cases on rape in India, inspiring public protests, feminist organizing, and widespread, and at least partially successful, calls to amend criminal laws relating to sexual violence (Basu 2013). In March 1972, a young tribal woman by the name of Mathura went to a police station in western Maharashtra to lodge a complaint against her brother, who was harassing her for having a boyfriend (Anandan 2012). While at the station, she was raped by two policemen. After lengthy legal proceedings, the Supreme Court of India acquitted the accused in 1979. The justices contended that Mathura had been unable to prove that she had withheld consent to intercourse. In their verdict, the Justices reasoned that Mathura did not raise an alarm till after she left the police station and that she had no visible marks or injuries on her body. The verdict also added that, since the accuser was a tribal woman, she could not possibly have been violated. They concluded that she was accustomed to having sex and may therefore have incited or encouraged the police to have sexual relations with her (Armstrong 2013; Tukaram v. State of Maharashtra 1979).[1]

Mathura's case was by no means the first (or the last) instance of custodial rape.[2] However, the verdict of the Supreme Court, which was shocking in its odious sexism and stereotyping, garnered the attention of some prominent legal scholars. Delhi University law professor, Upendra Baxi, along with three other academics, Lotika Sarkar, Vasudha Dhagamwar, and Raghunath Kelkar, wrote an open letter of protest to the Court. The letter challenged the Supreme Court's assessment of Mathura's "chastity" and situated the case within larger questions of justice for women from marginalized communities. It noted "the young victim's low socio-economic status, lack of knowledge of legal rights and lack of access to legal services, and the fear complex which haunts the poor and the exploited in Indian police stations…" (Lakshmi 2013). The letter urged the Supreme Court Chief Justice to review the case, asking:

> Must illiterate, labouring, politically mute Mathuras of India be condemned to their pre-constitutional Indian fate?… What matters is a search for liberation from the colonial and male-dominated notions of what may constitute the element of consent, and the burden of proof for rape…Nothing short of the protection of human rights and constitutionalism is at stake.
>
> (Lakshmi 2013)

The letter was one of the first instances when the Supreme Court of India had been challenged in such a public manner. Its powerful call for gendered social justice became the catalyst for protests in Delhi and elsewhere in the country. In 1980, after facing sustained and organized demonstrations, the central government of India presented a bill to the Parliament that reshaped India's legal definition of rape. The bill was ultimately passed into law in 1983. While it fell short of the demands made by several women's rights groups, it did introduce some significant legal changes. Under the new law, the onus of proof of consent shifted to the accuser. In other words, if the rape victim says she did not consent to having intercourse, the courts would have to presume likewise. In addition, the law stipulated that custodial rapes would be punishable by no less than seven years in prison. Revealing the identity of a rape victim during legal proceedings became a punishable offense (Sircar 2006). These were the first set of changes to the rape laws since those laws were first enacted in 1860, while India was under British colonial rule (Basu 2013).

As noted above, the open letter to the Supreme Court set the ball rolling for the protests that followed. Readers might be surprised to know, however, that no media outlet in India agreed to publish the open letter immediately after it was written. Initially, members of the Indian press expressed concern that the letter bordered on contempt of court (Savery 2007: 204). The written protest garnered interest in the India media only after it was reprinted in a Pakistani publication, *The Dawn*. As news of the effort spread, Indian feminists came to coalesce around the issue. A number of demonstrations were held in Indian cities such as Ahmedabad, Nagpur, Bombay, and Delhi (Gothoskar and Patel 1982; Savery 2007). The demonstrations were particularly widespread and well-attended on March 8, 1980, which marked International Women's Day. Word of the protests was disseminated by methods such as petitions and street plays. As the issue gained more public attention, it also garnered the interest of rival political parties. While the partisan politicization of custodial rape may not have been the goal of feminist groups, it served to push the government into action (Savey 2007). The resulting turmoil was enough for the government to enact legislative change. The relative success of the Mathura campaign spurred the formation of women's rights groups such as Saheli and Forum Against Rape[3], that have gone on to playing significant roles in the country's non-governmental and activist sectors.

The Intervening Years

Between 1983 and 2012, India's laws regarding rape remained unchanged. However, during this period, women's rights groups continued to agitate for further legislative changes related to gender violence. One seminal case was that of Bhanwari Devi. Bhanwari Devi was a social worker working with the Government of the State of Rajasthan on a campaign against child marriage. In 1992, Bhanwari Devi was gang raped by a group of upper caste men as "punishment" for her efforts against entrenched social practices. Bhanwari Devi battled significant obstacles, including ostracization and hostile medical and law enforcement personnel, to bring the perpetrators to justice. In 1995, three years after the attack on her, a sessions court acquitted the men on the grounds that upper-caste men could not have raped a Dalit woman (Chakravarti 2003).[4] The court further argued that the accused, who were relatives, would not have raped the same woman, and that Bhanwari's husband could not have passively watched the attack on his wife. The obvious failure of justice in this case, and the unwillingness of the state government to stand up for its employee, provoked women's organizations to file a petition in the Supreme Court asking for clearer guidelines on sexual harassment at the workplace. The apex court judgment, which came on August 13, 1997, issued the Vishaka guidelines that hold employers responsible for providing a safe work environment for women.[5] However, despite legislation passed during this period on other gender equality issues, such as dowry harassment, the first legal change regarding sexual violence would not occur till three decades later, in 2013.

Jyoti Singh

In December 2012, a twenty-three year-old woman, Jyoti Singh, accompanied by a male friend, Awindra Pandey, boarded a bus in Delhi. The six men on the bus attacked and beat both passengers and gang raped Jyoti. The woman eventually died of the injuries sustained during the ordeal. Even in Delhi, a city so accustomed to reports of sexual violence that it is known as the rape capital of India, the brutality of this particular assault came as a shock. In response, Delhi was rocked by citywide street protests that shut down large parts of the capital city. Other cities and towns across India also witnessed huge demonstrations.

The protests that swept through urban India during this time demanded speedy and retributive justice for Jyoti Singh. The demonstrators, many of whom were college students and first-time participants in protests, also demanded changes to existing laws and to prevailing social norms. While the Mathura protests addressed socioeconomic questions, such as the marginalization of tribal women, the Delhi protests were more individualistic. Posters with statements such as "My body, my right," "My dress is not a yes," and "Don't tell your daughter not to go out. Tell your son to behave properly" communicated the concerns of the urban middle class and were widely covered in the print and electronic media (Ashok 2013; Lodhia 2015).

At a pace rarely seen in Indian politics, the central government of India instituted a committee, headed by Justice J. S. Verma, former Chief Justice of the Supreme Court of India, to suggest changes to laws regarding sexual violence. The Verma Committee submitted its recommendations on January 23, 2013, just a month after it had been constituted. In March 2013, the Indian Parliament enacted a bill that included several of the Verma Committee's suggestions.[6] Under the new law, stalking and acid attacks would now be considered criminal offenses. In addition, the death penalty can now be applied to cases where the act of sexual assault causes death (Khalsa and Khambatta 2013). The definition of rape has been expanded to include oral sex and rape with the insertion of objects. It also addressed other forms of violence against women, creating separate offenses for stalking, voyeurism, acid attacks, and the forcible stripping of women. These provisions, along with the promise of speedier trials, were aimed at providing a stronger legal framework for combatting and deterring sexual violence. Some of the legal provisions, such as the criminalization of stalking had been the long-standing demand of women's rights activists. Others, such as the application of death penalty, are more controversial. Some long-standing demands of women's groups, such as the issue of marital rape, were not addressed at all. Overall, despite their limitations, the changes made to existing laws in 2013 marks a significant policy change to tackle, deter, and punish sexual violence in India within the legal framework. Further, the intensity of the protests that formed the catalyst for the 2013 law shows that public reaction to gender violence can be impactful in the policy sphere.

Similarities and Differences

The public protests surrounding these two sets of cases, the Mathura verdict in 1979 and the Jyoti Singh attack of 2012, were both seminal in their scope and outcome. They highlighted the power of public mobilization to affect legislative change. A comparison of the two sets of events can help us understand the similarities and differences in the protest environment between the two periods.

The Mathura case was, as described above, the first case in independent India that saw public protests against the judiciary's decision regarding sexual violence. The agitation occurred within an environment of greater sociopolitical awareness regarding women's rights and the dismal record of Indian law enforcement in protecting those rights. In 1978, a controversy erupted over the rape of Rameezabee, a Muslim working class woman from Hyderabad, in the southern state of Andhra Pradesh. Her husband, who was with her at the time, was beaten severely and later succumbed to his injuries. The police, backed by the state, claimed that Rameezabee was a prostitute and that her husband was a pimp. An investigation committee found that these allegations were unfounded and castigated the police and other state actors for their complicity in covering up the injustice inflicted upon Rameezabee and her husband (Prasad 1978). In 1980, Maya Tyagi, a young woman in the northern state of Uttar Pradesh was stripped in public and gang raped by the police. Her husband was shot dead, along with two of his friends. It was only eight years later, in 1988, that the accused in this case were found guilty and sentenced to life imprisonment (Bonner 1990; Gangoli 2011).

Taken together, these three episodes—Mathura, Maya, and Rameezabee—put India's custodial rape laws in a harsh light. Occurring in the immediate aftermath of the traumatic Emergency period, they served to mobilize activists and the public consciousness in an unprecedented manner (Agnes 2013). A multiplicity of tools was used to generate popular enthusiasm for the campaign to change the legal framework. This included public meetings, poster campaigns, skits, street theatre, signature campaigns, rallies, and demonstrations. Coverage by the print media served to enhance awareness about the salience of these cases. As a result of the success of the Mathura campaign in changing state policy, the women's rights movement was able to gain a national character and presence (Agnes 2013).

The 1983 legal changes were just one element of a long struggle against India's patriarchal norms and structures. In many crucial areas, including marital rape and the importance of character evidence as a way of protecting 'honorable men', the legislation did *not* address the pressing concerns of women's groups in India. Still, it was a significant one in that it created the space for a more progressive set of verdicts. For example, in a case in 1991, the Supreme Court said:

> The unchastity of a woman does not make her open to any and every person to violate her person as and when he wishes. She is entitled to protect herself if there is an attempt to violate her person against her wish. She is equally entitled to protection of law. Therefore, merely because she is of easy virtue, her evidence cannot be thrown out.
>
> (Mahapatra 2013)

The Mathura protests and ensuing policy changes helped the Indian social and legal environment to at least formally reject that the assumption that a rape victim enables or invites her accuser.[7] Nonetheless, India remained a country in which few convictions resulted from rape charges and regressive interpretations of existing laws continued (Agnes 2013; Savery 2007).

Three decades later, the protests surrounding the Jyoti Singh case built off the foundation placed by the Mathura verdict protests, as well as the activism of women's groups in the intervening years.[8] The resulting changes were the next major step in reforming Indian legislation with regard to sexual violence. At the same time, the character of the Jyoti protests marked a significant shift from Mathura in at least three ways, each of which is addressed below.

The Media

It is useful, at this juncture, to consider how the role of the media changed between the Mathura and Jyoti Singh cases. In the Mathura case, as noted above, newspapers were reticent in speaking out against the Supreme Court. By 2012, the media landscape of India had changed considerably, with an exponential increase in its scope, reach, and intensity. Television channels are now the largest players in Indian news coverage and these played a seminal role in disseminating information about the attack and its aftermath. Their persistent coverage of the victim, her family, and of the brutality of the case encouraged the public to take to the streets and demand justice.[9] The international media also covered the case and the resultant protests extensively, not least because India's presence on the global stage had been enhanced in the intervening years. As such, both print and electronic media became an important mobilizing tool for what was essentially a leaderless movement.[10] Rather than simply reporting on the issue, newspapers and TV channels engaged in active editorializing and exhorting the public to agitate for change.

A new feature of the 2012 protests, as compared to Mathura, was the use of social media platforms. Such forums were, of course, simply not present in the 1970s. It is worth noting that most of the protests occurred in urban areas and thousands of Indian youth used platforms such as Twitter and Facebook to mobilize protestors. The government's own missteps, including police crackdown on unarmed protestors using tear gas and water cannons and statements by prominent politicians questioning the victim's "morality", were all widely covered and disseminated through both social and electronic (televised) media. These served to further outrage public opinion and encourage the protestors (Bennett-Smith 2013; "Foot in Mouth" 2013; Hullinger 2013; Lakshmi 2013).[11]

As we consider the long-term policy implications of such mobilization, we should note that social media usage in India is limited to high-income sections of the population. By some estimates, nearly 80% of Indians now have a mobile phone, but only 11% have Internet access, and fewer than 5% use social media. A strong gender skew affects the use of information technologies. Men are 25% more likely to have cellphones than women and are 62% more likely to use the internet. Male smartphone or feature phone users in India are three times as likely as women users to have used Facebook (Lucini 2016).

Notwithstanding these income, gender, and urban-rural divides, social media platforms did serve as an important mobilizing tools for affluent and middle-class urban protestors. While only a small section of the Indian population may have access to social media, this section of society tends to be wealthy, vocal, and influential (Belair-Gagnon, Mishra, and Agur 2013; Poell and Rajagopalan 2015). The Jyoti Singh protests demonstrate that new media technologies, while not a substitute for traditional protest mechanisms, can help create a social and political space where citizens can effectively agitate for change (Chattopadhyay 2011; Subramanian 2013).

Organizational Structure

The structure of the protests themselves were quite different between the two cases. Recall that, in the case of Mathura, it took years between the custodial attack and the protests against the Supreme Court verdict. The protests themselves were shaped by a detailed, open letter drafted by prominent legal scholars and carefully organized by committed activists. In contrast, the Jyoti protests occurred spontaneously and almost immediately after news of her ordeal had been covered in the media. The first demonstrations, which were organized by students of Jawaharlal Nehru University, occurred in Delhi on December 18, 2012, less than forty-eight hours after the bus attack. As the protests spread throughout the city and the country, the movement remained leaderless. Perhaps because of the amorphous structure of the Delhi campaign, it did not build a sustained presence and the protests dissipated soon after the 2013 legislation was passed (Chaudhuri and Fitzgerald 2015). Nonetheless, the 2012–2013 occurences created, at the very least, a template for future mass mobilization, using both traditional protest tools such as demonstrations and new media technologies such as Facebook, to effect policy change.

The Voices of the Victims

While Mathura took the bold step of filing a complaint against her attackers, she was largely reticent during the protests surrounding her case. In sharp contrast, both Jyoti and her family were very vocal. Jyoti Singh herself gave statements to the police from her hospital bed and was widely lauded for her courage in doing so. Her father, Badri Singh, released his daughter's name to the press stating that he "hoped it would give courage to other women who have survived these attacks" and called for speedy justice for her and other victims. He added that "I know one day people will forget her. But they will remember her death led to changes. Changes in the anti-rape laws, a change in consciousness" (Farhoud and Andrabi 2013; Lodhia 2015). His statements challenged the pervasive norms of shame, secrecy, and family 'honor' that surround gender-based violence in India. It is notable that Jyoti Singh's family is of modest means. Her parents' active role in supporting the protests belie the claim made by some that the movement was entirely about elite concerns (Ghosh 2013a, b; Kumar 2013).

A Demonstration of the Power of Protests

The Mathura and the Jyoti protests demonstrate the power of public protests. In both cases, mass mobilization of a nonviolent nature was able to successfully challenge the state in order to enact policy change with regard to sexual violence in India. Demonstrators engaged in disruptive activity, such as road blockades and mass public gatherings, in order to press for change. At the same time, they remained peaceful, even in the face of police violence.[12] These dimensions of the protest movements are consistent with existing literature, which highlights the success of nonviolent resistance in affecting government decisions (Chenoweth and Cunnigham 2013; Roberts 2010).

The Jyoti Singh protests also help us understand the enormous mobilizing power of a networked population. As discussed above, social media played an important role in coalescing protestors. Potential activists who have access to electronic and social media often have a greater ability to undertake collective action, because their costs of coordination and participation are relatively low. The use of social media also helps individuals develop a shared awareness of issues and of their own political power (Shirky 2011). Coordinated action of non-formal groups of people demonstrate their willingness and ability to develop and act upon a shared area of understanding and interest. The use of social media enables this shared arena to grow without the barriers of hierarchy and time (Shirky 2011). At the same time, as noted above, this medium of shared meaning has its own barrier—that of access. Hierarchies of income, gender, and location all serve to limit the use of new media technologies to select segments of the population (Lucini 2016). Mobilization that relies on a networked population restricts participation to those that can afford to be networked.

The Historical Context: Feminism, Protests and the State

This section places the Mathura and Jyoti Singh protests in the context of the feminist movement in India. Emerging out of a larger social reform movement, the campaign for greater empowerment of women can be traced to the mid-nineteenth century. Initiated by Hindu upper-caste men, the focus was on educating women and giving them more social and political rights (Guha Ghosal 2005). This orientation had some parallels to the first wave of feminism in the United States, which also demanded more education opportunities for women. India gained independence in 1947 and the Indian Constitution, adopted in 1956, recognized men and women as equal citizens with equal political rights (Chitnis 2004). This was in stark contrast to the American experience, where women gained the right to vote only after a protracted struggle. In India, the constitutional and legal framework was supportive of equal rights for women in a number of areas. Consistent with the overall national policy towards development, women's groups sought to work with the government in promoting education and employment, rather than engaging in grassroots activism (Sen 2000). Gender violence was not explicitly addressed.

In the 1970s, a more activist movement, one that was critical of the Indian state, marked the beginning of the second wave of feminism in India. Activists pointed out that the state had shown itself to be unable or unwilling to implement legal protections for women. Grassroots mobilization and protests about social justice issues became more prevalent in the feminist movement (Sen 2000). The Mathura protests, demanding the recognition of the rights and dignity of tribal communities and other vulnerable groups, arose out of this context of social justice. Similarly, the campaign for legal changes in light of Bhanwari Devi's experience explicitly called upon the state to do more to protect women in general, and women belonging to vulnerable groups in particular.

As noted earlier in the paper, the 1980s and 1990s saw continuing efforts at social and legal change by a number of women's groups in India. We did not, however, witness the emergence of a cohesive national feminist movement in the country. In fact, women's rights came to be subsumed under many other polarizing demands on social issues, including caste and religion (Vijaya and Biswas 2016). As India embarked on a path of neoliberal economic policies, the focus of the middle class (and those aspiring to join the middle class) shifted away from social justice towards the pursuit of material prosperity. It was in this context that the Jyoti Singh protests occurred. The demonstrators were vociferous in asking for speedy arrests, fast-track trials, and, in many cases, capital punishment (Amrute 2015). Placards with statements such as "Give us Justice, Hang the Rapists" and staged, mock hangings in public sites were clearly visible during the protests (Huffington Post 2013). It is ironic that, while they were in direct confrontation with state authorities (such as the Delhi police), the young demonstrations were asking for a more assertive projection of coercive, state power. With a few exceptions, the social justice questions that marked the Mathura and Bhanwari Devi protests were absent. Concerns about state-sanctioned or condoned abuses of power were, for the most part, overwhelmed by the protestors' demands for speedy and retributive justice (Gangoli 2007; Poell and Rajagopalan 2015).

Undoubtedly, the state has an important role in promoting feminist goals, including providing effective policing, criminal justice, and legal measures in order to support women in their ability to move, work, make choices, or otherwise live freely. On the other hand, we also know that state authorities and policies can undermine the position and rights of women. For example, the Verma Committee identified the controversial Armed Forces Special Powers Act (AFSPA) as being highly detrimental to the safety and freedom of women. AFSPA was first introduced in 1958 in India's northeastern provinces and then expanded, in a modified version, to Jammu and Kashmir in 1990. In the provinces where it is in force, AFSPA gives considerable powers to military personnel, who can, among other things, arrest or detain civilians indefinitely and without a warrant. The military cannot be held accountable for any actions carried out under the provisions of the Act except by direct dispensation of the central government (Ministry of Home Affairs 1990). In effect, these provisions give military personnel near total impunity. Human rights organizations have recorded a number of abuses perpetrated as a consequence, including disappearances, torture, arbitrary detention, and extrajudicial killings (Biswas 2014; Human Rights Watch 2008). The

Verma Committee noted that "impunity for systematic or isolated sexual violence in the process of Internal Security duties is being legitimized by the Armed Forces Special Powers Act, which is in force in large parts of our country." (p. 149) The Committee recommended that allegations of sexual violence perpetrated by members of the armed forces or other law enforcement agencies be brought under ordinary criminal law and that AFSPA be reviewed (Verma, Seth, and Subramanium 2013). AFSPA is a law that is designed to enhance state capacity in the area of hard security (counterinsurgency efforts). At the same time, it clashes with the state's obligations to protect the human security of its citizens. Noting this, the Verma Committee asked for changes that would allow victims of sexual assault by security forces easier recourse to justice.[13] This was, however, rejected by the Parliament.

It is not surprising that the Government did not accept the recommendations of the Verma Committee with regard to security force abuses, given that it has been notably reluctant to consider requests to reform or repeal AFSPA (Biswas and Goel 2014). What is interesting, however, is that the public protests that rocked India in 2012–2013 made few references to AFSPA or to other instances where state security policy clashes with human rights and human security. The mainstream media also gave almost no coverage to this issues. It focused instead on demands for harsh punishment for the Delhi rapists. For example, *The Times of India* ran front page articles suggesting that those found guilty of rape should be subject to chemical castration (Singh 2012). The selective orientation arguably ignores marginalized groups in India that have long protested state-sanctioned or state-condoned abuse and violence (Mani 2014; Shah 2012). Far from the glare of national media and high-decibel protests, women from marginalized communities have remained targets of routinized sexual violence before, during, and after the 2012–2013 protests. In effect, the impact of the Delhi rape protests was circumscribed by the implied assumption that dignity and freedom of movement matter only when they concern specific segments of Indian society.

In the United States, third-wave feminists have argued that women, people of color, and others have multiple and shifting identities and experiences (Walker 1992). They have sought to move away from political agendas that relate to the demands of particular groups of women. Third-wave feminists argue that such an approach unfairly simplifies the complexities of individual, personal narratives. The Delhi protests can be seen as a mark of third-wave feminism because of its focus on the individual liberties of women in public spaces. This is certainly an important, and unmet, demand for many in India. At the same time, the focus on individualized rights and the affiliated demand for punitive justice does not fully address the needs of women from marginalized communities. Dalit, Muslim, Kashmiri, and *adivasi* women, among others, find their most basic economic, social, and political rights circumscribed by their assigned group identity. The protests of 2012–2013 did little, if anything, to ameliorate the abject lack of justice that the most vulnerable groups in India face on a daily basis.

A Temporary Mobilization or a Social Movement?

Did the Delhi rape protests represent a social movement? In order to answer this question, we must first define what a social movement is. A social movement represents a collective action based on common purpose, social solidarity, and *sustained* [emphasis added] interaction (Melucci 1996; Tarrow 2011). The Mathura protests clearly helped create a sustained interaction on women's issues, as witnessed through the creation of women's groups, such as Saheli and the Forum Against the Oppression of Women, that have gone on to be a resolute voice for women's empowerment in India.

It is still early to assess whether the Jyoti protests will be the harbinger of such long-term solidarity. Much of the initial emotional resonance of the case has ebbed and the protestors have, as it were, gone back to their day jobs. The media has continued its round the clock coverage of assaults of women. However, observers have noted, with concern, the sensationalist and even salacious tone of much of this coverage. For example, Prannoy Roy, one of India's most well-known television journalists and co-founder of New Delhi Television (NDTV), has lamented the tabloid-like nature of Indian journalism today. In 2013, he spoke of a news channel anchor who "twirled her hair with her forefinger, looked into the camera and said 'Break *ke baad aapko ek* rape *dikhayenge*'—'After the break we will show you a rape.'" (Roy 2013: 13).

At the same time, both the Jyoti and the Delhi protests show us that ordinary people have power because they can organize, demand, challenge, and lend, through individual and collective action, meaning to a particular situation (Melucci 1996; Tarrow 2011). The open letter in response to the Mathura verdict galvanized sections of Indian society and the state to reject pernicious assumptions about the "character" of women who have been raped. Similarly, when the Delhi protestors demanded the right to move in the city without being the target of sexual assaults, they served to delegitimize those, including public figures, who were engaging in "blame the victim" typecasting. Many of these critiques were disseminated through both social media and televised programs. As such, the two cases showcase the ability of peaceful protests to give rise to intense contention and resulting policy change.

Interesting parallels can be drawn between the Delhi protests and the anti-corruption demonstrations that had had swept India in 2011. Like with the anti-rape campaign, these protests were spread all over India, with the largest protests in Delhi. In both cases, large numbers of young, middle-class, and urban demonstrators were able to agitate, successfully, for policy change.[14] In both cases, social media became an important tool of mobilization. Neither movement was able to maintain a sustained presence after the passage of the relevant legal bills.

In sum, the similarities of the two movements include demographics, use of social media, and the rapid disintegration of the movement after the initial attainment of significant policy changes (Poell and Rajagopalan 2015). It would be interesting to assess, in future research, the extent to which the Jyoti Singh protests and the anti-corruption protests as well as other movements illustrate, if at all, a new middle-class activism. Such activism has intersections—and divergences—with feminism, but it also has the potential to shed light on larger questions related to contentious politics. Scholars should also investigate and compare protests around the world to ascertain if there can be a global compact on the issues of gender violence in both public and private spaces. Finally, the challenges of reconciling group-specific experiences with the individual narratives of third-wave feminists should be subject to greater exploration.

Conclusion

This chapter has shown us that, when collective actors join forces to confront and challenge elites and authorities through peaceful but forceful contentious politics, significant changes to policy and norms can result. Had it not been for the mass protests following the Supreme Court justice, Mathura would have been just another name among many of tribal women who have been denied justice.[15] The mass, nationwide protests of 2012–2013 pushed an otherwise lethargic government in Delhi to enact significant changes to legislation on sexual violence. The Verma Committee Report itself noted that:

> ...the constitution of this Committee is in response to the country-wide peaceful public outcry of civil society, led by the youth, against the failure of governance to provide a safe and dignified environment for the women of India, who are constantly exposed to sexual violence.
> (i)[16]

Yet, as evidenced by continuing concerns about the safety of women in India, and lack of access to speedy and reliable justice, much remains to be done with regard to the enforcement of laws and diffusion of new norms. Furthermore, the calls for increased state capacity that marked the Jyoti Singh protests ignored the fact that, in numerous parts of the country, state actors are actively engaging in sexual violence and oppression. It should also be a matter of concern that the women in marginalized communities and/or minorities, including Dalits, *advisasis*, religious minorities, and others, have little or no recourse to justice. The need for a sustained and persistent call for changes in social mores, state policy, and structural inequities remains as urgent today as it was in 1979.

Notes

1 Tribal communities in India, classified as Scheduled Tribes (ST) under the Indian Constitution, refer to a number of indigenous groups or *adivasis*. STs are among the most socially, politically, and economically deprived groups in India. As such, they are provided certain protections under Indian law, including preferential access to educational institutions and jobs and protection from discrimination (Vijaya and Biswas 2016). *Adivasi* communities often have social and cultural mores that are distinct from caste Hindus and other religious and ethnic groups in India. In their verdict, the Justices were reflecting a widely held view that tribal women have more sexually permissive lifestyles than other women in the country.

2 Custodial rape refers to assaults that occur while the victim is in police custody. This is viewed as a widespread occurrence in India. According to the National Crime Records Bureau of India, in 2014, 197 cases of custodial rape were recorded in India. Given the overall climate of police impunity in the country, the number reported by NCRB is likely a significant underestimation of the actual numbers of custodial assaults. Human Rights Watch and other nongovernmental groups note that the vast majority of women subject to custodial rape are from marginalized and disadvantaged backgrounds (National Crime Records Bureau Data, available at http://ncrb.nic. in; Human Rights Watch 1991).

3 This organization is now called Forum against Oppression of Women.

4 A term popularized by the Dr. B. R. Ambedkar, the architect of the Indian constitution, Dalits refers to those Hindus who have traditionally been called "untouchables." Dalits fall outside or below the four-tier hierarchy of the Hindu caste system and were historically relegated to professions considered "impure," such as cleaning human waste. Traditionally, any physical contact between caste Hindus and Dalits was forbidden as it would make the former impure. Dalits are part of the constitutionally protected category, Scheduled Castes, who are accorded a series of special considerations under Indian law. The term now encompasses lower caste Hindus (traditionally called *shudras*) who are also part of the Scheduled Caste category.

5 This demand was in response to the fact that the Government of Rajasthan, with whom Bhanwari Devi was working, did not take any steps to protect or to support her legal efforts to get justice. Actual parliamentary legislation that formally adopted these guidelines were adopted only in 2013.

6 The full text of the Verma Committee's report can be found online at www.prsindia.org/parliamenttrack/report-summaries/justice-verma-committee-report-summary-2628/.

7 It is notable that some political figures questioned Jyoti's "morality" in being out late at night. Nonetheless, the dominant public discourse, and the policy changes that were to follow, seemed to reject such assumptions.

8 Saheli, for example, has worked on a number of issues, domestic violence, dowry, and reproductive health. Forum against Rape/Forum against Oppression of Women has long advocated for a variety of policy measures to tackle gender-based violence and other issues. For more information, please see Economic and Political Weekly (2010).

9 For example, on January 4, 2013, as the protests were well underway, the popular Zee News Channel published a searing interview with Awindra Pandey, who discussed police apathy after he and Jyoti Singh were thrown off the moving bus. On December 30, 2012, the Times of India published a front page article entitled "Rest in Peace Nirbhaya, We Won't until India is Safer for Women," http://timesofindia.indiatimes.com/india/Rest-in-peace-Nirbhaya-we-wont-until-India-is-safer-for-women/articleshow/17813319. cms.

10 While the statements and actions of certain individuals, such as Kavita Krishnan of All India Progressive Women's Association and Arvind Kejriwal of Aam Aadmi Party, were widely covered in the media, they were viewed as spokespersons for their respective organizations, rather than the movement as a whole (Chaudhuri and Fitzgerald 2015).

11 The 2012–2013 protests were not, it should be noted, the first time that social media was harnessed to protest the moral policing of, and attacks on, women. The 2009 Pink Chaddi Campaign (PCC), which protested an attack on women in a pub in the southern city of Bangalore, was largely the result of mobilization through Facebook. See Chattopadhyay (2011).

12 Police violence was widely covered—and condemned—by the Indian print and electronic media.

13 www.prsindia.org/parliamenttrack/report-summaries/justice-verma-committee-report-summary-2628/.

14 In response to the 2011 protests, the central government of India enacted the Lokpal Act in 2013. This bill provides for an institutional framework for investigation into allegations of corruption against public officials.

15 The perpetrators of the attack on Mathura were never convicted. Nonetheless, her name remains alive in the annals of India's history of feminist and social justice mobilization.

16 The full text of the report is available at www.prsindia.org/parliamenttrack/report-summaries/justice-verma-committee-report-summary-2628/.

References

Agnes, Flavia. "No Shortcuts on Rape: Make the Legal System Work." *Economic and Political Weekly* XLVIII.2 (2013): 12–15.

Forum against the Oppression of Women. "Feminist Contributions from the Margins: Shifting Conceptions of Work and Performance of the Bar Dancers of Mumbai." *Economic and Political Weekly* 45.44/45 (2010): 48–55.

Amrute, Sareeta. "Moving Rape: Trafficking in the Violence of Postliberalization." *Public Culture* 27.2 (2015): 331–359.

Anandan, Sujata. "Remember Mathura?" *The Hindustan Times*. 26 December 2012. www.hindustantimes.com/columns/remember-mathura/story-20s5V27y2c HkCbTNCy9XlI.html. Accessed September 8, 2016.

Armstrong, Elisabeth. *Gender and Neoliberalism: The All India Democratic Women's Association and Globalization Politics*. London: Routledge, 2013.

Ashok, Sowmiya. "It Is Not Delhi that Has Changed, Rather the Women Have Changed." *The Hindu*. 17 December 2013. www.thehindu.com/todays-paper/tp-national/tp-newdelhi/it-is-not-delhi-that-has-changed-rather-the-women-have-changed/article5468237.ece. Accessed August 8, 2017.

Basu, Moni. "The Girl Whose Rape Changed a Country," *CNN*. 2013. www.cnn.com/interactive/2013/11/world/india-rape/. Accessed August 8, 2017.

Belair-Gagnon, Valerie, Smeeta Mishra, and Colin Agur. "Emerging Spaces for Storytelling: Journalistic Lessons from Social Media in the Delhi Gang Rape Case." *Neiman Lab* 2013. www.niemanlab.org/2013/04/emerging-spaces-for-storytelling-journalistic-lessons-from-social-media-in-the-delhi-gang-rape-case/. Accessed August 7, 2017.

Bennett-Smith, Meredith. "New Delhi Gang Rape Victim Partly to Blame for Brutal Attack, Lawyer Manohar Lal Sharma Suggests." *The Huffington Post.* 11 January 2013. www.huffingtonpost.com/2013/01/10/new-delhi-gang-rape-victim-blame-attack-lawyer-manohar-lal-sharma_n_2451398.html. Accessed February 8, 2017.

Biswas, Bidisha. *Managing Conflicts in India: Policies of Coercion and Accommodation.* Lanham, MD: Lexington Books, 2014.

Biswas, Bidisha, and Anish Goel. "In Kashmir, They Disappear: Civilians, Militants, and Democracy". *Foreign Policy: The South Asia Channel* (7 November 2014). http://southasia.foreignpolicy.com/posts/2014/11/07/in_kashmir_they_disappear_civilians_militants_and_democracy. Accessed August 8, 2017.

Bonner, Arthur. *Averting the Apocalypse: Social Movements in India Today.* Durham, NC: Duke University Press, 1990.

Chakravarti, Uma. *Gendering Caste: Through a Feminist Lens.* Kolkata: Stree, 2003.

Chattopadhyay, Saayan. "Online Activism for a Heterogeneous Time: The Pink Chaddi Campaign and the Social Media in India." *Proteus* 27.1 (2011): 61–67.

Chaudhuri, Soma and Sarah Fitzgerald. "Rape Protests in India and the Birth of a New Repertoire." *Social Movement Studies* 1.5 (2015): 1–7.

Chenoweth, Erica and Kathleen G. Cunnigham. "Understanding Non-Violent Resistance: An Introduction." *Journal of Peace Research* 50.3 (2013): 271–276.

Chitnis, Suma. "Feminism: Indian Ethos and Indian Convictions." *Feminism in India.* Ed. Maitrayee Chaudhuri. New Delhi: Kali for Women, 2004. 8–25.

Farhoud, Nada and Jalees Andrabi. 2013. "India Gang Rape Victim's Father: I Want the World to Know My Daughter's Name Is Jyoti Singh." *The Mirror* 5 January 2013. www.mirror.co.uk/news/world-news/india-gang-rape-victims-father-1521289. Accessed March 8, 2017.

Gangoli, Geetanjali. *Indian Feminisms: Campaigns against Violence and Multiple Patriarchies.* Aldershot: Ashgate.

Gangoli, Geetanjali. "Controlling Women's Sexuality: Rape Law in India." *International Approaches to Rape.* Eds. Nicole Westmarland and Geetanjali Gangoli. Bristol: Policy Press, 2011. 101–46.

Ghosh, Palash. "Delhi Gang-Rape Protests: What about the Sex Crimes against Untouchable Women?" *International Business Times* 5 January 2013a. www.ibtimes.com/delhi-gang-rape-protests-what-about-sex-crimes-against-untouchable-women-992666. Accessed August 8, 2017.

Ghosh, Palash. "Delhi Gang-Rape: One Year Later, What Has Really Changed in India?" *International Business Times* 16 December 2013b. www.ibtimes.com/delhi-gang-rape-one-year-later-what-has-really-changed-india-1510494. Accessed August 8, 2017.

Gothoskar, Sujata and Vitubai Patel. "Documents from the Indian Women's Movement." *Feminist Review* 12.1 (1982 October): 92–103.

Guha Ghosal, Sarbani. "Major Trends of Feminism in India." *The Indian Journal of Political Science* LXVI.4 (2005): October–December.

Huffington Post. "India Gang Rape Case: Death Penalty Demanded by Protesters in New Delhi" (21 January 2013). www.huffingtonpost.com/2013/01/29/india-gang-rape-case_n_2573444.html. Accessed August 8, 2017.

Hullinger, Jessica. "India's Deadly Gang Rape: 6 Troubling Attempts to Blame the Victim." *The Week* 9 January 2013. http://theweek.com/article/index/238542/indias-deadly-gang-grape-6-troubling-attempts-to-blame-the-victim. Accessed August 8, 2017.

Human Rights Watch. Prison Conditions in India. 1991. www.hrw.org/sites/default/files/reports/INDIA914.pdf. Accessed August 8, 2017.

Human Rights Watch. *Getting Away with Murder: 50 Years of the Armed Forces (Special Powers) Act*. 2008. www.hrw.org/legacy/backgrounder/2008/india0808/india0808web.pdf. Accessed August 8, 2017.

Khalsa, Guruamrit and Persis Khambatta. "New Sexual Assault Laws in India: Only the Beginning." *The Asia Foundation* 2013. http://asiafoundation.org/in-asia/2013/03/06/new-sexual-assault-laws-in-india-only-the-beginning/. Accessed August 8, 2017.

Kumar, Sunaina. 2013. "The Biggest Change Is That Nobody Is Calling Her a 'Zinda Laash': Flavia Agnes". *Tehelka.com* 26 August 2013. www.tehelka.com/the-biggest-change-is-that-nobody-is-calling-her-a-zinda-laash-flavia-agnes/. Accessed August 8, 2017.

Lakshmi, Rama. 2013. "India Struggles with Social Media following Rape Uproar." *The Washington Post* 25 January 2013. www.washingtonpost.com/world/asia_pacific/india-struggles-with-social-media-following-rape-uproar/2013/01/04/7896933e-559a-11e2-89de-76c1c54b1418_story.html. Accessed August 8, 2017.

Lodhia, Sharmila. "From 'Living Corpse' to India's Daughter: Exploring the Social, Political and Legal Landscape of the 2012 Delhi Gang Rape." *Women's Studies International Forum* 50 (2015 May/June): 89–101.

Lucini, Barbara Arese. 2016. *Connected Society: Consumer Barriers to Mobile Internet Adoption in Asia*. GSMA Intelligence. www.gsmaintelligence.com/research/?file=c52d213ec6288da6b31248df71e370a3&download. Accessed August 8, 2017.

Mahapatra, Dhananjay. 2013. "After Anti-Rape Ordinance, Change in Mindset Needed." *The Times of India* 4 February 2013. http://timesofindia.indiatimes.com/india/After-anti-rape-ordinance-change-in-mindset-needed/articleshow/18327035.cms. Accessed August 8, 2017.

Mani, Lata. "Sex and the Signal-Free Corridor: Towards a New Feminist Imaginary." *Economic and Political Weekly* XLIX.6 (2014): 26–29.

Melucci, Alberto. *Challenging Codes: Collective Action in the Information Age*. New York: Cambridge University Press, 1996.

Ministry of Home Affairs. "Armed Forces (Jammu and Kashmir) Special Powers Act, 1990." New Delhi: Government of India. 1990. http://mha.nic.in/pdfs/Armed%20forces%20_J&K_%20Spl.%20powers%20act,%201990.pdf. Accessed March 3, 2017.

Poell, Thomas and Sudha Rajagopalan. "Connecting Activists and Journalists: Twitter Communication in the Aftermath of the 2012 Delhi Rape." *Journalism Studies* 16.5 (2015): 719–733.

Prasad, P.S.N. "The Police and Rameeza Bee: Muktadar Commission's Findings." *Economic and Political Weekly* 13.35 (1978): 1497–1499.

Roberts, Adam "Introduction." *Civil Resistance and Power Politics*. Eds Adam Roberts and Timothy Garton Ash."Oxford: Oxford University Press, 2010. 1–24.

Roy, Prannoy. "More News Is Good News: Democracy and Media in India." *India's News Boom: The Good News and the Bad*. Ed. James Painter. Oxford: Reuters Institute for the Study of Journalism, 2013.

Savery, Lynn. *Engendering the State: The International Diffusion of Women's Human Rights*. New York: Routledge, 2007.

Sen, Samita. "Toward a Feminist Politics? The Indian Women's Movement in Historical Perspective." *The World Bank Policy Research Report on Gender and Development Working Paper Series No. 9*. 2000.

Shah, Nishant. "Resisting Revolutions: Questioning the Radical Potential of Citizen Action." *Development* 55.2 (2012): 173–180.

Shirky, Clay. "The Political Power of Social Media: Technology, the Public Sphere, and Political Change." *Foreign Affairs* (January/February 2011): 28–41.

Singh, Smriti. "Case for Chemical Castration?" *The Times of India* 19 December 2012. http://timesofindia.indiatimes.com/city/delhi/Case-for-chemical-castration/articleshow/17672881.cms. Accessed September 1, 2017.

Sircar, Oiskhik. "'Women Make Demands, But Only Ladies Get Protection'." *InfoChange Agenda Special Issue: Sexual Rights in India* 4 (2006): 13–15.

Subramaniam, Suchita. "Indian Supreme Court's Departure from Judicial Activism." *Jurist*. http://www.jurist.org/forum/2013/12/sujitha-subramanian-india-departure.php (2013). Accessed August 7, 2017.

Tarrow, Sidney. *Power in Movement: Social Movements and Contentious Politics*. New York: Cambridge University Press, 2011.

The Times of India. "Foot in Mouth Statements." *The Times of India* (8 January 2013). www.timesofindia.indiatimes.com/Foot-in-mouth-statements/articleshowpics/msid-17937085.cms. Accessed August 8, 2017.

Tuka Ram and Anr vs State of Maharashtra. 1978–1979. http://indiankanoon.org/doc/1092711/. Accessed August 8, 2017.

Verma, J. S. Leila Seth, and Gopal Subramaniam. Report of te Committee on Amendments to Criminial Law. http://www.prsindia.org/uploads/media/Justice%20verma%20committee/js%20verma%20committe%20report.pdf, 2013. Accessed August 7, 2017.

Vijaya, Ramya and Bidisha Biswas. Indian Immigrant Women and Work: The American Experience. New York: Routledge, 2016.

Walker, Rebecca. "Becoming the Third Wave." *Ms*. 1992. http://www.msmagazine.com/spring2002/BecomingThirdWaveRebeccaWalker.pdf. Accessed August 8, 2017.

Part II
Social Media

3 Gathering Online, Loitering Offline

Hashtag Activism and the Claim for Public Space by Women in India through the #whyloiter Campaign

Sonora Jha

Introduction

In the aftermath of the brutal gang rape and murder of Jyoti Singh, a medical student in New Delhi taking the bus home with a male friend after a movie, outraged citizens of India, its diaspora, and people with ties to or interest in the state of women in India took to Twitter and other social networks to aggressively campaign against the rampant violence against women in the country. This solidarity, built online and offline, led to massive protests on the streets of New Delhi and throughout the country. It also provoked reactions from around the world, including international human rights groups, the international media, scholars, academics, and the United Nations (Kapur 2013). Massive protests and social media campaigns found their way to politicians and lawmakers, and rape laws were changed in the country in 2013, based on the recommendations of the Justice Verma Committee. Stalking and acid attacks were now deemed as criminal offenses, the definition of rape was expanded to include oral sex and insertion of objects, and cases where sexual assault led to death became punishable with the death penalty, among other long-awaited changes.

Perhaps more important to long-term change, the response to the case disrupted and redirected previous discourses on gender norms and expectations and gave a voice to previously unexplored subjects of sexuality and violence across diverse class, caste, and geographical boundaries. Among the repertoire of protest strategies is the case of the #whyloiter feminist hashtag campaign as a digitally launched feminist social movement campaign.

This paper provides a theoretical critical analysis of the online discursive (textual and visual) representations of women claiming public spaces across India through the #whyloiter hashtag campaign in December 2014, protesting "rape culture" following the 2012 Delhi gang rape and murder. Using feminist media theory and the theory of digital social movements—cyberfeminist protest in particular—I examine the strides and limitations of online and offline repertoires of the #whyloiter campaign. Comparing the #whyloiter campaign with earlier hashtag activism in India such as the #SlutWalk and #BlankNoise campaigns, this paper examines the political choice of this campaign to foreground pleasure in public space as a carnival of protest (Figure 3.1).

The campaign grew out of a 2011 book titled "Why Loiter: Women and Risk on Mumbai Streets," by feminist scholars Shilpa Phadke, Sameera Khan, and Shilpa Ranade, in which they argue that although political and economic visibility has brought women increased presence in urban public space, this has not automatically translated into greater claim to public space for them. Based on more than three years of research in Mumbai, the book maps women's exclusion from several public spaces and discusses the experiences of women from different

Figure 3.1 Poster released by the #whyloiter campaign in 2014.

localities, classes, and communities in negotiating with real and implied risks of being in public every day (Phadke et al. 2011).

The #whyloiter hashtag event was launched online in December 2014 as a campaign responding to what the campaign leaders (which included the authors of book as well as others supporting the cause) describe as "the increased victim blaming and the restrictions on women's mobility that takes place when a woman is sexually assaulted in public space" (#whyloiter, Facebook, 2014). The #whyloiter campaign set up a worldwide, multi-day event on social media, urging women to go out and loiter in physical, public spaces in real life. The event was publicized on all manner of social media, inviting women globally to "hang out in the city, to make use of its public spaces, to loiter aimlessly and to use the hashtag #whyloiter" (#whyloiter, Facebook, 2014) when women posted their loitering status on Facebook, Twitter, Instagram, Snapchat, etc.

The December 2014 timing was chosen by the campaign's organizers to coincide with and commemorate the second anniversary of the Jyoti Singh rape and murder. Grounded in the theory of feminist geography and in feminist media theory—cyberfeminist protest in particular—this paper examines how the #whyloiter hashtag campaign extended and expanded on the resistance to rape culture in India by focusing on women's claim to public space, thereby adding another facet to the growing anti-rape movement in India. I also discuss the complex fabric of gender politics into which this campaign arrives in India, including the intersectionality of gender, class, caste, religion, and geography as well as the resistance of powerful mainstream, largely neoliberal media to moving along the cause of ending a shame-driven rape culture, all of which serve as severe stumbling blocks for this campaign.

The campaign began on December 16, 2014. An interesting part of its timeline of public protest is that it encouraged an offline component prior to an online one, in that women were asked to loiter in public spaces and then post their pictures, statuses, and check-ins online. The focus was on seeking pleasure in public spaces, that is, *exhibiting* one's person in the city, and seeking pleasure in the exhibition of this public presence, then, online, with the use of the hashtag #whyloiter.

Public Space, Fear and Risk

Feminist geographer Doreen Massey (1994) has discussed space as the product of interconnected social relations and as negotiated sites based on power dynamics and geographies grown from politics and ideology. Within its brief history, feminist geography has studied the negotiations and navigation of space by women within private space, public space, the workplace, cities, rural areas, and also the nation state as a political construct (Hanson and Pratt 1988; Hanson 1995; McDowell and Sharp 1997; Fenster 2005; Nelson and Seager 2005).

In her analysis of women's inhibited use of space as an expression of patriarchal repression, Gill Valentine (1989) points out that "an understanding of women's use of space necessitates an awareness of their geography of fear" (p. 386). Studying the experiences of women in the town of Reading in England, Valentine found that women developed mental maps quite early in life of places where they feared male violence and sexual assault. These maps were based on personal experiences, parents' differential spatial fears for boys and girls, and from secondary information. In particular, Valentine found, women believed that "the behavior of any stranger encountered is potentially unpredictable and uncontrollable" (p. 386). Reading's women, Valentine found, reported their personal space frequently invaded by male behaviors like whistling, commenting, or actual physical assaults by strange men, which added to the sense of unpredictability, lack of choice in interaction, and insecurity in public for women.

More recently, and in the South Asian context, geography and gender have been discussed also in the context of patriarchal structures and emerging market forces and the impact of these on the lives of women (Raju 2011). Shilpa Phadke, who co-authored the "Why Loiter" book in 2011, began documenting narratives from a cross-section of Mumbai women about their negotiation of public space in the mid-2000s over a three-year study published in 2007, finding that women in cities like Mumbai were constantly engaged in taking calculated and intuitive risks regarding their public safety. They risked physical assault; risked their reputations; risked being blamed for being in public space in case they were victims of consequences such as violence, sexual assault, molestation or verbal abuse; and risked the loss of opportunity to engage public space (Phadke 2007). What is most remarkable in the case of these women that was not a factor in the case of Valentine's study of women in England is that "the discourse of gendered safety then is inextricably linked to the manufacture of respectability... staking a claim for safety is critically dependent on being able to demonstrate that one is worthy of being protected." (p. 1510). In the context of Indian patriarchy, such protections are granted to women who observe the norms such as being home before dark, going out for specific purposes (work, household shopping, visiting relatives, etc.) dressing demurely in public, staying out only when accompanied by male relatives, etc. So, to combat this whole narrative, Phadke argues that what women need in order to maximize their access to public space as citizens is not greater surveillance or protectionism (however well-meaning), but the right to engage risk and thereby expect the same unharmed and unfettered mobility that men can expect in public spaces.

Feminist protest against fear of violence in and claiming the right to public space and safety in recent years in India has seen an extensive repertoire through campaigns like Blank Noise, Safe City Campaigns, Take Back the Night, and SlutWalk (Sharma 2011; Borah and Nandi 2012). However, Slutwalk, which was hugely successful in Toronto, Canada and inspired an off-shoot in New Delhi in 2011 (before the 2012 Jyoti Singh rape case), was controversial and left feminists divided—especially along generational lines—over the relevance of the word "slut" to Indian contexts. Some feminists asserted that it was a healthy expression of female sexuality and others argued that it was classist, urban, and western in its understandings. While Ratna Kapur (2012) suggests that SlutWalk may present an incarnation of feminism in a different guise and thereby call for an expansion of feminist theoretical positions, Rituparna Borah and Subhalaksmi Nandi (2012) point out that "the feminist community in India, due to its limited participation in SlutWalk, lost a great opportunity for mobilization, organization, and strategizing on feminist politics" (p. 419). They point out, however, that the movement found greater support on social media and blogs. They called for "reclaiming our feminist politics in the notion of the 'slut' because it encapsulates the politics of the body, of pleasure and of challenging social and sexual norms" (p. 420).

The #whyloiter hashtag campaign appears to inhabit this exact space that the politics of SlutWalk opened up. It extends the notion of female bodies going beyond the narratives of fear and risk and seeking pleasure in their presence in "public space" instead. This activity of protest, as designed by #whyloiter, starts with organizing online, loitering in public space, and then returning to cyberspace to share stories, both written and visual, of their physical sites of pleasure (Figure 3.2).

In extending this examination of women's relationship with space into the themes of identity within feminist and cultural studies, the case of #whyloiter positions "loitering" as a radical act of claiming public space legally offered by the nation state yet interrupted and forbidden by political and patriarchal norms. #whyloiter positions an agenda that imbues a fluidity of motion between "safe spaces" (private and online) that are constructed as feminist discourse and "unsafe spaces" (offline and public) that are claimed as feminist acts of dissent.

Safety in Cyberspace vs. Public Space

How safe are online spaces for feminist connections, however? While on the one hand scholars have discussed how social networks expand the opportunities to humiliate women and encourage sexually violent discourse (the latest and most visible horrifying case being #GamerGate), they also acknowledge that hashtag campaigns and movements facilitate a feminist takeover with online debate such as a discussion of rape culture: for

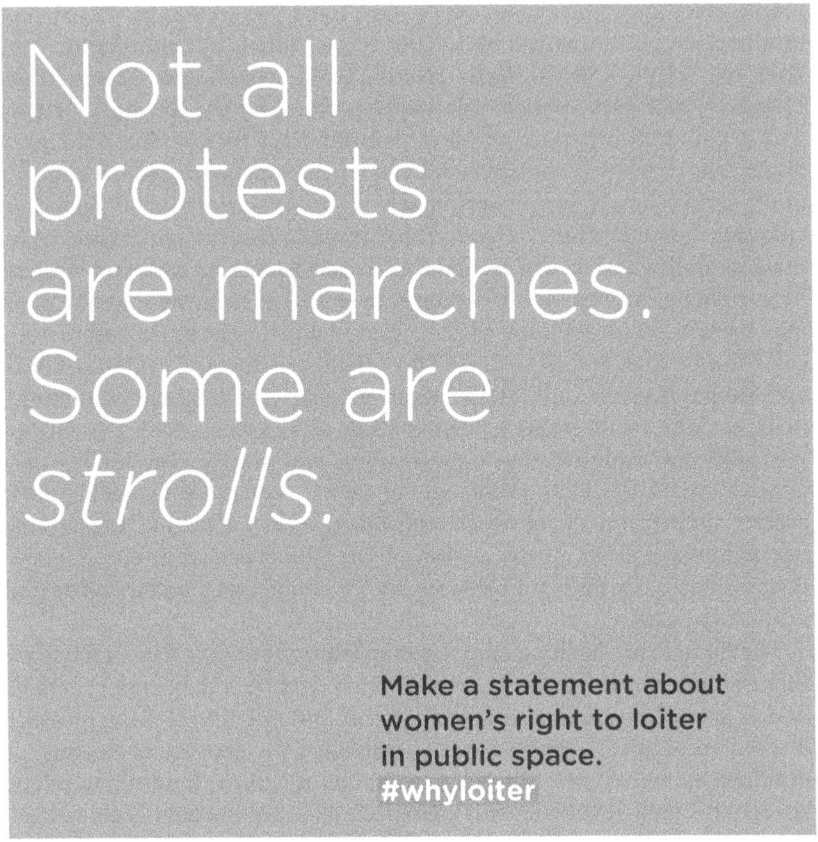

Figure 3.2 Poster released by the #whyloiter campaign in 2014.
Credit: #whyloiter, Nishant John and Abhishek Prakash

example, the cases of the #AskThicke campaign based on the 2013 song "Blurred Lines" and the #YesAllWomen campaign following the Santa Barbara mass shootings in the same year (Horeck 2014; Rodino-Colocino 2014; Solnit 2014). Scholars have also found that "tone policing" on on-line feminist networks on Twitter and Tumblr can turn conflicts into positive and teaching moments and allows for the realization of the potential strengths of feminists' diversity and Twitter, in particular, can be a strong democratic feminist media due to the fact that it allows for on-the-ground reporting and democratic activism (Small 2011).

Feminist scholars have envisioned cyberspace as a natural location for technofeminism or cyberfeminism (Wilding 1998; Wajcman 2004; Blair, Gajjala and Tully 2009), a space for feminist community and a network in which women may seek both pleasure (of self-expression, sharing of stories, community building, etc.) and political organization (Oh 2012).

Wilding uses the metaphor of cyberfeminism as "a browser through which to see life" (Wilding 12). In her study of cyberfeminism online, Yeon Ju Oh found that Unnine, a cyberfeminist community and webzine initiated by a group of young Korean feminists, helped to "speculate about gender politics in cyberspace in relationship to offline spaces and envision the ways in which cyberspace can deconstruct power relations."

Of particular interest to me for its many parallels with the #whyloiter case as an instance of cyberfeminism is the study by Natalia Rybas of the Facebook group "Hey Facebook, breastfeeding is not obscene!" Rybas examined the gendered technology and politics of Facebook activism for the case of public breastfeeding as a contribution to the understanding of social networks online, technology, and public space. The Facebook group was formed to challenge the practice of the social networking site of removing profile pictures of women nursing their babies. Similar to #whyloiter, this group extended its activism in both online and public, physical dimensions, including organizing virtual nurse-ins. The questions that Rybas uses to frame her study are relevant to the study of #whyloiter. She asks: "When the issues of breastfeeding spill into the digital realm, what cultural values come to the surface in online conversations and actions? What is at stake when breastfeeding occupies public space online?" (Rybas 2012: 264).

#whyloiter, meanwhile, envisions the deconstruction of power relations as a discourse in online space but also a display in offline spaces, with women returning with the "spoils," as it were, of their offline battles. The use of Facebook and a closed group such as #whyloiter in itself can be seen as a radical act of claiming "safe spaces" for women. Unlike the case of the breastfeeding photos, where the display in online space was as much a point of "offense," as breastfeeding in physical spaces, #whyloiter's photographs—of fully clothed women in public spaces— did not pose such problem wherein the content of the pictures in itself may be deemed "objectionable" by sexist patriarchy.

One reason for the strength and success of the #whyloiter campaign may come also from its minimal reliance on online debate or policing, with the focus being on pictures of revelry. In the Indian context, it would appear to be the perfect storm of feminist protest. An aspect of this kind of gender performativity and subversion of politics in digital and physical spaces is that in the case of #whyloiter as opposed to the case of #FreetheNipple or other breastfeeding campaigns, these women in India were not *performing* gender. Contrary to the identity construction within gendered norms and heteronormativity of breastfeeding mothers online and offline, the #whyloiter women[1] are, by their mere physical presence in the act of "doing nothing," breaking away from not only the performance of gender, but are actually performing an act of rebellion against the "doing" dictated by gendered constructions of females in public or private space. It is of some consequence that, in fact, breastfeeding in public in India is not frowned upon in the manner it is in the West. This is in large part owing to the fact that it fits in comfortably with the social construction of gender and the performance of motherhood. Ironically, it is easier for a woman in India to nurse her infant seated on a street corner than it is for her to simply stand there and stare at the world passing by, an activity quite amply enjoyed by Indian males. Breastfeeding fits in comfortably with gendered expectations of the woman and the deification of motherhood itself, particularly in Hindu patriarchal contexts.

It becomes important to examine the existing social media environment in which #whyloiter came into being. While scholars are only now beginning to study the use of Facebook in India, the use of Twitter in a significant way in India as an alternative to mainstream news media was first noted during the 2008 terror attacks in Mumbai when citizens provided eyewitness accounts of the unfolding tragedy soon after the first shots were fired in multiple attacks across the city (Beaumont 2008). Since then, Twitter has established itself as a phenomenal means of political commentary and also a statement of feminist critique and protest mechanism in cases as varied as Bollywood stars like Deepika Padukone who took on newspaper giant The Times of India via Twitter in 2016 when it published a picture of her cleavage and drew sensationalist attention to her body, to feminist Kavita Krishnan on the other hand, who actively uses Twitter and blogs on Huffington Post as part of her repertoire in her work as secretary of the All India Progressive Women's Association (AIPWA) to maintain an ongoing feminist critique of matters relating to gender inequality as it surfaces in the news.

#whyloiter's combination of the social media zeitgeist with the call for pleasure as protest was significant—more than 4.5 thousand attendees signed into the Facebook page, mostly in India but also across the world: New Delhi, Bangalore, Mumbai, Srinagar, Jaipur, Chicago, Hong Kong, Bharuch (Gujarat), and women hiking the summit of the Kedarkanta Peak in Uttarakhand. The campaign garnered news media coverage, both through essays published by participating feminist writers as well as mainstream media taking note of the event and its mandate (Figure 3.3).

Participants on Facebook posted photographs of themselves on streets, riding cycle-rickshaws, sipping tea on street corners, and more. One woman wearing a motorcycle helmet and leather jacket (thereby performing gender disruption) in her picture posted this update:

> #whyloiter because there was a bike, bone chilling wind, and an inviting road.

Another woman posted on her timeline, with her post set to "public,"

> As a young girl, I told my mother I wanted to be a boy. 'Cause boys could hang about on their bicycles after school, play football after

Figure 3.3 Poster released by the #whyloiter campaign in 2014.

the sunset and not have to ask anyone before going out. That is why. No more. 'Cause loitering women seem dangerous, 'cause loitering is political. #whyloiter

A young woman riding a late-night bus posted a "selfie" on the bus and said,

> #whyloiter? Because women's presence in the last bus for the day is a protest against patriarchal codes of time-space and will remain so until no bus is the last one.

A brightly dressed young woman riding a cycle-rickshaw in the streets of Old Delhi posted a picture with this status:

> The spooky streets of Old Delhi are not so grim after all. #whyloiter because I refuse to sit on the fence.

In a tweet of a blog post on dailyo.in, writer Neha Dixit (2014) made a list of reasons why she wanted to lay claim to public space, among which was this one:

> The roadside paranthawala next to the Moolchand flyover in Delhi offers an affordable and delicious fare. When I asked for a plate, the dhaba owner said, "Madam, let me pack your order. It will not be okay for you to sit and eat here." When I insisted, he said, "Madam, please try and understand. If something happens, the police will shut my shop."

To a significant degree, the posts, tweets, and photographs that emerged with the #whyloiter hashtag over the days of the campaign seemed to provide a festive representation of the idyllic landscape of gender equality in public space that the #whyloiter activists envisioned.

Further, by involving Indian diaspora from across the world—a successful move, given the posts that came in over the days of the campaign—the #whyloiter campaign slyly co-opted or appropriated the narratives of the "globalization" campaign in modern India and of India's self-perception as a global player. Still, while studies of cyberspaces created by women for women have discussed the possibilities for empowerment, they continue to also point out the difficulties and fragilities of determining safe spaces online for women (Blair and Takayoshi 1999; Gajjala 2002) because such spaces continue to be negotiated within the spectrums of gender, class, and caste.

Who Loiters? Negotiating "Space" for the Subaltern

#whyloiter states that the online campaign is not limited to cis-women but is inclusive of trans-women and anyone who identifies as woman. "In doing so," the #whyloiter page states, "we hope to create a conversation and target victim blaming in order to assert women's right to the city, the right to take risks."

The #whyloiter case, given its online and offline participations for social change, invites examination through the lenses of privilege, access, and representation. I will first discuss the online participation. A successful model of a digital social movement has been described as one that is both collaborative and decentralized (Garrett 2006; Joyce 2010; Salter 2011). With particular regard to feminism online, Radhika Gajjala and Yeon Ju Oh have noted in their seminal book on cyberfeminism that "the exploration of what it means to be a cyberfeminist necessitates priv-ileging 'decentered, multiple, and participatory practices'" (Gajjala and Oh 2012).

In her analysis of the negotiations of representation and voice for the subaltern by the privileged, Radhika Gajjala points out that while "the 'subaltern' does not have a voice online in the same sense as female South Asian intellectuals and professionals who may have greater access and privilege in cyberspace, the latter would do well to examine the speaking roles they are assigned as well as the locations from which they speak" (Gajjala 1998; Gajjala 2002). Although Gajjala's analysis refers to South Asian women's voices online challenging Western hegemony, the same principles and recognitions, I believe, can be extended to priv-ileged South Asian women challenging South Asian patriarchal hege-mony. In effect, we must examine whose voices arrive at the forefront of social movement media, whose voices recede, and whose do not make the cut at all.

The first group within which to examine issues of access and repre-sentation on social media would be cis-gendered women themselves. In her ethnographic study of the adoption and use of Facebook among urban Indian youth from socioeconomically disadvantaged commu-nities, Neha Kumar found that while young men from these com-munities negotiate social (and special) boundaries and technological hurdles to become legitimate members of a global community, young women had more restricted access and activity. Kumar notes three reasons for this: parental restrictions on young women for the fear of negative influences, priority given to boys for access to household assets like laptops and smartphones, and poor access for females to the physical spaces that allow for a participatory culture of upward mobility (Kumar 2014).

It becomes important, then, to discuss the issues of representation and participation offline and raise this question—while the #whyloiter fem-inist movement takes online hashtag activism into the public, real life realm, what are the limitations we see with regard to the digital divide between the urban middle class, English-speaking, and digital-native feminists versus lower class/caste, rural, and regional language speaking women? It is important to note that while the #whyloiter hashtag move-ment saw some posts from smaller towns and villages in India, these posts were, clearly, from urban women visiting these places rather than residents of these places.

Not too far from Kedarkanta Peak, for instance, in Uttarakhand, a state that has often made headlines for its record of violence against women with intersecting dimensions of caste and religion such as the rape of two teenage Dalit girls in Badayun in April 2014 and the gang rape of a young girl in Fatehpur in 2011, partisan politics is seeing a dif-ferent kind of movement that appears to, quite disturbingly, appropriate some of the rhetoric of recent feminist campaigns in India (Joshi 2014). The Bajrang Dal in India recently launched the "Bahu Lao Beti Bachao" campaign, which urges Hindu males to marry non-Hindu women to convert them to Hinduism and to prohibit their daughters from associating with non-Hindu males. The campagin has been launched with the ostensible claim to women's empowerment by offering "protections" to non-Hindu women by inviting them into Hindu families by way of converting through marriage.

So, an emerging question, of course, is about the extent to which the hashtag activism that leads to offline protests or cultural change promoted by urban feminists may in fact make an impact in smaller towns or villages (where we see frightening consequences for women violating the patriarchal norms on access to public spaces). More disturbingly, it remains to be seen whether any such impact may in fact be re-routed and completely appropriated by conservative activists who may actually have access to both, the discourses of the digital natives of the nation (and beyond) as well as the discourse of the grassroots. Moreover, what lack do we see in access to social media and its language when it comes to feminist activists working at the grassroots?

A multifaceted analysis of grassroots feminist activism in India has been provided by Joti Sekhon (2006), who notes that a much needed rethinking of feminist politics and democracy in recent years has led to measures to promote women's participation in politics in rural India, where 70% of Indians reside. In particular the 73rd Amendment to the Constitution of India in 1993, granting the reservation of at least 33% of elected positions in village councils to women, resulted in the election of nearly one million women within the first five years since it was passed, empowering women as independent agents in the democratic social process. (Sekhon 2006). Such empowerment is key to democratic politics in India, lending visibility to patriarchal structures in community and domestic life, where, historically, women and minority groups have been oppressed, Sekhon notes. Such feminist rethinking of politics is necessary to re-envision democracy as a broad participatory process in which women may "take part directly in decisions affecting them, their community, their work, their interpersonal relationships and of course, their formal political institutions" (Sekhon 2006).

Returning to the physical sites of the #whyloiter protests in particular, we come upon the complex intersectionality peculiar to India. While Valentine's (1989) study in Reading, England laid the framework for such understanding by stating that "a woman's ability to choose a coping strategy and therefore her consequent use and experience of public space is largely determined by her age, income and lifestyle," (p. 386), the Why Loiter scholars and activists (Phadke 2007; Phadke, Khan and Ranade 2011) state up front that their study consciously focused on women in the city of Mumbai, particularly middle class women, who would indeed be the most privileged in their access to public space and yet are afforded "only conditional access to limited spaces." (Phadke 2007: 1510).

Other scholars would argue that greater risks are assumed and challenges are posed to the received and established order by lower class urban women. Datta (2007), studied women and their environment in a squatter settlement near New Delhi, and argued that, while feminist gains are not their explicit political concern, their trespass into the public square is a symbolic movement into forbidden spaces that function as a political act and present a "collective resistance against the injustices of the state" (Datta 2007: 228).

This tension between politicization and feminist action by women of different classes becomes particularly important when one considers that campagins and protests such as #whyloiter are situated in the conveniences of choice, timing, and the ability to *leave* for some women versus others. The general perception is that middle and upper class women move in a bubble of sorts, within the protections and human barriers created by chauffeurs and maids, building watch staff and guards at hotels, shopping malls, movie theaters, restaurants, schools, colleges, and other business establishments. It is also, indeed, a reality that these women would have greater access to the enforcement of law and order. In the perceptions and cultural realities of urban India, these women also are seen as protected, in some manner, by western ideology within the imagined community of western feminist norms rather than patriarchal Indian cultural dictates.

As mentioned by the Why Loiter authors as well as the organizers of the #whyloiter campaign, the focus of this campaign was middle-class women. So, when it comes to hashtag-activism, the demographics of those who may feasibly take part are considerably limited, and this spells difficulty for the growth of the campaign into a movement.

Facebook and Twitter posts "situated" the women not merely in their geographical surroundings, but also, by way of it, in their class environment. For instance, Ragamalika @rgmlk, who describes herself as "Wannabe traveller. Intermittent writer. Diagnosed nomad," tweeted two nighttime pictures of swings in an empty playground that appears to be within a housing complex:

"Because when kids are gone & the night is still, winter + empty park + swinging = merry! #whyloiter, @whyloiter" and –
   Slept in the metro on the way home last night #napctivism, #whyloiter

Naushina Shaikh on Facebook posted a nighttime picture of a street on December 17 after an evening at an upscale Mumbai theater:

#whyloiter #NarimanPoint #NCPA #NarimanPoint #Contem-poraryDanceSeason #AstadDeboo #RhythmDivine Just because a woman hang (sic) out late night in the dark, doesn't mean she's inviting assault. Enjoyed a spectacular night show alone at NCPA #LiveWithoutAnyFear.

Several tweets and Facebook posts were used as notice boards of sorts, announcing physical loitering venues and urging women to gather at those. This negotiation of both geographical space within the realms of relative safety as well as the gathering in groups for loitering, seem to be in keeping with the literature on women's instinctual sense of safety, fear, risk-taking, and a navigation of public space and gendered privilege within it.

In the physical realm of the #whyloiter protest, i.e. the actual loiter-ing in real life inasmuch as it was then represented through posts and pictures on Twitter and Facebook, it would appear that women were frequently out with male companions, or in large groups, and, rather than loitering, were mostly in transit from one place to another, going to see a movie, on public transportation, or at a coffee-shop or corner tea-stall (locations Phadke explicitly marks out in her article as not part of public space accessible to women). It seemed, then, that the hashtag may have served mostly political networking purposes and to promote these women's empowerment as temporary or ongoing activ-ists (Figure 3.4).

In discussing the need for such a campaign and of their experiences, women articulated the gamut of responses they encountered also from males—from opposition to protectiveness—both of which women encounter as patriarchal responses. An article by journalist Kareena Gianani (2014) in the Mumbai newspaper Mid-Day discussed #whyloiter activist Devina Kapoor's experiences with reactions to her loitering during the December 2014 campaign:

> The ideal reaction was that of her father, who, after being aghast that his young daughter was out on the streets even late at night as part of the campaign, supported her after understanding the con-cept and announced it on the Why Loiter blog. "On other days, we have tried to photograph a man who was masturbating in front of us on a Juhu street (he fled) and another time, a man tried to hail an autorickshaw for us because 'women from good families shouldn't loiter', says Kapoor with a smile."

Similar discussions about the safety factor of the campaign emerged on blogs, teasing out the nuances of the call to loiter and the reali-ties of loitering. On a blog titled "Everydayfeminisms," blogger Payal Tiwari (2014) echoed scholar Gill Valentine's (1989) discussions of the

Figure 3.4 Poster released by the #whyloiter campaign in 2014.

relationship between women's fear of male violence and their perceptions and use of space.

> While I agree to every ounce of what this movement says, my heart sinks when I imagine loitering in public places alone. I flip through some news pieces that hit the newspapers over 2014 only to find news articles about rape cases at home, school, workplaces, and streets. And we are urging women to loiter? Where? These very places? .... The movement is symbolic. But the women who work on the streets of Mumbai for a daily living—the ragpickers, the garbage collectors, the cleaners who mostly are lower caste women, will this movement make things easier for them? Is 'symbolic' enough?

While the Why Loiter authors have, in their book as well as academic work, drawn attention also to the constraints in negotiation of public space by lower class and lower caste women in urban spaces, one aspect that seemed like a missed opportunity in the #whyloiter hashtag campaign, to my mind, was a documentation of the "loitering" or the navigation of public spaces by lower class and lower caste women. While photographs would likely be an invasion of privacy or even elitist intervention exploitative of the lives of these women, perhaps a series of written updates or tweets by women with access to social media, about sighting women of less economically and geographically privileged classes in their everyday negotiations with public space as construction workers, homeless dwellers, ragpickers, maids, fisherwomen, etc. may have served to provide a greater sense of women's totality of experience in urban public spaces. Although one may argue that these working women inhabit these public spaces as their "workplace," it bears noting that these women are also more comfortable or at least considered commonplace when it comes to, say, lingering over a cup of tea while sitting outside a tea stall.

Another nuanced yet deeply significant layer of documentation needed would be the presence and behaviors and interactions between lower class men and upper class or middle class women during the loitering. While pictures posted often showed curious men in the background either looking at the women or even leering into the camera, it was hard to find longer descriptions of women's experiences with the "jostling" for space on the street corner, as it were, as women loitered in spaces predominantly loitered upon by unemployed men or men enjoying a breeze or even loitering for the sake of catcalling or "eve-teasing" women. A larger question is what shifts may take place in the perceptions of privilege, class, and space for lower class or unemployed men as upper class and middle class women either deliberately or unwittingly "clear" spaces for themselves, say, by requesting a clearing by local police constables or by seeking the assistance of male friends, relatives, chauffeurs, shop owners, watchmen, and the like? While social media spaces provide avenues for middle class women to connect and discuss and enact a safe gathering and solidarity online, outside the presence of lower class men, what kind of tilting and inadvertent flushing out of under-privileged males may take place given a larger success in the garnering of public space by privileged women?

The notion of "other minorities" was also encountered within the discourse of the #whyloiter hashtag campaign by those belonging to other marginalized groups. In this post, a Muslim male activist, Abul Kalam Azad, complicates the arguments for women's access to public space by using his position as a Muslim male to draw attention to the multiplicity of subaltern groups and their relationship to public space:

> A Muslim, or anyone who can be identified to be so from his hair style, dresses etc. cannot loiter in many public spaces without generating the ire and stigma of the society surrounding him/her compromising his/her safety. So are many spaces prohibited by overwhelming social consensus to lower caste and class folks. Who can loiter where? How much and how far? Spaces are segregated in myriad intersectional ways but reducing it to a question of gender alone (the same woman who is loitering in a space restricted to her can get queasy when she finds a bearded man roaming in her locality) can leave many glaring holes in the fight for and vision of a society with egalitarian spaces #whyloiter

In the comments that followed, the campaign organizers, authors of the 2011 book, agreed with Azad and drew attention to their contention in their book that women's access to public space cannot be seen in isolation from the access available to other marginalized groups.

Such intersectionality in the social media public sphere will, in the coming years, provide much material for continued study and development of feminist media theory. In one such analysis, Michelle Rodino-Colocino (2014) has pointed to the #YesAllWomen Twitter hashtag, which she called a "key moment in the genealogy of feminism that underscores the old-in-the-new and suggests an urgent course of action for media scholars" (p. 113). The tweets in the #YesAllWomen campaign provided an opportune moment to study the problems with "grounding feminist solidarity in white, middle class, US-centric, heteronormative privilege" (p. 1113). Yet, feminist solidarity across transnational lines may serve to buttress campaigns like #whyloiter. Ryan Bowles Eagle (2015) has discussed such transnational solidarity in hashtag activism through #BoardtheBus, #StopStreetHarassment, and the #EverydaySexism Project, all of which served to lend support to the feminisms emerging in India after the 2012 rape (Bowles Eagle 2015).

Social Media Feminism vs. Mainstream Media

In their studies of the representations of women in and their access to mainstream media in India, scholars have pointed to a poor commitment on the part of print media to women's issues. On television and in film and advertising, women are given patriarchal and home-based representations. (Rao 2001; Srivastava and Agarwal 2004; Manohar and Kline 2014). So, women as well as feminist media researchers have faced a challenge in the lack of equity in quantitative "space" as well as qualitative "identity" in the representations of women in Indian media.

Although the 2012 rape case and the protests that stemmed from it garnered wide media coverage across the country and overseas, several feminists drew attention to the fact that this was likely because this as a case of rape of an urban, middle-class, and young woman. Shakuntala Rao's (2014) analysis of this media coverage pointed out that Indian television news media, in particular, rarely turns its lens to poor, marginalized, lower caste, and non-urban women and the sexual violence wrought upon them. She also discusses the larger cultural environment of shame and the disapproval of women being seen in public space, all of which bleeds into the language and coverage of television news media. This, she found in her interviews with journalists after the 2012 gang rape, was also true of globalized and newly liberalized media thriving in India, focused as they were on serving what they believed to be the narrow, urban, and upper class focused repertoire of news coverage that their audiences were interested in. Somehow, the larger global journalistic ideals of inclusiveness and human dignity did not seep into the patriarchal journalistic ethics of Indian media.

With particular emphasis on the mainstream media coverage of the 2012 gang rape and murder, Meenakshi Gigi Durham (2015) points at the dangerous dichotomies that some of the media frames and tropes created by obscuring rape culture in the First World/Global North and representing India as a nation steeped in patriarchal norms. Such representation in American news media, Durham suggests, undermines the possibility of cross-national feminist collaborations and feminism without borders.

The current challenge in studying social movements and their relationship with the use of digital technology is that one cannot isolate digital constructions and narratives of dissent from the larger media environment. Any case study of such online activism needs examination of the broader organizational process that takes place simultaneously online and offline and also within its interplay with other media.

Pallavi Guha (2015) discusses the failure of some feminist hashtags, in particular, to gain traction in mainstream media. She cites a case on September 23, 2013, when the hashtag #victimblaming emerged on Twitter in India, in response to a satirical video about sexual abuse, rape, and victim blaming but was ignored by mainstream media. Guha believes that "for a successful feminist campaign to take off, there needs to be a convergence of social media hashtagging and news media discussion" (p. 155). Guha compares this with the hashtag #Nirbhaya (Fearless) that emerged from mainstream media (in a leading newspaper, The Times of India) as a name given to Jyoti Singh, the victim of the 2012 Delhi gang rape and murder. The name and hashtag made a huge impact and became a catchword and a sentiment employed by the successful protest movement that led to a change in Indian rape laws.

Quite unlike earlier hashtag campaigns, however, the #whyloiter campaign, even though it wasn't related to a breaking news story, was covered widely by mainstream media ranging from leading Indian newspapers like The Hindu, The Times of India and Business Standard, to the French newspaper, Le Monde, among other international media. Part of the reason for this success of a hashtag campaign with mainstream media may be because, given that the Facebook group celebrated the ritual of pleasure in public loitering, several female journalists who would otherwise eschew direct political involvement for the sake of professional objectivity now found themselves willing participant-observers within the Facebook group. This could be seen by the several messages that participants posted, alerting the group to being contacted by journalists from within and outside the group for media coverage.

Kumar (2014) has also noted that it is important to study the use of Facebook for networking through entertainment such as the sharing of Bollywood (the Mumbai film industry's Hindi language films) music, since such leisure-driven technological engagement can lead to development-friendly outcomes in the global south (Arora and Rangaswamy 2013; Kumar 2014). In the #whyloiter case, in fact, participants used the celebratory power of Bollywood songs by asking each other to post songs that were about the pleasures of loitering or wandering. Participants noted that while several Bollywood songs celebrated the free and exhilarating explorations of the world and loitering by men, few songs did the same with women. Participants took on the challenge and posted songs that alluded to loitering and the independent movement or wandering by women.

Conclusion

The #whyloiter hashtag campaign provides a strong model of online social movement organizing within Indian contexts. While drawing upon the protest repertoire of campaigns that have gone before it within the larger movement across India to end rape culture, #whyloiter employs a sly political strategy of focusing not so much on street protest but on pleasure-seeking in public space by women. It also drew partnerships from feminists and feminist partners (such as leading Indian feminist Kavita Krishnan and also the Blank Noise social media-based feminist movement) in the Indian public sphere, thereby attracting some news media coverage and disseminating the message into the larger audience networks outside social media. While the campaign may not have been very effective in raising larger public awareness beyond the camaraderie of its participants and some discussion in mainstream media, it served well to mobilize and direct a well-informed but previously unorganized/ non-mobilized sector of the population and give coherent expression to a desire that was already present.

Further study may examine what #whyloiter activists and organizers consider to be the measures of success for the #whyloiter feminist campaign and how successful this campaign can expect to be in creating a lasting and far-reaching impact on women's claim to public space.

In particular, given that almost 70% of the Indian population is in rural and small town India, it becomes imperative to study the reach, strategies and success of the #whyloiter campaign outside the urban and English-speaking digital natives. If the #whyloiter campaign and other such digitally constructed campaigns fail to draw those women who would want to participate from rural and regional India, where patriarchal hierarchies and rape culture may be harder to dismantle, do they risk deepening a divisive and elitist/hierarchical access to public space and negate the ethos upon which their campaign is founded?

In the larger environment of patriarchal norms and the navigation of public space via the negotiation of fear, one could also argue that the risk involved with "loitering," per se, could be high. In the context of a movement, such risky actions could be termed civil disobedience and are given a codified justification. If this manner of protest grows into a movement and loitering is conducted with some regularity, reactions against loitering could be expected be explicitly politicized and connected with a *program* of some sort, presumably from the well-entrenched patriarchal norms that motivated the movement. Outside the context of a campaign or movement, these actions are, in themselves, unlikely to result in some sort of gradual change in the public perception of the role of women that enables female loitering. Rather, they may bear the risk of perhaps endangering women. Evidence in support of the notion that such actions lead to greater equality, minus a broader, well-formed program, remains to be seen. Still, the #whyloiter model of celebrating female presence in public space and its experiences with an initial jab at taboos appears to have created a strong sense of community and collaboration that continues through the use of this hashtag for building feminist solidarity online and posting relevant material long after the designated dates of the physical campaign were done.

A significant part of such a long-term and substantive program for change would involve critical participation from mainstream media, which still have a stronger hold than social media across the length and breadth of the subcontinent. A sustained critical cultural analysis is called for to lay bare the patterns of gender bias not only at the level of the politicians and those wielding patriarchal power and given voice in the media but also the media themselves, for the frames of coverage they feel compelled to follow, not the least of which is the orientalist othering in news coverage of India's rape crisis in international, western media.

Note

1 I refer here only to cis-gendered women; transgender women or the hijra community in India have an entirely different relationship to public space, characterized by religious exoticization, sexual exploitation, and violence, and yet, as Tara Atluri (2012) points out, a unique ownership of sexual dissidence and sexual citizenship.

References

Atluri, Tara. "The Prerogative of the Brave: Hijras and Sexual Citizenship after Orientalism." *Citizenship Studies* 16 (2012): 721–36.

Azad, Abul K. 2014. Facebook. March 28, 2015, www.facebook.com/search/str/%23whyloiter/keywords_top.

Beaumont, Claudine. "Mumbai Attacks: Twitter and Flickr Used to Break News." *The Telegraph* 27 November 2008. Accessed June 29, 2015. www.telegraph.co.uk/news/worldnews/asia/india/3530640/Mumbai-attacks-Twitter-and-Flickr-used-to-break-news-Bombay-India.html.

Blair, Kristine, and Pamela Takayoshi. *Feminist Cyberscapes: Mapping Gendered Academic Spaces*. Stamford, Conn.: Ablex Pub., 1999.

Borah, Rituparna, and Subhalakshmi Nandi. "Reclaiming the Feminist Politics of 'SlutWalk'." *International Feminist Journal of Politics* 14.3 (2014): 415–21.

Bowles Eagle, Ryan. "Loitering, Lingering, Hashtagging: Women Reclaiming Public Space Via# BoardtheBus, # StopStreetHarassment, and the# Everyday-Sexism Project." *Feminist Media Studies* 15.2 (2015): 350–53.

Datta, Ayona. "'Samudayik Shakti': Working-class Feminism and Social Organization in Subhash Camp, New Delhi." *Gender, Place and Culture* 14.2 (2007): 215–31.

Fenster, Tovi. "Gender and the City: The Different Formations of Belonging." *A Companion to Feminist Geography.* Ed. Lise Nelson and Joni Seager. Oxford: Blackwell Publishing Ltd, 2005. 242–256.

Gajjala, Radhika. "An Interrupted Postcolonial/Feminist Cyberethnography: Complicity and Resistance in the 'Cyberfield'." *Feminist Media Studies* 2.2 (2002): 177–93.

Gajjala, Radhika. 2001. "Studying feminist e-spaces: Introducing transnational/post-colonial concerns." *Technospaces: Inside the New Media.* Ed. Sally Munt. Continuum 113–25.

Gajjala, Radhika. *Cyberfeminism 2.0.* New York: Peter Lang Pub, 2012.

Garrett, Kelly R. "Protest in an Information Society: A Review of Literature on Social Movements and New ICTs." *Information, communication & society* 9.2 (2006): 202–24.

Gianani, Kareena. 2014. "Who's afraid of women loitering?" www.mid-day.com/articles/whos-afraid-of-women-loitering/15856193#sthash.ng8Ty2Em.dpuf. Accessed August 1, 2015

Guha, Pallavi. "Hash Tagging But Not Trending: The Success and Failure of The News Media to Engage with Online Feminist Activism in India." *Feminist Media Studies* 15.1 (2014): 155–157.

Hanson, Susan, and Geraldine Pratt. *Gender, Work, and Space.* New York, Routledge: Psychology Press, 1995.

Horeck, Tanya. "#AskThicke: "Blurred Lines," Rape Culture, and the Feminist Hashtag Takeover." *Feminist Media Studies* 14.6 (2014): 1105–107.

Joyce, Mary. *"Digital Activism Decoded: The New Mechanics of Change."* New York: International Debate Education Association, 2010.

Kapur, Ratna. 2012. "Pink Chaddis and SlutWalk Couture: The Postcolonial Politics of Feminism Lite." *Feminist Legal Studies* 20.1 (2012): 1–20.

Kapur, Ratna. "Gender, Sovereignty and the Rise of a Sexual Security Regime in International Law and Postcolonial India." *Melbourne Journal of International Law* 14.2 (2013): 317.

Kumar, Neha. "Facebook for Self-Empowerment? A Study of Facebook Adoption in Urban India." *New Media and Society* 16.7 (2014): 1122–37.

Joshi, Bhoomika, and Umar Sanober. "Bleak Outlook for Women's Empowerment in Uttar Pradesh." *Business Standard.* 2014. www.business-standard.com/article/news-ians/bleak-outlook-for-women-s-empowerment-in-uttar-pradesh-comment-special-to-ians-114123000131_1.html.

Manohar, Uttara, and Susan, Kline. Sexual Assault Portrayals in Indian Cinema. *Sex Roles* 71.5/8 (2014): 233–45.

Massey, Doreen. *Space, Place and Gender.* Minneapolis: U of Minnesota P, 1994.

Oh, Yeon Ju. Cyberfeminist Movement for Space Online. *Cyberfeminism 2.0.* Eds. Gajjala Radhika and Yeon J. Oh. New York: Peter Lang Publishing, 2012. 245–61.

Phadke, Shilpa. "Dangerous Liaisons: Women and Men: Risk and Reputation in Mumbai." *Economic and Political Weekly* 2007 Vol. 42, No. 17: 1510–18.

Phadke, Shilpa, Sameera Khan, and Shilpa Ranade. *#whyloiter?: Women and Risk on Mumbai Streets.* New Delhi, India: Penguin Books India, 2011.

Raju, Saraswati. *Gendered Geographies: Interrogating Space and Place in South Asia.* Malden, Massachusetts: Oxford U P, 2011.

Rangaswamy, Nimmi, and Arora Payal. Mobile technology in the wild and every day: Case studies from the slums of urban India, *Revisiting the emancipatory potential of digital media in Asia symposium,* 24–25 January 2014, Leiden, NL: Leiden University.

Rao, Shakuntala. "Covering Rape in Shame Culture: Studying Journalism Ethics in India's New Television News Media." *Journal of Mass Media Ethics* 29.3 (2014): 153–67.

Rodino-Colocino, Michelle. "# YesAllWomen: Intersectional Mobilization against Sexual Assault is Radical (Again)." *Feminist Media Studies* 14.6 (2014): 1113–15.

Rybas, Natalia. "Where Is My Profile Picture? Multiple Politics of Technological Mothering and Gendered Technology." *Cyberfemism 2.0.* Eds. Radhika Gajjala and Yeon Ju Oh. New York: Peter Lang, 2012.

Salter, Colin. "Going Online for Social Change: Techniques, Barriers and Possibilities for Community Groups." *Social Alternatives* 30.1 (2011): 19.

Sekhon, Joti. "Engendering Grassroots Democracy: Research, Training, and Networking for Women in Local Self-Governance in India." *NWSA Journal* 18.2 (2006): 101–22.

Sharma, Kamayani. 2011. "Slutwalk: Walk of Shame or McFeminism?" July 11. Accessed June 30, 2015. http://openspaceindia.org/express/articles-a-essays/item/747-slutwalk-walk-of-shame-or-mcfeminism?.html.

Small, Tamara A. "What the Hashtag? A Content Analysis of Canadian Politics on Twitter." *Information, Communication & Society* 14.6 (2011): 872–95.

Solnit, Rebecca. "Listen Up, Women are Telling Their Story Now." *The Guardian* 30 December 2014. Accessed June 30, 2015.

Valentine, Gill. "The Geography of Women's Fear." *Area* 1989 Vol 21, No. 4: 385–90.

Wajcman, Judy. *Technofeminism* (Réimpr. 2005. ed.). Cambridge: Polity, 2004.

4 From *Bombay Dost* to Global Host

Mobile Imaginings of Cybergaysians in Contemporary Queer India

Rahul K. Gairola

Beginnings of an Era

In 2015, *Bombay Dost* (hereon referred to as *BD*), India's oldest LGBTQ periodical, celebrated the publication of its twenty-fifth anniversary issue. This moment in some ways commemorates the nascence of a queer public sphere in the realm of print media and its wide presence on social media (*Economic Times* 2016) in the world's biggest and youngest democracy. The magazine's 1999 issue, only nine years following its initial publication in Bombay in 1990, featured stylized cover art at a time when Y2K hysteria was predicting a global computer meltdown. An accompanying cover story titled "CyberGay" prognosticated the radical and transformative role that technology would have on the meteoric formation of a public, if clandestine, culture for LGBTQ South Asians around the globe (Figure 4.1). Produced and edited by Ashok Row Kavi, widely recognized as one of India's most prominent queer rights activists, the cover proclaimed, "The internet is changing the gay scene in India," and below the tagline strategically listed URLs of the publication and of The Humsafar Trust, its sister organization that promotes sex education and awareness.

According to Vikram Phukan, the early issues of *BD* included "tear-me-out condom questionnaires," while the classified section espoused homonormative desires for "fair, slim, young, masculine" men (2015). As the magazine evolved, it definitively expanded its audience as it "brought lesbians into the fold with many women-centric pieces" (Phukan). Today, the publication and its online presence arguably shape queer identity, which includes a wide range of genders and sexualities, more than any other periodical in South Asia. The expansion of its subject matter, on the one hand, and its conscious infusion into the queer cybersphere, on the other hand, are marked by a contradiction in public identity disclosure and life even as recent, critically acclaimed films like Hansal Mehta's *Aligarh* (2016) and Shakun Batra's *Kapoor & Sons (since 1921)* (2016) present empathetic cinematic portraits of lesbians and gays on the Hindi silver screen. This contradiction crystallizes in the public sphere

Figure 4.1 The cover of the 1999 issue of *Bombay Dost*, courtesy of Ashok Row Kavi and *Bombay Dost*.

between the representation of LGBTQI Indians in print and online culture into the millennium, on the one hand, and the prohibition of queer sexuality in Indian law on the other. This disjuncture looms large when we survey the emergence of a queer public against the persistence of the highly controversial Section 377 of the Indian Penal Code, which governs erotic lives in India.

The Section capitulates to the erstwhile British colonizers, and enshrines into law the Victorian prudishness at the heart of the repressive hypothesis that Michel Foucault critically interrogates in his opening chapter of *The History of Sexuality, Volume I*. This notion, argues Foucault, strived to portray sex and sexuality as a muted social discourse although, conversely, it yielded a "proliferation of specific pleasures and the multiplication of disparate sexualities" (1976: 49). The queer public sphere imagined by the magazine would be an anathema to Section 377, whose strange history exposes its fundamental instability. The British Raj enshrined the statute in 1860 to criminalize all non-heteronormative sex acts between consenting adults. The law criminalizes *any* sexual act "against the order of nature," and thus often facilitates corruption by authorities who harass, blackmail, and extort bribes from sexual minorities and sex workers in India. The Supreme Court of India upheld the statute in December 2013 amidst widespread criticism at home and abroad despite a Delhi High Court ruling against it in July 2009.

A wide swath of critics in India have condemned the statute, with Vikram Seth memorably declaring, "We cannot suppress the happiness of 50 or 100 million people," and Indian television journalist Rajdeep Sardesai stating, "Despite the sexual revolution taking place in India, and the fact we are modern in many ways, there is a deep conservatism at work here. Until sexuality is debated in the public sphere we will have these laws" (Ramesh 2006). The apex court's move was decried by social justice advocates around the world, with Seattle's *Socialist Alternative* leader Kshama Sawant insisting that "a globally-linked mass movement for LGBTQ rights" is inextricably linked to the global eradication of poverty and oppression (Franceschini and Gairola 2015: 20). As such, the statute brings into question India's global, socio-economic potential as the world's largest and youngest democracy at the same time that it undermines the Government of India's April 2014 legal recognition of transgender people, the so-called "third sex." While at first glance this legal recognition appears to be a positive move for queer folks in contemporary India, it does nothing to mediate against the criminalization of queer sexuality. The status quo defaults back to Victorian, colonialist ideologies of sexuality.

The goal of this essay is to draw on third world feminism as a means for reading transgender women's identities on the social media platforms of *BD*. I engage in this research as a means for complicating and extending the ways in which feminism and transgender identities come together in the purview of publications in Digital India. The heuristic which I hereon use as a baseline—feminism—has indeed had a fraught relationship with M2F (male to female) subjects. For example, as early as 1979, Janice Raymond has forcefully damned transexuals as anti-feminist. In what reads as a second wave feminist manifesto against queer identities, she writes:

> All transsexuals rape women's bodies by reducing the real female form to an artifact, appropriating this body for themselves. However, the transsexually-constructed lesbian-feminist violates women's sexuality and spirit, as well. Rape, although it is usually done by force, can also be accomplished by deception.
>
> (Raymond 1979: 104)

Raymond's likening of transexuality to sexual violation in the crucible of second wave feminism likely stoked the very discriminatory attitudes which are today crystallized in ongoing battles of gender-neutral bathrooms in the United States and housing discrimination in South Asia.

In opposition to this pathologization of transsexuals, Eleanor MacDonald argues that:

> ...what transgendered identity politics generates is new motivation to move beyond identity as the basis of social movement politics and into new exploration of the ethical bases of alliances and formation of communities. As well, and critically, it demands an exploration of the structural and systemic production of 'contested' and 'liminal' sites within every political community, including feminism, and the responsibility for breaking down the exclusionary and limiting effects that these boundaries have on us all.
>
> (MacDonald 1998: 10)

I would here venture that we can draw on such varied prescriptions from second- and third-wave feminism in thinking about LGBTQ representations on contemporary social media platforms in postmillennial India. I turn to the social media platforms of Digital India because they are arguably the safest and most popular forums on which queer South Asians can meet one another. As Bhavya Dore notes, there were other queer print publications in India before *BD*, but the latter "became India's first gay publication to be registered, which is a bureaucratic requirement that allows a publication to be sent in the post...In the first four years, the magazine wasn't just a printed publication, it was an all-purpose platform" (2016). This difference between *BD* and all other LGBTQ publications in India at the time is a crucial one with respect to availability and dissemination, especially for those who reside outside of major metropolitan center like Mumbai (formerly called "Bombay").

I turn my critical acumen to *BD*'s social media platform because it reconfigures accessibility on the "all-purpose platform," in Dore's words, of social media in the twenty-first century. It is on this electronic stage of hyperlinked identities and data conglomerations that contemporary, queer identities in India are transformed and made visible to a digitally literate public. According to Sandip Roy, such internet sites moreover globally enable safe, anonymous spaces while facilitating e-commerce and even the sale of condoms (Roy 2003: 188). This timely re-formatting of print into digital media engenders innovative applications of third-wave and third world feminisms in the digital public sphere that enable re-materializations of gender and sexuality in South Asia despite punitive prohibitions in postmillennial society.The evolution of *BD*'s print culture to hypertext (cross-referenced, or "linked," electronic texts that contain graphics and often other links), from 1990 to 2016, demonstrates the contradictory position of queer South Asian subjects as free and active agents in the world's largest democracy whose erotic and reproductive lives are defined by a colonial-era statute that invalidates their existence.

We may thus critically read queer activist journalism and its on-line discourses through many heuristic lenses. However, the universal pathos promised by limitless cyberspace and online netizens ostensibly challenges the geographical limitations of traditional print culture. Frameworks for theorizing subjects represented in print culture range from Benedict Anderson's "imagined communities" enabled by "historical amnesia" that represent, as in the case of Section 377, post-colonial, democratic plurality to Lee Edelman's notion of "homographesis" as a means for writing the gay male body into social and literary existence. The technological turn's impact on queer identity in India as suggested by the magazine's cover further complicates post-millennial queer identities—perhaps even more so in the complex web of hyperlinks networked throughout interlinked websites. This turn also has far-reaching implications for how digital social media and gender fluidity are shaping one another in contemporary India. Given the dramatic rise in the use of mobile phone use in the subcontinent, the implications for punitive human connections nurtured by internet connectivity are vast and full of potential.

Anderson's original contention that the nation is imagined as a limited, sovereign community is substantiated by the bittersweet logistics of localized inclusion within simultaneous national exclusion in the context of print versions of *Bombay Dost*. For example, Anderson cites the nation as an "imagined community" that is limited yet sovereign because:

> ...regardless of the actual inequality and exploitation that may prevail in each, the nation is always conceived as a deep, horizontal comradeship that espouses democratic ideals even as it dictates who is included and within which geo-political space. Ultimately it is this fraternity that makes it possible, over the past two centuries, for so many millions of people, not so much to kill, as willingly to die for such limited imaginings.
>
> (1983: 7)

This formulation of "horizontal comradeship" is historically more or less global yet selective in the frame of European colonialism, and even in the postcolonial nationalisms that depended on print culture to challenge the hegemony of colonial and neo-colonialism. Many scholars, notably Ranajit Guha of the Subaltern Studies Group, have forcefully detailed the distinction between "colonialist" and "bourgeois-nationalist" discourses that fail to engage with a "politics of the people" (Guha 1988: 37–43). There are yet many lessons left to learn from subaltern studies, third world feminism, and queer studies in working towards a nuanced vision of how technology and gender come together in Digital India for queer agents whose mobile phones are their lifelines to community, home, belonging, identity, and safety.

Facebook and Queer Feminisms in and beyond South Asia

In re-formulating Anderson's notion of "imagined communities" in the context of contemporary South Asia, Radhika Gajjala (2004) hails Indira Karamcheti's turn to the "cyborg-diaspora," a figure that challenges the sense that Indian diasporas retain an unmitigated and unchanged essence of "India." She writes:

> The disruption implied by the term cyborg-diaspora can occur if there are counternarratives of present real-life material, social and cultural conditions within the geographical region mapped out as 'India.' The counternarratives to those offered by most diasporic Indians, who live in communities created through memory, could come, for example, from Indians actually living in India, as well as through cross-generational and across rural-urban and class/ caste narratives.
>
> (2004: 13)

For Gajjala, the term also empowers a strategic kind of imagining, with respect to Anderson's paradigm, in which "media play a key role in the circulation and sharing of such alliances, creating an 'imagined' community of people around the world" (2004: 14). In post-millennial India, Gajjala's observation is key for re-thinking the interplay between the prevalence of social media and reconstructions of gender and sex identities.

While most scholars agree that the printing press revolutionized the world and people absorbed print identities and affiliations, these have evolved in unpredictable yet compelling ways that force recalibrations of data intake in the new millennium. This shift, I would argue, also imbibes a shift in how we mentally configure truth and testament, an "imagined community" marked by inclusivity/plurality/hybridity, if you will, as it is digitally transmitted from place to place. Just as some viewed the first printed Gutenberg Bibles as a manifestation of the word of God as human truth, hyperlinks, screen shots, selfies, and instant messaging have re-shaped what counts as evidence and truth in the world of ubiquitous mobile devices. Such reformulations of evidence and truth on the relatively small handsets with compact displays facilitate the transference of information (even private data is in closed groups and private list serves) and surreptitious movements of queer South Asians both within the family home and beyond in the queerphobic world. The portability of these devices is augmented by their abilities to transfer multi-layered referents and evasive, electronic signifiers. There are new vectors to identity formulation, connectivity, and anonymity that we are witnessing today that defy that which was previously imaginable only a decade ago. Indeed, in the formulation of Patrick Jagoda, mobiles facilitate what we can call a "network imaginary" wherein networks "are not only theoretical figures of technological infrastructures. They also serve as organizational blueprints for different forms of economical, political, and social life" (2016: 13–14).

For example, in his pioneering study of hypertext, George Landow defines both hypertext and hypermedia as linking "one passage of verbal discourse to images, maps, diagrams, and sound as easily as to another verbal passage...Electronic links connect lexias 'external' to a work— say, commentary on it by another author or parallel or contrasting texts—as well as within it and thereby create text that is experienced as non-linear, or, more properly, as multilinear and multisequential" (2006: 3). While the reading experience of the text(s) is indeed "multilinear and multisequential," the meaning conveyed is still aimed toward producing multimedia explanatives and explications from the sender to the recipient. They give rise to the notion of truth on the go, testament in motion although it is perceived to be fixed in time and space as truth. That is, the digital fungibility of evidence is disseminated throughout a network of other audio-visual highways including hyperlinks, GIFs, screen shots, live streamings, digital signatures, etc., that substantiate things we are trying to claim in with life constantly on the move. Even truth and evidence must go with the (migratory) flow.

The mobility of identities as facilitated by the mobile phone has a profound impact on space, where, as observed by Leopoldina Fortunati,

> The use of the mobile in fact means that the non-univocity of space, already put into crisis, by that ubiquity which the fixed phone ensured, deepens. You have in fact the possibility of choosing more easily between the physical space which you physically go through and the psychological space of the intimacy of your networks of relationships.
>
> (2013: 157)

This twenty-first-century discourse of electronic evidence production at the tip of our fingers is nonetheless subject to historical moors that anchor South Asia's booming mobile phone market. In "Queer Mobiles and Mobile Queers," Nishant Shah deftly opines,

> It [the mobile phone] is an object, a metaphor, a process, and an embodied reality that shapes the social, cultural, and political life of defining space, place, bodies, and conditions of being governed in emergent economies like India. The mobile has to be imagined as being

in motion, as moving, as generating movement, and catalyzing movements, in the process of creating conditions of queerness which are not
just embedded in sexual choices and practices. Instead the metaphor of
the mobile thinks of queerness as a condition of temporary activation,
where bodies, in their mobility, accrue queerness, thus creating queerness as a potential radicalism available to us all in our mobile states
of being rather than a state of pathology that configures only certain
bodies which are marked for punishment and regulation.

(2015: 283)

Fortunati's focus on the mobile phone's relationship to space and Shah's
focus on the mobility of queer identity in South Asia are crucial to consider
in the context of queer agency and the reformulation of gender and identity
following the April 2014 Supreme Court Ruling of the so-called "third
sex." This is because such a ruling is undercut by the colonialist Section
377 that undercuts any hope of queer erotic expression despite the fact that
the male/ female gender binary has implicitly been recognized as inadequate in contemporary India. Despite the demise of British colonialism,
therefore, these queer bodies and their terms of identification are shaped
by colonialist histories as well. In Sherry Joseph's account,

The impact of colonial history and concepts of orientalism upon
world-views and perceptions has played a central role in how non-
white people have been defined, how they are perceived, and how
white-non-white relations evolved socially and on personal levels...
south Asian gays and lesbians have had to invent themes, often with
new terms of identification.

(1996: 2229)

Joseph's account compels us to here ask: how are contemporary, queer
identities in post-colonial India re-shaped by both the digital medium
and the message? How can we most effectively analyze *BD*'s Facebook
group page for content, form, access, and transformative capabilities for
juridical-political subjects excluded from queer materials offline? One
formulation of the impact of digital mediums on the formation of identities is the notion of "the fourth screen" formulated by Rajinder Dudrah,
Sangita Gopal, Amit Rai, and Anustup Basu. They write,

We have barely scratched the surface of [the] Fourth screen—The
Mobile (for the uninitiated the first three screens are the Silver screen,
TV screen, and Computer screen), it is perhaps the most ubiquitous
of all screen in our lives today. Going by the mobile penetration
level India is perfectly poised to leapfrog the internet revolution to
land directly into the mobile broad band revolution. It has already
begun with the fast changes on all fronts of digital media including

improvement in handset features, network band with and quality & variety of content. [The]Mobile has fast evolved from just being a device to talk to a centerpiece of our lives [sic].

(2013: 2)

Indeed, mobile phones in general and smart phones in particular have radically re-shaped how we transmit, read, absorb, and behave around variant sexual identities. Mobile hyperlinks reconfigure what we think of as evidence since so often, in texts, emails, social media messages, and innumerable other messaging apps, we nimbly use "Cut/ Copy and Paste" features to teleport recipients between windows, into alternate yet intersecting states of mind. We use hyperlinks, in other words, to cite/substantiate/emphasize what we are often intending to express in brief. Few, if any, studies examine the ongoing policing of Section 377 and the mobile closets that it produces. This reality of millennial technoculture warrants further theorization, especially in acceptable domains of online presence the hyperlink is a synecdoche for ultimate truth. Hypertext is a lightning-fast shuttle between meanings and representations on visual displays which also impacts the way that testament is electronically disseminated.

It is within this frame of hypertextuality and shifting notions of electronic evidence on the Fourth Screen that I want to critically read *BD*'s social media platform on Facebook from which I here share some screen shots. In doing so, I want to explore how queer and feminist identities are reconfigured on the portable Fourth Screen with respect to India's oldest gay periodical, and which facilitates imagined communities of queers that are yet outlawed by the governing statute. Screen shots of the magazine's Facebook page offer rich perspectives on what it chooses to post, and how the material addresses the needs of the queer South Asians whom it identified in the 1999 issue's cover story. In particular and as if in response to the oppressive societal undercurrents of Section 377, the webpage congregates the politically minded, even by inviting them to socio-political events that are framed as Socratic questions that solicit viewers to think of answers even if they are afraid or unable to attend.

One event in January 2016 was titled "Queer & Political! How Political is your Queer?" and visually encourages viewers to imagine the event as part of a queer democracy that is also struggling. With its rainbow-colored dialogue bubble, the Fourth Screen representation of the event is arguably as significant as the event itself. It creates multiple queer publics—imagined, material, and hoped for. Despite the divergent social articulations of this queer public sphere, we must keep in mind what nonetheless binds them together: that despite being imagined, material, and hoped for, they are all mobile and thus potent due to their quick mobile transmissions that can reach out, in seconds, to a borderless, "imagined community." In the moment of interception, they are all in motion, and as such empowered by movement and maneuvers of space

22 **Queer & Political!**
JAN **How Political is**
your Queer ?
Queer & Political

★   ✓   •••
Interested   Going

Fri, Jan 22 at 5:30 PM - 8:30 PM
Fri, Jan 22

Humsafar Trust
3rd floor, Manthan Plaza, Nehru Road, Opp. Vakola
Masjid, Vakola, Santacruz East, Mumbai, India 400055

Figure 4.2 An event hosted by the Humsafar Trust uses social media to query
hypertext readers on the relationship between sexual and political
identity, screenshot courtesy of Rahul K. Gairola.

and locale in ways never before possible by simple print media. As portable GPS devices, they empower their holders with instantaneous shifts of
location of a person or event, or guide their holders through city streets
and byways as, in Michel de Certeau's city, the walker compels them to
"become liberated spaces that can be occupied" (de Certeau 1984: 105).
In other words, the Fourth Screen facilitates mobility for *BD's* event
page where queerness surreptitiously circulates in public space despite
the punitive constraints of Section 377.

The publication's Facebook page moreover anchors issues that are
timely for feminism and anti-rape activism in India in addition to championing LGBTQ issues and events. For example, the May 2015 issue of
the magazine features Kalki Koechlin in an article titled "Breaking Stereotypes!" alongside a multi-authored story titled "The 377 Dossier"

by authors Manil Suri and Ruth Vanita. Koechlin, who belongs to the French diaspora that settled in Pondicherry (now Puducherry) during France's colonialist forays in the south. Kochelin is widely viewed as a feminist role model; she is viewed as a rare actress in the Hindi film industry based in Mumbai (Bombay) who is able to "subvert stereotypes by playing characters who are nothing like each other" (Groves 2016). Critically acclaimed for her flexible acting oeuvre, which challenges stereotypes on the silver screen, she is in real life also respected for being outspoken and honest. In March 2016, Kochelin starred in a black and white advertisement with strong lesbian overtones as Brand Ambassador for IICE Vodka. The digital advertisement for the "Kinki Chili" flavor of the spirit arguably features two women in sexualized, suggestive lingerie and postures that underscore lesbian desire. Koechlin's privilege as a postcolonial, French Indian diasporic woman (and indeed her light skin color in an ardently colorist nation) perhaps allows her to cross such borders.

Figure 4.3 Kalki Koechlin's cover story in the May 2015 issue of *Bombay Dost,* courtesy of Ashok Row Kavi and *Bombay Dost.*

The vodka advertisement moreover panders to heterosexual male fantasies concerning threesomes and simultaneously pleasing multiple women even as the women in the advert seem intimate with one another. If Koechlin functions as a "brand ambassador" in such qualified queer roles, her image and presence circulate to a far wider audience for those who access *BD*'s Facebook page on their mobile phones. From silver screen to Fourth Screen, she represents queer feminism in a manner that ultimately subverts and undermines the hegemony of a male gaze that is legally codified by the ideals enshrined in Section 377. For example, the notorious law tacitly enables corrupt police officials to troll (engage in online harassment and aggressive behavior) and blackmail LGBT people who are casually seeking sex. Such financial extortion is viewed as a small price to pay for men and women, many of whom are married and live in joint households, and whose lives would be utterly ruined if news about their extracurricular sexual activities became public. In a bid to mediate against unethical law enforcement, the *BD* Facebook group page offers counsel and support by posts by The Humsafar Trust, which functions in real time with the mobility of smart phones. Because the May 2015 cover of *BD* featuring Koechlin is the profile picture of the publication's group page, her image appears in the upper left corner of

Figure 4.4 Sonal Giani's warning post is shared by *Bombay Dost*'s Facebook page, screenshot courtesy of Rahul K. Gairola.

a post that informs and instructs queers in motion who risk entrapment by corrupt police officials.

In this captured moment of space and time, even as bodies are in motion with mobiles in hand, Koechlin's image and reputation for challenging stereotypes complements the text written by LGBT activist Sonal Giani. Giani's story, which is visibly linked to the presiding thumbnail of Koechlin on the cover of *BD*, offers a sharp and compact contrast to Section 377's ostensible goal to protect social morale by directly outlining how and where police entrap queer interlopers. Not only does the post detail characteristics of those who corrupt police officers prey on, but also, it details the two main social media platforms, Grindr and Planet Romeo (PR), through which they are able to victimize gay men. Yet, I would argue that in the realm of the Fourth Screen and how it re-shapes queer identity in motion in contemporary India, the thumbnail image of Koechlin along with the miniature portrait of Giani set the visual tone for the online demography which reads this post, which is presumably comprised of closeted, queer folks. The image rubber stamps the text of the warning post, thus recalibrating testament on the mobile device. In other words, the shared post hosted by *BD* endorses Giani's post and in doing so lends a sense of veracity to the legal advocate's counsel. It allows the fact of queer identity to be shared and circulated amongst many imagined communities even as it nails down into reality the existence of a community whose hyper reality might otherwise be taken as digital mythology.

In the cybersphere of digital social media, celebrity endorsement has far-reaching implications that historically include "teaching" an adoring public what passes as hip, cool, trendy, and right. In a country that produces more films per year than any other and where familiar faces are plastered throughout South Asia, celebrity appeal carries more sway than democratic appeal in shaping people's opinions. As P. David Marshall observes,

> The pedagogy of the celebrity has served very particular purposes throughout the twentieth century. Celebrity taught generations how to engage and use consumer culture to 'make' oneself. In a number of treatises on advertising and consumer culture, cultural critics have identified how the individual had to be taught how to consume and to recognize the value of consumption for their own benefit.
>
> (2013: 428)

Such forms of public pedagogy in the digital world through high profile social figures are having revolutionary effects in contemporary India, and also spearheading many movements for social justice here that have also spread around the globe (Nayar 2016). I would add that the seemingly innocuous thumbnail has a pedagogical effect, as described above, in the digital milieu: it imparts knowledge to queer readers in motion as it also adds celebrity endorsement to the presented data. However, as I have earlier suggested, the post also allows us to critically read Koechlin as a stereotype-breaking feminist in a different light of the image's affiliation with the Giani post.

For even if the actress is consolidating a heteronormative, male gaze in her vodka advertisements, her thumbnail image does the contrary; that is, it visually affiliates with transgressive sexualities as the post verbally mediates against police corruption. As such, it minoritizes the male gaze's encounter of the objectified women in the liquor company's commercial by augmenting the queer pedagogy of a digital public that is both local and global. I would moreover assert that *BD's* catalyzation of this process on the Fourth Screen produces a global network of "cybergaysians." These online agents are queers in and beyond India who form affiliations and alliances with LGBTQ people and events in India through the backdrop of Section 377's colonial agendas on the erotic experiences of contemporary India. Cybergaysians are agents in motion, whose unfixed parameters allegorize the interface of queer sexuality with the flexibility of mobile smart phones. As such, they challenge the parameters of the social media platform in addition to the gender binary. Matthew G. Kirschenbaum delineates a major distinction between Facebook, the most popular social media platform in India, and Twitter: "Unlike *Facebook*, *Twitter* allows for asymmetrical relationships: you can 'follow' someone (or they can follow you) without the relationship being reciprocated [sic]" (2013: 200).

While the "asymmetrical relationship" certainly disrupts the pressure of reciprocity, especially in terms of "liking," "friending," and "trending" that coalesce in Facebook groups, comments, and posts, the latter's multimedia reach is unparalleled in India. According to the *Economic Times*, India will have the world's largest number of Facebook users by the end of 2016 (2013). The social platform's popularity in India reflects the country's penchant for busy and colorful media in films, religious festivals, cultural events, and ethnic diversity. While the *BD* Facebook Group page provides a venue for queer Indians to invite and share events that are not advertised to the general public, it also consciously unites folks fighting against Section 377. For example, it introduces queers living in rural areas of India away from the underground lifestyles and communities of Mumbai, Delhi, Bangalore, Chennai, and other metropolises, to resources like the Centre for Civil Society. A feature section on the group page includes brief quotes and links concerning legislative responsibility in terms of safeguarding civil rights. While I do not want to suggest that the dominance of the English language and access to resources transcend rural/ urban and rich/ poor divides, I would argue that such posts provide queer-positive agency in motion at one's fingertips. They also, perhaps most importantly, allow South Asian queers in motion to engage and confront Section 377's bigoted legacy in real time, together.

Figure 4.5 Centre for Civil Society battles the erotic bigotry of the colonial-era Section 377 on its Facebook page, screenshot courtesy of Rahul K. Gairola.

Third Sex on the Fourth Screen

Such a strategy in motion to combat the spread of anti-queer laws, regulations, attitudes, and violence (especially as perpetuated through conservative ideologies of religious extremism) is especially crucial at a time when pink washing in India masks the government's uneasy love affair with neoliberal capitalism and anti-Islamic ideologies. These days, the nation seems to be coming closer to recognizing the fluid possibilities of gender and how it may be legally codified as it has been informed by the first two waves of feminism. But I would venture that we instead witness the tensions and contradictions produced between the Victorian ethos surrounding sexuality and India's ancient tradition of honoring third sex people in addition to non-heteronormative, sexual identities. On April 15, 2014, the Supreme Court of India ruled to recognize hijras as the Third Sex to much applause and fanfare of queer rights activists in India. An umbrella term not just for those who live non-heteronormative and non-homonormative lifestyles, "third sex" includes those whose gender categories stretch beyond the over-determinations of the Western fe/male binary. For example, myriad conceptions of "third sex" beyond normative taxonomies of gender include "eunuch," "transgender" (khusras), "hijra," "kothi," "chhakka," "hermaphrodite," "genderqueer," "intersex," "transsexual," "*aravani*," "jagappa," "cross-dresser" (zenana), "Shiv-Shakthi," and other specifications which appear in sacred Hindu texts including the *Kama Sutra* and The *Mahabharata*.

Such histories of flexible gender roles stand in stark contrast to the relatively recent domination of the colonialist gender binary in India. This verdict literally permits those who identify as Third Sex to tick "third gender," rather than "male" or "female," on passports, government documents, job applications, school registrations forms, and other documents requiring gender selection. This juridical order from the apex court legally underscore's Judith Butler's recent query:

> If queer means that we are generally people whose gender and sexuality is 'unfixed' then what room is there in a queer movement for those who understand themselves as requiring—and wanting—a clear gender category within a binary frame? Or what room is there for people who require a gender designation that is more or less unequivocal in order to function well and to be relieved of certain forms of social ostracism? Many people with intersexed conditions want to be categorized within a binary system and do not want to be romanticized as existing 'beyond all categories'.
>
> (Ahmed interview with Butler 2016)

The Supreme Court of India has moreover mandated the establishment of Third Sex reservations, which constitute affirmative action around gender and sexuality, in education and employment with material benefits that will mediate against years of gender discrimination.

In this frame, it would seem that contemporary Indian statutes that regulate gender identity are quite progressive with transgender people, or the so-called "third sex." But closer scrutiny at the history of hijras and the contradictions that arise from the Supreme Court of India's legal recognition of the third sex while upholding the constitutionality of Section 377 suggests otherwise. Legal codification of the third sex provides new grounds for criminalizing queer sexuality anchored to intelligible gender roles—hijra and/ or fe/male—and some historical framing is in order to understand precisely why. While popular belief in South Asia holds that the appearance of hijras at births, weddings, and other auspicious occasions bestows blessings (or curses if the visitors are ill-treated or not paid properly for their merry-making) on the spot, this particular colonial-era statute breaks the ancient tradition of venerating members of the third sex. The legal reservations accorded to hijras by the new law deliver paltry remedies in contrast to the dominant mentality of patriarchal male privilege that looks down on femininity as an abject ontology and haunts social acceptability. This comes into sharp focus in a brief titled "Hijras/ Transgender Women in India: HIV, Human Rights, and Social Exclusion," submitted to the United Nations Development Programme (UNDP), India, by Dr. Venkatesan Chakrapani, M.D.

The report is of importance to this discussion of queer feminism and the Fourth Screen because it details the many forms of "social exclusion" experienced by third sex peoples, including exclusion from familial, social, and cultural participation; discrimination in healthcare settings; exclusion from economic participation and lack of social security, which includes lack of livelihood options and health and life insurance schemes; and exclusion from political participation (Chakrapani 2010: 8–9). As one might have correctly guessed by now, this break can be traced back to anxieties about Hindu women and "the family" during the days of the British Raj. The British colonial administration instituted the Criminal Tribes Act of 1871 which criminalized those who transgressed normative gender roles. According to Nancy A. Naples and Barbara Gurr,

> By specifically regulating gender/ sex identities, the colonial project in India legally imposed a heteronormative binary which marginalized those who stepped outside of the legal bounds of gendered sexuality...The British colonial powers incorporated hijra into a grander, criminalized category which included all non-heterosexual identities without distinction.
>
> (Naples and Gurr 2012: 314–315)

This brief reflection back to the historical roots of criminalizing in South Asia those whose gender identities do not match Occidental, social norms demonstrates how and why social activism for transgender rights are timely in the wake of legal recognition yet the ongoing institutionalization of Section 377.

The *BD* group page promotes, in addition to gay and lesbian cultural and legal information, supportive representation and data for hijras. For example, in one update, the *BD* platform features pictures of 6 Pack Band, India's first ever transgender band. This visibility, sponsored by Red Label Tea, is arguably a landmark for India's stigmatized third gender class of citizens who constitute one of India's most impoverished communities and one that is also victim to trans-misogyny on a regular basis despite legal recognition under law. While corporate sponsorship of such bands arguably taps into a market of young and hip twenty-somethings in the middle-class market of mainstream India, I would conclude that the *BD* social media platform on Facebook facilitates the formation of an online community of what I have previously called "cybergaysians." This online, imagined community anchors content that is on the move as it is re-presented through social media apps, location services, and screen shots on mobile phones. This has revolutionized queer representation in South Asian journalism, and further tracks the shift of the ephemeral print issue as a hub of LGBT information in India to the queer public sphere in Digital India.

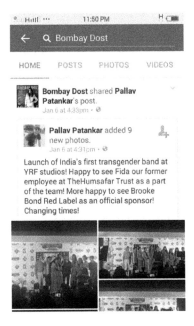

Figure 4.6 Bombay Dost's Facebook page promotes 6 Pack Band, screenshot
courtesy of Rahul K. Gairola.

Yet, beyond rehearsed arguments about queer invisibility or visibility that
have become institutionalized in white and homo-nationalist queer studies
(Puar, 2007), the Fourth Screen in South Asia enables the movement of
queer visibility. Here, that visibility and its further electronic disseminations and use of hyperlinks, screen shots, and other digital, multimedia tools
re-calibrate witness, testimony, and truth. To end with the words of Nishant
Shah:

> Computing ontologies and computational geographies are wedded
> to the relentless action of the individual and its actions—the user is
> at the centre of the networked universe, rhizomatic and yet hierar-
> chical, empty of signifiers, and yet so invested with micro-meanings
> that it implodes under the weight.
>
> (2015: 24–25)

The flows, disruptions, and consequences of these individuals in queer
India will continue to foster and shape, through online communities
fostered by *Bombay Dost*'s Facebook group page, and how they come
together online as a cohort of cybergaysians. These cybergaysians,
which include those who stretch the limitations of gender—and thus
feminism—also stretch the spatial configurations of identity and place
as they renegotiate identities as they are absorbed and inflected by the
dawning of cybercultures in the queer public sphere.

Bibliography

Ahmed, Sara. "Interview with Judith Butler." *Sexualities* 19.4 (2016): 1–11.

Anderson, Benedict. *Imagined Communities: Reflections on the Origin and Spread of Nationalism.* London: Verso, 1991.

Benjamin, Walter. "The Work of Art in the Age of Mechanical Reproduction." Illuminations. *Bombay Dost* 7.1 (1999).

Chakrapani, Venkatesan. 2010. "Hijras/Transgender Women in India: HIV, Human Rights, and Social Exclusion." *United Nations Development Programme* (UNDP), India. Accessed January 11. www.undp.org/content/dam/india/docs/hijras_transgender_in_india_hiv_human_rights_and_social_exclusion.pdf.

de Certeau, Michel. *The Practice of Everyday Life.* Trans. Steven Rendall. Berkeley: U of California P, 1984.

Deleuze, Gilles, and Felix Guittari. *A Thousand Plateaus.* London: Continuum Books, 1987.

Dore, Bhavya. "The Rise, Fall, and Resurrection of India's Oldest Surviving LGBT Magazine." *Pacific Standard: Stories that Matter.* Accessed October 24, 2016. https://psmag.com/.

Dudrah, Rajinder, Sangita Gopal, Amit Rai, and Anustup Basu. "Intermedia Emergence: the fourth screen." *InterMedia in South Asia: The Fourth Screen.* Eds. Rajinder Dudrah, Sangita Gopal, Amit Rai, and Anustup Basu. London: Routledge, 2013. 1–5.

Edelman, Lee. *Homographesis: Essays in Gay Literary and Cultural Theory.* New York: Routledge, 2013.

Economic Times. 2015. "India to Have World's Largest Facebook Users by 2016." Accessed 14 May 2016. http://telecom.economictimes.indiatimes.com/news/internet.

Fortunati, Leopoldina. "The Mobile Phone: Towards New Categories and Social Relations." *The Media Studies Reader.* Eds. Laurie Ouellette. New York: Routledge, 2013. 156–65.

Foucault, Michel. *History of Sexuality: Volume I.* London: Allen Lane, 1976.

Franceschini, Robert, and Rahul K. Gairola. "Two Years Later: Catching Up with Kshama Sawant." *Salaam: The Newsletter of the South Asian Literary Association* 39.1 (2015): 14–20.

Gairola, Rahul K. "Re-Worlding the Oriental: Critical Perspectives on Madonna as Geisha." *Madonna's Drowned Worlds: New Approaches to Her Cultural Transformations (1983–2003).* Eds. Santiago Fouz-Hernandez and Freya Ivens-Jarmin. Aldershot: Ashgate Publishers, 2004. 104–19.

Gajjala, Radhika. *Cyber Selves: Feminist Ethnographies of South Asian Women.* Lanham, MD: Altamira/Rowman & Littlefield Press, 2004.

Gopinath, Gayatri. *Impossible Desires: Queer Diasporas and South Asian Public Cultures.* Durham, NC: Duke University Press, 2005.

Groves, Dan. 2016. "Bollywood Star Kalki Koechlin Discusses Upcoming Films and Breaking the Stereotype Boundaries." *Forbes.* 16. April, 2016. www.forbes.com/sites/dongroves/2016/03/10/bollywood-star-kalki-koechlin-discusses-upcoming-films-and-breaking-the-stereotype-boundaries/2/#f4d8a43fa717. Accessed July 17, 2016.

Guha, Ranajit. "On Some Aspects of the Historiography of Colonial India." *Selected Subaltern Studies.* Eds. Ranajit Guha and Gayatri Chakravorty Spivak. Oxford: Oxford University Press, 1988. 37–41.

Haraway, Donna. *Simians, Cyborgs, and Women: The Reinvention of Nature.* New York: Routledge, 2013.

Jagoda, Patrick. *Network Aesthetics.* Chicago: University of Chicago Press, 2016.

Joseph, Sherry. "Gay and Lesbian Movement in India." *Economic & Political Weekly* 31.33 (1996): 2228–33.

Kirschenbaum, Matthew G. "What is Digital Humanities and What's It Doing in English Departments?" *Defining Digital Humanities: A Reader.* Eds. Melissa Terras, Julianne Nyhan, and Edward Vanhoutte. Aldershot: Ashgate Publishers, 2013. 195–204.

Landow, George. *Hypertext 3.0: Critical Theory and New Media in an Age of Globalization.* Baltimore: Johns Hopkins University Press, 2006.

MacDonald, Eleanor. "Critical Identities: Rethinking Feminism through Transgender Politics." *Atlantis* 23.1 (Fall/Winter 1998): 1–10.

Mallapragada, Madhavi. "Rethinking Desi: Race, Class, and Online Activism of South Asian Immigrants in the United States." *Television & New Media* 15.7 (2014): 664–78.

Marshall, P. David. "The Promotion and Presentation of the Self: Celebrity as Marker of Presentational Media." *The Media Studies Reader.* Eds. Laurie Ouellette. New York: Routledge Publishers, 2013. 427–38.

Naples, Nancy A., and Barbara Gurr. "Genders and Sexualities in Global Context: An Intersectional Assessment of Contemporary Scholarship." *The Wiley-Blackwell Companion to Sociology.* Eds. George Ritzer. Oxford: Wiley-Blackwell, 2012. 304–32.

Nayar, Pramod K. "How UoH and JNU Have Taken Us from Public Protest to Public Pedagogy."

O'Riordan, Kate, and David J. Phillips. 2007. "Introduction." *Queer Online: Media, Technology, and Sexuality.* Eds. Kate O'Riordan and David J. Phillips. Bern: Peter Lang Publishing, 2007. 13–30.

Puar, Jasbir. *Terrorist Assemblages: Homonationalism in Queer Times.* Durham, NC: Duke UP, 2007.

Raymond, Janice. *Transsexual Empire: The Making of the She-Male.* Boston, MA: Beacon Press, 1979.

Roy, Sandip. "From Khush List to Gay Bombay: Virtual Webs of Real People." *Mobile Cultures: New Media in Queer Asia.* Eds. Chris Berry, Fran Martin, and Audrey Yue. Durham: Duke University Press, 2003. 180–97.

Shah, Nishant. "Internet and Society in Asia: Challenges and Next Steps." *Inter-Asia Cultural Studies* 11.1 (2010): 129–35.

———."Queer Mobiles and Mobile Queers: Intersections, Vectors, and Movements in India." *Routledge Handbook of New Media in Asia.* Eds. Larissa Hjorth and Olivia Khoo. New York: Routledge, 2015. 275–84.

———."Identity and Identification: The Individual in the Time of Networked Governance." *Socio Legal Review* 11.2 (2015): 22–40.

Vikram Phukan. "Bombay Dost, India's First LGBT Magazine, Turns 25!" http://www.mid-day.com/articles/bombay-dost-indias-first-lgbt-magazine-turns-25/16587189.

5 Writing New *Sastras*

Notes towards Building an Indian Feminist Archive

Padmini Ray Murray

Janaki Nair (1994) in her important articulation on the emergence of an Indian feminist historiography describes how, in 1928, the women of the All India Women's Conference (AIWC) demanded 'new sastras' in response to Madan Mohan Malaviya's assertion that the age of marriage could not be raised due to the diktats of Hindu scriptures. This moment, Nair asserts, "anticipated by several decades the demand of feminist historians not just for new histories but for a reinvention of the historical archive" (82). While the volume of work both inside and outside the academy has demonstrated feminism's coming of age in the country, it is undeniable that it is time again to provoke another reconsideration of the archive as an epistemological site.

Nair goes on to describe how the historiographical exercise of considering the feminist archive has always been complicated by tensions wrought by class, caste, and religion. Indeed, as she says, those perspectives which *cannot* speak of lower castes (due to lack of documentary sources) "reverberate through successive interpretations of Indian history which continue to use such constructions as if they were gender and class neutral" (87). However, despite the increasing visibility and articulation of non-dominant-caste feminist work, especially online, I will argue that there is still a great danger of the narrative of our multivalent feminist heritage being overwhelmed by those who are English-educated and/or from dominant castes, whose levels of access to institutional knowledge and status mean that their work is often parsed as definitive. Despite efforts by feminist publishers and academics in India and elsewhere to amplify less-represented voices, there are invariably archival silences created by the lack of access and means of non-dominant-caste and tribal communities to publish in traditional modes of dissemination such as academic journals and monographs as well as the mainstream press.[1]

The adoption of social media tools such as Facebook and Twitter by middle-class Indian feminists served to create a new archive, but one which still perpetuated these silences, as access to technology devices and internet connectivity is still difficult for those who are socio-economically disadvantaged—as of 2016 only 21% of Indians use the internet or possess a smartphone (Poushter 2017). What makes this threat even more troubling is that the ubiquity and rhetoric of techno-utopianism gives the impression that the digital will ensure everything will be preserved, and that content on born-digital news and social networking sites will be easy to search and retrieve. But however convenient and tempting it might be to believe in this vision of the future, the stark reality is that most online content hosted by a third party, such as Google or Facebook, holds that content to ransom, and its preservation is contingent on such exigencies as government policy or diktat, or financial precarity.

However, while digital feminism rapidly gains momentum in India, there is little attention paid to the future of this prodigious output—as to how this sort of content might be archived, or the implications of not archiving such material in a responsible and representative fashion. It is essential, therefore, to conceive of an alternative space that might represent Indian feminism in inclusive, expansive, and representative ways. As Jarret M. Drake, a radical digital archivist who has supported projects such as the *A People's Archive of Police Violence in Cleveland*, puts it: "Archives have never been neutral." However, he also reminds us of the "liberational value" of the archive, and in the pages that follow, I will demonstrate how it might be possible to harness that value for the Indian feminist movement, though it might require considerable rethinking of our current attitudes towards the archive and what it represents in historiographical terms.

Considering the archive requires a deeper examination of the politics of the archive itself, requiring an alertness to how "seemingly neutral Western criteria and classifications" which were inherited as a colonial legacy, are "in fact tools for maintaining the role of an archive as an imperial project of domination and affirmation" (*Decolonising Archives*, 5). It is worth flagging up at this point that the Indian feminist archive lies somewhere between the reified and metaphor—defined both by material and cultural production and as a historiographical site of inquiry. The notion of a feminist archive, of course, is complicated by its relationship to that of the modern nation-state where the archive serves as, as Wolfgang Ernst puts it, "a foundational narrative of its temporal genealogy" where, via "the historical discourse, the administrative state which is an infra-structural function (and represents the symbolic order of power) could be transformed into an imaginary called 'nation'" (11). In the particular context of India, it is tempting to envision the archive as a locus of power for its colonial leaders—but, significantly, the postcolonial archive also followed this flattening logic. Georges Perec in "Think/ Classify" (1974) stated "Behind every utopia there is always some great taxonomic design: a place for each thing and each thing in its place" and it was precisely this utopian ambition that led Jawaharlal Nehru, the first prime minster of the Indian republic, to design his vision of the nation along "scientific Marxist" lines—what has come to be known as Nehruvian socialism.

Nehru preferred to leave the emotionally messy work of appealing to the "masses" (comprising of the peasantry and/or non-dominant-caste people) to Gandhi, imagining (in a rather patronizing fashion) that they were unlikely to appreciate his dedication to the larger nationalist cause of "scientific progress." This vision basically entailed championing large-scale industry over small-scale or cottage industry, which he felt were colonial throwbacks that would only hamper India from taking its rightful place on the international stage. Nehru was confused by the spontaneous uprisings of the peasantry, who were by and large non-dominant caste, envisioning another idea of India which valued their labour and their ties to their land—such as in the Tebhaga movement, which was one of the first challenges to the appropriative claims of feudal landowners. In the wake of independence, such protests were seen as an inconvenient, messy resistance that undermined the much-vaunted "national" agenda that challenged Nehru's vision of a "scientific" route to postcolonial progress. This vision of a technosocial citizen as the ideal Indian gained more momentum in post-liberalization India, reaching its apogee under Narendra Modi's strategies such as "Make in India" and "Digital India."

The emergence of feminist thought as a defined mode of inquiry was largely made possible by the "historical recovery of the precolonial and colonial past" and "the postcolonial formation of the nation-state" has unsurprisingly dominated postcolonial feminist thought in South Asia. Indeed, as Maitreyee Chaudhuri asserts, it was "feminist *historical* research" that laid the grounds for theorizing feminism in the region (4, qtd. in Loomba et al. 2012). However, it might be that the understandable preoccupation with undoing the legacy of colonial epistemologies and knowledges meant that the archive was only perceived as a site of imperial control rather than one that might be activated to produce new epistemological formations. As Uma Chakravarti argues:

> ...even as feminists have been very strong in critiquing the cultural basis of nationalism, they have not been as mindful of the class (and caste) and regional bases of this nationalism and the implicit assumptions that have shaped our own ideologies of nationalism, nation-states, and their territorial arrangements, as reflected in borders and boundaries, and the way we ourselves have been constructed to invest in our own nation-states in this process.
>
> (2008: 2–3)

What these accounts demonstrate is that, while writing the struggles of non-dominant groups out of the archive is evidently due to lack of institutional will, it is also politically and tactically expedient as a strategy and has been since India gained independence in 1947. In the current climate, while it might be imagined that digitization could be a democratizing tool to challenge the authority of the archive, it is only too easy to replicate "established Western narratives" and "turn into a pseudo-democratic end in itself, resulting in an overload of the material available online" (*Archives*, 6). A meaningful act of digital archiving therefore must be performed at the level of epistemological understanding, ontological authenticity, and scaffolded appropriately by interface and code in order to interrogate the existing archive as well as to expand its scope.

The Archive in the Time of the Digital

Pre-digital archives are underpinned by an understanding that the subject becomes the object, or artifact after its death. "In order for ethnology to live," Baudrilliard asserts, "it's object must die; by dying, the object takes its revenge for being 'discovered' and with its death defies the science that wants to grasp it" (1981/1994: 7). Similarly, Achille Mbembe gestures to the necessary death of the author of a document for it to enter the archive and acquire archival value, focusing on the historian's handling of dead and living time, with the archive forming both the original point from which historical time is constructed as well as the sign of death (qtd. in Balachandran, 2011: 22). The post-Web 2.0 archive, however, complicates this notion of death as the starting point of the archive—where event, documentation, and comment collapse the category of the "mortal" by inhabiting a state of always becoming. Social media, then, is a constant narration of historical event, accelerating our relationship with a polyphonic archive—challenging the Western taxonomic tradition of privileging one authorial voice over another. The articulation of protest online attempts to stand in for embodied activism in the streets, and this has particularly interesting implications for an Indian feminist culture that has manifested itself both in terms of visible and physical action—the Chipko movement for example—but also through different modes of knowledge making and sharing. This shift from the visibly embodied to the virtual is neatly encapsulated in the anecdote below, ushering in a significant moment in feminist protest in India:

> A casual conversation with my Gender Studies professor a few years ago revealed her deep sense of apprehension about the future of feminism. "Apathetic" and "apolitical" is how she described whom she called the "younger generation of feminists." To me, who had always held my peers in high regard for their feminist politics, this came as a surprise. While I would not admit this out loud, I had learnt more about feminist theory through interactions with my friends than I had inside the classroom. Where was this disjunction in opinion coming from? I realised then that while I sought feminist

interaction and politically charged conversations with fellow feminists on Facebook, my professor saw the empty streets as evidence of
our lack of interest in feminist politics. In the span of a generation,
the political actors had not changed, but the space of politics had
been transformed.

(Subramanian 2015: 71)

As Subramaniam goes onto describe, Nisha Susan's "Pink Chaddi"
campaign (2009) came to be seen as a watershed moment in the mobilization of social media for feminist activism in India. Susan's plan to
send three thousand pairs of pink knickers to the head of the right wing
Hindu outfit Sri Ram Sene was an audacious response to the equally
outrageous moral policing enacted by members of the group, who reinforced their disdain by physically assaulting a group of women who were
seen as flouting "traditional Indian norms of decency" by drinking un-
accompanied in a pub in Mangalore. By any measure, Susan's Facebook
campaign enjoyed considerable engagement, growing from five hundred
followers on the first day itself, burgeoning to forty thousand within a
week (Chattopadhyay 63).

But the "Consortium of Pub-going, Loose and Forward Women" as
Susan's group was monikered, also represented a dramatic break with
traditional feminist work in India, by unapologetically embracing its
urban, middle-class, English-speaking identity, speaking only for itself
rather than laying any claims to speak for a larger community and cause.
Undoubtedly, the Pink Chaddi campaign inaugurated a certain form of
feminist work that was new to the movement in India, and consequently
has generated a considerable amount of coverage by observers and
feminist thinkers both in India and abroad. Saayan Chattopadhyay
comments on how the campaign, which garnered support from many
followers abroad as well as locally, succeeded in activating an international solidarity. It modeled participation along the lines of a global citizenship, enacting the inevitable shift from "the notion of citizenship tied
to the terrain and imagination of a nation-state" to ""new entitlements
are being realized through situated mobilizations and claims" "within
the conditions of globalization" (Ong qtd. in Chattopadhyay, 64).

Hemangini Gupta's work references Susan's as well as other consecu-
tive feminist projects (Blank Noise, The Friday Convent) to describe how
"neoliberal subjectivities shape a new feminism" which she describes
as shifting "its attention from legal redress and state intervention to
cultivate entrepreneurial activists who adopt responsibility for their experiences of urban space as agentive actors" (152). While Gupta, Chattopadhyay, and many others have spoken to the implications of digital
feminist work in India, there has been little focus on the implications and
impact of the tools and technologies deployed, or how the ways in which
these actions shaping this mediascape (after Appudurai) are bound to

affect the archive. Elizabeth Losh's work on the aftermath of the Delhi rape case and mobilization of digital spaces is notable in this regard, being one of the few scholars to address with nuance how, showing "solidarity with those who are protesting 'live' is complicated by new forms of digital participation in which 'the metadata is the message'" (13). While Losh carefully addresses the paradoxes and tensions created by using corporate hegemonic platforms complicit in neoliberal economic and labour practices for social activism, she does persuasively argue the advantages of using "walled gardens" such as private Facebook groups or protected Twitter streams to provide a "safe space" for talking about assault and sexual violence, such as in the case of Jasmeen Patheja's initiative, Blank Noise (17). Losh highlights the "important hashtag activist labor" that human rights NGO and Blank Noise undertake, trying to influence the conversation online by "choosing, using, and appropriating online hashtags" and offline, by addressing the limitations of India's conditions of limited literacy and access to smart technologies by using different forms of media, such as Breakthrough's use of:

> ...'video vans' with content that responds to the needs of particular linguistic and ethnic communities and live stagings of 'theatre of the oppressed' scenarios that solicit audience participation and community deliberation about the appropriate course of action for treating the fictional women in the play with justice.
>
> (17)

There is already a danger of certain voices being amplified over others, even on a platform like the internet where everyone can be a publisher: a television feature by NDTV broadcast in March 2017 entitled "Feminism Online—The New Wave" featured a number of organizations that speak to largely English-speaking, upwardly mobile, urban women, and completely omitted *Savari* and *Dalit Women Fight*—both significant online platforms for non-dominant-caste women. *Khabar Lahariya*, the rural weekly newspaper staffed entirely by women from non-dominant-caste communities, is only mentioned as an after-thought following a talking head snippet advocating the need for intersectionality, despite the paper having a robust online presence in several Indian languages, including English. These omissions and elisions corrupt the historiographical record and the archive, and thus it is absolutely vital to begin addressing these misrepresentations and appropriations through proactive archiving work.

Pathfinders

The limitations of the digital historical record are not only evident at the level of content, but also at the level of infrastructure and storage. These susceptibilities have been highlighted by no less a figure than Vint Cerf, vice president of research at Google, and whose work informed the very foundations of the internet itself. Cerf has sounded a note of caution regarding the lack of integrity of digital files, vulnerable as they are to bit rot and obsolescence, thus raising the stakes for the archivist community who have to respond and strategize accordingly. Guidelines are emerging to ensure the longevity of these records, in order to guarantee both preservation and access, paying close attention to metadata, format, and storage. Projects like "Dodging the Memory Hole" hosted at the Reynolds Journalism Institute in Missouri, are dedicated to another historically significant online archive, that of digital news—creating strategies to include and educate numerous stakeholders to ensure the future of that record.

To paraphrase Itza Carbajal, one of the researchers on the project, and her discussion about online news: if social media "now represents a unique testimony of humanity's existence then there must exist a mandate to preserve it" (2017: 2). Given the vast volume of social media and online activism in India that defines itself as feminist, it is crucial to begin a consideration of how this archive will be curated, designed, and preserved. The irony is that the platforms themselves are ephemeral—as Kimberly Springer points out, the overreliance on the cloud means that the bulk of activist output on social media platforms puts the "ephemera, strategizing, and documentation of contemporary social movements [...] at risk" (2015). Springer goes on to describe how in her own research, she found "plenty of magazine clippings in archives that normalized feminism as 'a white thing,' the purview solely of white feminists," and that it was in fact the exceptionalist attitude exemplified by some sources in that archive (such as a 1973 *Newsweek* article called Feminism: 'The Black Nuance') that inspired her to recover narratives of black feminist organizing during that period. Consequently, she found that "more [relevant] records existed un-archived rather than in institutional archives" and that in a grotesque irony, the FBI actually maintained the most robust records of the movement due to their minute monitoring of the activities of the Third World Women's Alliance.

She writes:

> Should we thank the federal government for their spying, which resulted in an accidental archive that no other historical archive possessed? It would have been unheard of for the TWWA to consider the FBI their organization's official archivist. So why are we letting Facebook or even blogging platforms like WordPress be the de facto archivist of our calls to action, poster PDFs, organizational records, and other born-digital materials?
>
> (2015)

Springer then flags up the work of organizations such as Activist Archivists, who describe their aims on their website:

> ...to share knowledge and provide assistance on archiving and preservation matters in order to improve the discoverability of the media content that is being produced; to support the usability of digital media as evidence and as a creative resource; to ensure that the rights and intentions of media creators are respected; preserve the legacy of social movement for future generations; and to help give voice and history to those who may have traditionally been left out.

Though Activist Archivists concluded their activities in 2015, they inspired a legacy of similar organizations, some of which were set up by former members, such as the Community Archiving Workshop, the Interference Archive, WITNESS, and the XFR Collective. While none of these specifically address archiving social media, they focus on other uses of technology such as video, recording oral histories, and photography to create an alternative, grassroots historical record that necessarily, in some cases, deviates from the national or government narrative.

Springer's case study is instructive, demonstrating how the nature of the archive can threaten to obscure a whole strand of activism and how crucial documentation is to our understanding of social movements. For the purposes of thinking through how this sort of precarity might be avoided with regards to the contemporary Indian feminist archive, especially by focusing on social media, the US-based project DocNow might serve as an inspiration. DocNow, which emerged during the time of the Ferguson protests in 2014, was a response to the transformative power of social media to alter how we think about history. As one of its founders and their community manager, Bergis Jules puts it, "We're thinking ahead to how we'll look back."

Representation and the Archive

There is very little infrastructural and governmental support for creating archives in India, of any sort, on or offline—unlike the Library of Congress or the British Library, there are few initiatives and mandates to actively create, build, and maintain archives without those that uphold a hegemonic nationalist narrative. Against this backdrop, the advent of the Google Cultural Institute initiative has offered a platform for organizations who wish to build an outward facing archive. However, recent efforts in collaboration with feminist publishing house Zubaan, have led to a slightly tone-deaf resource entitled *Women in India: Unheard Voices*, which draws on a range of collections that purport to fall under the remit of the topic. The homogenous interface common to all Google Cultural Institute projects sets up a hierarchy of information, highlighting and reinforcing some narratives over others—even while the title purports to give voice to women whose stories are untold, the archive appears fragmented and random, due to its drawing on several disparate sources. A particularly confounding example is a page/portal entitled "Images and objects that represent the lives of women across India" which pulls up works of prominent Indian women artists cheek in jowl with statues of goddesses, alongside testimonies from women who were subject to sexual violence during the Partition of 1947. The visual presentation creates a jarring, decontextualized experience and serves as a salutary experience for a future vision of an archive; this establishes, in no uncertain terms, how essential it is to observe an ethics of curation when trying to design such a resource. Mitchell Whitelaw's formulation of "generous interfaces" with regards to cultural collections embodies such an ethical approach, where he articulates the need for the display of such collections to "support exploration as well as the focused enquiry where search excels [and] would also enrich interpretation by revealing relationships and structures within a collection." The Google site, on the other hand, conforms to static presentations of images that cannot be reordered, nor their metadata altered without considerable intervention.

There are several factors to consider in order to fulfil these ethical obligations: the current nature of such archives means that they are likely to be subject to scrutiny by governments and law enforcement agencies. Digital privacy is also an issue with regards to social media—one might choose to publish a tweet or a Facebook status but not to have it archived, and DocNow is working to create a tool which would allow users to opt-out of the archive. The primary concerns of "consent, context and access" need to be prioritized when considering the building of such an archive, especially since there is a long history of editing subaltern voices out of the record, but what the contemporary digital moment and networked communications do allow is for all stakeholders to participate and contribute, if they so wish. The grassroots project Mukurtu, directed by Kim Christian Withey, takes cognizance of the fact that different communities might have different protocols for navigating and understanding the world, and takes these into account as the basis for creating a content management system that privileges these values. Mukurtu does not prioritize access for all, and instead focuses on creating a "safe space" for cultural content, something which a transactional model such as the Google Cultural Institute cannot achieve, as its mandate is one of complete openness.

Mapping Mediascapes

In 1993, in her seminal work *A History of Doing*, Radha Kumar pointed to how it was a "bleak irony for contemporary feminists that queries and self-doubts raised about representation should have come back to roost in recent times" (13) born out of the incommensurability of the category of "woman" in the Indian context, due to the fault lines of caste, religion, and class. Ten years later, in her introduction to *New South Asian Feminisms*, Srila Roy sounds the same note of uncertainty regarding the resistance of the category to classification:

> The liberal inheritance of women's movements, most manifest in their privileging of 'woman' as a rights-bearing subject to be protected by the state, is consequently seen to have come to its logical conclusion (Menon 2004; Madhok 2010). The presumed transparency of this subject, unmarked by community, caste or religious affiliations, has, moreover, lent to majoritarian and essentializing impulses *within* women's movements as well as to fierce identity-based politics and cleavages (see Sunder Rajan 2003). Globalization, privatization, (neo) liberalization, and increased and excessively militarized ethnic and religious nationalisms and violence are fundamentally transforming the terrain upon which feminists must wage their struggles, as well as the nature and form of such struggles. The future, it seems, has never been more uncertain.
>
> (John 2005: 2)

Much of these anxieties stem from a consideration of how something like representative intersectionality might be performed in an Indian context, given that the constant tension between privilege, patriarchy, and caste often threatens to destabilize these efforts. However, some of these anxieties might be countered by thinking of the archive as a space where agency, authorship, and curated metadata ensure representation and amplification rather than obliteration. What such an archive also might allow is to reconsider the epistemological stakes of contemporary Indian feminism, by carefully thinking through the ontological categories that would inform the building of such a site, which themselves can be radical re-inscriptions of institutionalized knowledge. The affordances of social media also facilitate recognition of transnational allegiances and struggles, such as those relationships forged between Dalit and #BlackLivesMatter activist communities, which allows issues to resonate far beyond national borders.

In a climate still dominated by patriarchal discourse, paying academic attention to both individual and institutional feminist performative labour and the formal and informal allegiances that are fostered on social media and then republishing it as historical (re)source is a feminist act in itself—militating against the idea that women's speech is insignificant. The choice of the name Zubaan, for example, was a reclamation of a pejorative term in Hindi denoting women's talk, or gossip. Kate Eickhorn typifies the Riot Grrrl movement of the 1990s as "defined by an explosive repertoire of gestures, styles, performances, rallying cries, and anonymous confessions reproduced on copy machines—it was also a movement that had been collecting, preserving, and preparing itself for the archive all along" (IX), a prodigious output that was precipitated by access to photocopying technology. Similarly, the digital toolkit that allows Indian feminists to publish prolifically and be heard, echoes that repertoire and deserves an archive which legitimizes and recognizes these multitudinous histories.

In order to conceptualize such an archive, it might be useful to outline some essential and definitive features that could lay the foundations for such a project. Such an endeavor must necessarily be designed as a community archiving project, which immediately allows participants to decide whether they wish to opt-in to the archive or not. Participation can be retracted at any point—the aim is not to create a complete archive but to foster many archives that intersect and speak to one another. Consequently, efforts should be made to ensure metadata schemas of such archives should be interoperable, and accommodate linguistic difference, and include conceptual categories that are not necessarily accounted for by Western ontological frameworks. The interface should be "generous" and allow users to encounter data in serendipitous ways, ensuring that the presentation of such data does not reinforce existing hierarchies. Users should be able to annotate and contribute metadata that speak to their own understanding of the content, which they can choose to make public, shared with specific audiences, or private. The archives created using these guidelines should have open APIs which can be moderated depending on the terms of use entered into by each participant in the archive. Researchers and users of the archive will be advised to be alert to the ever-emergence of the archive, and that it is always a work in progress—Michelle Moravec's feminist guidelines for working in a digital archival environment are illuminating:

1 Have individuals who appear in these materials consented to this?
2 Whose labour was used and how is it acknowledged?
3 What absences must be attended to among an abundance of materials?

Such insights could only benefit the archive, and possibly inspire proactive outreach to those who are not visible, for whatever reason.

Building such inclusive feminist archive(s) will be an incredibly difficult, yet essential task that will not only grant both posterity and legitimacy to the various strands of thought and activism that have defined the movement, but also enlarge understandings of what it means to be a feminist in India by accommodating "contrasting and fluid ontologies" that are marked by local, regional, and other specificities. In a country marked by such a range of difference, it is imperative that the task of representing that difference is performed by the actors themselves, rather than technological corporations. Tejas Harad writes:

> By various estimates Brahmin population in India ranges between 3% and 5%. But even though a minority, they are the most visible group in the country as they occupy most positions of power, be it in the government, judiciary, media or academia. If you are a Deshpande or a Kulkarni or a Patwardhan, you will be easily recognised as a Brahmin by everybody. And people will also look at you with a certain amount of respect, implicit or explicit.
>
> (2016)

This visibility also replicates itself and algorithmically re-embeds itself in the social media archive, especially in spaces such as Facebook which prioritize relationships with other individuals based on such class/caste markers such as neighbourhoods lived in, schools and universities attended, and professional affiliations. But the subversive potential of a digital archive becomes apparent when we use technology to help us re-narrate these relationships, and when we understand that to name is to own. To name is to lay claim on culture, as sure as planting a flag on the shores of another. To name is to assert authority, authorial control of the narrative, to write the world into being. And never has the act of naming been so significant; as we try to navigate our digital universe, the stars that shine the brightest and are the easiest to find are the constellations we care to name on our maps, and that outshine the others by sheer conviction of being. But, of course, we all hold up the sky and so must write our names across it together.

Note

1 See, for example, Dhrubo Jyoti's piece 'Covering Dalit Atrocities in a Savarna Newsroom' for the difficulties experienced by Dalit journalists in an industry dominated by urban, dominant-caste reporters.

Bibliography

"Archives have never been neutral": An NDSA Interview with Jarrett Drake. http:// ndsa.org/2017/02/15/archives-have-never-been-neutral-an-ndsa-interview-with-jarrett-drake.html. Last modified: February 15, 2017. Accessed March 14, 2017.

Balachandran, Aparna, and Rochelle Pinto. *Archives and Access*. Researchers at Work. Bangalore: Centre for Internet and Society, 2011.

Baudrillard, Jean. *Simulacra and Simulation*. Trans. Sheila Faria Glaser. Ann Arbor: U of Michigan P, 1994.

Carbajal, Itza A. "Web Archivability: A Path towards Dialogue." www.rjionline. org/stories/itza-carbajal-web-archivability-a-pathway-towards-dialogue. Last modified: February 13, 2017. Accessed March 16, 2017.

Chakravarti, Uma. "Archiving the Nation-State in Feminist Praxis: A South Asian Perspective." Centre for Women's Development Studies Occasional Paper, no. 51, 2008.

Chattopadhyay, Saayan. "Online Activism for a Heterogeneous Time: The Pink Chaddi Campaign and the Social Media in India." *Proteus* 27.1 (2011): 63–69.

Eichhorn, Kate. *The Archival Turn in Feminism: Outrage in Order.* Pennsylvania, PA: Temple U P, 2013.

Ernst, Wolfgang. 2016. "Radically De-Historicising the Archive. Decolonising Archival Memory from the Supremacy of Historical Discourse." *Decolonising Archives.* L'Internationale. PDF ebk. www.internationaleonline.org/bookshelves/decolonising_archives. Accessed March 7, 2017.

Google Cultural Institute. "Women in India: Unheard Voices." www.google.com/culturalinstitute/beta/project/indias-women-in-culture. Accessed March 21, 2017.

Gupta, Hemangini. 2016. "Taking Action: The Desiring Subjects of Neoliberal Feminism in India." *Journal of International Women's Studies* 17.1 (2016): 152–168. http://vc.bridgew.edu/jiws/vol17/iss1/11. Accessed March 14, 2017.

Harad, Tejas. 2016, April 29. "What's in a Surname: Caste and So Much More." *Round Table India.* http://roundtableindia.co.in/index.php?option=com_content&view=article&id=8596:what-s-in-a-surname&catid=129:events-and-activism&Itemid=195. Accessed March 16, 2017.

Introduction. *Decolonising Archives.* L'Internationale, 2016. PDF ebk. www.internationaleonline.org/bookshelves/decolonising_archives. Accessed 1st March, 2017.

Loomba, Ania, and Ritty A. Lukose. *South Asian Feminisms.* Durham and London: Duke University Press, 2012.

Losh, Elizabeth. "Hashtag Feminism and Twitter Activism in India." *Social Epistemology Review and Reply Collective* 3.12 (2014): 10–22.

Moravec, Michelle. "Feminist Research Practices and Digital Archives." Australian Feminist Studies 32.91–92: 187–202.

Nair, Janaki. "On the Question of Agency in Indian Feminist Historiography." *Gender and History* 6.1 (April 1994): 82–100.

Poushter, Jacob. "China Outpaces India in Internet Access, Smartphone Ownership." Pew Research Center, March 16, 2017. www.pewresearch.org/fact-tank/2017/03/16/china-outpaces-india-in-internet-access-smartphone-ownership/. Accessed March 25, 2017.

Springer, Kimberly. "Radical Archives and the New Cycles of Contention." October 31, 2015. www.viewpointmag.com/2015/10/31/radical-archives-and-the-new-cycles-of-contention/. Accessed March 5, 2017.

Subramanian, Sujatha. "From the Streets to the Web: Looking at Feminist Activism on Social Media." *Economic and Political Weekly* 1.17 (April 25, 2015): 71–78.

Whitelaw, Mitchell. "Generous Interfaces for Digital Cultural Collections." *Digital Humanities Quarterly* 9.1 (2015). www.digitalhumanities.org/dhq/vol/9/1/000205/000205.html. Accessed March 18, 2017.

6 The Two Faces of Afghan Women

Oppressed and Exotic

Shahnaz Khan

Introduction

Said's (1978) seminal work on Orientalism helps us identify two prominent aspects of Western discursive construction of the other: violence and sexuality, both of which help to inform our material reality and are present, I suggest, in the images of Muslim women. Focusing on the story of Bibi Aisha as articulated by *Time Magazine* in 2010, this discussion examines the oppressed and mutilated Afghan woman who generates spectacle through imagery and the accompanying narrative, in the process inviting rescue attempts. Although it continues to fascinate the reader/viewer, the other type of Orientalist image, exemplified by the sexualized and exotic young Afghan girl, Sharbat Gula, whose 1985 image appeared on the cover of *National Geographic*, has receded into the background. In this discussion, I examine the politics surrounding the narrative construction of the Muslim exposed by *WikiLeaks* documents as well as the Taliban response to Aisha's mutilation. I conclude that few pay attention to the many invisible Afghan women who live and struggle in first world countries, including Canada.

Introducing Bibi Aisha

The cover of the July 2010 issue of *Time Magazine* presents an image of the oppressed Muslim woman. She is a violated and mutilated Afghan woman with a hole where her nose had been. A caption next to the image reads, "What Happens if We Leave Afghanistan." The accompanying article by Aryn Baker (2009) identifies the woman in the picture as eighteen-year-old Bibi Aisha, and there is a brief description of her brutalization and the fact that she had been rescued by U.S. forces and was now safe.

Aisha's account is part of the repertoire of images of the brutalized third-world woman whose stories, social scientists argue (Mohanty 1991; Thobani 2003), are presented to us as narratives of violence and trauma in Western accounts. These narratives are accompanied by imagery that promotes stereotypes of the women as timeless and ahistorical while locating their oppression within local barbaric patriarchies. National, regional, or international links to the local conditions that constrain women's choices, and that at times brutalize them, are never interrogated. What we are presented with are sensationalized images and accompanying narratives that float with little or no context and, in the process, endorse the workings of power. In recent years stories have focused on Afghan women (Armstrong 2008; Ellis 2002), presenting de-contextualized accounts that Mackie (2012) notes have much to say about US perception of its place in the world and little about the lives of women themselves. Such accounts present modern-day spectacles of the brutalization of Afghan women, inviting rescues, and, dare I say, military interventions. A WikiLeaks document (2010) that identifies the importance of Afghan women's narratives in shoring up support for the Afghan war in the west, supports my assertions. I will return to that document later in the discussion.

The impact of Bibi Aisha's image on the *Time* cover is extremely powerful. Selected as the 2010 World Press Photo of the Year, it has won prestige for its South African photographer, Jodi Beiber. We do not even need to read the article; the visual impact of Aisha's brutalization speaks volumes about the urgent need to save her, and makes a plea for the liberation of other Afghan women from their context and, by extension, from their Islamic culture.

For those who do decide to read Baker's article, "Afghan Women and the Return of the Taliban," we are introduced to eighteen-year-old Bibi Aisha, who ran away from an abusive husband and who, Baker claims, was punished under orders from a Taliban commander. Her brother-in-law held her down while her husband sliced her ears and nose off. Baker meets Aisha in a shelter in Kabul, where she was taken after receiving care from U.S. forces. The *Time* website informs us that upon leaving the refuge in Kabul, Aisha flew to the United States, where she is undergoing reconstructive surgery and receiving counseling. Aisha's narrative as articulated by Baker leaves many people with the impression that she has been rescued by the liberating forces in Afghanistan—a narrative that leads to a logical conclusion: NATO and the United States should stay in Afghanistan to continue to rescue women from the Taliban who want to brutalize them. Logically, Western forces are set up as saviors of the Afghan woman.

Elsewhere (Khan 2008) I note that, unable and/or unwilling to fully guarantee the civil rights of racialized and impoverished women at home, Western states deflect attention to Afghan women's issues as a way of maintaining popular support for a war whose main priority may not include the securing of women's rights. Abu Lughod (2002) points to the dangers of such processes, which she claims draw upon reified images of Muslim women that tend to mask complicated processes of history and politics. She notes that the desire to rescue the authentic yet oppressed

Afghan woman is a Western liberal desire that has its roots in colonial feminism and missionary rhetoric. To examine such processes I turn to a discussion of colonial feminism and its connection to Orientalism and the oppressed Muslim woman.

Orientalism, Colonial Feminism, and the Oppressed Muslim Woman

Yegenoglu (1998) notes that Orientalism constructs the Orient as a place of "sensuality, corrupt despotism, mystical religiosity, sexually unstable Arabs, irrationality, backwardness, and so on" (1998: 17). While Orientalist accounts render suspect the heterosexuality and thus masculinity of the Muslim man (Massad 2008), accounts of the Muslim woman by Lewis (2004) and Lal (2005) remind us, focus on the highly sexualized and exotic figure of the harem girl, who in years past was ever-present in Western imagination. The Muslim woman's image in European paintings, and accounts of her life in travelogues, provided a tantalizing sexual invitation to Europeans for hundreds of years. After the social and political realignments that accompanied the Iranian revolution of 1979, the exotic Muslim woman receded to the margins. She has been largely replaced by the veiled, oppressed one. Particularly since 9/11, it is the Afghan woman who exemplifies this role, and her image is used to justify military intervention by Western states.

Saving Muslim women from their oppressive cultures, along with the use of this trope in war and occupation, is not a recent phenomenon. Using the limited agency of Victorian womanhood as a model for Egyptian women to strive for, the British colonial authorities in nineteenth-century Egypt attempted to exchange Egyptian patriarchy for a European one, in the process endorsing what Ahmed (1992) calls a colonial feminism. Such a process, she claims, uses the language of women's rights to advance colonial interests. For example, Lord Cromer, the British consul general in Egypt, used the "plight" of Egyptian woman to help justify British rule of the country. Feminist language was appropriated, Ahmed notes, to serve as a "handmaid" to colonialism. Fanon (1965) has identified similar tendencies in colonial Algeria, where French colonial policy identified Algerian woman's liberation as a major component in their strategy for the pacification of its men and control of its society.

These examples from the past point to an overt language and accompanying arguments about the superiority of European civilization and culture, language that identifies the freedom European women enjoy as proof of their exalted status in "civilized" European states. Assumptions about a superior European culture and an inferior Islamic one continue in a more coded language today and inform, as Abu Lughod (2002) has noted, ongoing conversations about equality, freedom, and rights. Abu Lughod argues that such conversations, which seek to save the Muslim woman, entail a form of violence on the other as historical subject. Recent laws enforcing the unveiling of Muslim women in France (Chrisafis 2011) and restrictions on veiled women in the Canadian province of Quebec (Talaga 2010) provide an example of Abu Lughod's position.[1]

Colonial feminism also rears its head in the United States. The Feminist Majority Foundation's (FMF) campaign launched in 1997, and entitled *Stop Gender Apartheid in Afghanistan*, provides an example. At a time when the US administration saw the Taliban as a force for stability in the region, the FMF was one of the first major organizations to challenge the latter's gender policies. Long before Afghan women became the women that Americans loved to rescue, their plight under the Taliban regime was vividly described through FMF documents and presentations to U.S. officials. Russo (2006) acknowledges the contributions of FMF in making visible in the United States the conditions of Afghan lives. She notes, however, that their discourse identifies an "imperial feminism" tied to U.S. policies of military expansion. Jasbir Puar appears to support Russo's position when she names those who influence FMF as "hegemonic, U.S.-centric feminists enamored by the plight of Afghan women under the Taliban" (Puar 2007: 6). Yet, as Hirschkind and Mahmood (2002) note, FMF narratives minimize the US role in creating conditions that allowed for the emergence of the Taliban and present what appears to be a tacit American acceptance of their hold on power in Afghanistan. It is important to note, however, that despite weak critiques of Orientalism within FMF documents and its scant analysis of the Afghan woman as historical subject, the organization has provided tremendous support to women's groups in Afghanistan and continues to be a primary fund-raiser for them.

While the current imagery of Afghan women focuses on her oppression, the other face of Orientalism - the sexualized exotic woman - has receded to the background. It is to her I now turn.

The Sexualized Muslim Woman

Bibi Aisha is the authentic oppressed woman who needs to be saved. As such, she represents one side of the Orientalist spectacle. There is another side to the Orientalist spectacle, the exotic sexualized woman. Featured on the June 1985 cover of *National Geographic*, the image of the Afghan girl photographed by American Steve McCurry in 1984 provides an example. Famous for her green piercing eyes and a ragged red *dupatta* covering her head, thirteen-year-old Sharbat Gula's image continues to be among the most recognized photographs in the history of *National Geographic* and was widely used on brochures, calendars, and posters by Amnesty International. Her beautiful haunting face confirms her as the exotic face of the other. For many years her identify was unknown, but after a well-publicized search by McCurry she was "found," seventeen years after the picture was made famous on the cover of *National Geographic*. This led to Gula's image appearing on another *National Geographic* cover in April 2002. The more recent cover shows her as a burkha-covered woman holding the photograph of the girl with the striking eyes, suggesting that the promise of beauty and splendor of the young girl has mutated into the burkha-clad oppressed woman victimized by her men, her culture, and especially by Islam. The exotic woman is no longer a standalone figure as she was in 1985. Instead, the force of her beauty has receded when faced with the much-more-powerful image of the oppressed victim. Gula's transformation from exotic to oppressed woman in the context of her life and her "search" were documented for television in *Search for the Afghan Girl*, which aired in March 2003. In recognition of Gula's life, *National Geographic* set up the Afghan Girls Fund, a charitable organization with the aim to educate Afghan girls and young women. In 2008, the scope was broadened to include boys, and the name was changed to Afghan Children's Fund (Newman 2002). Gula's haunting image and life history disrupted by war situate her as the exotic other whose story has not only reconfirmed the rescue narrative but also provided a marketing windfall for the magazine. In both cases, the image is used to construct a narrative that obscures a wider history. It functions as testimony about broader uses of individual images to construct narratives that serve the needs of the teller. As such they speak to representational practices that display the media and military power of the United States. Women do not speak in such photographs; instead the readers project their own ideas onto these images. In recent years the decontextualized twin images of the Muslim woman, particularly those of the oppressed Afghan woman, are used to legitimize her rescue. I now turn to a brief description of the context that structures her life.

Geo-Politics and the Afghan Woman

The mountainous terrain in Afghanistan has contributed to the lack of a strong central state able to impose a social and political order over the whole country, particularly in the countryside, where a majority of Afghans live (Daulatzai 2008; Saikal 2006). As such, the center rule from Kabul has not always been able to implement its laws and policies in the rural areas. Islam, too, is contested along class, regional, and ethnic lines. Within a context of these competing narratives, various regimes have attempted to implement social reforms, with an aim to educating Afghan women and integrating them into the waged labor economy. Challenges to such reforms have frequently emanated from rural areas where, as Ahmed Gosh (2003) points out, control over women's lives and their gender roles is largely determined by tribal patriarchies and their interpretation of Islamic codes. In such a context, the rights of women have been unevenly implemented. By the 1920s, changes in administration meant that reforms passed earlier were canceled due to pressures from rural areas (Massels 1974). A period of reforms began anew in the early 1940s, when a secondary school for women was established in Kabul in 1941. By 1959, veiling was no longer mandatory, and the 1964 constitution gave women the right to vote and allowed them to enter politics (Afghanistan Online 2011).

Reforms that gave women greater freedoms accelerated in April 1978 when a coup brought an underground Marxist group, the People's Democratic Party of Afghanistan (PDPA), into power. The new regime committed itself to changing the political and social structure of Afghan society, and in particular to changing gender relations. Although the PDPA programs promoted gender justice, Ahmed Gosh (2003) argues that the accelerated pace of change demanded by urban-based government decrees facilitated neither organic nor what many in rural areas considered culturally appropriate change.

In the summer of 1978, prior to the 1979 Soviet military incursion in Afghanistan, many Afghans began to flee as refugees to Pakistan. Land reforms and the compulsory implementation of literacy programs were some of the reasons that refugees gave for leaving their country (Moghadam 1993). Others pointed to the heavy-handedness of the PDPA regime and the fast pace of change imposed against the will of the people, particularly those in the countryside (Anwar 1988). Resistance to the regime was organized in the refugee camps in Pakistan and soon spread to parts of Afghanistan. With the Soviet invasion in 1979, Islamic forces in the region linked the issue of the "defense" of Islam with the defense of the Afghan nation against the communists (both local and international). Such processes allowed Islam to crystallize as the major ideology of resistance.

The tenure of the PDPA regime (1978–1992) coincided with international attention to the situation in Afghanistan largely due to the superpower rivalry between the United States and the Soviet Union. The Soviets intervened militarily in Afghanistan in 1979, and their advisors had considerable power in the affairs of the PDPA government (Anwar 1988). Military support for the Mujahadeen resistance was provided by Saudi Arabia and the United States, while Pakistan helped with the logistics. An influx of foreign arms had significant repercussions in Afghanistan as well. After the fall of the PDPA regime in 1992, the various Mujahadeen factions turned on each other for supremacy and control in a civil war (1992–1996) that continued to destabilize the region. The Taliban became engaged in the latter part of this conflict and emerged as victors. Although women's lives were influenced in some way by all the various political regimes, it is their situation under the Taliban regime (1996–2001) that stands out in the Western imagination and provides much of the fuel for the rescue missions.

The Taliban were initially students who received military training using CIA manuals in *madrasas* (schools) set up in Pakistani camps that housed Afghan refugees, large numbers of whom were Pukhtoon. Later, the schools came to include other impoverished Pukhtoon children from the Pakistani side of the border as well. The madrasas received much of their funding from Saudi Arabia and became, many believe, bastions of political indoctrination and religious extremism (Rashid 2002). At the same time, the schools were encouraged by the CIA to provide recruits for the emerging jihad against the Soviets. Their puritanical zeal of the Taliban helped propel them to victory over Mujahadeen groups in 1996, but as they consolidated power, only Pakistan and the United Arab Emirates gave the regime formal recognition. The United States had a more ambivalent attitude. Although US officials criticized the regime's human rights record, many in Washington also viewed the Taliban as a stabilizing force and seemed to give it silent backing (Knightley 2001, Maykuth 2001).

The various military interests at play encouraged a state of conflict in Afghanistan for decades, during which there was a virtual collapse of stable, functioning civil, legal, and political institutions. During this period, Jacinto (2006) notes that the ancient patriarchal Pukhtoonwali code helped regulate lives, particularly in southern Afghanistan. This rural code, which was largely alien to urban Afghans, was insular, influenced by tribal rivalries, and relied on revenge-based justice. The consolidation of Taliban power in much of Afghanistan brought Pukhtoonwali-influenced policies to the cities. In rural areas, women had lived in insular communities where they were largely away from the gaze of unrelated and unfamiliar men. But women in the larger cities, including Kabul, had enjoyed many freedoms, particularly during the PDPA regime.

Women's lives changed with the chaos of the civil war: veiling provides an example. Although veiling was a customary practice for rural women, women had not been mandated to veil in the cities since 1959. During the period when the Mujahadeen (freedom fighters) factions were fighting for power and control (late 1980s–1996), some urban women began to veil because they saw it as a means of securing their safety in very turbulent times. It was under the Taliban, however, that urban women faced the greatest challenges. Faced with a very strict and puritanical interpretation of Islam and of Sharia law heavily influenced by the Pukhtoonwali code, women were forced to veil and had to submit to other restrictions regarding their mobility.

With the presence of NATO in Afghanistan and its support for the Karzai government, one might assume that there would be an improvement in women's lives in areas outside of Taliban control. To determine whether this is indeed the case, I now turn to the current situation of women in government-controlled Afghanistan and note that women and men have equal rights under a new constitution that came into effect in 2004. Moreover, in August 2010, the Elimination of Violence against Women law was passed by the Afghan President and Cabinet. This law criminalized violence against women, including domestic violence; however, parliamentary approval of the law has remained pending. While these laws provide legal equality to women and criminalize violence against them, the Shi'a Personal Status Law, which contained several discriminatory provisions against Shi'a women, was passed in 2009. Further, Karzai's recent backing of a "code of conduct," written by leading clerics of an Ulema (religious scholars) council, sanctions women's status as secondary to that of men. The code of conduct demands that women wear hijab and recommends that they avoid mixing with men in the public space and travel only with a male chaperone (Ward 2012). Karzai's endorsement suggests that women's hard-won rights are fragile at best in Afghanistan.

Uneven access to rights for women accompanies other kinds of hardships. Despite the billions in aid poured into the country, the UN has ranked Afghanistan 155th out of 169 countries in its index of human development. The country had the second-highest maternal mortality rate in the world, with only 22% of Afghans having access to clean drinking water (Kanani 2011).

Regardless of the harsh conditions under which Afghan women live, 6.3 million children have been provided access to education (USDS 2010). An Oxfam report (2011) claims, however, that the quality of education varies from district to district and from school to school and that 47% of schools have no building yet, a problem that is particularly severe in the rural areas. Many of these schools are located a considerable distance from where students live.

Let us examine how these factors might affect Bibi Aisha. Although her chances at receiving an education would have significantly improved since the invasion, her access to education would likely be limited unless she lived in a well serviced area. Furthermore, her chances of obtaining a secondary education were also slim, as many young girls do not progress beyond primary school. But there is more. Recall that women and men are equal under the current Afghan constitution, but also that this equality is not always operationalized through policies and practices. Should Aisha have escaped the clutches of her in-laws and complained to the police in the areas under the control of the Karzai regime, she might not have found justice. Motlagh (2011) reminds us that women are frequently jailed for the "crime" of running away from husbands. This is just one way that the legal system appears unable to serve the needs of Afghanistan's most vulnerable citizens. In its national report to the UN Human Rights Council in February 2010, the Afghan government acknowledged that the justice system was inadequate, corrupt, and fell below international standards of fairness (AI 2010).

Aisha would have had little recourse had she turned to her elected politicians for help. Although women politicians hold a quarter of the seats in their country's parliament, many are mere mouthpieces for warlords. Comments made by Suraya Pakzad, an Afghan women's rights activist, to a meeting in the U.S. Congress to mark International Women's Day 2010 suggest that many female politicians were elected with the support of warlords and are now obliged to answer to them. Moreover, once released from jail, Aisha would either be sent back to her family or end up on her own with few employment prospects. Many women have lost hope about their lack of options and have resorted to burning themselves to death (Mong 2009; Rubin 2010), while some have become sex workers (Tang 2010) because of a lack of other employment opportunities.

If Aisha had been fortunate enough to find refuge in a woman's shelter she might have faced an uncertain future. The Afghan government recently announced that it is considering regulation that would allow the government to control the management of women's shelters that at present are operated by NGOs and the United Nations. Such a move, a Human Rights Watch report (HRW 2011) suggests, would have negative repercussions for women seeking refuge, including a movement toward institutions with greater restrictions on women's freedom of movement, compulsory forensic examinations, and the expulsion of many still in need of refuge (because they do not fit in with a narrow eligibility criteria). Moreover, there would be a closure of some facilities. According to HRW, conservative forces within the government are fuelling this initiative.

Many Western sources believe that veiling is a major issue for Afghan women. A report released by the United Nations Assistance Mission in Afghanistan (UNAMA 2010) suggests otherwise. There is widespread violence against women, including through such practices as giving away girls in marriage as a means to resolve disputes (where the young bride is treated as a servant because of the circumstances of her marriage), honor killings, and exchange marriage. Amnesty International (AI 2010) endorses the conclusions of the UNAMA report, and further notes that the culture of violence in Afghanistan also targets groups that help women and defend their rights. Such groups suffer harassment, discrimination, and intimidation from government figures as well as from the Taliban and other armed groups. Aisha and others in her situation have more to fear then the brutality of the Taliban. They live in a country where the government is corrupt, weak, and unable to guarantee the rights of its most vulnerable citizens. Yet, it is a government that many countries support with tax dollars and a military presence. These practices are common despite the presence of NATO and US forces in Afghanistan, and these forces have either been unwilling or unable to stop such abuse. In essence, the conditions of Afghan women's lives are reflective of a culture of corruption and government incompetence even though billions of dollars are pouring into the country in the form of military assistance and for nation-building projects. Despite the marginal concern that policy-makers in Washington and Kabul appear to have for Afghan women's rights, I argue that narratives that seek to save them continue to be used in the West.

Uses of Afghan Women's Suffering

The vision of the Afghan woman as a victim needing to be rescued is one that is endorsed by policy-makers in Washington and European capitals, it seems. Yet, this concern also has an imperialist and political agenda that come to light in a WikiLeaks CIA document, (2010) that expresses alarm about the fragility of support in Western Europe for the International Security Assistance Force (ISAF) mission and suggests that further casualties might cause a backlash in Europe and America against the mission in Afghanistan. The authors recommend that:

> Afghan women could serve as ideal messengers in humanizing the ISAF role in combating the Taliban because of women's ability to speak personally and credibly about their experiences under the Taliban, their aspirations for the future, and their fears of a Taliban victory. Outreach initiatives that create media opportunities for Afghan women to share their stories with French, German, and other European women could help to overcome pervasive scepticism among women in Western Europe toward the ISAF mission.

In the *Time Magazine* issue in which Aisha's account appeared, an editorial comment by managing editor Stengel (2010) suggests that Baker's article might have been tailor-made to respond to CIA concerns:

> Aisha posed for the picture and says she wants the world to see the effect a Taliban resurgence would have on the women of Afghanistan, many of whom have flourished in the past few years. Her picture is accompanied by a powerful story by our own Aryn Baker on how Afghan women have embraced the freedoms that have come from the defeat of the Taliban—and how they fear a Taliban revival.

Despite the seemingly obvious link that the image and accompanying text have to military policy, Stengel insists that *Time* is merely contributing to the ongoing debate surrounding American involvement in Afghanistan, and is not taking sides. He notes:

> We do not run this story or show this image either in support of the U.S. war effort or in opposition to it. We do it to illuminate what is actually happening on the ground. As lawmakers and citizens begin

to sort through the information about the war and make up their minds, our job is to provide context and perspective on one of the most difficult foreign policy issues of our time.

In spite of Stengel's assertion that *Time's* story provides "emotional truth and insight into the way life is lived in that difficult land and the consequences of the important decisions that lie ahead," I argue that a case is being made by Baker and endorsed by *Time* for continued NATO and U.S. presence in Afghanistan. The significant gaps in *Time's* decontextualized account of Aisha's life, and by implication of the lives of other Afghan women, facilitate such processes.

Two other factors need to be considered in this analysis. The mutilated image of Bibi Aisha and her story appeared at a time when the American public was beginning to question the cost and goals of the Afghan war, and it advanced the perspective of those who wanted to continue US involvement in the conflict. An article that accompanied the story challenged the US dialog with the Taliban, a dialog that sought to involve the Taliban in a future government in Afghanistan, a step toward Western military disentanglement in the country. Writing for the *New York Observer*, however, journalist John Gorenfeld (2010) notes that there is something missing from the *Time* story. It does not disclose the ways in which journalist Baker's husband, Tamim Samee, benefited from the awarding of contracts and development in Afghanistan. Although *Time* stated that "Aryn Baker's husband has no connection to the U.S. military, has never solicited business from them and has no financial stake in the U.S. presence in Afghanistan whatsoever" (Gorenfeld 2010), records suggest that Samee is an Afghan-American information technology (IT) entrepreneur who has run two companies, Digistan and Ora Tech. In addition, Gorenfeld records, Samee, who is a board member of an Afghan government minister's $100 million project advocating foreign investment in Afghanistan, noted that ISAF presence in Afghanistan provides significant business opportunities.

Another aspect of this discussion is the Taliban response to the *Time* piece. In a communique posted on Jihadology.net (2010), the Taliban deny any connection to Aisha's mutilation. The statement also claims that Aisha's case was not adjudicated by one of their roaming judges (which many Afghans turn to because, unlike the government judicial system, the Taliban judges deliver timely justice and don't ask for bribes). The statement claims that the story of Taliban involvement in Bibi Aisha's mutilation was a fabrication and an attempt to turn the conversation away from an impending US defeat in Afghanistan. Further, the Taliban condemn Aisha's mutilation, which they call un-Islamic and against the Sharia law. The Taliban continue with some propaganda of their own: Violence against women is against Islam, they maintain, but such violence, they note, is common in the United States, including in the US army. They reference various US surveys from 1996 to 2008 to support their claims. In effect, the Taliban statement uses selective data to support their assertion that women are safer under Taliban rule and face violence in the United States. While the Taliban may not have ordered Bibi Aisha's mutilation, they are certainly responsible for implementation of some of the harshest laws in the name of Islam, laws that many scholars of Islamic law claim are against their religion. Moreover, the Taliban communique denies the absence of civil and human rights that women and men faced under their rule as well as the lack of protection for women from domestic violence, lack of mobility options for women, and lack of education and employment. While narrow in its breadth of analysis, the communique certainly reveals a sophisticated understanding of putting together a referenced report (albeit the data used is skewed and cannot withstand rigorous analysis) and belies the impression that one gets of an unsophisticated group who lives largely in a medieval society. Their communique reveals that the Taliban are as able as the international community to engage in strategic narrative construction. I do not mean to imply that the IT the Taliban have at their disposal is as sophisticated and cutting edge as that employed by ISAF. I merely want to suggest that there appears to be a competition between the two for ownership of the Afghan women's narrative, a competition that suggests that the narrative is used for their own interests, not those of the women.

Bibi Aisha's mutilated face functions as a silent but potent reminder about the need to rescue her; moreover, the message it sends is thus: NATO/ISAF have saved Afghan women and if we leave Afghanistan, atrocities against women will resume. I find this message disturbing. It focuses on the local, that is, Aisha's immediate family and a supposed Taliban commander's sanction for her mutilation. Yet, Stengel in his editorial piece notes:

> In the end, I felt that the image is a window into the reality of what is happening—and what can happen—in a war that affects and involves all of us. I would rather confront readers with the Taliban's treatment of women than ignore it. I would rather people know that reality as they make up their minds about what the U.S. and its allies should do in Afghanistan.

This message, however, does not examine how women are treated in the larger national context, that is, in the state of Afghanistan under the Karzai regime. Further, Aisha's narrative does not tell us about how Afghan men are also brutalized through the inability of state policies and programs to protect them from corruption or police brutality, to provide them access to a living wage, or to safeguard them from the indiscriminate killing, detention, and torture by state and non-state actors.

By leaving out many contributing factors to Aisha's reality, the spectacle of her image as the "oppressed woman" generates a desire to rescue Afghan women and becomes another instance of colonial feminism. Some liberal feminists participate in this, because they emphasize equality and individual rights for women while minimizing the role that social systems play in their lives (Weston 2011). Inderpal Grewal notes that, in addition to minimizing the role of systems of power, such impulses are connected to a moral superiority that "has become part of emergent global feminism, constructing American women as saviors and rescuers of the 'oppressed women" (Grewal 2005: 150). Indeed, some feminists have used Aisha's narrative to further the liberal feminist project of benevolence toward and rescue of the third-world woman. ABC's World News anchor Diane Sawyer revisits Aisha's story in a program that aired October 11, 2010. It is the kindness of an American medical team, Sawyer reminds us, that helped Aisha through her ordeal and sent her to the US for reconstructive surgery. There, fitted with a temporary prosthetic nose, she is feted by former First Lady Laura Bush, who notes that "she looks so great," and honored by Maria Shriver, the wife of then-governor of California, Arnold Schwarzenegger. Those seeking a quick happy ending would have to wait, however, claimed Tzemach Lemmon (2010), deputy director of the Women and Foreign Policy Programs at the Council on Foreign Relations. Despite the significant numbers of Americans who wished to help (or rescue) her, Aisha's ordeal was not over. The many years of family abuse and trauma left her unable to undergo the painful and temporary disfiguring re-constructive surgeries required until she is emotionally and physically stronger (Ravitz 2012).

Comments that support Aisha's rescue present the face of liberal feminism, a philosophy with powerful adherents in the United States. While such comments encourage rescue missions they also tend to minimize, like the authors of the *Time* articles, the multilayered circumstances that allow individual women to be abused in Afghanistan and elsewhere in the Third World. They also do not identify or work to eradicate with the same amount of energy the many obstacles that impoverished and racialized women's face in the United States. Instead, as colonial feminists, they frequently spend their energies in saving women in third-world countries, Afghanistan being a hot location for such ventures at present. In so doing, they also endorse military agendas of various dominant groups. In addition, little attention is paid to corporate interests that such spectacles support or to the opportunistic journalists and their families who may be involved in constructing the spectacle.

In view of recent commitments by the Obama administration to withdraw all U.S. military personnel from Afghanistan by 2014, let us take stock of comments from within Afghanistan, including from women's groups and other progressive organizations. To what extent has nation building been successful? A poll released in 2011 by the Asia Foundation noted that 45% of the people surveyed said that Afghanistan is moving in the wrong direction. They cite an incompetent government, a culture of corruption, and high unemployment. More than half of the respondents feared for their safety. Over 80% want the government to negotiate with the Taliban and offer them a chance to reintegrate into society.

Speaking at a seminar sponsored by The Swedish Institute of International Affairs in December of 2011, Masood Aziz, a former Afghan diplomat in Washington, supported these views and noted that the corruption within and the weakness of the Karzai regime will likely lead to its collapse once ISAF troops withdraw in 2014 (Pavellas 2011). Statements on the website of the Revolutionary Association of Women of Afghanistan suggest that activists who are anti-invasion and are disappointed by the effects of the invasion are also fearful of likely developments in Afghan governance following the departure of ISAF. They note that you cannot put in place programs and policies geared toward ending inequality for women and fostering an environment where women can live their lives in dignity and peace as long as the political situation in the country remains dire. Statements made by the group's spokespersons adamantly challenge both the US occupation and the warlords, even as they speak out against life under the Taliban. Malalai Joya, an activist and a former member of the Afghan Parliament, also demands that warlords be disarmed (Joya 2009). Despite her strong rejection of all international forces (which she considers occupiers) in Afghanistan, Joya's comments contain an expectation that the disarming of warlords will be done by foreigners. While she proclaims that Afghans can and should govern themselves, she too is fearful that a civil war will result when ISAF withdraws.

Where, then, will the urgently needed leadership for the future come from? And what is the way forward? Unfortunately, there is no clear direction. Perhaps a combination of the following suggestions will put us on the right path. People outside Afghanistan might consider sending money to Afghan women's NGOs with a history of making a contribution in the education and health sectors and other service deliveries, including training for income generation and legal aid support. Such contributions will certainly help women and their families but probably will not suffice to stop the abuses and effects of the incompetence of the Karzai regime.

Frequently, Orientalist arguments help legitimize the unethical foreign policies of Afghanistan's neighbors and friends both near and far. Perhaps voters in those countries might pay closer attention to their governments' foreign interventions and the politics that they promote. Moreover, political leaders frequently cut funding for vulnerable groups, including refugees, to help reduce their budgets. These groups cannot vote against such policies, but those of us who are able to vote can register our dissatisfaction.

It took several decades for disastrous foreign interference and unhelpful local policies to produce the quagmire in Afghanistan and it will take decades of rational and steady nation building to stabilize the country. Particularly those states that helped create the Afghanistan of today have a responsibility to build a strong and viable nation of the future. Citizens of the states who have interfered in Afghanistan have to hold, I believe, their politicians to account for their past and present actions as well as any that might be planned in the future, so that women and men in Afghanistan may live in peace and dignity, which is the human right of all.

Conclusion

How then might we move from a colonial feminist perspective that focuses on "helping" and "saving" Afghan women to feminist politics that imagines solidarity with Afghan women? Used to silence critics of Western military intervention in Afghanistan, the ever-present image of the oppressed Afghan woman focuses on spectacular instances of cruelty, leaving us with a desire to rescue women from their cultures. At the same time, the spectacles intensify stereotypes about the third world and about Islam in particular.

I want to suggest that the desire to save the oppressed Afghan woman disregards the fact that she and her sisters, mothers, and grandmothers have spent decades resisting the violence and dislocation resulting from decades of war and conflict. In a sense, they are veteran resistance fighters who have struggled for safety, education, health care, and food security for themselves and their families. The activities of the group Afghan Women Leaders Connect and former MP Malalai Joya remind us that women in Afghanistan have run underground schools and health clinics for decades. Revolutionary Association of Women of Afghanistan (RAWA) is another group that has been actively involved in the struggle for human rights and for social justice. Its members under the leadership of twenty-year-old Meena struggled against the Soviet supported Communist government in Afghanistan and advocated for democracy since 1977. Meena's activism resulted in her assassination in 1987. With the overthrow of the Communist government, RAWA struggled against the excesses of the various Mujahadeen groups and the Taliban for decades. They currently challenge the corruption of the Karzai regime and the brutality of the warlords (RAWA 2011). Such women, who likely need assistance that strengthens their projects, present an alternative to the twin stereotypes of the oppressed and exotic woman. To view them as oppressed in need of rescue, as many do through mainstream imagery and discourse, is a Western middle-class construction that ultimately colludes with hegemonic interests and incorporates itself into the larger imperial undertaking. A viable Afghan nation, I believe, is only one project of the ISAF war machine, and perhaps a minor one at that. Unable and/or unwilling to fully guarantee the civil rights of racialized and impoverished women at home, Western states deflect attention to Afghan women's issues as a way of maintaining popular support for a war whose aim may not include, certainly not as its main priority, the securing of Afghan women's rights. As the state sends young women and men to fight in Afghanistan, ostensibly to rescue the oppressed woman, it secures its human rights and feminist credentials.

The liberal feminist, along with other likeminded groups, risks being recruited into this undertaking. Should she take up Bibi Aisha's cause without interrogating Afghan women's history, she is endorsing the imperialist project of political and economic domination of third world societies by the first. Supporting this position are Gayatri Spivak's comments that "[t]he most frightening thing about imperialism, its long-term toxic effect, what secures it, what cements it, is the benevolent self-representation of the imperialist as saviour" (Spivak 1999: 54). Setting herself as the savior of Afghan women, the liberal feminist deflects her own hopeless encounter with the first-world state in which she lives. She struggles largely in vain to restore the reduction in funding for projects at home that support women's health, housing, and a violence-free environment and is faced, particularly in the United States, with the weakening of laws that give women the right to make reproductive choices. By promoting Aisha's cause in faraway Afghanistan, she recovers her own agency. But it is a colonialist feminist agency. And this is not the sisterhood that feminists have struggled for.

I want to identify another type of woman who is largely invisible in these Western media accounts. She and her sisters are the racialized immigrants, permit holders, and illegal aliens in first-world societies. Their invisible presence forms the silent backdrop of the images of the oppressed and exotic Muslim women that confront us through television, films, and print media and filter through our everyday conversations. Instead of using a charity framework to rescue third-world women from their cultures, I suggest we make visible the historicity of women's lives both at home and abroad. Such a process challenges oppressive local and international systems and makes visible the operations of power within nations and between women so that feminists can think about global issues and their effects on women's lives in ways that challenge dominant forms of hegemony over their communities and societies.

Acknowledgments

Funding from the Social Science and Humanities Council of Canada has enabled the research for this article.

Note

1 I realize that veiled women have faced restrictions in Iran in the past and continue to do so in Turkey. These restrictions are connected to the state's complicated relationship with modernity and a discussion of these processes is beyond the scope of this paper.

This article was previously published in Women's Studies International Forum 44 (2014), 101–109 and has been reproduced her with copyright permission.

References

Abu Lughod, Lila. "Do Muslim women Really Need Saving: Anthropological Reflections on Cultural Relativism and Its Others." *American Anthropologist* 104.3 (2002): 783–90.

Afghanistan Online. Last Modified, April 24, 2011. Accessed May 6, 2011. www.afghan-web.com/woman/afghanwomenhistory.html.

Ahmed, Leila. *Women Gender and Islam: Historical Roots of a Modern Debate*. New Haven, CT: Yale UP, 1992.

Ahmed Gosh, Huma. "History of Women in Afghanistan: Lessons Learned for the Future, or Yesterdays and Tomorrows." *International Journal of Women's Studies* 14.3 (2003): 1–14.

Amnesty International. "Human Rights in the Islamic Republic of Afghanistan." Last modified 2011. Accessed May 10, 2010. www.amnesty.org/en/region/afghanistan/report-2010.

Anwar, Raja. *The Tragedy of Afghanistan: A First Hand Account*, trans. Khalid Hasan. London: Verso Press, 1998.

Armstrong, Sally. *Bitter Roots, Tender Shoots*. Toronto: Penguin Books, 2008.

Baker, Aryn. "Afghan Women and the Return of the Taliban." *Time Magazine*, August 9, 2009, 20–28.

Chrisafis, Angelique. "Full Face Veils Outlawed as France Spells Out Controversial Niqab Ban *Guardian.co.uk*." March 3, 2011. Accessed June 17, 2011. www.guardian.co.uk/world/2011/mar/03/niqab-ban-france-muslim-veil.

Daulatzai, Anila. "The Discursive Occupation of Afghanistan." *British Journal of Middle Eastern Studies* 35.3 (2008): 429–35.

Ellis, Deborah. *Parvana's Journey*. Oxford: Oxford UP, 2002.

Fanon, Frantz. *A Dying Colonialism*. New York: Grove Press, 1965.

Gorenfeld, John. "*With its Horrifying Cover Story. Time* Gave the War a Boost. Did its Reporter Profit?" *The New York Observer*, August 12, 2010. Accessed May 11, 2011. www.observer.com/print/130693.

Grewal, Inderpal. *Transnational America: Feminisms, Diasporas, Neoliberalisms*. Durham, NC: Duke UP, 2005.

Hirschkind, Charles, and Mahmood, Saba. "Feminism, the Taliban, and Politics of Counter-Insurgency." *Anthropological Quarterly* 75.2 (2002): 339–54.

Human Rights Watch. "Afghanistan: Government Takeover of Shelters Threatens Women's Safety." February 3, 2011. Accessed May 10, 2011. www.hrw.org/news/2011/02/13/afghanistan-government-takeover-shelters-threatens-womens-safety.

Jacinto, Leela. "Abandoning the Wardrobe and Reclaiming Religion in the Discourse on Afghan Women's Islamic Rights." *Signs: Journal of Women in Culture and Society* 32.1 (2006): 9–13.

Jihadology.net. "New Statement from the Islamic Emirate of Afghanistan: Response Regarding a Picture Published by Time Magazine." August 7, 2010.

Accessed May 12, 2011. http://jihadology.net/2010/08/07/new-statement-from-the-islamic-emirate-of-afghanistan-response-regarding-a-picture-published-by-time-magazine.

Joya, Malalai. *Woman among Warlords: The Extraordinary Story of a Woman Who Dared to Raise Her Voice.* New York: Scribner, 2009.

Kanani, Rahim. *Maternal Mortality in Afghanistan: A Way Forward.* Huffworld March 8, 2011. Accessed May 16, 2011. www.huffingtonpost.com/rahim-kanani/maternal-mortality-in-afg_b_490107.html.

Khan, Shahnaz. "Afghan Women: The Limits of Colonial Rescue." *Feminism and War.* Eds. Rovin Riley, Chandra Mohanty, and Minnie Bruce Pratt. 161–178. New York: Zed Press, 2008.

Knightley, Philip. "U.S. Gave Silent Backing to Taliban Rise to Power." *The Guardian,* October 2, 2001.

Lal, Ruby. *Domesticity and Power in the Early Mughal World.* Cambridge: University Press, 2005.

Lewis, Reina. *Rethinking Orientalism: Women Travel and the Ottoman Harem.* London: I.B. Tauris, 2004.

Mackie, Vera. "The 'Afghan Girls': Media Representations and Frames of War." *Continuum: Journal of Media and Cultural Studies* 26.1 (2012): 115–131.

Massad, Joseph. *Desiring Arabs.* Chicago, IL: University of Chicago Press, 2008.

Massels, Gregory. *The Surrogate Proletariat: Muslim Women and Revolutionary Strategies in Soviet Central Asia: 1919–1929.* Princeton, NJ: Princeton UP, 1974.

Maykuth, Andrew. "Afghan Rebels Ambivalent About U.S. Effort." *Philadelphia Inquirer,* October 21, 2001.

Moghadam, Valentine. *Modernizing Women: Gender and Social Change in the Middle East.* Boulder, CO: Lynne Reinner Press, 1993.

Mohanty, Chandra. "Under Western Eyes: Feminist Scholarship and Colonial Discourses." *Third World Women and the Politics of Feminism.* Eds. Chandra Mohanty, Ann Russo, and Lourdes Torres. 51–80. Indianapolis: Indiana UP, 1991.

Mong, Adrienne. "Afghan Girls Burn Themselves to Escape Marriage." *Worldblog from NBC News,* October 29, 2009. Accessed May 10, 2010. http://worldblog.msnbc.msn.com/_news/2009/10/29/4376694-afghan-girls-burn-themselves-to-escape-marriage.

Motlagh, Jason. "Fleeing Violent Husbands Puts Afghan Women in Jail." *Time-World,* January 3, 2011. Accessed May 10, 2011. www.time.com/time/world/article/0,8599,2039564,00.html.

Newman, Cathy. "Afghan Girl: A Life Revealed." *National Geographic,* 2002. Accessed June 8, 2011. http://ngm.nationalgeographic.com/2002/04/afghan-girl/index-text.

Oxfam. "High Stakes: Girls' Education in Afghanistan." February 24. Accessed 10 May 2011. www.oxfam.org.uk/resources/policy/education/downloads/bp-high-stakes-girls-education-afghanistan-240211-en.pdf.

Pavellas, Ron. "The Pavellas Perspective." 2011. Accessed January 30, 2012. http://pavellas.com/.

Puar, Jasbir. *Terrorist Assemblages: Homonationalism in Queer Times.* Durham, NC: Duke UP, 2007.

Rashid, Ahmed. *Taliban, Islam, Oil and the New Great Game.* New Haven, CT: Yale UP, 2002.

Ravitz, Jessica. "Saving Aisha." 2012. Accessed September 23, 2013. www.cnn. com/interactive/2012/05/world/saving.aesha/index.html.

Revolutionary Association of Women in Afghanistan, 2011. Accessed January 30, 2012. www. rawa.org/index.php.

Rubin, Alissa. "For Afghan Wives, a Desperate Fiery Way Out." *New York Times*, November 7, 2010.

Russo, Ann. "The Feminist Majority Foundation's Campaign to Stop Gender Apartheid." *International Feminist Journal of Politics* 8.4 (2006): 557–80.

Said, Edward. *Orientalism.* New York: Vintage Books, 1978.

Saikal, Amin. *Modern Afghanistan: A History of Struggle and Survival.* New York: I.B. Tauris, 2006.

Spivak, Gayatri. *A Critique of Postcolonial Reason: Toward a History of the Vanishing Present.* Cambridge and London: Harvard UP, 1999, 54.

Stengel, Richard. "To Our Readers: What's Hard to Look at Time." August 9, 2010, 4.

Talaga, Tanya. "Quebec Niqab Bill Would Make Muslim Women Unveil." *The Star. com*, March 25, 2010. Accessed June 17, 2010. www.thestar.com/news/canada/article/785036-quebec-niqab-bill-would-make-muslim-women-unveil

Tang, Alissa. "Sex Trade Thrives in Afghanistan." *USA Today*, June 15, 2010. Accessed May 10, 2010. www.usatoday.com/news/world/2008-06-15-460899821_x.htm.

Thobani, Sunera. "War and the Politics of Truth-Making in Canada. *Qualitative Studies in Education* 16.3 (2003): 399–444.

Tzemach Lemmon, Gayle. "Bibi Aisha's Pain Isn't Over." *The Daily Beast*, November 21, 2010. Accessed August 10, 2011. www.thedailybeast.com/articles/2010/11/21/bibi-aishas-pain-isnt-over-tragic-afghan-story-one-year-on.html.

United Nations Assistance Mission in Afghanistan (UNAMA). *Harmful Traditional Practices and Implementation of the Law on Elimination of Violence against Women in Afghanistan.* Geneva: Office of the United Nations High Commissioner for Human Rights, December 9, 2010.

United State Department of State USDS. "Human Rights Report: Afghanistan." April 8, 2011. Accessed May 17, 2011. www.state.gov/g/drl/rls/hrrpt/2010/sca/154477.htm.

Ward, Olivia. "Afghan President Endorses Cleric's Code That Downgrades Women's Rights." *The Toronto Star*, March 7, 2012. Accessed May 10, 2012. www.thestar.com/news/world/article/1141804-afghan-president-endorses-clerics-code-that-allows-wife-beating-segregation-of-sexes.

Weston, Sarah. "Liberal Feminism: The Individual is the Key." *Workers Liberty.* November 24, 2011. Accessed September 19, 2013. www.workersliberty.org/story/2011/11/24/liberal-feminism-individual-key.

WikiLeaks. "CIA Report into Shoring up Afghan War Support in Western Europe. March 26, 2010. Accessed May 7, 2011. http://mirror.wikileaks.info/leak/cia-afghanistan.pdf.

Yegenoglu, Meyda. *Colonialist Fantasies: Towards a Feminist Reading of Orientalism.* Cambridge: University Press, 1998.

Part III
Film

7 Feminist Masculinism

Imagined Response to Violence against Women in Pradeep Sarkar's Hindi Film, *Mardaani* (2014)

Shreerekha Pillai Subramanian

From early anecdotal productions of myth, folklore, and history in silent films—embedded and entangled in the discourse of an incipient nationalism—Indian cinema, perhaps unconsciously, invested energy in producing feminine power for a putative "We the People" protesting against iniquities of statist patriarchal power. Such a premise informs comments in this chapter on a contemporary Indian film, a blockbuster produced under the sign of Bollywood[1] titled *Mardaani* (2014), starring Rani Mukerji in the role of Shivani Shivaji Roy, Senior Inspector, Crime Branch, Mumbai. From this vantage, she unravels and brings to justice a sex trafficking cartel[2] and liberates in the process a number of young girls held captive from their abductors.[3] The theme is a popular current in global cinema: a hyper fit vigilantress bringing down a shady syndicate of Late Capital Slavery in a spectacular valorization of human rights. I focus here on the Indian strain of such a global 'mardaani' or feminist masculinity, which purports to demolish the Man with payback in his own coin: killing, in the climactic sexual act, the monster with bare hands. This complex, as disposed in Sarkar's film, is in my reading, an intertextual thematic in Indian feminist dissent.

Mardaani harks to the Rani of Jhansi, a major historical muse for Subhadra Kumari Chauhan, poet-laureate of anti-colonial Hindi literature. Chauhan enshrined the Rani in the famous refrain: "Khub ladi mardaani, voh to Jhansivaaali Rani thi!" (She fought like a man, that Queen of Jhansi!) *Mardaani* saw light of day about a year and a half after the tragic and violent death in 2012 of a twenty-three year-old physiotherapy student in Delhi referred in public sphere as the Nirbhaya case.[4] That appalling event of rape and murder precipitated national and global-diasporic civil-society mobilizations protesting the abominable levels of public and private violence against women in India. *Mardaani* appeals, no doubt, to call for an urgent and long-overdue revision needed in discursive practices relating Indian women to performance of power.

The 2012 case involved harrowing levels of violence that gripped national and international attention. The young woman was gang raped in a moving bus, disemboweled using a metal rod, then thrown off the bus into the dark streets along with her male companion, naked and severely wounded.

Despite concerted medical efforts to save her and her own fierce battle to survive, she died nearly two weeks later in a hospital in Singapore. The great number of local and global protests that arose in the wake of this incident provoked unexpected alliances formed amidst demands waged by the far right and the far left. Sareeta Amrute's project on reading the vectors of liberalization that go into trafficking within the moving vehicle informs us of new aporetic spaces where different classes and genders—upwardly mobile women and lower caste/class males meet within the confines of private cars that transport workers to and from call centers. Amrute notes, "The "moving rape" on the Delhi bus and the call center driver rapes can be understood through this twinning of the upwardly mobile lower-class woman and the dangerous lower-class man."[5] In contrast, the film reflects men of privilege, education, and of the upper class ready to capitalize on their power by brutalizing and trafficking all available bodies—from orphans and vendors on the street to privileged girls attending elite private schools: ready to "do down just about anyone,"[6] as Terry Eagleton has remarked on capitalism's insatiable appetite for any and all bodies.

Ratna Kapur's "Brutalized Bodies and Sexy Dressing on the Indian Street" speaks of the Slutwalks (2011) and the massive mixed order of people and positions that took over the streets especially in Delhi after the rape and death of Jyoti Singh. Slutwalks,[7] a response to repeat observations that it is the sexily dressed woman that invites such violence upon herself, remained dismissed by mainstream feminists and conservative groups that nevertheless all showed great support in the aftermath of the incident. I am informed in my reflections also by Shruti Iyer's "Taking a Break from the State: Indian Feminists in the Legal Reform Process"[8] wherein Iyer alerts us to the detriment of a governmental approach to remedying violence against women. Iyer raises questions about attempting a structured mitigation of violence upon the vulnerable body through violence doled out by the state often rendering greater vulnerability upon the most disenfranchised bodies. Iyer's provocative conclusions find more general articulation in Jose Medina's philosophical approach to epistemologies of resistance. Both scholars articulate from different perspectives the limits of widely held liberal fallacies regarding individual heroism. In closely reading the historical figures of transcendence such as Rose Parks and Sor Juana Ines de la Cruz, Jose Medina cautions against a valorization of a single action or a single hero, key in the annals of state glorification and historical narratives. According to Medina, resistance often arises out of "chained action, which is both individual and socially extended"[9] and the narratives pivoted around the singular titular hero need further interrogation.

Informed and abetted by the urgency palpable in these scholars' thoughts, this chapter examines the promise of liberation and limitations of liberalization that underline the film's premise. The feminist performative herein expresses a central paradox: state-approved, citizen-sanctioned vigilante violence ultimately brings "freedom" and "futures" to forsaken subjects commodified in the global sex market.[10] The film's resolution revives discourses of absolute state power, and in doing so, corroborates a logic of *parens patriae*, reminding audiences of the role of the state as parent, especially for those who cannot protect themselves, such as the powerless and vulnerable children, but also legitimizing the punitive parental arm of the state and reifying an older patriarchal order. Despite the material limit of its failure to resolve, I suggest there are elements of a cultural reading that enrich critical approaches to the central paradox of rights of women and laws of man.

In the final act of retributive justice, the climactic encounter between huntress and hunted, Mukherji-as-Shivaji Shivani performs a *taandav* while kicking the prostrate body of the impenitent cartel boss, much like the mythical God Siva dancing on the body of the demon in the process of slaying him. She turns her back on the bad guy's cynical version of a corrupt India where he need never live in fear of comeuppance. He receives condign punishment for thinking that systematic corruption guarantees freedom from retribution. Inspector Roy's retort is that a person practicing such a politics can always be "encountered"[11] as an exception sanctioned by a justice excepted from obligations to legal-liberal norms. The subaltern's[12] justifiable demand for ethical behavior from their 'consumers' is circuited through the hegemonic assignation of legalized brutality embodied in a heroic policewoman. In all this, the violated body as well as the protesting body disappear or emerge as one, the body that needs protection through the authority of law. Ratna Kapur's incisive comment is worth recalling, "The vulnerable and frightened female body, repackaged in a protective bubble wrap and regulated by a new sexual security regime, ultimately displaced the body in protest."[13] The Law of the Father, ironically embodied in the sexed figure of the policewoman, guarantees a suspension of law when it comes to exercising acts of extra-judicial violence. In the colonial triangulation Spivak famously sums up as an alibi for colonial violence, she states:

> As a product of these considerations, I have put together the sentence 'White men are saving brown women from brown men' in a spirit not unlike the one to be encountered in Freud's investigations of the sentence 'A child is being beaten'.[14]

Spivak's continual dissembling of Freud's pronouncements, a way to reveal his latent misogyny, is utilized to refer to her own political agenda and call attention to the ways in which social progress becomes the cover for cementing colonial authority. The film, arising under the sign of Bollywood, amnesiac and ahistorical, bound within modes of late capital and new empire, points to a more muscular and violent state, albeit in the figure of a woman to set wheels of justice in place.

Problematics of Protest in Feminist Mediascapes

> It is a well-known fact that the worst victims of the recent exacerbation of the international division of labor are women. They are the true surplus army of labour in the current conjecture. In their case, patriarchal social relations contribute to their production as the new focus of super-exploitation.[15]

In the making of this film, the director, Pradeep Sarkar, and script writer, Gopi Puthran, speak of a "net" and "web" of activities nucleated at a seat of power in the capital city, Delhi. Siddharth Kara, in the first of his powerful studies on the global sex trafficking industry, identifies the victims of this labyrinth as "slaves" named in the system of western capitalism where their bodies are captured, isolated, commodified, violated, and utilized for maximum profit and pleasure of the buyers in a macro-movement of enslaved workers across a world market. Kara writes:

> Every minute of every day, the most vulnerable women and children in the world are raped for profit with impunity, yet efforts to combat sex trafficking remain woefully inadequate and misdirected. There are several reasons for this insufficiency. First, despite increased media attention, sex trafficking remains poorly understood. Second, the organizations dedicated to combating sex trafficking are underfunded and uncoordinated internationally. Third, the laws against sex trafficking are overwhelmingly anemic and poorly enforced. Finally, despite numerous studies and reports, a systematic business and economic analysis of the industry, conducted to identify strategic points of intervention, has not yet been undertaken.[16]

The film takes on this problem, and in doing so, the filmmakers speak to cops, undercover senior crime branch professionals, as well as people affected by this labyrinthine stateless industry that adds possibly $200 million USD or more to the national GDP.[17] There is an awareness and sensitivity in the making of the film: consider the observations of casting director, Shanoo Sharma, who speaks of the difficulty of casting girl-actors for the harrowing scenes of sex trafficking and exploitation. She shows us footage of a teenage actor speaking to her parents to explain why she wants to play the role of a sex-worker. She finds the task disturbing but is moved by the fact that there are "real" girls, her peers in age, trapped in conditions of abysmal exploitation. Sarkar speaks of filming with care so that the diegetic sequences are not titillating but meant to convey harsh material realities. The young actor, Tahir Raj Bhasin, who describes the problem of this character precisely through his globally recognizable 'cool', says, "Age is no longer relevant to capacity and capability."[18] As a villainous figure who poaches on the vulnerable in the market and violates the bodies of young girls, Bhasin underlines the need for a young actor to play this character, reiterating how the technological know-how of a newer generation can be utilized for furthering global circuits of exploitation and misogyny.

Bhasin plays the villainous ring-master, Karan Rastogi, a video-gaming mastermind racketeer. Influenced by western media and television, he chooses Walt as his identity, in homage to American TV's popular epic "Breaking Bad." The similarity ends there: Indian Walt is moving a drug far more potent that high-grade meth. In profiting from the vulnerable women Rastogi runs through his circuits of global sex trade, the spectacularity of his entrepreneurship rests on the women's abjection. As Kristeva wrote, "...abjection is elaborated through a failure to recognize its kin."[19] This critical turn in the ethical gaze signifies the distance between Walt and his slaves. Kristeva explains, "...discourse will seem tenable only if it ceaselessly confronts that otherness, a burden both repellant and repelled, a deep well of memory that is unapproachable and intimate: the abject."[20] In establishing the cold reality of the machinery running this business, we are made to witness a harrowing sequence where the kidnapped girls are "broken" and readied for various sites of purchase—cities in the nation, sites abroad. The fairer-skinned and more educated girls, after they are ordered to display their naked bodies, are dispatched to places in Europe, the Middle East, and commercial hubs like Hong Kong and Singapore. One girl puts up a fight and most others tremble, weep, and struggle, but all walk towards Walt and drop their towels, akin to slaves on an auction block. To the girl who fights, Walt concludes his summary of her position with a statement in English, "But the way I look at it, you don't have much of a choice, do you?" The scopophilic order is resisted by limiting the spectatorial gaze in a way distinguishing this cinematic gaze from the normative one where women's bodies are present on screen to be consumed and titillate; instead we look at the flippant "commodifying" gaze of the perpetrator via over-the-shoulder shots of the girls' backs. Much of the film's diegetic sequences relish this mode of subjective treatment since production is premised on Sarkar's desire to bring out the fighting spirit in viewers, girls and women alike. In its framing devices, cutting, close-up angles, and unflattering extreme close-ups of the racketeers, its discursive order approaches Kristeva's unapproachable, naming the abject. Abjection is beyond ambiguity and repugnant; Kristeva explains how the subject does not disappear but instead finds, "...in that sublime alienation, a forfeited existence."[21]

Shuddhabrata Sengupta, in analyzing the invisible labor of cameramen in Hindi cinema, notes, "Cinema in India has had a global outreach from its very inception ... Particularly in cinematography, German and American technicians continued to have a significant presence in both Bombay and Madras cinemas till the mid to late 1950s."[22] Artur Zurawsky, director of photography, speaks of un-Bollywoodizing the film with "less color, less light, less special effects, no high speech effects, and no slow motion. We wanted to make the action more natural, but not cheap." He speaks of arriving in India and seeing a lot of everything, "a lot of colors, a lot of different foods, too much ... too much. In this film, we are trying to get less, less, less, so we get more."[23] To arrive at the bleakness of these liminal lives, the cameraman reduces what is made visible to illuminate the leitmotif. Manohar Varma, action director, says about the action sequences, *"Aadmi log mard nahi hote, aurtein log bhi mardaani hote hain"* (The men are not men; women are men too). Attending to the thick parallel text[24] of actors' lives and how it animates the filmic text, Rani Mukerji's well known preference for method-acting compelled her to take rifle training, police combat sessions, and lessons in Israeli self-defense, Krav Maga, which teaches its practitioners to overwhelm opponents with technique rather than size. The director, in speaking about awakening the *mardaani* in all women, says regarding his film, *"Bahut ho gaya, candle jalaana. Ab maaro!"* (Enough already with candle-light vigils. Now beat them!). In attending a Women's Beat Marshall Unit opening ceremony, Rani Mukerji speaks of films as a mirror and inspiration for society so that as more audiences watch her film, more girls will join police units and, as she advises female cops at the launch, *"Apne andar ki Shakti jagayiye, apne andar ki mardaani jagayiye"* (Awake your inner Goddess; awake your inner Mardaani).[25] The actor here deputizes state power through an authorization of more girls in the police force leaving little room for an empowerment that arises apart from or in spite of state-implemented apparatuses. Here, I return to Shruti Iyer's caution about the dismissals inherent in state authorizations of resistance movements:

> Positioning the victim-oriented governance feminism forged by Western feminists and Third World elites on offer as only feminism means dismissing alternative resistances, and losing narratives that would contribute immensely to a full account of the female experience under patriarchy and the state.[26]

Laura Mulvey's critique of film spectatorship as male authorial gaze foregrounded scopophilia as the pleasure surplus of mass consumption.[27] Rendering all spectators male also queers the cinematic audience at inception. Mulvey's theories of the gaze were given new life in the 1980s by the feminist film theorists' collective, which relied also for its theoretical stance on Joan Copjec's quasi-axiomatic comment: "subjectivity assigned to femininity within patriarchal systems is inevitably bound up with the structure of the look and the localization of the eye as authority."[28] In any reading founded on notions of panoptical surveillance, *Mardaani* would appear as screen-mirror in whose reflective depth, the central subject Shivani Roy, becomes an extension of our moral selves. We are invited to be awed by her warrior-like female body towering over us. In our look lies the localization of authority, embodied in the sign of Woman-as-Law, violating the violator under the aegis of an approbative gaze of the state. As Copjec's project aims to identify limitations in the Foucauldian position, her critique of the panopticon is quite productive in reading the figure of the warrior woman on screen. Copjec probes the undecidability and refusal of panopticon-based theories to acknowledge resistance; in her reading, they are totalizing and remain "resistant to resistance."[29] Copjec maintains that the Lacanian subject is inaugural and can be distinguished from predecessors in film theory. The latter are mired in the central problematic of the panopticon itself: "the desire that it precipitates *transfixes* the subject, albeit in a conflictual place, so that all the subject's visions and revisions, all its fantasies, merely circumnavigate the absence that anchors the subject and impedes its progress."[30]

The spectatorial projection upon the uniformed police woman on screen remains locked in a narcissistic circuit; falling in love with the ideal self of the modern Indian woman, the story further reifies statist discourse while undercutting long years of feminist anti-imperial anti-patriarchal activism on the ground. Under the sign of woman as "legal vigilante," the simulacrum is structured by an absence at the core of this mediatized text: the complete erasure of the courage of women who fight sex trafficking every day in quotidian institutional and personal work. In fighting without being named, the uncinematized protagonist remains in the liminal zone, not entirely outside the law of the father, but at the threshold selling flowers by the bushels like Pyaari, the sex-worker rescued by Inspector Shivani Roy.

In 2015, Leslee Udwin made a film called "India's Daughter" as part of the BBC Storyville series. In it, she interviews the defense lawyer as well as the rapists in the Nirbhaya case. One of the rapists states, "A girl is far more responsible for rape than a boy." He maintains girls should be home doing housekeeping chores rather than roam around discos and bars at nine o'clock PM "doing wrong things, wearing wrong clothes."[31] The defense lawyer evinces similar misogynistic views where he declares that were his own daughter to be seen gallivanting about at night, he would readily take her to their ancestral farmhouse and in the presence of extended family, set her on fire, his imaginary clearly undergirded by patriarchal class and feudal mechanisms of bringing the errant woman into line. Udwin's documentary pits male depravity against women's original sin of desire,[32] and the kind of binary it creates to pitch its message has been complicated by scholars like Aswini Tambe. She addresses systemic structural inequalities and ideologies that allow men and women to practice misogyny in their daily lives in India as well as across the western world. While the nation foments around the case of the gang rape of a young student, in over 94% of rape cases, the assailant is known to the victim. In speaking about "rape culture" Tambe speaks to the larger systemic problem of violence by the powerful and educated against the powerless, like the laboring classes whose violation is not even read as violence.[33] No national movements have mobilized in a widespread sense[34] to speak out against endemic structural violence that assails indigenous, Dalit, and other women left in the shadows of civic enfranchisement.[35]

Female leaders, members of parliament and establishmentarian voices in India's public and political spheres spoke up passionately on the 2012 rape case referred to as "Nirbhaya" in many ways epistemically coding a larger feminist grass-roots movement for "*Bekaouf Azaadi* or Freedom Without Fear"[36]: governmental feminists bemoan a nation where goddesses are worshipped and women are raped on a daily basis. Ruchira Gupta—an activist who started the human rights organization *Apne Aap*—reaches 20,000 children of prostitutes, providing them refuge, work, and education in a language that engages the same vocabulary of promise used to keep them enslaved. Gupta works to bring down the edifice of centuries-old hereditary system of prostitution and her organizational activism testifies to nodally linked practices of resistance at sex trafficking epicenters in India.[37]

Rani Mukerji is right when she asserts that the film mirrors society; it reflects the very limitations of public discursive ordering around this issue. In the productive confluence of activism in the wake of the 2012 tragedy, much is made of a change in the rape culture that is all-pervasive, a desire to radically alter the collective unconscious around physical and emotional acts of violence directed toward women, and the renewed pride in India's women as being goddess-like in their powers of chastity and ferocity as well as a more radical global movement to shake off the yoke of oppression, establishing solidarity with international women's movements such as "One Billion Rising,"[38] and, most crucially, taking back their bodies from *Baap, Bhai, and Khaap* (father, brother, and village council that traditionally formed the familial juridical order governing and regulating women's bodies/lives). However, the portrayal of women as all-powerful and divine can be disabling and disempowering in that it does not allow for the material redress of actual conditions of violence against women: much of the violence is perpetrated by family and friends upon women and girls they know or newly produced contested spaces of liberalization such as private cars and buses shuttling women to and from corporate IT work sites wherein the solutions of further protecting women by offering an opportunity to work from home would "enfold women in patriarchal domestic space through a technocratic rationale that sidesteps women's rights"[39]; many of the victims of rape and related sex trafficking industry are poor, indigenous, and disen-franchised people of historically marginalized communities, and marital rape is still not seen as rape under the juridical order in India. Amartya Sen's point that most of the rape in India goes unreported speaks to the truth that when relatives rape women and girls in the family, it is gener-ally not considered acceptable to make this family secret public through a First Information Report, or FIR.[40] When women in vulnerable social circumstances are raped, it is such a common occurrence that it is not even recorded or registered as an act of violence; it is normalized instead as a reflection of the real world. The Filmic Fable, while touching upon structural iniquities in new imperialisms, elides the more urgent prob-lematic of rape culture. In conveying speech from the woman-as-victim, much of the derivative homespun videography inspired by this spectacle of protest continues to cement the woman-as-victim who needs to be rescued and placed back on her pedestal as any of the following tired tropes: goddess of strength and chastity, the woman as nation, the girl as standard bearer for cultural mores.

The neat encapsulation of a rescue narrative, wherein a "lost girl" is "found" and supposedly rendered happy, distorts the material real-ity of millions of lives numbered in grim human rights statistics pre-sented during the end-credits: one child abduction every eight minutes in India. Rani Mukerji's voice-over narrates poetic justice meted out as condign punishment as she concludes, "Today we could bring back the smile on Pyaari's face but there are many more Pyaaris that have to be rescued from this muck." The double bind in this civilizing mis-sion presents an enclosure both to the liberated "girls" and scores of "enslaved" bodies waiting to be rescued. Rescue missions (framed in statist imperial ideologies) promise salvation, while the rescued are enshrined in a return to childhood and the innocence of happiness (flower sales). Neither option is generally on offer for the average sex worker whose life expectancy is under forty. The repetitive and cycli-cal nature of trauma returns survivors to episodic dehumanization so that "getting on with life" is a chimera. As Sara Ahmed put it, "Ethics cannot be about moving beyond pain toward happiness or joy without imposing new forms of suffering on those who do not or cannot move in this way."[41]

Significations of Feminist Masculinity

For women, nationalist liberation theology has always begged the question of gender because ousting the despot is meaningful only if one can step out of the home and inhabit the streets of the liberated nation. Speaking on this nearly a century ago, Subhadra Kumari Chauhan cel-ebrated the woman warrior, "Jhansi ki Rani" (Queen of Jhansi) and inaugurated an Indian imaginary of feminist *mardaani*, raising further critical questions on why quests of female empowerment have to be authorized through masculinity.

Prachi Deshpande[42] has shown how the Rani of Jhansi demands a critical historiography in the context of Indian nationalism and anti-colonial feminist thought. Chauhan's valorization of the historical Rani was part of a feminist nationalist mode of revitalization within the collective mythos of an emergent nation. Chauhan, a committed activist in the Indian freedom struggle against British rule, was imprisoned twice for promoting women's rights. Below are some excerpts from Chauhan's 125 lined, much quoted and memorialized poem that describes the symbolic and literal victories of Rani of Jhansi:

> *Gumi hui azadi ki kimat sabne pahchani thi...* (1.3)
> *Lakshmi thi ya durga thi vah svaya virta ka avatar...* (1.15)
> *Jaha khadi hai lakshmibai mard bani mardanon mein...* (1.85)
> *Mila tej se tej, tej ki vah sacchi adhikari thi...* (1.113)
> *Hamko jivit karne aayi ban svatantrata nari thi...* (1.115)

> We recognized the value of our lost freedom
> Lakshmi or Durga, she was an avatar of courage
> She stood there, Lakshmibai, men amidst men
> As steel met steel, she is the true inheritor of this light
> She came to bring us to life, a freedom-woman she was
> (translation mine)

While translation fails to convey the gender politics of Rani as a *mard bani mardanon mein* [she became a man amidst men], *mila tej se tej* [brilliance meets brilliance] and *svatantrata-nari,* [freedom woman/Lady Liberty], it suggests Chauhan saw no disconnect between her nationalist struggles and her feminist social work. As poet/activist/writer, her Self is as *woman warrior*, with rich and fraught connections to twentieth-century latter day feminism of India. The multiple valences of women fighting for freedom within the Indian context suggest that the lost freedom signifies more than the native mourning her agency under imperial rule. Cloaked within the rhetoric of anti-imperial struggle is also the melancholy and temerity of a specifically female voice transgressing the threshold of privacy by demanding in public that dignity of human rights, freedom, and equality, which implicates gender and nation simultaneously. The poem, in attempting to transcend the limitations of time and space, relapses into the familiar and limiting apotheosis of woman as goddess. Yet, it teases out a gendered refrain of becoming a greater man than most men, or in other words, an equal-or-greater rather than secondary/marginal figure.

Here, Mary Wollstonecraft's first wave feminist call for universalist ethics is braided with the particularist/identitarian politics of second-wave feminists who symbolically cohere around the coeval nature of the personal and political, insisting that the one is the other. Ursula McTaggart provides literary insights into Virginia Woolf's 'room of one's own' as an always-already present motif at the Hogarth Press that allows a perfect blurring between the private and the public. This insight enables too, a reading of this early twentieth-century Indian poet, except for the fact that she is "Indian" and nationalist questions are always already entwined with the "woman question" in early twentieth-century colonial India. Thus, when Woolf declares in McTaggart, "I have no country. As a woman, I want no country. As a woman my country is the whole world"[43], Chauhan's vantage point unravels the unconscious colonial complicity of such a declaration. For Chauhan, whose country is at the time waging a full-scale resistance against their English overlords, global sisterhood is politically impossible: the gender struggle has to be articulated within the *limit* of nation.

Gayatri Spivak's deconstruction of the historiography around Rani of Sirmur offers spectral possibilities and insight. Ultimately pessimistic in accounting for the fact that there is no real Rani to be found, Spivak elucidates the conundrum around a Rani who is enthroned instead of her deposed husband and in lieu of the child prince. In the forced erasure of the native sovereign, Spivak claims the *unnamed* woman guards the dismemberment of native authority because "caught between patriarchy and imperialism, she is almost in an allegorical predicament"[44] and thus, the spectral figure of the Rani of Sirmur moves us toward Chauhan's re-evocation of another historical royal woman who emerges to contest both laws of the father—native patriarchy and foreign imperialism re-signed as woman warrior. Chauhan's poiesis projects a woman crowned for bravery; Chauhan gives her the titular lead of *freedom woman* and thus discursively plays with an excess of meaning: freedom for the imperial subject and the subjugated woman at once. The Rani of Jhansi (1835–58) died defending her fortress at Jhansi in present day Madhya Pradesh, the state where Chauhan (1904–48) spent most of her married life as a wife, mother, and activist. The connections between the poet and her subject are much greater than mere mechanics of history or coincidences of geography; the Rani is assigned as resistance to British imperialism, she signifies the deficiency of law, especially as it poses iniquitous adversity to female inheritance and women's rights. Those themes are tackled with even more nuance in Chauhan's short stories.[45] Ramya Sreenivasan's meticulous deconstruction of nearly five hundred years of interpretations of the Queen of Mewar's self-immolation[46] compels us to place Mardaani in a patriarchy ever invested in dismembering and re-membering women's histories. To the critical interpreter of Bollywood, Pradip Sarkar's masala film[47] evokes these cultural histories through the figure of the vigilantress cop. The projector, in this sense, does not simply beam the movie from behind the audience. The screen itself juts out as a geological promontory comprising layers of feminist resistance.

Radha Kumar's *The History of Doing: An Illustrated Account of Movements for Women's Rights and Feminism in India 1800–1990* foregrounds an active women's movement to which Chauhan was an heir.

> The nineteenth century was a period in which the rights and wrongs of women became major issues: if early attempts at reforming the conditions under which Indian women lived were largely conducted by men, by the late nineteenth century their wives, sisters, daughters, protégées and others affected by campaigns, such as that for women's education, had themselves joined in movements. By the early twentieth century women's own autonomous organizations began to be formed, and within a couple of decades, by the thirties and forties, a special category of 'women's activism' was constructed.[48]

Kumar shows how tensions rise between reformists (those arguing in favor of modernity and against superstitious or dehumanizing religious mores) and nationalists (whose primary antagonist is imperial rule). The latter utilize religious iconography to sustain their nationalist sentiments but feminist dialectics in both movements wrack the debate on anti-colonial agenda. The nationalists—especially in Bengal where Durga and Kali Puja[49] become popular cultural practice in the nineteenth century—elevate the place of the goddess and see her as *Mother India* and mothers in general while also limiting the participation of Indian women in the public sphere. Kumar (1993) writes,

> Moreover, some women now began to express the view that women, in order to be free, had to engage in a struggle with men. And the demand for equality between the sexes was itself based on the principle of sameness rather than complementarity.[50]

Chauhan's oeuvre reflects the nuanced shifts in consciousness that brings together the reformist and nationalist binary together in the feminist movement of the early twentieth century. Sarkar's *Mardaani* arrives as sign for female empowerment while presenting an ahistorical Bollywood text without memory, without predecessor, or peer;[51] Deshpande theorizes the birth of a new male hero in the 1990s in the shadow of Bollywood who has a certain amnesia, is more global than local, comfortable in any vacation spot in the world, but hardly Indian or rooted in the nation in any visible way. Sarkar's film, in entering a global conversation on sex trafficking, presents a narrative with the villain and cop in one-on-one conversations, but the histories of feminist activism remain deep in shadow. Female empowerment stands alone severed from its long history of radical feminist activism. It is this severance that informs the concluding remarks in this paper.

Mythic Retributions of the Feminine Divine

The film, shorn of the song and dance sequences that are normative to Bollywood formulae, gives a nod to this tradition by weaving together the climactic sequence of bloodthirsty female-led vengeance on the broken body of the perpetrator though song. Indian cinema, an amalgam of premodern traditions—folk, indigenous and balladic dance theatre forms—that have informed its discourse since inception in late nineteenth century, utilizes song and dance to portray and disseminate ideas of modern love that could otherwise be curtailed by the Indian Censor Board. Often the song and dance sequences framed the *rasa* of *Sringara* (erotic) representing the blossoming love between hero and heroine and suggesting through gesture, what would be surveilled and edited out in dialogue. Thus, this sequence is diegetic and crucial to story; in this film, the violent denouement refers to the more disturbing *rasas*, such as *raudra* (terrible), *bhayanaka* (fierce), and *bibhatsa* (odious). In representing a gruesome level of female upon male violence through song, the film values and translates these disturbing *rasas* as positive performance, an agential and ancient restoration of order, so the suturing occurs and the audience is to take away *veera* (heroic) *rasa* of this collective correction of societal malaise, industrialized forms of violence against women.

To emphasize this sentiment of cosmic balance, the song's refrain refers to a generic prayer to the goddess Devi, who lives in all human beings in the form of strength and peace. It is also critical that heavy thumping of female heels on the male body is matched by a male voice invoking the mother goddess figure of Hindu antiquity, "*Ya Devi sarvabhuteshu/ Shakti rupena samasthita/ Ya Devi sarvabhutesu/ Shanti rupena samasthita/ Namasthasyai namasthasyai namasthasyai namo namah.*"[52] The song invokes the Goddess of retribution and peace, not binary opposites within Indic cosmogony, Kali, whose arrival functions in mythology as the gruesome and physically charged annihilation of ungodly elements, any men or kings who have lost their ethical way as they reign bloated with power. The grand narrative of a mythic epic violence remains limited within the modern imaginary; for the average audience member, the possibility of reckoning with one's power by awakening the "man" within who can perform vigilante violence is not an option. Such a logic also equates man with violence and the solutions remain blood-soaked in a way that continues to keep women locked within phallogocentric conservative Hindu hegemonies. On first glance, the film elides the difference between Roy, the police officer, and Roy, the woman, aunt, mother figure, and friend. Seemingly, the script has reversed Spivak's refrain that haunts postcolonial literary and mediascapes of the white man rescuing the brown woman from the brown man. With Roy as super cop at the action's center, ideologically, the story reifies old imperial statist patriarchal notions of the arm of the state squelching the outlaw; the brown woman continues to be rescued; the brown man continues to victimize.

The song, an anthem for a renewed and reinvigorated women's movement now marked by protest marches that include men and children, emphasizes a binary between the physical and the spiritual, a binary that is present as early as the epic text, *Ramayana*, where the oft-tested princess, Sita, speaks of the lack of autonomy over her body compared to the indomitability of her soul and spirit.[53] Here, the voice claims that while the body can be laid to siege through violence, the voice argues for a refusal to let anyone touch her *aan* (dignity, prestige) and *maan* (esteem, respect). These similar sounding alliterative words, while difficult to fully translate with the load of cultural implications, have separate gendered registers. When being claimed in maleness, they suggest warrior codes of honor and the implacability of the word. When engendered female, the words cloak an ambiguity where the violation of the body simultaneously suggests a violation of dignity, esteem, and respect, thus reifying long-standing patriarchal ideologies that equate the violated woman's body as site of disrespect and indignity. This regulatory order generated by the powerful mythic figure of Sita perpetuates the punitive fallacy that rather than indict the violence of the perpetrator, it is indeed all right to further punish the woman's body.

Even while the song expresses a binary between body and spirit, it espouses a welcome to physical violence that takes life rather than contest violence that violates the female body. Stanzas buried within the song do invoke various spheres of historical resistance in the Indian women's movement, such as the move to take back the streets, raise bulwarks against the sex trafficking industry, and, in larger ways, resist the linguistic and systematic devaluation of women. In an extradiegetic move, the song critiques collective habits of mourning which are marked by candle-light vigils and on occasion, depending on the gravity of the crime, outrage against eve-teasing,[54] and with it, the epidemic of violence against women that continues unabated. Thus, the song is a clear winner as an anthem for the contemporary movement sparking across the Indian and South Asian subcontinent. Yet, it remains limited and bound to older traditions of female resistance couched within patriarchal frameworks where it is the voice of the inviolate body proclaiming its purity that rises above the din. In many ways, the song reifies the phallic order that values a woman's body in its virginal state; once penetrated, her *aan-maan* are besmirched and the goddess arises as the redeemer. For the spectator, especially those outside the Hindu order or have belief systems that do not subscribe a fealty to the goddess, the song offers a chimera rather than a concrete exit from spectacles of violations and violence. When unpacking the gendered significations and surveillance of women's bodies during the period of anticolonial nationalist struggles, Mrinalini Sinha notes that she was not necessarily a traditional woman but rather, "She was more likely the "modern-yet-modest" woman who both symbolized the nation and negotiated its tension between tradition and modernity."[55] In thinking through the misogyny that is ideologically present and so deeply institutionalized in modernity and contemporary pixilation of religion, I am taken back to what Mary Gossy once declared, "At the heart of each western text is the body of a dead woman."

My rejoinder has an element of the fantastic in that what can be noted is that the raped female body continually disappears from the body of the living text. The rape narratives are both foundational and marginal to the canonic discourse in western and non-western traditions; in cataloguing the rape events of monumental mythic figures that are remembered through painting and balladic art forms, from the Sabine women in Livy's account, to Dinah in the Book of Genesis, or Saraswati the Goddess of wisdom and music in Indic traditions, the female figures are essential in founding new empires and yet, their body continually disappears as rape becomes part of the vernacular, a new normal in the establishment of civilizations. As the angry sons of Jacob, Simeon, and Levi avenge their sister, Dinah, by killing all the Shechemites, recovering from the circumcision ritual undertaken to be yoked as one community on word given by Jacob, all one learns about Dinah is that the two brothers led her back home from Hamor's son, Shechem.[56] In the case of the Sabine women, all that is promised to them in terms of citizenship and rights to property by the Romans is quickly forgotten as they become the vessels to found a new empire. Goddess Saraswati, escaping from the carnal desirous gaze of her procreator, God Brahma, turns into every creature on earth, and is raped at every turn, producing all the animals of the earth, an etiological tale of creation.

While the raped body of the female disappears continually, her womb generates new worlds unto which patriarchal ideology is writ large; theodicy here is irrelevant to an extent as the question of evil around rape hardly rises. Rape is a normalizing event of violent creation stories, the woman's body the ground upon which new worlds are founded. Misogyny, then, is a layered (H)Indic narrativizing that legitimates and celebrates the foibles of God Krishna who steals the clothes of the Gopis bathing in the river, or Lakshmana who chops off the ears and nose of Surpanakha, or Ahalya, who is turned to stone for unknowingly betraying her husband with God Indra, or Indra of the thousand phalluses and wives, and on and on.

In thinking through the cataclysmic event of a son beheading his mother, the case of Parasurama and Renuka, Wendy Doniger arrives at a curious concatenation of affect. Once Parasurama asks his father to reconsider his wrath and forgive the mother, the son patches together the head of his "Brahmin" mother with the body of a lower caste woman so that the hybrid recreated body suggests a defilement that is expressed vividly in temple architecture; the goddess's head is placed often in the inside room of reverence and sanctity, *garbagraha* while her body is kept at the threshold. Doniger writes,

> So great is the tension within her that she does not remain integrated in ritual; she is split up once again, the divine head at last purified by being divorced from its polluting body, and the outcaste body made literally liminal, placed on the doorstep, forever marking the pale of the Hindu society that sees woman as a divine-headed and outcaste-bodied monster.[57]

It is this amalgam that haunts the Indian discursive order where at one end, the apotheosis of the female as divinity is corralled against the other extreme of the degraded female body, both as virginal victim and colonized subject. In sorting through women's bodies as an index of cards on the global commodities market through phenotypic markers of age, race, color, and size, such an ideology enables the male gaze to collectively look past the humanity of the populations ensnared in the sex trafficking auction blocks. If the woman's body is always already a sexualized monster in a state of transgression, the machinery of violence in many ways permits the mythic exercise of beheading, not only the "rational" head that would raise the specter of theodicy, thereby questioning the evil of this mercantile trade in female flesh, but the "hymenic" head that might otherwise turn around and devour its other. In arrogating the female body to a liminal site, neither God nor monster, what is eliminated within language, and by extension, culture, are the lives[58] of women.

Notes

1 Ashish Rajadhyaksha's addresses the Bollywoodization of Indian cinema and speaks of the flattening of grand narratives under pressures of globalization, late capital, and an active western diasporic consumer market ready to engage the corporate market to subsidize nostalgia and Indian nationalism. Feminist scholars have productively engaged with the mimetic and self-enclosed loops of films, film-makers, and the actors that constitute this simulacrum, deconstructing the filmic text and its feedback loop to speak on how it regulates female sexuality. For more, read Ashish Rajadhyaksha, "The "Bollywoodization" of the Indian Cinema: Cultural Nationalism in a Global Arena," 17–40 and Padma Govindan and Bisakha Dutta, "From Villain to Traditional Housewife!: The Politics of Globalization and Women's Sexuality in the "New" Indian Media," *Global Bollywood*, Anandam P. Kavoori and Aswin Punathambedkar, eds., (New York: New York University Press, 2008), 180–202.

2 According to the International Labor Organization, 21 million people are victims of forced labor. Though the numbers are an estimate since so much of this labor pool remains invisible, made visible in films like these, three out of one thousand people worldwide are in work situations that are the result of coercion, deception, and offer no exit. Out of the 18.7 million people trapped in conditions of forced exploitation, 4.5 million are estimated to be in conditions of sexual exploitation. While the largest numbers in this group are adult women, 21% or higher in this population could be children. "International Labor Organization," last modified June 12, 2015. www.ilo.org/global/about-the-ilo/newsroom/news/WCMS_181961/lang–en/index.htm.

3 According to a recent US report on India's booming underground economy in forced labor:

> Sex trafficking of women and girls within the country is widespread. Religious pilgrimage centers and cities popular for domestic tourism continue to be vulnerable to child sex tourism. A large number of Nepali and Bangladeshi females—the majority of whom are children—and an increasing number of women and girls from Uzbekistan, Ukraine, Russia, Azerbaijan, Serbia, Kazakhstan, and Afghanistan are also subjected to sex trafficking in India. There are increasing reports of women and girls from northeastern states and Odisha being sold or coerced into forced marriages in states with low female-to-male gender ratios, including Haryana and Punjab, some of whom are subsequently forced into prostitution or labor by their new "families." Indian women and girls are also subjected to transactional sexual exploitation in the Middle East under the guise of temporary marriages. Women and girls—including those in child marriages—fleeing domestic violence from their husbands are particularly vulnerable to human trafficking. The Naxalites, or Maoist armed groups, forcibly recruited children into their ranks. Sex trafficking establishments continue to move from more traditional locations—such as brothels in densely populated urban areas—to locations that are harder to find, such as to residential areas in cities and to rural areas. Sex traffickers increasingly procure false identification documents for child victims to evade detection by police. Traffickers are increasingly better organized and adapting to state government crackdowns on well-known establishments or routes of human trafficking.

United States Department of State, 2013, Trafficking in Persons Report—India, last modified June 19, 2013. www.refworld.org/docid/51c2f3b7c.html. According to the same report, the Indian state had not reached the minimal standard of compliance in fighting or dismantling this underground economy of sex traffic. Although new police units were established specifically to counter these networks, as evidenced in this film, the complicity and lethargy within the political and police ranks makes the work all the more challenging.

4 Nirbhaya case refers to an event that rallied a nation together and brought world-wide condemnation upon the actors in the case. A young woman, Jyoti Singh, and her friend, returning from an evening after watching the film, "Life of Pi," were assaulted in a bus. Her male partner, beaten and rendered helpless, bore witness to the brutal gang rape and assault of the woman by six men, a tragedy so extreme that the young woman died of her wounds less than two weeks after the assault on December 16, 2012. Instead of her given name, the nation, coming together in protests, candle light vigils, and other public outcry to speak on violence against women addressed more endemic and institutional sanction of a culture of violence

and misogyny, marked her death as a symbol of resistance and dignity by referring to this case and her as "nirbhaya" or fearless. While one of the central actors of the crime, Ram Singh, committed suicide in Tihar Jail during the fast track court case proceedings, four of the other guilty parties were sentenced to death for committing crimes that were deemed to be the rarest of rare category. http://timesofindia.indiatimes.com/india/Delhi-gang-rape-Case-diary/articleshow/22455125.cms.

5 Sareeta Amrute, "Moving Rape: Trafficking in the Violence of Postliberalization," *Public Culture* 27, no. 2 (2015): 338.

6 Terry Eagleton, *After Theory* (New York: Perseus, 2003), 19.

7 Ratna Kapur, "Brutalized Bodies and Sexy Dressing on the Indian Street," *Signs* 40, no. 1 (Autumn 2014), 9–14.

8 Shruti Iyer, "Taking a Break from the State: Indian Feminists in the Legal Reform Process," *Journal of International Women's Studies*, 17, no. 2 (2016), 18–29.

9 Jose Medina, *The Epistemology of Resistance: Gender and Racial Oppression, Epistemic Injustice, and Resistant Imaginations* (New York: Oxford University Press, 2013), 237.

10 Dennis Altman, in his now dated work from the late 90s, references global sex trafficking through the lens of autonomy, agency, and the psychic map of eros and affect, but he does note the rising iniquity in this porous market between the metropolitan north and sites in the global south when he notes,

> In both rich and poor countries the rapidity of economic change is increasing the sex trade. From the copious literature available take this example from Nepal. Says NGO activist Rana: 'Sex has begun to play a major role in Nepal's tourism earnings, which is unfortunate.' Another facet of the sex trade is trafficking in women and girls, a huge business in Nepal…According to a recent estimate by UNICEF, more than 300,000 Nepali women are reported to have been sold to Indian brothels.

Dennis Altman, *Global Sex* (Chicago: University of Chicago Press, 2001), 112. The numbers are clearly not able to capture the gravity of a situation that has been spinning out of control; recent numbers are even more chilling in stating that a record 200,000 Nepali girls might be sold into prostitution in various cities in India, a business that averages about 5000 girls a year.

11 The intertextual references of this moment cannot be lost within postcolonial feminist and deconstruction studies, especially around the discursive order laid by Gayatri Spivak in her now-canonic translation of Mahasveta Devi's "Draupadi." In Devi's story, Dopdi is the indigenous outlaw figure who, after the event of brutal violation by officials of the state once captured by them, she turns her naked body to her captors, and refuses to clothe or cover her bloody and bruised body. Under the threat of the "encounter" a word that needs no translation into indigenous languages, she turns to her assailants and proclaims, "Come on, counter me!" In the current filmic text, the "man in uniform" is instead the woman who represents both the law and women's empowerment, and in speaking back to the violator of girls and women with the threat of the "encounter," we have a stark reversal that shows, in some ways, how far mainstream bourgeois hegemonic feminism has come within India, and how complicit women are within structures of power and patriarchy. See Gayatri Chakravorty Spivak, trans. Mahasveta Devi's "Draupadi," *Critical Inquiry: Writing and Sexual Difference* 8, no. 2 (1981): 381–402.

12 Gayatri Chakravorty Spivak, "Can the Subaltern Speak?" in *Marxism and the Interpretation of Culture*, eds. Cary Nelson and Lawrence Grossberg (Urbana: University of Illinois Press, 1988), 271–313.

13 Kapur 11.

14 Spivak 92.

15 Gayatri Chakravorty Spivak, *In Other Worlds: Essays in Cultural Politics* (New York: Routledge, 1988), 167.

16 Siddharth Kara, *Sex Trafficking: Inside the Business of Modern Slavery* (New York: Columbia University Press, 2009), 3.

17 Repeatedly, studies on the subject of global sex trafficking and trafficking in South Asia arrive at the same point of consensus that reiterates Kara's thesis as well; along with individual and community empowerment, more economic resources provided to impoverished sites of the global or rural south that are poached upon for disposable bodies, large-scale structural interventions need to be made to turn the tide against this unchecked multi-headed hydra of an industrial complex. Read J. G. Silverman, M. R. Decker, J. Gupta, A. Maheshwar, V. Patel, B. M. Willis, and A. Raj, "Experiences of Sex Trafficking Victims in Mumbai, India," *International Journal of Gynecology and Obstetrics* 97, no. 3 (2007): 221–26. In a more recent research article, the scholars conclude on the perfect storm of forces that embattle the sex worker to be at the mercy of perpetrators who are often violent, and leave the worker vulnerable to HIV and other sexually transmitted illnesses. Read Jhumka Gupta, Elizabeth Reed, Trace Kershaw, Kim M. Blankenship, "History of Sex Trafficking, Recent Experiences of Violence, and HIV Vulnerability among Female Sex Workers in Coastal Andhra Pradesh, India," *International Journal of Gynecology and Obstetrics* 114, no. 2 (2011), 101–105.

18 "Making of the Film—Part 2—Mardaani: Casting," YouTube Video, 9:36, posted by Yash Raj Films, August 23, 2014, www.youtube.com/watch?v=3iJ07mLnavk.

19 Julia Kristeva, "Approaching Abjection," in *Routledge Critical and Cultural Theory Reader*, eds. Neil Badmington and Julia Thomas, (New York: Routledge, 2008), 248.

20 Kristeva 249.

21 Kristeva 251.

22 Shuddhabrata Sengupta, "Reflected Readings in Available Light: Cameramen in the Shadows of Hindi Cinema," in *Bollyworld: Popular Indian Cinema through a Transnational Lens*, Raminder Kaur and Ajay J. Sinha, eds., (New Delhi: Sage, 2005), 122.

23 "Making of the Film—Part 3—Mardaani: The Image," YouTube Video, 5:32, posted by Yash Raj Films, August 24, 2014, www.youtube.com/watch?v=Xa4rnWUq68A. The rest of the interviews in this paragraph are also provided in this video clip.

24 For more on the cross-animation of material and filmic lives of the actors as well as their audiences, read Vijay Mishra's extended analysis of the fanzines around the actor, Amitabh Bachchan. Vijay Mishra, *Bollywood Cinema: Temples of Desire* (New York: Routledge, 2002).

25 "Rani Mukerji—At the Launch of the Women Beat Marshal Unit of the Mumbai Police," YouTube Video, 9:15, posted by Yash Raj Films, August 30, 2014, www.youtube.com/watch?v=S2uZQck_IcA. Trans. mine.

26 Iyer 21.

27 Laura Mulvey, "Visual Pleasure and Narrative Cinema," *Screen* 16, no. 3 (1975), 6–18.

28 Quoted in Joan Copjec's *Read my Desire: Lacan against the Historicists* (Cambridge: MIT Press, 1994), Mary Ann Doane, Patricia Mellencamp, and Linda Williams, eds., *Re-vision* (Los Angeles: The American Film Institute, 1984), 14.

29 Copjec, 1994, 18.

30 Copjec, 1994, 38.

31 Leslee Udwin, "India's Daughter," documentary film, interviews Mukesh Singh, one of the convicted rapists serving life imprisonment (UK-India Co-Production of Assassin Films and Tathagat Films, March 4, 2015) — BBC aired it on March 4th as part of its ongoing Storyville series even though it was blocked from being aired on Indian TV and the government had it removed from YouTube in India after deeming the perpetrator's direct interview as inflammatory for public viewing in India. While Udwin's film provokes quite a bit of reaction at home and abroad, hers is only the first of probably many attempts at understanding the culture that precipitates such violence rendering precarious women's bodies in India. Along with a multitude of digital films and amateur attempts at marking the moment, Deepa Mehta, a renowned feminist film maker, releases, "Anatomy of Violence" on September 12, 2016 interrogating the ontologies of violence underlying this tragedy.

32 To add some depth to the artificial gendered binary, one can surmise, in the Lacanian sense, that the neo-liberal order generated by Late Capital in India produces the endless quest for the objet petit a positing a new crisis in Indian masculinity. Owning capital is the only way to truly become a man in the new order.

33 "Professor Ashwini Tambe discusses feminism in US and India," Anand Naidoo interviews on her for the show, "The Heat," YouTube Video, 7:25, posted by CCTV America, March 13, 2015, www.youtube.com/watch?v=UCNIVtu_hv0.

34 While national sentiment has risen and women's rights have cemented against the innumerable acts of violence suffered by women in recent history, the Mathura case (Maharashtra, 1972) and Bhanwari Devi case (Rajasthan, 1992) pivots and mobilizes public sentiment around the condition of tribal and indigenous women who raise their fists against unjust practices of child marriage and/or upper caste iniquities.

35 Arundhati Roy's entire corpus of essays and books serve as witness and account of the structural violence faced by the indigenous, the poor, the Dalit, and other disenfranchised peoples of India. For more, read Arundhati Roy, *Walking with the Comrades* (New York: Penguin, 2011) and *Broken Republic* (New York: Penguin, 2012). In a recent interview, Roy addresses the Nirbhaya case specifically for its unexceptionality in terms of horrific violence faced by women in the nation, but exceptional in that when the narrative shows a middle-class woman violated by the migrant and the poor, it is worthy of attention. "Arundhati Roy on India's Rape Culture," YouTube Video, 3:57, posted by Outlook India, December 22, 2012, www.outlookindia.com/blogs/post/arundhati-roy-on-indias-rape-culture/2927/31.

36 Iyer 22.

37 Ruchira Gupta, Founder, "Apne Aap," YouTube Video, 22:18, posted by Apne Aap Women Worldwide, March 19, 2015, http://apneaap.org/ruchiras-keynote-speech-at-ngo-cswny-forum-consultation-day-before-the-start-of-un-csw-59/.

38 www.onebillionrising.org/37155/indias-official-obr-newsletter-march-issue-an-overview-of-the-2016-campaign/.

39 Amrute 353.

40 Amartya Sen, "India's Women: The Mixed Truth," *New York Review of Books* (New York), October 10, 2013.

41 Sara Ahmed, *The Promise of Happiness* (Durham: Duke University Press, 2010), 216.

42 Prachi Deshpande's argument which traces a movement from the early modern to the colonial modern and speaks of an archive-based historiography also sheds critical light on how literary biographies, by late nineteenth century, valorize Rani of Jhansi as a symbol of Indian modernity, tradition, and female heroism. By the time Chauhan scripts her most famous lines on the Rani, she is fortifying an already cemented literary history, but adding to it, as expressed in this paper, the female voice of authorship to the canon. Prachi Deshpande, "The Making of an Indian Nationalist Archive: Lakshmibai, Jhansi, and 1857," *Journal of Asian Studies* 67, no. 3 (2008): 855–79.

43 Virginia Woolf, *Three Guineas* (San Diego: Harcourt Brace, 1966), 109, quoted in Ursula McTaggart, "Opening the Door: The Hogarth Press as Virginia Woolf's Outsiders' Society," in *Tulsa Studies in Women's Literature* 29, no. 1 (2010), 65.

44 Gayatri Chakravorty Spivak, "The Rani of Sirmur: An Essay in Reading the Archives," *History and Theory* 24, no. 3 (1985), 267.

45 Subhadra Kumari Chauhan, *Sidhe Saade Chitra: Short Stories* (Allahabad: Hans Publications, 1983).

46 Sreenivasan traces the important changes in the narrative around Padmini, the Queen of Mewar who self-immolates in the early fourteenth century. From the earliest Jayasi records inflected by Sufi and Afghan traditions to nineteenth- and twentieth-century nationalistic Hindu Aryan appropriations, Sreenivasan offers a magnificent bird's eye view of five hundred years of historiography and its effects on the materiality of a queen's narrative that has grown in consequence in the social and public culture of northern India. It is interesting to note that, though Chauhan belongs to the Hindi canon during the active reconstitution of the nation as Hindu, Aryan, and ancient, she stands apart in her choice of language and politics as explained in this paper. See Ramya Sreenivasan, *The Many Lives of a Rajput Queen: Heroic Pasts in India, c. 1500–1900,* (Seattle: University of Washington Press, 2007).

47 Masala (spiced/spicy) film, suggesting a grab at mainstream audiences and with it, a comeback for Rani Mukerji, yielded lower than expected profit margins. Nevertheless it is significant to note that Sarkar is aiming to capture the broadest audience possible rather than the more rarefied or specialized groups who attend art house or alternative productions. *Mardaani* has aspirations for diasporic and non-Indian audiences also, as evident in its availability in an online film viewing database like Netflix.

48 Radha Kumar, *The History of Doing: An Illustrated Account of Movements for Women's Rights and Feminism in India 1800–1990* (New York: Verso, 1993), 1.

49 *Puja* indicates a way of worshipping by paying obeisance to the gods. Here, Durga and Kali who are mentioned are both powerful and fierce goddesses who are forms of Parvathi.

50 Kumar 66.

51 Sudhanva Deshpande, "The Consumable Hero of Globalised India," in *Bollyworld: Popular Indian Cinema through a Transnational Lens,* eds. Raminder Kaur and Ajay Sinha (Delhi: Sage, 2005), 186–203.

52 The goddess chant, much longer in its full form, loosely translates as: To that Goddess who resides in all beings abiding in the form of power/ To that Goddess who resides in all beings abiding in the form of peace and forbearance/ I bow to her, again and again.

53 "That which was under my control, my heart, has always been yours; how could I prevent my body from being touched when I was helpless and under another person's control?" Sita asks Rama at the penultimate moment

of epic victory when Rama reunites with his wife after the Great War but instead of embracing her, questions her virtue. *Ramayana*, trans. Swami Venkatesananda, in *Bedford Anthology of World Literature: Ancient World, Beginnings-100 CE*, Eds. Paul Davis et al. (New York: Bedford/St. Martin's, 2004), 1420.

54 Sexual harassment in all its many guises including comments, whistles, groping, and any other forms of aggression women face on the street, is included under an innocuous title in South Asia, "eve teasing" further cementing a culture of violence against women. www.womenwelfare.org/Eve%20Teasing.html.

55 Sinha cites Deniz Kandiyoti who is citing Afshaneh Najmabadi in Kandiyoti's, "Identity and its Discontents." For more, see Mrinalina Sinha, "Gender and Nation," in *Feminist Theory Reader: Local and Global Perspectives*, eds. Carole R. McCann and Seung-Kyung Kim (New York: Routledge, 2010), 221.

56 Genesis 32: 25–31.

57 Wendy Doniger, *Gender and Myth in Ancient Greece and India* (Chicago: University of Chicago Press, 1999), 204.

58 "Lives" here is a stand-in for humanity, textuality, wholeness, and most importantly, authorizing agency, which albeit promised through various instances of epistemological histories of the world, still remains very much a work in progress. Rather than end on a note that reifies neoliberal feminisms very much in vogue in the public sphere today, I am insisting on a deconstruction that addresses the piecemeal commodification of women's bodies and a radical feminist gesture at re-constitution of women's lives in the shadow of new imperialisms and late capital.

8 *Silent Waters*

Mapping Silence and Women's Agency in Post-Partition Pakistan[1]

Amrita Ghosh

Film scholar and critic Bhaskar Sarkar in his exhaustive study on film and Partition notes, "[the Partition] brings into sharp focus the problematic of the national as a structuring principle of film historiography: what remains of the category of national cinema, when the national itself is in question?"[2] Sarkar's work is particularly remarkable in its understanding of the construction of nation through cinema, and it argues for cinema as enabling a space for mourning the nation post-Partition, since except for literature and history, Partition has been shrouded with silence in the subcontinent. Since the 1990s, the filmic representations of Partition on both sides of the border have been mostly one-sided in their approach—that is, most filmic representations of Partition have performed as deployment of nationalized narratives[3]. This essay focuses on a relatively recent Partition film titled *Khamosh Pani* (2003) and argues that it subverts patriarchal religio-nationalism and re-envisions the totalized history of the two national constructs through the liminal figure of the female protagonist Ayesha. My discussion of *Khamosh Pani* focuses primarily on two things, the notion of female agency and honor killings during Partition, to explore Ayesha's liminal subjectivity against the twin discourse of patriarchy and a virulent religious fascism. I also focus on the "Recovery Act" of Partition to argue for a nuanced understanding of agency in understanding Ayesha's subjectivity. Ayesha/ Veero's final plunge into the silent waters serves as a moment of agentic revelation that reminds us that she refuses to be pinned into fossilized religious-ethnic identities and transgresses the boundaries of a statist notion of religious identity. The reception of the film was controversial and one may argue that the film presents a monolithic version of Islam under the reign of General Zia ul Haq in Pakistan. This essay shows the women characters' resistance and agency in constructing a varied account of Islam in the film that goes against any notions of an essentialized understanding of the Islam.

Khamosh Pani is a relatively recent independent film, made in 2003, by Pakistani female director Sabiha Sumar. Translated as "Silent Waters," the film is set in 1979, in the small border village of Charkhi, in Pakistan's Punjab province. The film focuses on Ayesha and her son Salim, living in a seemingly harmonious setting in Charkhi far away from the memories of Partition. Through exposition the narrative hints at Ayesha's past and her broken memories from 1947. The film "performs" the rupture of Partition visibly on the screen by breaking the linear narrative of Charkhi in present times, and flashing back to hazy images of a girl running with men in pursuit. Ayesha's voiceover narrates the events of the summer of 1947 as the viewer faces the violence and trauma experienced by Ayesha. Through such cinematic flashbacks fragmenting the linear cinematic repeated narrative, Ayesha tells the story of thousands of abducted women from both sides of the border—"fathers killing daughters"—and brutal violence against women, all in the "name of honor." Ayesha, initially known as Veero by her natal family, refuses the accepted familial practice inscribed by patriarchy to end women's lives. Unlike other women in the community, she refuses to be coerced into ending her life to uphold patriarchal honor. The film leaves the consequence of her defiance of her family orders unclear. She is shown to frantically flee violent men in pursuit of her, but the nature of violence against her, possibly rape, is not entirely clear from the narrative. The cinematic narrative then cuts to the present showing "Veero's" transformed identity as Muslim Ayesha who is happily settled in Charkhi with her son. She lives on her dead husband's pension and by her meager earnings through teaching the Quran to young girls. Haunted by violent memories of the forced deaths and suicides in the well, Ayesha never goes to fetch water from the village well. Allabi, the water-fetcher, and her daughter Shanno come to her house daily to deliver water to her. Ayesha also keeps an old locked trunk in her room and occasionally opens it to view the items inside—they form the remnants of her secret past as a Sikh woman.

Into this almost idyllic setting of Charkhi, Punjab, begins the slow social transformations as the village starts undergoing fundamental Islamization under the dictatorial leadership of General Zia Ul Haq. Ayesha's son, Salim, a sensitive young man who plays the flute in solitude, grows increasingly radical and shuns his love for Zubeida, a village school-girl. Following the establishment of a peace treaty with India, many Sikh pilgrims come to their natal home of Charkhi from pre-partitioned times and visit the Gurdwara that is now located in Pakistani territory.[4] In this group, one of the visitors, Jaswant, keeps searching for his lost sister, Veero, and Salim eventually learns of his mother's "real" identity. The radicalized men, turned to fanaticism under General Zia's rule, doubt Salim's defiled blood as he is rendered to be a "fake" Muslim. Ayesha is once again forced to confront her past and the complicated notion of belonging with her 'real' identity being found and is disowned by the entire village, including her son, after a gradual alienation from the village people, including friends who stop visiting her in their daily lives. Ultimately, Ayesha ends her life by jumping into the same well from which she had fled thirty years ago.

During Partition's massive gendered communal violence, it was expected that women would choose death as the only alternative, rather than facing violence at the hands of men of the other faith. Urvashi Butalia in her study on the gendered violence, *The Other Side of Silence,* especially emphasizes the shocking strain of "sexual savagery" during Partition, and her research estimates that about 75,000 women were raped or abducted "by men of religions different from their own (and indeed sometimes by men of their own religion)."[5] Although that number has been debated elsewhere as an officially catalogued list, the "real" number was stated to be 100,000 or more.[6] Here, the patriarchal code assumes women to be responsible for the status of honor and purity, which is then mapped through their bodies in the delineation of the nation's body politic. Butalia's exhaustive study particularly underscores these kinds of 'honor' killings of women by men in the family to protect them from sexual violence because the honor of the family resided with the women. Unfortunately, sometimes the violence towards women occurred by local men from the same community. Within the history of such gendered violence, the State responded to the displacement and violence against women by constructing the Abducted Persons Act and Restoration of Women Ordinance which was recognized by both governments as a Bill and then made into an Act in 1949. This Indian act categorized the "abducted person" as:

> A male child under the age of 16 years or a female of whatever age who is, or immediately before the 1st day of March 1947, was a Muslim and who, on or after that day and before the 1st of January, 1949, had become separated from his or her family and is found to be living with or under the control of any other individual or family, and in the latter case includes a child born to any such female after the said date.[7]

Jill Didur also stressed that this gave the state complete authority to arrest any woman or persons it thought had been abducted.[8] In the same context, Butalia also points out that any woman who was living with a man of the other religion was "taken by force" by the state and marriages or voluntary religious conversions were not recognized. As she states, "Many things were left unresolved by the fixing of this date in the Act: women who had children from mixed unions after the cut-off date—were they also to be considered abducted women?"[9] Most importantly, the legal apparatus makes the question of women's choices totally irrelevant in the bill. Thus, whether these women wanted to be rehabilitated in their erstwhile families, or remain with the "other" community, or what their silence meant in the larger statist discourse was entirely dismissed or erased.

This history of the Recovery Act is significant in the context of Veero. Throughout the film, the present time in Charkhi is undercut by flashbacks to the past when scores of Sikh women are seen standing on the edge of the village well in Charkhi, waiting to jump into the waters. Veero is urged forcibly by her father to jump and the scene then cuts to show her running away first from her father, going straight into the hands of the abductors. The flashbacks hint at Veero being saved by one of the abductors whom she later marries. Veero's act of defiance by refusing to commit suicide is thus an act of direct transgression. As stated earlier, the Recovery Act reveals the State as being brutally complicit in patriarchal norms and codifying women as objects lacking agency. The assumption that women would be "recovered" to their original families even after they had settled into a life post-abduction affirms the government's final erasure of their agency.[10] Read in the light of the Recovery Act, the film also suggests that Veero's second transgression of the legal discourse was by refusing to return to her natal family and "home." As her brother returns after several years in search of her, Veero refuses to "recognize" him. She pronounces underscores her Muslim identity as Ayesha by her own volition, thereby claiming her agency and subjectivity and refuses to grant responsibility and the role of rescuers to men of such "fallen women."

I want to emphasize Ayesha's nuanced agency against Mahatma Gandhi's epigraph that praises "brave women" of India who are courageous enough to accept death and who have "not sold away their honour."[11] Ayesha clearly violates this notion since she is fleeing from two sets of patriarchal subjugations—one that forces her to death, and the other which subjects her to physical and sexual violence. Shahnaz Khan argues that, during Partition riots, the ritual of women killing themselves in fear of violence or abduction was a practice "that suggest[s] a desire to control their destiny, a desire for agency—a nihilistic agency, one that Veero refuses."[12] Yet, Veero's flight from her family presents a striking rupture in the history of abducted women that necessitates the question whether such women chose death courageously or submitted to the wishes of the men in their family. Men would have perhaps killed them nevertheless, to maintain the assumed "honor" of the family and nation.

In fact, Veero's first dialogues in the film against her father, stating "No, not me," to his request that she jump into the well, is a reclamation of her agency, which challenges the very notion of conflating and mapping national honor and purity through women's bodies. Aparajita De in a different light discusses another "parallel" Partition film, "Pinjar," based on Amrita Pritam's famous novel and argues that "abducted women occupy strategic positionalities... to potentially contest the nature and socio-legal apparatus of the State."[13] This kind of nuanced understanding of agency is important in understanding Ayesha's subjectivity and strategic agency in her refusal to accept death initially as Veero. Even when thirty-three years later, her brother Jaswant comes looking for her across borders from the Indian side of Punjab, to tell her that their dying father wants to see her before his death, Ayesha replies *"he had once tried to kill me for his mental peace"* (translation, italics mine). It is a striking scene, which again reminds us of Ayesha's negotiation of agency, which led her to her first subversion of patriarchal apparatus.

In the penultimate scene that marks the erasure of both Ayesha and Veero, and her religious-ethnic identities, Ayesha reclaims her agency even in her death. In her resistance to patriarchal and statist domination, her final silencing in death then becomes a way to claim her agency. Interestingly, this is strongly reminiscent of Spivak's investigation of "sexed-subaltern agency" through Bhubaneswari Bhaduri's death by hanging herself. Spivak in "Can the Subaltern Speak?" reminds us that "there is no space from which the sexed-subaltern can speak"[14] and in such a state she explains Bhaduri's strategic agency when she chose to commit suicide during her menstrual cycle to "tell" everyone that her suicide should not be categorized as one of death from a case of illicit love affair and pregnancy.

In Veero's case, this retrieval of agency through the final silence marked in her death may be read as a glorification of agency. Shahnaz Khan reads this act of ending her life as "her acceptance of defeat at the hands of communalism and the processes of history."[15] However, what I am suggesting here is a re-envisioning and reevaluation of agency outside of its literal meaning. It is not a simple "action embodying or personifying concrete existence";[16] rather, I have tried to locate a more nuanced understanding of agency within specific socio-economic and cultural contexts. Moreover, if we consider, agency as "free will" then for subaltern women, it becomes more problematic because as Spivak reminds us, subaltern women are "doubly effaced" from acts of speech or barred from even being heard. A viable definition can perhaps be found in understanding agency as "situational," which means that one cannot be an "agent" by completely wrenching himself/herself from the "situational networks" and contexts.[17]

In a telling scene with a close-up shot on Ayesha that highlights her feminist perspective, Ayesha confides in her friend Shabbo, telling her that for a woman "there is nothing to call her own, no land, no family or son" (my translation). Ayesha's declaration in this scene also forebodes her rejection of her dual religious identities as the Muslim Ayesha or the Sikh Veero—moreover, the scene locates her resistance to move beyond the State's imposition of any hegemonic religious-ethnic identities as the only domain of constructing subjectivity for women. Thus, with her refusal to adhere to any land or family, she also subverts the notion of conformity to a re-inscribed religious-national identity and territorial spaces. Ayesha's suicide becomes a way to narrate her final resistance against the statist discourses of belonging and citizenship rather than to accept defeat at the hands of the socio-legal state apparatus.

The ultimate plunge into the silent waters serves as a moment of agentic revelation that reminds us that Ayesha refuses to be pinned into fossilized religious-ethnic identities and transgresses the territorial spaces of the India and Pakistan that only allow women to be molded into a statist notion of religious identity. And, the only way it is possible for this articulation is through her death by plunging into the waters of the well. I read her death by drowning as a final negation of territorial divisions and embracing the water as her final "home."

The film's treatment of Ayesha's character is interesting in the way it emphasizes the dangerous liminal space she posits in which her religious and national identity is always suspect. The brilliant cinematography underscores her liminality as all the fragmented flashbacks portraying haunting scenes of Ayesha standing at the precipice of the well are in sepia tones. Sepia flashbacks are especially used in the film in the unfolding of Veero's past that becomes an interesting undercutting against the use of regular black and white flashback images. These sepia scenes foreground Veero's liminality; they form an in-between space between white and black images and create a chiaroscuro effect. Also, throughout the film's narrative the cinematography consistently presents dark, shadowy moments whenever Ayesha remembers her past. One instance of this is a scene in which Ayesha sits beside a window and opens her wooden trunk that contains remnants of her childhood locked in it. The scene closes up on Ayesha and is shot in a dim light, revealing a kind of chiaroscuro where light from the window seeps into her surrounding darkness. Consistently, this kind of interplay between light and darkness, silence and speech highlights Ayesha's liminality in the film.

Here, I want to turn to the film's use of silence and light to understand Ayesha's agency. Throughout the film, the moments of trauma and the revelation of Ayesha's Sikh identity are located in silence.[18] The images of Ayesha staring at the dark waters of the well interwoven in the film's diegesis have no background sound (in a few instances they present muffled voices and screams, but mostly they are covered in silence). The use of silence in the film, as well its appropriation in the title, does not denote lack of speech or voice; rather, Sumar uses silence to perform a critique of the fascist state that usurps all freedom of its subjects to secure an Islamic nationalist zeal. The unspeakability of Ayesha's horror and trauma manifests itself in silence in the mnemonic encounters with her past. Yet, the film also uses silence as a powerful device to demonstrate that for liminal subjects like Ayesha silence is a means of resistance.

I once again turn to the most haunting scene of the film: the penultimate scene of Ayesha's suicide. The viewer encounters a moment of shocking silence in this scene. The scene, shot in an obscure blue light with Ayesha standing, arms outspread at the edge of the well, produces a stunning shock effect. The wide angle shot of the barren landscape with the well in the distance shrouded in a ghastly blue light transforms the

figure of Ayesha almost into an apparition-like state before she jumps
into the well. This haunting scene works in many layers—first, it reminds us that liminal figures like Ayesha, whose identity is a constant
source of state anxiety, cease to be human subjects. Thus, Ayesha in the
final scene has transformed into an apparition. The purported effect of
shock in this scene also acts as a poignant reminder for viewers that
Ayesha has met with the final silence of death. Hence, the silence located
in the most traumatic moments of the film are not devoid of a voice;
rather, they work as a tool to protest the statist ideology and to shock
the audience into thinking. Such silent scenes also perform to highlight
the patriarchal discourse, as her suicide stems more from her disap-
pointment with the men ordering her around than the state attempting
to repatriate her. Another instance of silence as a performative tool in
the film is the very last scene with Zubeida wearing Ayesha's childhood
locket, given to her by Salim. This scene closes up on Zubeida's face
wearing the locket in silence and indicates her importance in the narrative. It shows that Ayesha's story is not lost in silence—it stays with
women like Zubeida. In a brief voiceover Zubeida finally states, "I think
of Ayesha chachi often; she comes in my dreams" (translation mine).[19]
This scene represents Zubeida as the new face of female agency in the
contemporary Pakistani nation.

Connected to the larger notion of Ayesha's agency in a religio-fascist
state, is my point of the film's revisioning of Islam through the women
characters. Shahnaz Khan charges Sumar with "orientalizing" Islam
for the masses with her stereotypical portrayal of Islam as fundamentalist and backward in the film. Although my take on her argument is
vastly different, I do acknowledge the importance of Khan's discussion
of the socio-historical and international context of 1979 that is crucial
to the understanding of the film. In the post 9/11 severed world, Islam is
generally stereotyped as a backward, fundamentalist faith that harbors
insurgency and *Khamosh Pani*, seen in this light, may appear to churn a
similar orientalist narrative of representing a monolithic view of Islam.
Yet, as traced throughout the film, the radicalizing of Islam is through
a very specific socio-historical context of late seventies South Asia under the regime of General Zia. Far from a stereotypical, normative view
of Islam, the film actually reconstructs Islam through the woman like
Ayesha and Zubeida. Apart from the women, the film also posits constructs of gentler masculinities through the village men who form new
definitions of Islam; as they daily gather around the barber shop discussing the politics on television, they are gradually aware of the intensity of
religious fanaticism shrouding them.

To dwell briefly on the *Sharia Law* under General Zia, Khan elaborates
on the political scenario in 1979 which created a radical Muslim State
where the "Muslim male had the greatest rights.[20] Laws and ordi-
nances were passed that ensured diminished citizenship for minorities

and women."[21] For General Zia, the nation's acute problems since independence, over poverty, inequality, debt, labor strike, etc. could only be solved with the principles of *Nizam-e-Mustapha* (Governance inspired by the Prophet) that ushered in a severe rubric of Islamization of Pakistan.[22] The film shows this change in the village of Charkhi, too, as the two jihadi leaders attempt to sway the masses with reverberating speeches on how the "true voice of the Muslim will save the land" (my translation). In this political climate that already severely marginalizes women to the lowest possible strata in society, "Ayesha's claims to [Pakistani] citizenship are in doubt."[23] Yet, it is the women characters who produce an intense alternative vision for Islam against the radical state-religiosity. For instance, a powerful scene instigates viewers into critically thinking about the state's religious policies: when Salim stops all communications with Zubeida, and reminds her of her religious duties and priority as a Muslim woman, she responds by saying—"*I also pray, but that doesn't mean I don't think*" (translation, italics mine). This becomes a pivotal moment in the film's narrative that compels the audience to not only rethink stereotypical versions of radical Islam, but also re-enforces the notion that Muslim women are capable of thinking and questioning dangerous totalitarian narratives.

Sumar distinctly sets another feminist perspective of re-envisioning Islam in a sequence in which Ayesha teaches Quran to the young girls in her house. She explains to them that God sends any honest, good soul to heaven, it doesn't matter if he/she is a Muslim. The scene cuts to jihadis standing at her door, overhearing Ayesha's Islamic teachings with their faces expressing acute disapproval of her subversion of their Islamic ideas. The scene is another reminder of Ayesha's challenging the normative religious understanding of Islam. In another scene, Ayesha measures Shabbo's daughter for her wedding trousseau and makes the garment's sleeves shorter than expected even though Shabbo cautions her that her husband would not like this—here, Ayesha subverts the religio-patriarchal standards of conforming to the representation of a covered bride. She finds newer spaces and ways to thwart the expected gender and religious codes in a deeply religious society. The film's feminist politics also strikes at the root of religio-heteronormativity through the unique hybridity of Ayesha's faith, her challenging of Salim's understanding of Islam, and her commiseration with Zubeida emphasizes the solidarity of a feminist vision.

Alka Kurian in her essay, "Gender, Home and Displacement in Sabiha Sumar's *Khamosh Pani*" also argues for the film's unique feminist vision and reconstruction of agency in the "powerful expressions of rebellion (through speech, gaze, silence, dismissal and exile) by which women subvert institutionalized structures of control and literally and figuratively refuse their bodies to be used as battlefield for sectarian and communal conflict" (98–99). Kurian's analysis of the film underscores the conflictual notion of belonging of the woman subject in the post-partitioned nation-state of Pakistan where Veero and many like her find themselves caught between patriarchal and statist forces. Significantly, Kurian argues for the film's "feminist aesthetics" that presents an alternative construct of the nation, beyond the limited "women as nation" narrative, in which the nation is narrativized through different gendered ideals, both male and female (104). Both subversive female and subaltern minoritized masculinities perceive a different national imaginary against the fundamentalist postcolonial nation-state. Kurian's emphasis on Veero's hybrid identity is particularly important in her defiance of the larger labels the community forces upon her. Ayesha/Veero's hybrid identity becomes marked in her wearing of the necklace she had as a young Sikh girl, and in her saying the Muslim prayers with faith and in other instances of privately referring to God as "Rab" (Kurian 110). As Kurian highlights, these instances of a fluid hybrid identity provides dynamic spaces of empowerment and transformation against a strict patriarchal and statist control in the Pakistani nation-state.

Silent Waters also uses interesting intercutting shots to highlight the dangerous effects of religious fundamentalism on women. When Salim and his jihadi friends visit the city of Rawalpindi, the scene opens to a mosque where a large number of fundamentalist men are gathered, screaming about recreating the nation of Pakistan in light of the bloody lessons of 1947. The interior shots of the mosque with aggressive men shouting to protect the nation's women intercuts to a panning shot of a little girl learning to ride a bicycle on the street. Ultimately, the scene pans from the girl and the jihadis and freezes on a large banner of General Zia's headshot. The entire sequence critiques the fundamentalist laws prescribed by the State that relegates women to the private spheres of "zenana." It also foreshadows the end of the little girl's freedom to ride a bicycle on the streets. In the same speech, when the jihadi inspires the masses by asking "how to save our nation of Pakistan," he responds by explaining that it is through the women of the land. This scene illustrates the construction of nationalism that shows how "patriarchal nationalist interests situate women as bearers of a reconfigured notion of 'tradition.'"[24] It emphasizes how women become "contested site[s]" for advancing the patriarchal state agenda.[25] These details are necessary to chart how Sumar separates the state-sponsored religio-nationalism from the women's resistance who construct a varied account of Islam in the film that goes against any notions of a monolithic representation of the religion.

Apart from the women's subversion of a religious state, the film also produces a consistent critique of radicalized state-religion through the minor characters of Charkhi. Beyond the scope of my argument, it is significant to note that through characters like the Charkhi barber, Mehboob, and other villagers, Sumar provides the subaltern resistance against the State's growing link with religious jingoism. As the gradual radicalization of the village happens under the General Zia regime, these subaltern people question the socio-economic conditions rather than dwell on Hindu-Muslim animosity. In a vital scene, Mehboob questions one of the extremists, Rasheed—"The question is whose voice General Zia is representing, yours or mine, or naïve people like me from the village?" (translation mine) The Muslim people of Charkhi clearly do not share such a version of extreme radical Islam and most importantly, it also shows a consciousness of resistant ideology that critiques such state-crafted religious indoctrination. In an analysis of media, culture and hegemonic practices, Brian Ott and Robert Mack explain that the hegemonic ideology persists and "never goes away." Using Antonio Gramsci's idea, they state that the "spontaneous consent" of hegemony is sometimes challenged when the "consent fails and socially marginalized gain visibility in a culture... [their] resistant ideologies represent a challenge to that society's overarching hegemonic ideologies."[26] The marginalized villagers of Charki, too, represent such resistant ideologies, asking critical questions against the state policies.

Finally, I want to comment on the film's viewership and distribution in South Asia and its connection to the film's larger significance. In the political context of the subcontinent, it is a very telling situation that Sumar did not find any distributorship or access to Pakistan's film industry, whose reins are mostly controlled by statist censorship. Instead of a South Asian production supporting the film, Sumar's film was ironically produced by a French-German production house. It did receive viewership space and a producer in India, but it was shown only in large metropolitan cities in selective theatres. The "enthusiastic" response that the film garnered in India has been often critiqued by many, including Khan, who argues that India obviously allowed the Pakistani film to be released in its territory because of the negative light in which Pakistan is portrayed in the film. And yet it seems dubious to dismiss the film's enthusiastic response by critics and people in India by relegating it to the politics of South Asia: this is because, *Khamosh Pani* is still not a well-known film in the mainstream Indian population. Most people do not even know the name of the film and it was "enjoyed" by an alternative audience who also show support for the parallel art house productions in India. The larger problem is also to demote the film's substantial critique of fundamentalist politics as a form of xenophobic appreciation in India, which completely negates the film's subversion of the hegemonic ideologies.

One wonders if the critics of the film's reception also credit the film's overall international response based on the production of a monolithic version of Islam, which already is a problematic idea, as explained earlier. Instead of the portrayal of radical Islam, I would insist that the biggest critical moment of the film is the haunting image of Ayesha jumping into the well, followed by the last scene showing Zubeida as a single woman working and living alone in Rawalpindi. She walks alone assertively on the streets of the city, signaling hope for an alternative future for women with a nuanced negotiation of agency by them.

Film theorists Fernando Solanas and Octavio Gettino coin the term "cinema of subversion" to define films that carry with them "an impulse to emancipation" against statist reality (Octavio et al. 267). In this light, *Khamosh Pani* produces a significant cinematic intervention that emerges as a "cinema of subversion" against the majoritarian twenty-first-century divisive politics of South Asia. The women figures enact subversive subjects existing within the in-between spaces and margins of the national construct, who tell a subversive tale of rewriting the nation-state. Characters like Veero and especially Zubeida, who forms the new face of feminist politics in South Asia, create spaces to resist patriarchal-statist control over women's agency and bodies in the Indo-Pakistani context. Sumar's focus on subversive women ultimately challenges the order of the polis, which dismantles the nationalist project, enabling newer spaces of choice and belonging. It may be argued that I run the risk of totalizing this hybrid space in its potential to re-envision the nation-state and the concept of belonging. How 'real' is such a gendered third space in its subversion of the state since it may be said this hybrid space is also an essentialized concept? Yet, it is important that we do not bar such political gestures, even small, from getting obliterated. The subversive subjects discussed in the film challenge statist ideologies to better understand questions about inheritance and official citizenship in postcolonial South Asia. Thus, *Khamosh Pani* creates subversive possibilities that raises radical questions on the gendered national subject, and who can become "valid" citizens of post-partitioned India and Pakistan within the frame of a patriarchal hegemony.

Notes

1 This essay is a part of Ghosh's doctoral dissertation, "Towards Alternate Imaginaries: Rethinking the Nation-State in Partition Texts" and it was also an invited talk at the University of Washington, Seattle's Continuing Conversations on Gender Speaker Series, on April 26, 2013.

2 Bhaskar Sarkar, *Mourning the Nation: Indian Cinema in the Wake of Partition* (Durham, NC: Duke University Press, 2009), 3.

3 This is not to suggest that there have been no other radical cinema on Partition beyond the selected film here. Ritwik Ghatak's famous Partition films, his trilogy on the Partition, are highly critically acclaimed films that present the plight of Bengali refugees in the aftermath of Partition. M.S. Sathyu's *Garam Hawa (Hot Winds)* is another example of cinema of resistance which revolves around the question of Muslim belonging in post-Partition India. My selection of *Khamosh Pani* is based on the "othered" figure within the national construct whose belonging in both nations is complicated because of her inhabiting liminal spaces.

4 Gurudwara is a place of worship and prayer for Sikh people. Post-Partition places of worship were often found across the borders in the newly carved territory, and people of the opposite religious sect found it difficult to cross the border and visit them.

5 Urvashi Butalia, *The Other Side of Silence: Voices from the Partition of India* (Durham, NC: Duke University Press, 2000), 3.

6 Khosla, quoted in Veena Das, *Life and Words: Violence and the Descent into the Ordinary* (Berkeley: University of California Press, 2007), 20.

7 Jill Didur, *Unsettling Partition: Literature, Gender, Memory* (Toronto: University of Toronto Press, 2006), 37.

8 Didur, *Unsettling Partition*, 37.

9 Urvashi Butalia, *Other Side of Silence*, 115.

10 Urvashi Butalia also reveals that in most cases the recovered women were unaccepted by their families, and eventually a large group of women formed the category of "fallen women" who resided in camps organized by women's welfare organizations.

11 Mohandas K. Gandhi, "Speech at a Prayer Meeting," *Collected Works of Mahatma Gandhi* (Delhi: Publications Division, Ministry of Information and Broadcasting, Government of India, 1958–1994), 96: 388–389. Gandhi's epigraph urges Hindu men to kill the women in their families, which in turn serves the glory of the nation.

12 Shahnaz Khan, "Floating on Silent Waters: Religion, Nationalism and Dislocated Women in Khamosh Pani," *Meridians: Journal of Feminism, Race, Transnationalism* 9, no. 2 (2009): 138.

13 Aparajita De, "The Caged Bird Sings: The Politics of Subaltern Agency in Pinjar," (conference paper, South Asian Literary Association (SALA) Annual Conference, Philadelphia, December 2009).

14 Chakravorty Gayatri Spivak, "Can the Subaltern Speak?," in *Colonial Discourse and Postcolonial Theory*, ed. Patrick Williams and Laura Chrisman (New York: Columbia University Press, 1994), 103.

15 Khan, "Floating on Silent Waters," 141.

16 Definition of *Agency* from Oxford English Dictionary, Second Edition.

17 Guy Poitevin, *The Voice and the Will: Subaltern Agency, Forms and Motives* (New Delhi: Manohar, 2002), 54. Poitevin explains agency as "situational" and contextualizes the concept. For him, agency needs to be traced through situational networks and cannot be understood as a free term devoid of context.

18 I am grateful to Amit Rahul Baishya for pointing out the use of silence in the film.

19 *Chachi* is a Hindi/Urdu word for aunt.

20 The *Sharia Law* may be different under different approaches to Islam, but it usually entails a very fundamentalist and extremist view of Islam in every sphere of culture, politics, women's role, sexuality, and violated human rights in society.

21 Khan, "Floating on Silent Waters," 134.

22 Khan, "Floating on Silent Waters," 135. Shahnaz Khan traces this encroachment of religious fascism as every sphere of Pakistani society including education transformed to incorporate a heavy influx of radical Islamic teachings. Khan further points out that this process of radical Islamization in Pakistan also enabled the Afghani jihad, which had a significant role to play in the cold war between the US and the Soviet Union.

23 Khan, "Floating on Silent Waters," 135.

24 Didur, *Unsettling Partition*, 23.

25 Sangeeta Ray, *Engendering India: Woman and Nation in Colonial and Postcolonial Narratives* (Durham, NC: Duke University Press, 2000), 8.
26 Brian L. Ott and Robert L. Mack, *Critical Media Studies: An Introduction* (Oxford: Wiley-Blackwell Publishers, 2010), 131–32.

Bibliography

Butalia, Urvashi. *The Other Side of Silence: Voices from the Partition of India.* Durham, NC: Duke U P, 2000.

Das, Veena. *Life and Words: Violence and the Descent into the Ordinary.* Berkeley: U of California P, 2007.

De, Aparajita. "The Caged Bird Sings: The Politics of Subaltern Agency in *Pinjar*." Conference paper, South Asian Literary Association (SALA) Annual Conference, Philadelphia, December 2009.

Didur, Jill. *Unsettling Partition: Literature, Gender, Memory.* Toronto, ON: U of Toronto P, 2006.

Gandhi, Mohandas K. "Speech at a Prayer Meeting." *Collected Works of Mahatma Gandhi,* Vol. 96, 388–89. Delhi: Publications Division, Ministry of Information and Broadcasting, Government of India, 1958–1994.

Khan, Shahnaz. "Floating on Silent Waters: Religion, Nationalism and Dislocated Women in Khamosh Pani." *Meridians: Journal of Feminism, Race, Transnationalism* 9.2 (2009): 130–52.

Kurian, Alka. "Gender, Home, and Displacement in Sabiha Sumar's *Khamosh Pani*" *Narratives of Gendered Dissent in South Asian Cinemas,* New York: Routledge, 2012. 98–122.

Ott, Brian L., and Mack, Robert L. *Critical Media Studies: An Introduction.* Oxford: Wiley-Blackwell Publishers, 2010.

Poitevin, Guy. *The Voice and the Will: Subaltern Agency, Forms and Motives.* New Delhi: Manohar, 2002.

Ray, Sangeeta. *Engendering India: Woman and Nation in Colonial and Postcolonial Narratives.* Durham, NC: Duke U P, 2000.

Sarkar, Bhaskar. *Mourning the Nation: Indian Cinema in the Wake of Partition.* Durham, NC: Duke U P, 2009.

Silent Waters. Directed by Sabiha Sumar, featuring Paromita Vohra, Kiron Kher and Aamir Ali Malik. Vidhi Films with Unlimited, Arte and Flying Moon FilmProduktion, 2004. Film.

Solanas, Fernando, and Gettino Octavio. "Towards a Third Cinema." *In Film and Theory: An Anthology.* Eds. Stam Robert and Toby Miller. Malden, MA: Blackwell, 2000. 265–86.

Spivak, Chakravorty Gayatri. "Can the Subaltern Speak?" *Colonial Discourse and Postcolonial Theory.* Eds. Patrick Williams and Laura Chrisman. New York: Columbia U P, 1994. 68–74.

9 Gender, War, and Resistance
Documentary Cinemas of Kashmir, Sri Lanka, and Nepal

Alka Kurian

In areas ridden by political conflict, women's narratives tend to mostly go un-reported. Instead, what gets highlighted is their victimization. However, an increasing number of women use art as a tool to resist this narrative of systemic and interlocking structures of oppression. In this chapter, I attempt to surface the political embeddedness in women's work in art that is implicitly defiant and contestatory so as to unravel moments of "resistance in subaltern historiography" (Sunder Rajan: 3) that are articulated against statist, militaristic, political, legal, and social injustices in South Asia. I see this as a bold gendered engagement with postcolonial nation states marked by forces of new orientalistic regressive cultures, neoliberalism, indigenism, tribal dispossession, and anti-Enlightenment rhetoric at a time of emergent and revitalized nationalisms. I see women's creative work as what Boyce-Davis refers to as "uprising textualities" that has the power to decolonize received knowledge and statist authority (108) and move us "from postcoloniality and the state of 'postness' or afterness' ... into a more radical consciousness of our creativity" (112). To substantiate my argument, I examine a range of documentary films that form part of women's resistance movement. Set in Kashmir, Sri Lanka, and Nepal, three of South Asia's most troubled spots, these films explore the gendered fallout of a brutal state-led militarized repression. An exploration of these films will be accompanied by an investigation of the following set of interrogations. In what way do these films constitute a political force? How do they decolonize received knowledge and subvert oppression? How does raising awareness, sharing hope, and coping with trauma help reconstitute identities? Are these films undergirded by a genuine humanitarian appeal or are these simply rescue narratives of humanity at risk? Given the material exigencies of filmmakers, would these films always be considered progressive and transformative?

Kashmir

In August 1947, as the Indian subcontinent gained independence from Britain, it was also divided into India and Pakistan along religious lines:

the Muslim majority areas went to Pakistan and the rest remained in India. However, Raja Hari Singh, the Hindu ruler of the Muslim-dominated Kashmir, chose to side with India and violently suppressed Kashmiri people's demand that they be allowed to independently choose India or Pakistan as their home. Hari Singh formally acceded to India in October 1947 when the latter helped him pushback an attack on Kashmir by a Pakistan-led group of tribal militias. The signing of the "Instrument of Accession" that India offered as a condition for its support to Singh, led to a total war between the two newly independent states. The United Nations helped bring the conflict to an end and suggested that the Kashmiris be allowed to decide their future by means of a referendum. India went back and forth on its promise of the referendum, and tried to appease the Kashmiris by giving them the special status of internal autonomy through promulgating the Article 370 of the country's Constitution. This, in addition to a series of rigged elections in the state, tested the patience of the Kashmiris, especially its youth, whose peaceful resistance eventually turned into a violent armed struggle for self-determination, which India responded to by a brutal military repression.

Pakistan and India consider Kashmir as an unalienable part of their territories and have engaged in three full-scale wars over the region. The struggle over ownership of Kashmir is not simply, however, about the Hindu-Muslim nationalism (Kaul 2010–11). While India projects Kashmir (which is part of the Himalayan range) as a crucial geopolitical buffer for its safety against potential imperialistic incursions, it regards Kashmiris as alien, untrustworthy, and inherently tainted people (Kaul 44). Further, it has never bothered to consult the Kashmiris in any of the decisions about the future of their state, dismissing them as "irritants / separatists /traitors / terrorists" (Kaul 49). The Indian state denies them their fundamental human rights and freedom, and defines their movement for national self-determination as anti-national and even criminal. Today, with 750,000 troops of the Indian army stationed in the region, Kashmir is the world's most militarized zone. The five-decade-long conflict in the region has left nearly 100,000 people dead, more than 350,000 people internally-displaced, countless women raped, and 8,000 people involuntarily disappeared.

Memory as a Political Tool

Iffat Fatima is a prolific Kashmiri feminist artist who uses the medium of film to illuminate the issues of human rights abuse, social justice, and gender. Her films are a personal "act of active citizenship," (Jayashankar and Monteriro 2016: 98) that foregrounds women's lived experiences over masculinist-centric grand narratives on militarization, communalism, insurgency, and war across regional, national, and international borders. Many of her films, including *Lanka—The Other Side of War and Peace*; *In the Realm of the Visual*; and *Boojh Sakey to Boojhi*, have received critical appreciation. Her documentary film *Khoon Diy Baarav* (*Blood Leaves its Trail*) (2015) offers a powerful representation of the blight of enforced disappearances in Kashmir, which is the subject of our analysis here. *Khoon Diy Baarav* explores the daily struggles and challenges suffered by the families of the disappeared, and uses their recall and memory in the film as a means of resistance. The film is a result of nine years (Joshi 2016) of extensive travel, research, and conversations with people into the interiors of the region.

Most of the scholarship on Kashmir tends to focus on the political and territorial conflict between Pakistan and India keeping a muffled silence on the ways in which people experience this conflict in their day-to-day lives, and on the lived reality of the loss and grief that results from this conflict. This section attempts to tackle the physical and emotional fallout of the conflict in Kashmir represented as a site of pain, trauma, and resistance to brutal state repression. At the core of its examination is an exploration of the effects of enforced disappearances carried out by members of the Indian Security forces who have official impunity for their actions under the protection of the infamous 1990 Armed Forces Special Powers Act (AFSPA). The disappeared are abducted against their will, subjected to torture, threatened with death or killed, and their whereabouts or fate are never disclosed to their families. Disappearances scar the lives of survivors and their families, especially women, given that most of the disappeared are usually men. Despite India being a signatory to the International Convention for the Protection of All Persons from Enforced disappearances, protected by AFSPA, the perpetrators of this crime are not held to account in Kashmir.

As Fatima follows the lives of the female relatives of the disappeared, she turns their personal testimonials into political articulations, their individual lives into part of a collective. Their shared memory becomes an ultimate form of resistance, and an act of "defiance against powerful instruments of the state that try to erase their individuality" (Lamakaran 2015). The excess of grief and despair become vehicles to strengthen their recall: the time and place of the abduction, the emotional reactions of those that were left behind, and the shared grieving of their loss. Drawing on Nancy C M Hartsock's contention that feminism is a "mode of analysis, a method of approaching life and politics, rather than a set of political conclusions about the oppression of women" (cited in Khan 21), I locate female family members of the disappeared within a feminist standpoint from where they use their experience of oppression to critically understand the world, think through what strategies to work around, and challenge their oppression.

The film becomes "a testimony, a consequence of [the filmmaker] bearing witness," of the gross violation of human rights in a brutalized Kashmir, a valley of death in the Himalayas, that is far from the desirable tourist destination that it used to be. Using Parveena Ahangar's loss as a point of departure, Fatima accompanies her across Kashmir to unravel the anguish of the families of the disappeared, tracing their deeply networked organization that was launched at Srinagar's Batamaloo Sahib Shrine in early 1990s. After losing her son to enforced disappearance in 1987, Ahangar co-founded the Association of the Parents of Disappeared Persons (APDP) in 1994 to provide a collective space of grieving for the families of the disappeared. Its objective is to seek justice and obtain information on the whereabouts of the missing people. Its members document involuntary and enforced disappearances and organize campaigns to put an end to this practice at national and international platforms. Since its inception, families of the disappeared have followed APDP's public protest in Srinagar to commemorate the lives of the disappeared and demand that the state provides information about their whereabouts.

For twenty years, Ahangar has been looking for her disappeared son, desperate to see him, or at least his dead body so she can have a closure. She has made her individual struggle into a collective one by connecting with the families of the disappeared, inspiring them to join protests, giving speeches, participating in demonstrations and in sit-ins, disparaging the army's occupation of Kashmir, accusing it of being above the rule of law, and urging government officials in Delhi to sanction prosecution. "Where did they disappear," she asks. "Has the sky devoured them or has the earth swallowed them? Have they become ether?" Clearly, Ahangar's activism stems from an unambiguously "Muslim feminist standpoint" (Khan 21) precisely because of her focus on human rights that are imperiled in a militarized, misogynistic, Islamophobic, and nationalist state. As a filmmaker, by having Muslim Kashmiri women take ownership of their stories and using "cinema as an activist tool," Fatima documents and interrogates the specific challenges of human rights issues in a society that they live in.

Fatima's camera pans across the lake, going past spiral shaped razor wire. This is normal in Kashmir: a spectacular and ubiquitous presence of the army and its apparatus of control and death that visiblizes Kashmir's colonization and facilitates disappearances. The narrative moves on to Halima Begum in Handwara: she misses her militant husband who went across the border in 1989 for training to mark his resistance to Kashmir's occupation by the Indian military. She refuses to testify against the militants, despite being bribed by the army with the potential of a job and money. From the fields nearby, one can hear her friends sing songs, beckoning the Mujahidins to come down from the mountains and "burst upon them bullet spray." As a mother of slain sons, Kupwara district's[1] Jana Begum's life is steeped in memory. Festive wedding songs intersect with eerie evocations from women who implore imprisoned heroes to bring them newspapers so that they can sing their truth. As Hajra Begum looks at her son working in the field, she recounts his experience of torture: he was blindfolded by the Indian army, stripped naked, drenched in water, given electric shocks, and returned after eleven days, leaving him practically blind. After losing four sons, this old widow from Bandipore suffers from survivors' guilt, and is harassed by the army as the Mujahids used to come to her house.

Subhan Tantray from Pattan recalls how safe he felt in the company of the battas (Hindus) who used to live near his house. As doctors and engineers, the Battas were good neighbors, he says. They have now fled Kashmir for their safety, leaving behind homes that the army has converted into detention camps, and land, which is now used for burying unidentified bodies. Accidentally coming across a shallow grave, Tantray pulls out the body of a young boy who, he was told, had run away along with his son. The narrative takes us to a run-down former army base in Pattan where a counter-insurgency militia, called Ikhwan, used to be trained by the Indian army to abduct, torture, rape, or disappear people. As the "eyes and ears" of the army, the Ikhwan are celebrated by the Indian army that gives them jobs and honors them with awards for their exemplary social service. Indian troops too are regularly awarded medals, promotions, and money for killing Kashmiri "terrorists" in encounters.

The camera pans over to mass graves with unidentified bodies where people recognize their children through birth marks, clothes, and shoes.[2] Mass graves constitute particularly distressing sites for offering a "contiguous display of death," the state's arrogance in killing with impunity, and its flaunting of its power to those who are forced to witness this drama of terror. On the insistence of family members, when some of the bodies are exhumed for DNA testing, violence erupts in the valley, thousands of men and women, risking gun fire, chant slogans for freedom, pelt stones at the army, and beat their vans with sticks. A group of women push and shove at the army, screaming at them. The army backs off, for they don't know to deal with women. As a procession of army trucks and vans leaves, women and men, young and old, jeer and clap. As many as 800,000 people gather in Eidgah, chanting slogans of *Azaadi*. In 2012, nearly 130 unarmed protesters are killed, most of them teenagers.

The film comes full circle with Ahangar, who warns that it was time that the rule of law was applied to account for the disappearance of nearly 10,000 men in Kashmir. The blood of the dead was leaving a trail, says Ahangar, Kashmir was frothing at the killings, and angry young Kashmiris were risking their lives by throwing themselves in a situation that had become uncontrollable. How many more lives must be lost? Going beyond active recall of violence, within these final dregs of the film's diegesis is a feminist challenge to the militaristic solution to a political problem that has destroyed the lives, dreams, and hopes of five generations of people in the Kashmir valley. Clearly, the film marks the purpose of consciousness-raising, promoting social change through women's empowerment.

The spotlight on the crimes perpetrated by the Indian army (the torture of abducted men at the detention centers, the terror unleashed by the Ikhwans, and the young graffiti artist being asked to wipe clean the wall with his tongue) and the highlighting of slogans of freedom (Go India, Drub India, and Scrub India) outline the price of Kashmiri dissidence. At the film's screening at IIT Delhi, some of the students protested, calling the film anti-national. And yet, undeterred, the filmmaker perseveres. *Khoon Diy Baarav* surfaces the importance of documenting people's testimonies before death takes over. The memory of loss, for Fatima, strengthens the resolve of victims and their families, and propels them into seeking redressal through political action. As she claims,

> Memory is a political act on their part, and they live and relive every moment. It hasn't ended and is continuing, and they have no choice but to remember. These details are internalized into their being, so there is no question of forgetting—these people are not dead for them but alive ... Theirs is a very active hope and it is a political act on their part.
>
> (Ramnath 2015)

While the disappearances peaked in the early stages of the militant movement in 1990s and early 2000s, if there is no closure, the wounds will not heal. Each family's loss is suffered both individually and collectively. Given the sheer scale of loss, the personal becomes political and the political personal.

Sri Lanka

Ethnic tensions between Sinhalese majority Buddhist and Tamil Minority Hindu communities in Sri Lanka can be traced back to the pre-colonial times and the country's movement for self-determination. The country was under colonial rule for nearly 450 years. First by the Portuguese, then the Dutch, and finally the British, who ruled the country right until 1948 before granting it independence. The British colonizers' policies of divide and rule favored the Tamil minority, in particular, in the British-style educational institutes in the Northern provinces, which led to the Tamils dominating universities and government-sector jobs. The colonizer-led mutual suspicion between Tamil and Sinhalese ethnic groups became exacerbated in the postcolonial period: the Sinhalese leadership that was at the forefront of the anti-colonial resistance movement attempted to fashion the newly independent country as a

Sinhalese nation-state. The pre-independence ethnic tensions came out into the open in the postcolonial Sri Lanka and reached their epitome in the 1960s as a result of youth unemployment and crushing poverty. The rising ethnic tension that resulted soon changed into mob violence and the Sinhala-led state intervention only ended up exacerbating the situation. Under newly imposed colonization schemes, large Tamil areas were taken away for Sinhala Buddhist settlers, referring to their land as sacred. The 1956 Official Language Act mandated Sinhalese, spoken by 70% of the country's majority Sinhalese population, as the official language. The resulting loss of linguistic rights and alienation from the country's educational and professional spaces can be well imagined. This was followed by state-led anti-Tamil pogroms in 1956, 1958, 1977, 1981, and 1983. In what's notoriously referred to as the Black July pogrom, nearly three thousand Tamil civilian men, women, and children were killed. In response to their persecution, thousands of Tamil youth joined armed resistance groups, seeking justice and independence for their minority group.

The Sinhalese Government's ethnocentric practices put in place in the aftermath of national independence therefore laid the basis of Tamil persecution, resulting in the movement for Tamil separatism. Pro-Sinhalese policies were implemented across the institutional structure of postcolonial Sri Lanka: schools, bureaucracy, the parliament, and the judiciary. The Sinhalese-politicians-led 'ethnic-outbidding' ended up marginalizing Tamil leaders and politicizing Tamil youth, who began allying themselves with groups and organizations—Liberation Tigers of Tamil Eelam (LTTE) being the most militant of these—seeking secession from the Sinhalese majority State. At the height of its power, the LTTE had developed its own highly sophisticated army, navy, and air force. Its supporters within the diaspora annually raised thousands of dollars' worth of funds to meet its running costs, and the organization controlled close to a quarter of the country's land mass, where it had already introduced a state-building project. The LTTE was internationally recognized as the most dangerous, ruthless, and efficient paramilitary organization that operated from 1987–2009. Several Sri Lankan Buddhist nationalists have tried to explain away the LTTE phenomenon as a simple terrorist problem, which prompted the State to engage in counter-terrorism activities—Sri Lanka's own 'war on terror'. Such claims, argues DeVotta (2009b), only conceal the majoritarian Sinhalese State's anti-Tamil ethnocentric practices that were at the root of the Tamil separatist movement, dehistoricize ethnic grievances of the Tamil minorities, and disregard the need for finding a political solution by means of devolution of power in the country.

Central to my thesis in this section of the chapter is an exploration of the claim about the transformative potential of revolutionary violence for the subaltern and, especially for women, located in postcolonial, deeply hierarchical, and gendered societies. By setting my argument against the civil war in Sri Lanka (1983–2009), I investigate the extent to which Tamil women's politics of armed resistance directed by the militarized minority group, the Liberation Tigers of Tamil Eelam, especially in its ideology of violence, led to their empowerment and coming into being of their agency. I will put forth my arguments by investigating the way women's anxieties around personal and communal victimization as members of a minority community, their sense of personal agency and its realization through internalizing a politics of violence, and their manipulation by heteronormativity are represented in Sri Lankan cinematic texts. I will compare my analysis of Beate Arnestad's documentary film *My Daughter the Terrorist* (2007) with Santosh Sivan's parallel cinematic narrative *The Terrorist* (1998).

Violence and Agency

Both films intertwine a multiplicity of characters and stories with the view to foreground a diverse range of subjectivities and social networks that intersect a plethora of classed, sexed, ethnic, and caste identities. The significance of these narratives inheres in being located in and influenced by key moments of the history of minority persecution and their suppression led by the neo-colonial state in various geopolitical locations in Sri Lanka. *My Daughter the Terrorist*, set in the 1990s Sri Lanka, gives a unique insight into the lives and points of view of two female suicide bombers living in the LTTE camps. *The Terrorist* underlines the coming into being of the agency and resistance of a potential Tamil suicide bomber being prepared for her mission in Sri Lanka. Through my analysis, I hope to come to the following conclusions: *My Daughter the Terrorist* is an Orientalist representation of the female suicide bombers due to their agency being located in personal and not political reasons, their resistance coming into being through internalizing a masculinist vocabulary of violence, aggression, obedience, and arrogance; their blind faith in the LTTE and its leadership; their inability to think beyond immediate gratification that comes with the power of the gun; their failure to see through the patriarchal, imperialistic nature of the LTTE; and finally their unwillingness to reflect on the instrumentalization of their (female) bodies. The film narrates the story of two LTTE female suicide bombers—Puhalchudar and Darshika. The narrative is offered in the form of a series of interviews where the two women give candid explanations of their decision to join militarized revolution. The third person in the film is Darshika's mother Antonia, who articulates her sorrow and grief at the choices made by her daughter who had run away from home at age twelve. Arnestad offers the starkness of the choices available to ordinary Tamil girls in a war-torn country, highlighting, however, the injustice of the situation that has left her a widow and perhaps will snatch away her daughter too.

The Terrorist, on the other hand, offers a nuanced exploration of the female suicide bomber. Santosh Sivan's film explores the life of a nineteen-year-old Tamil female militant, Malli, who is secretively training to be suicide bomber. A day before the assassination, however, she discovers that she is pregnant, a surprise that transforms her future course of action, as she is caught in a quandary between commitment to her cause, the love for her unborn child, and the support of the elderly couple in whose house she has been living. In the end, after an agonizing period of indecision, Malli chooses life over death and abandons her suicide mission. After initially internalizing the logic of 'necropolitics', Malli is shown to undergo a transformation as she begins to critically reflect on the meaning of her living body and the sanctity of life; the disregard for this body within the logic of the LTTE; the colonization by the LTTE of her mind and body; alternative modes of resistance to her persecution as a minority Tamil; her subversion of the violent mode of resistance through more humane, tender, and pacifist methods; and the significance of motherhood as a means of resistance.

The phenomenon of the female suicide bomber in the Sri Lankan context has posed ethical questions about the complex intersections between militarism, patriarchy, violence, and gender. The body of the so-called war machine is re-inscribed with meanings of subjectivity, choice, feminist agency, the discourse of martyrdom, and ideological commitment, which make it difficult to talk about it, as discussions get divided into opposing camps: those that completely sympathize with the suicide bombers' politics of annihilation for the benefit of the wider society and those that express their disgust at the ruthlessness of the inhuman killing machines, turning it into a moral discourse where one type of violence is justified over another form that gets pathologized. By locating herself outside the 'legitimate' violence of the dominant order, the suicide bomber turns herself into a statement underlining a powerful indictment of a history of suffering, marginalization, persecution, and erasure.

The documentary *My Daughter the Terrorist* claims to be the first film to foreground the choices made by two female LTTE terrorists—Darshika and Puhalchudar—articulated from their own point of view. It offers angst-ridden accounts of the personal, familial, and communal pathos that resulted from the civil war in their lives. After the loss of her father in an aerial bombing, Darshika's family was brutalized at the hands of the Sri Lankan army. Due to heavy artillery shelling of her neighborhood, as Puhalchudar was forced to flee to a safer area, she almost got separated from her family but for the timely help of the LTTE militants. While the ruthlessness of the anti-Tamil Sinhalese army, the loss of family members and home, and the overall volatility of life resulted in an extreme form of hurt and humiliation for Darshika and Puhalchudar, what emerges from their response to it all is a sense of fearlessness and non-submissiveness rooted in an essential pride of their gendered Tamil identity. Their transitioning across to armed rebellion can be seen as a way to restoring their agency and dignity, far more important than life itself, performed through conquering their fear for which they are prepared to do anything, including sacrificing their bodies. Violence for them became a Fanonian "cleansing force" (White 2007: 259) which would free them from their sense of secondariness, anguish, and inaction. Within the larger meta-narrative of the day-to-day life led by Darshika and Puhalchudar, the film offers a brief account of how the postcolonial Sri Lankan state-led persecution of the Tamil minority people was the reason why women like them had agreed to go on suicide missions. They are confident about the correctness of their choice, as working for the LTTE makes them fearless and repairs their damaged egos. Like Malli, dressed in army fatigues and leather shoes, they go about their business on motor vehicles, commanding respect within and outside the LTTE camps. Interjected in the film's powerful images of women engaged in rigorous military training sessions, undergoing strenuous physical exercise regimes, offering clinical justifications for the unimaginable scale of destruction (of human beings, buildings), are quieter intimate insights into their tender expression of care and love for each other, for communities, for families, and mothers and daughters. In each other, they have found life-long friends and confidants with whom they share intimate moments within a feminine homo-social space or train together in a cold-blooded warfare. By choosing the suicidal mission, they have decided to become a "mobile war machine, timing [their] final blow-up moment, the hidden female agency lurking in the body politics … [choosing] that moment of collective annihilation—the [woman's] body devouring and engulfing the nation" (M. De Silva 2007: 142).

In his "Appointment with Rajiv Gandhi" (Cited in De Mel 2009: 203), a fictional portrayal of the female suicide bomber Dhanu, the Sri Lankan author Charles Sarvan outlines the last day of her life as she prepares for the daunting mission of assassinating the Indian Prime Minister Rajiv Gandhi. Sarvan envisions the central character going over the details of the murderous plan: she would wear the plastic explosives around her waist and once inside the Sriperumbudur stadium, at the appointed time, she would not hesitate to press the trigger, going up in flames, her body exploding into smithereens, taking the Prime Minister with her. On this last day of her life, Dhanu is in a dream-like frame of mind, where she imagines herself as a bride, preparing for her wedding. Unlike her friends and female members of her family, male strangers will decorate her with metal and plastic wires instead of silk and flowers, rendering her body non-virginal even before her wedding.

Just like Dhanu, dressed in bridal finery, Malli too accompanies herself all the way to her cremation. Dissimilar to other women who, with their disturbing and hysterical wailing and crying defile the sanctity of the cremation ground and the last rites, she is in control of her mind and body. Unashamedly, she allows herself to be photographed, unveiling herself—the Tamil woman—for the world to see her moments before she would martyr herself. "On this morning of marriage and death," (Sarvan cited in De Mel 2001: 204) she is not afraid of the choices she has made or the moral rectitude of her actions. The question that comes to the forefront here is the extent to which the ruthless terrorist Malli views her act as agentic. To a certain level, the multiple levels of her subversions could be seen to shape her agency: she chooses her own 'bridegroom' (rather than having one chosen for her); she experiences the thrill of sexual indiscretion through the gaze and touch of unknown men, disregarding societal imposition of feminine prudery; she seeks pleasure in a public display of her photographs; and (like Dhanu) she delights in being the rare Hindu woman who would walk all the way to the cremation ground. And yet, if subverting patriarchal restrictions in a tradition-bound culture signals Malli's identity formation, the troubling question that remains unanswered deals with the price of liberation, as it only comes through the decimation of the self.

The complicated nature of what impels suicide bombers to take a radical ideological position and action means that it is not enough to interpret their choice as a simple "desire to self-destruct and a disinterest in living" (Hage, cited in Dillon 2009: 210). The normative understanding of a suicide bomber as a depressed individual is not credible enough either, given that several of them are attracted to the mission due to a longing for an enhanced self-esteem that results from the militant organization's glorification of the violent self-destruction performed by the suicide bomber. The LTTE, for example, observed an annual Black Tiger Day to commemorate the lives of Tamil Tigers who martyred themselves to the cause of Tamil nationalism and bestowed great stature to the families of the martyred girls (Keairns 2002, cited in Wessells 2005). In their celebration of the suicide bombers' families lay an unsaid LTTE promise of monetary reward for them, which too makes a career in suicidal militancy attractive for young Tamils. Moreover, scholars have attempted to unearth a 'geneology of martyrdom' in Sri Lanka through an exploration of the Sangam literature and poetry that celebrates a cult of sacrifice of the self (De Mel 2004: 77). While some members of the LTTE (especially Prabhakaran) saw its ideology of annihilation as rooted in ancient Tamil culture, one must not undermine the socio-political and material reality that impelled young Tamilians to vie with each other to be chosen as Black Tigers. Further, Tamil popular culture inspired by militarism also valorized and glorified the suicide bomber and their families. The Sinhalese oft-repeated question "What is it that Tamils have which we don't that they will die for their cause while a Sinhalaya will run a mile?" (De Mel 2004: 77) smacks of disingenuity and unwillingness to recognize their complicity in the Tamil minority persecution. This incomprehension and wonderment expressed by the Sinhala majority represents their disregard for arriving at a political settlement which further amplifies the Tamil struggle for a meaningful life marked by equal opportunity in education and in the professional sphere. Niloufer De Mel speculates whether there is a connection between this manifestation of extraordinary Tamil militancy and competitiveness, given the collective Tamil pride based on competitive militancy that used previously to be rooted in educational excellence (2004: 78).

War foregrounds normative gender categories of men as fighters and aggressors and women and children as victims of violence and in need of protection. The media and popular culture focus in particular on sexual brutalization of women that is used by the occupying enemy as a strategy of war leading to an erasure of ethnic purity, humiliation of men forced into situations of occupation and submission, and an overall sense of their emasculation due to their inability to protect their women and children.

However, when women fight alongside men, they end up chipping away at traditional gender stereotypes and foreground instead their physical strength, agency, and the violent side of their identity. The media, particularly in the West, represent such women as pathologically abnormal, unfeminine, unkind, ungraceful, rough, uncaring, unmotherly, monstrous, and masculine. This reversal of the situation gets further complicated by the arrival of the female suicide bombers in the discourse of insurgent war against state power because not only do they demonstrate disregard for the physical integrity of their own bodies, but also inspire terror in the psyche of their targets by the performative/public act of violence. Given that revolutionary groups do not have well-equipped armies and weapons, suicide acts of their members are performed in ways that are as violent as possible with the view to attract the widest possible attention from media and society. Since female suicide bombers, as opposed to their traditional images of femininity and nurturing, call upon their political agency and capacity for violence, their actions induce heightened worry and anxiety and inspire fear among people in ways that male suicide bombers do not.

Women taking on masculine actions confuse men. Malli inspires admiration among the boys in the LTTE camp and terror in the eyes of Lotus, who sees her beating a Sri Lankan military soldier to death. Further, men don't know how to rationalize such actions and look for personal reasons. Malli had lost her family to war and her brother to martyrdom. It's the death of family members, loss of home, and private grief which are shown to impel Darshika and Puhalchudar to join the LTTE. Both Arnestad and Sivam fail in constructing narratives that are structured around the women's political understanding of the historical Tamil persecution at the hand of the Sinhala State or the army. Similarly, in her analysis of Wafa Idris, the first Palestinian female suicide bomber, Dorit Naaman (2007) argues that the hetero-patriarchal Western media attributed her actions to personal (private) and not political reasons: her infertility, jealousy of her husband's second wife who bore him children, and her overall sense of worthlessness. Naaman challenges this logic and claims instead that many female suicide bombers were happy, engaged in committed relationships, did well in school and professionally, and had borne children. In the case of male suicide bombers, on the other hand, people usually do not hear about their personal lives or identities: they are automatically believed to be committed to their political, religious, or ideological cause. The actions of female suicide bombers, in contrast, are seen to be an anachronism and open to a psychological analysis of their pathological acts. This contradictory analysis clearly demonstrates the gendered nature of female and male suicide bombers which informs their representation in film.

The history of women's involvement in armed resistance and terrorism is older than the modern-day phenomenon of suicide bombing. While feminist writings have deployed gender as a category of analysis to determine the intricate ways in which nationality, race, and ethnicity produce interlocking systems of power stacked along hierarchies of difference, most analyses of the racialized body of the suicide bomber are based on assumptions which remain largely unexamined. Brunner (2007) points out that some of the recent scholarship on the topic (Davis 2003; Bloom 2005; Skaine 2006) tends to recreate an Orientalist and mainstream understanding of the female suicide bomber as the raced, gendered, and irrational other of the progressive and sane Western self. Brunner bemoans the persistence of a twentieth-century Western interpretation of the phenomenon of suicide bombing strictly in the context of the post 9/11 World Trade Center attacks. Such an approach, argues Brunner, dehistoricizes and simplifies a complex phenomenon, denying in the process multifaceted global geopolitical specificities. Simultaneously, the Western views of female suicide bombers are uni-dimensional too: their irrational desperation to commit acts of violence to redress personal grievances (sexual brutalization, death of a close family member) makes them fall victim to patriarchal leaders of militant organizations. Unlike male bombers who are ascribed political or religious motives, female suicide bombers are dehistoricized, decontextualized, and are denied complexity of political knowledge. Men are organizers of attacks, and women are followers of orders for a personal/private reason. The logic of the above arguments taken together projects the female suicide bomber as the "irrational other of the rational, enlightened Western self" (Brunner 2007: 958).

Given their marginalization and differential treatment at the hands of the recruiting heteronormative militias, the question that comes to the fore is the extent to which Black Tigers (suicide bombers) have, at times knowingly, volunteered their services for the LTTE and whether they view their choice as agentic. To some extent, the multiple levels of their subversions could be seen to shape their agency: Malli/Dhanu choose their own victims, are unafraid of the masculine gaze and proximity of their trainers, and escape objectification of their bodies by staring into the camera, constructing in the process a self-defined visual narrative.

If Darshika and Puhalchudar's fearlessness and pride signal identity formation, the troubling question that remains unanswered is to do with the price of liberation they are expected to pay, as their newly found freedom can only be realized through the decimation of the self. Neloufer De Mel (2001) underlines the loss that lies at the heart of identity formation, gender, female sexuality, and reproduction, and which, however, is replicated across gender, as it affects both male and female militants. Located outside the politics of self-representation, the suicide bomber is forced to forgo articulating her story from her own point of view. At best, her individuality is constructed at the behest of her leader. At worst, it is enunciated in the unreality of fiction. And when it is constructed in a truth-telling narrative of a documentary, the audience is disturbed by some of the facts that are either not elaborated or deliberately hidden. Within the context of such diminished possibilities, then, the construction of the self, argues De Mel, is further eroded for women participants in armed rebellion of the LTTE. Clearly, these women are not mistresses of their own actions and decisions. The fact that they end up being controlled by hetero-patriarchal nationalist movements undermines the basis of their actions being rooted in independent choices. *My Daughter the Terrorist* does not critique the actions of the central protagonists, nor does it delve into alternative peaceful forms of resistance that might have been open to them. As for the politics of violence, the film does not problematize their internalization of this very ideology of annihilation, nor does it question its potential to transform the society or change gender relations. In sidestepping some of these crucial questions, the film ironically ends up setting the parameters within which suicide bombers can speak, appropriating their voice in the process.

Both Arnestad and Sivan offer a one-sided insight into women's response to the politics of violence. They both internalize the incapacitating narrative of violence that leads to paralysis, death, or counter-violence. While Malli demonstrates the formation of her counter-resistance agency, one does not know the ramifications of her decision. Even though she refuses henceforth to be responsible for perpetuating violence, her action takes place far too late, is too individualistic, and in the end is ineffective. Going by research on the LTTE response to those that abandon the movement (Hoole et al. 1990; N. De Silva 2006), it is not difficult to imagine that most likely she would be viewed as a traitor to the cause and shot dead by the LTTE agents. As a result, by maintaining a studied silence on an alternative feminine subjectivity and strategy, the filmmakers essentialize Sri Lankan women as victims of hetero-patriarchal politics of violence.

Militarism promotes authoritarianism and a narrow, hyper-masculine view of manhood. Darshika and Puhalchudar are shown to have molded themselves into soldiers who will obey orders without thinking, and will internalize unquestioning loyalty to the leadership. Their eyes shine with pride as they take the leader's name and demonstrate blind faith in him. By their very nature, their actions undermine their autonomy and agency in particular because as women, they occupy a secondary position within the LTTE, which leaves them more prone to abuse. Further, sexual division of labor produced by revolutionary war does not give equal position to women in military forces. Malli, Darshika, and Puhalchudar are all shown to follow orders rather than be engaged in decision-making processes. Under the masculinist gaze of the LTTE agents, Malli partially disrobes herself to tie the hefty suicide belt around her waist. One of the men guides her hand to feel the red suicide trigger (one can easily read phallocentric symbolism in the action), while his peer orders her to turn around several times as he looks over her to make sure that her clothes conceal the belt. He roughly tells her that her job is to act and not think, contradicting the appellation earlier used for her as the "thinking bomb" (*The Terrorist*). Faced with this blatant show of masculine arrogance and superiority, Malli's lips tremble, sweat beads form on her brow, and her eyes become uncertain, distant. Her facial close-up underlines her anxiety about the logic of authoritarianism of the LTTE, which represents absolute domination, hierarchy, and obedience. Malli is shown to become aware of the slow erasure of free expression, egalitarianism, and transparency in decision making. This contrasts with Darshika and Puhalchudar's confidence in their decision and the LTTE, which I read as false consciousness.

Nepal

Nepal has been governed by autocratic and corrupt royal dynasties for more than 200 years since the time the King of Gorkha Prithvinarayan Shah established his Shah rule by forcefully unifying small Himalayan kingdoms under one kingdom in 18th century.

The monarchy was overthrown as late as in 1990 when the first People's Movement, Jana Andolan, launched by several political parties seeking greater economic, social and political equality for people, carried out months of agitation and street protests and established a multi-party democracy in the country. Subsequently though, when the dream of economic prosperity was disrupted by infighting between political parties, the new Communist Party of Nepal (Maoist) launched the People's War in 1996, an armed struggle which grew from a small insurgency in rural Nepal to a brutal full-scale war that left 13,000 people dead and 1,300 missing (Aryal 2016: 174). Making use of this period of instability, the king regained power in the country from 2002–2006 by means of a military coup, disbanded political parties and called a state of emergency. In 2006, the CPN(M), mainstream political parties, and a large civil society movement joined forces to launch the second People's Movement to overthrow the King and restore democracy. At the same time, the signing of the historic Comprehensive Peace Agreement ended the ten-year-old Maoist-led civil war in the country, at least on paper. The post-2006 period of transition saw the founding of a republic, pulling the Maoists from the shadows of an underground movement and including them in the interim parliament. The Maoists were invited to participate in the Constituent Assembly elections in 2003 and 2004 and to help with the writing of the constitution.

Set against the ten-year long internecine civil war and the movement for democracy in contemporary Nepal, Julie Bridgham 2009 documentary film, *The Sari Soldiers* brings together six disparate characters whose lives are shaped by the political positionalities located on a number of conflicting sides of the civil war. The film's diegesis unfolds through an insight into the lives of Devi, a Dalit woman, whose fifteen-year-old daughter Maina Sunawar has been disappeared by the Royal Nepal Army; Mandira Sharma, a human rights lawyer; Rajni, an officer in the Royal Nepal Army; Kranti, a Commander in the Maoist-led People's Liberation Army; Ram Kumari, a student activist engaged in the country's democratic movement; and Krishna, a Monarchist village leader. The narrative emphasizes the troubled journey of modernity undertaken by the Nepali consciousness that forces its various factions to interrogate the intersectionality of their identities along the lines of ethnicity, caste, class, language, geography, and religion, and their relationship with the state and within larger community. Devi's quest for her daughter's whereabouts offers the narrative hub that forms the premise through which the six characters unravel the core of the conflict in Nepal over the questions of rights and justice during the decade-long armed conflict that left nearly 20,000 dead, about 150,000 people internally-displaced, and thousands of women sexually abused with impunity.

Having witnessed in February 2004 the rape and extrajudicial murder of her niece by the soldiers of the Royal Nepal Army (RNA), Devi was targeted for making the case public and naming the officers involved. Five days later, while Devi was visiting her mother, the army abducted her daughter Maina Sunuwar from her home in Kharlethok in Kavrepalanchowk District, telling the family to reclaim her from the army barracks the following day. However, when Devi went to the barracks the next day, the soldiers flatly denied Maina's abduction.

With Nepal under a State of Emergency at that time, many fundamental rights of people had been suspended by the repressive regime, an anti-terrorist legislation was put in force - especially since the Obama administration put the Maoists on their official terrorist watch list, and the army given control of security operations. Maina's abduction happened at the height of the conflict that had normalized extrajudicial killings, unlawful abductions, torture, and enforced disappearances. Despite being barred from making unlawful arrests under the anti-terror legislation, the army continued to detain civilians in the barracks, denying these detentions pointblank. Moreover, while the atmosphere of fear and terror resulted in silencing people who dared not challenge the authorities, people within the wider society looked towards the army for protection from Maoists' human rights violations. as the state was too powerless (Murthy 332) and therefore refrained from challenging army activities.

As a human rights lawyer and founder of Advocacy Forum, Mandira Sharma is one of the strongest critics of the impunity with which the state apparatus and non-state Maoist rebels caused grave human rights violations: torture, illegal killings, forced disappearances (this number being the highest in the world at the peak of the conflict), sexual violence, and permanent displacement of thousands of people in the country during the civil war. In an atmosphere of mounting fear, peace-loving people in Nepal were caught between the state and the Maoists. Nepal's imaginary as a Shangri-La with "poor but happy" people stands, therefore, in sheer contrast with the reality of the armed struggle that stems from centuries of poverty and oppression of many Nepal's castes/ethnic groups.

On the one hand, the State muffled all dissent through the imposition of the State of Emergency and shielded members of the armed services from proper accountability for violating human rights. It did so by trying them in military courts, including in cases of crimes against civilians, which is not possible under Nepalese law (Murthy 2016: 322, 329). On the other, the Maoists harassed and attacked people for not supporting them in their war for social transformation. While looking at images of Nepali men in various stages of disfigurement and decomposition, Mandira condemns the Maoists obfuscating and manipulating people through their discourse on social issues, without revealing their true politics steeped in violence and senseless killing.

As a head of the village *Panchyat* (council), Krishna has everything to lose from the people's war on the monarchy. The monarchy was better for the country and losing the king, she believes, amounted to losing one's head. Maoists for her are trouble makers and a source of menace and danger. The camera following her walking through the village captures Maoist slogans graffitied on the huts: "Long live Maoism! The People and the Movement are Against Dictatorship and his Government." The villagers are forced to support the Maoists who threaten to abduct or even kill them if they don't. The anger and fear among the villagers is palpable as they watch out for the Maoists day and night. Krishna has no patience for democratic parties either as they have done nothing to protect them from Maoist oppression.

Although the film does not shed light on its significance in Krishna's life, the loss of Monarchy would spell the end of the *Panchayat* system and her leadership of the village. Introduced in the country in 1960, the *Panchayat* period came into being when the head of the Shah dynasty ended democratic government, banned all political parties, and imposed his autocratic rule. This declared Nepal as a Hindu state, undermining the country's caste, tribal, religious, and linguistic heterogeneity. In many ways, the *Muluki Ain* codified this way earlier, and despite casteism being illegal since long, it remains in practice today. Many women activists celebrated the *Panchayat* political system as a progressive phase in Nepal's history: recognized as part of a special interest group, women's legal status dramatically improved during this period. Maoists and other supporters of democracy, on the other hand, considered the *Panchayat* rule as regressive for women for the following reasons: the "Single Family Law" Introduced by the Monarchy was based on the heteronormative upper-caste Hindu family that naturalized women as mothers, daughters, and wives; institutionalized inequality for Dalit and *janajati* (indigenous) women; legitimized unequal gender relations; and increased sexual violence against women.

Because of this undemocratic system Kranti joined the Maoist party that had taken the right path to end oppression. As the Maoist brigadier Commissar, Kranti believes that the King was "inviting his own death" for taking away people's rights. Dressed in army fatigues and carrying a gun on their shoulders, Maoists claimed to have joined the party to fight against poverty, hunger, and gender oppression. During the ten-year war, the Maoist party played a key role in highlighting the intersectionality between gender, class, and ethnicity. It is useful to remember an important and often overlooked fact that the top brass of the Maoists were primarily high-caste men who sent their children to international boarding schools, and waged a people's war with the people's blood in order to further their internecine struggles. Offering an alternative to the stereotype of Nepali women as helpless and passive victims, the Maoists also presented themselves as tough soldiers and worked towards progressive structural change in the society with the aim to introduce a secular rule, end untouchability, guaranty citizenship rights to mothers, eradicate gender inequality by overthrowing feudal Brahminical patriarchy, introduce equal inheritance law for women, declare Nepal a secular state, and hold state-sponsored Hindu casteist feudalism responsible for women's oppression.

Given the fissures in the fabric of the legal structure and democracy, Mandira is not surprised at the increasing feminization of villages where most men have either fled, been arrested, or killed, placing tremendous burden on women to seek justice for human rights violations. It is important to note that Krishna forces her son to flee to Kathmandu and Devi's husband would eventually disappear under mysterious circumstances. In addition to the paralyzing effect of the above, Devi too faces structural challenges that exacerbate her struggle for justice. As a Dalit and economically depressed woman, she is triply disadvantaged by her gender, caste, and class positionality in a deeply hierarchical Nepali society. Dalit marginalization in Nepal can be traced to the 1854 *Muluki Ain*, the country's general legal code that reinforced Hindu supremacy by driving Dalits to the bottom of the caste hierarchy whose middle and upper rung were occupied by the Tibeto–Burman tribes and Bahun and Chettri caste respectively. Dalit persecution was reinforced during the period between 1960–90, when the king banned all political parties, replaced the democratically elected government with an autocratic *panchayat* democracy, and began a process of establishing an essentially Nepali identity based on the "triad of Hinduism, the Nepali language, and the monarchy" (Burghart 1994 cited in Tamang 2016: 56–7). The 1962 constitution declared Nepal a Hindu state, bypassing the heterogeneous nature of Nepal's social fabric resulting in the caste, linguistic, regional, and gender-based discrimination of lower caste Hindu, non-Nepali speaking, and Madhesi people living in the plains.

The flooding of Nepal with international aid for *bikas* (development) at the end of the Rana rule in 1950 only helped validate its feudalistic culture and lent a serious blow to gender relations in the country. The development discourse that resulted from *bikas* being led by international organizations and government institutions, with high-caste Hindu men at their helm, essentialized and homogenized Nepali women as disempowered and tradition-bound, across caste, class, ethnic, and religious differentials, in need of rescue by state-led development and welfare projects. It destroyed *janajati* people's gender-just traditions such as widow-remarriage and professional freedom (Bennet 1983). Accentuating their unequal citizenship as wives, daughters, sisters, etc., the 1990s state-led rescue narrative infantilized women, depriving them of freedom in the name of their safety. Faced with this protectionist vocabulary of national honor while the Maoists used violent revolution, women's NGOs relied on the welfare discourse, and upper caste women used their power within political parties to silence marginalized women.

Given, therefore, the breadth of political and structural disadvantages, and despite being displaced from her village and being forced to repeatedly relocate (Murthy 324), an undeterred Devi persisted. In the filmmaker's attempt at positioning her as a grieving mother and victim of circumstances, Devi's perseverance can be read as her coming into her agentic being and the politicization of her consciousness that had been occurring for many years. Her long-term membership in the Communist Party of Nepal (United Marxist Leninist), her brief tenure at the National Women's Commission, and her experience as a women's rights activist demonstrate her leadership qualities. The film surprisingly conceals Devi's political affiliations. Should one read this as an Orientalist erasure of a Third World woman's agency?

Battling the guilt, regret, and sorrow forever hovering on the surface of her heart about being the cause of Maina's abduction, Devi went from pillar to post: from one military barracks to the other, from the temple to the clairvoyant, finally landing at Mandira's human rights office. Seeing her determination to fight for justice, and her courage to testify against the state, Mandira chose Devi over other victims of human rights violations (Murthy 325), that no doubt helped the case garner national and international media attention, the support of the United Nations, and a meeting with the Chief of the Amy Staff, where she demanded criminal investigation into the case. The military court inquiry that was subsequently ordered was the first trial of this kind in Nepal where high level officers were investigated (*The Sari Soldiers*). Given the sensitivity of the case, and worried about the safety of all people involved, Mandira requested the UN to "intervene as a third-party witness" (Murthy 326) Although the army tried to cover up the case by claiming that Maina was killed while trying to escape, the truth behind her disappearance was ultimately unraveled. Suspecting the teenager of being a Maoist supporter, four army personnel tortured her to death through repeated water boarding and electric shocks, the intensity of which was too high for her frail body to withstand. Two days after she had been abducted, fifteen-year-old Maina Sunuwar succumbed to her injuries in the secrecy of the army custody. At a press conference that followed, Devi declared her intention to pursue the case until the perpetrators were caught, challenging the court's decision to try the perpetrators for "using inappropriate techniques of interrogation" instead of murder (Murthy 329). Devi asserted her right to perform the last rites for her daughter and to know where and how she was killed. The camera rolls over to a scene in the jungle, where a group of people are shown to be exhuming Maina's body. She said, "The Nepal Army thought that this day would never come. They thought they would get away with it" (*The Sari Soldiers*). However, it would take another thirteen years for the court to convict the perpetrators of Maina's death, which it did in 2017 (BBC.com, April 17).

Devi's persistence and courage catapulted her to the heart of the battle against the culture of violence and impunity in Nepal, leaving a legacy of Maina's name that has set a precedent for justice for families of the disappeared for all times to come (*The Sari Soldiers*). Devi would most likely not have been able to achieve what she did without Mandira's help. Screen shots in the film testify to her accessing spaces and people that an illiterate Dalit woman from a village would have been barred from. Along with her colleagues, Mandira continues to achieve justice for ordinary Nepali people and remains committed to the idea that peace without justice is illusory (Advocacy Forum website). By 2004, through filing writs of *habeas corpus*, the Advocacy Forum had hundreds of people released from illegal and incommunicado detention and is continuing to expand their human rights work (Murthy 333).

Following the 1990s pro-democracy movement (Jana Andolan) initiated by a range of political parties, and unprecedented mass agitations articulated through street protests and demonstrations, a multi-party democracy was finally established in Nepal. Yet, a growing economic equity and in-fighting in the political party, undermined the relative peace, social, economic, and political freedom that had been ushered in by the democratic movement. The Communist Party of Nepal (Maoist), led an armed "People's War" struggle in 1996 against the government, accused of exacerbating the country's political, social, and economic uncertainty. From what appeared to be an inconsequential revolt, it left thousands of people dead and missing as a result of extrajudicial killings, indiscriminate arrests and torture, enforced disappearances, and sexual violence in the brutal war that ensued between CPI(M) and the security forces of the government. During the second pro-democracy movement, with the signing of the Comprehensive Peace Agreement (CPA) between the Government of Nepal and CPN(M), the "People's War" finally came to an end.

Notes

1 At the height of the militancy in the 1990s, many young men slipped into Pakistan, with Kupwara district being their last stop before crossing the border. Located a mere forty miles away from the Line of Control (LOC), Kupwara has spawned some of the fiercest resistance fighters, such as the pro-*Azaadi* leader, Maqbool Bhat who, following his state-led assassination in 1984, came to be referred to as *Shaheed-e-Azam* (the great martyr). The region, therefore, has come under the most intense scrutiny by the Indian state, triggering the worst forms of human rights abuses of its inhabitants including slavery, torture, disappearances, extra-judicial killings, and mass rapes that are performed at the hands of the Indian army that uses its brute power to suffocate the *Azaadi* movement and to terrorize people into submission.
2 In 2011, the State Human Rights Commission confirmed the burial of 2156 unidentified bodies in unmarked graves across North Kashmir.

Bibliography

Aryal, Mallika. "Truth Silence, and Justice: The Maoists' View." *A Difficult Transition: The Nepal Papers.* Eds. Mandira Sharma and Seira Tamang. New Delhi: Zubaan, 2016. 174–204.

Bennett, Lynn. Dangerous Wives and Sacred Sisters: Social and Symbolic Roles of High-Caste Women in Nepal. New York: Columbia University Press. 1983

Bloom, Mia (2005) *Dying to Kill: The Allure of Suicide Terror,* New York: Columbia University Press.

Boyce-Davis, Carole. *Black Women, Writing and Identity: Migration of the Subject.* London: Routledge, 1994.

Brunner, Claudia (2007) "Occidentalism Meets the Female Suicide Bomber: A Critical Reflection on Recent Terrorism Debates; A Review Essay", *Signs: Journal of Women in Culture and Society,* Vol. 32, No. 4, pp. 957–71.

Chakravarti, Uma, ed. *Fault Lines of History: The India Papers II.* New Delhi: Zubaan, 2016.

Cockburn, Cynthia. "The Gendered Dynamics of Armed Violence and Political Conflict." *Victims, Perpetrators or Actors? Gender, Armed Conflict and Political Violence.* Eds. Caroline O. N. Moser, Fiona C. Clark. New Delhi: Kali for Women, 2001.

Davis, Joyce M. (2003) *Martyrs: Innocence, Vengeance, and Despair in the Middle East*, New York: Palgrave Macmillan.

De Mel, Neloufer (2001) "Agent or Victim? The Sri Lankan Women Militant in the Interregnum" in *Women & Nation's Narratives: Gender and Nationalism Twentieth Century Sri Lanka*, New Delhi: Kali for Women.

——— (2001) "Mother Politics and Women's Politics: Notes on Sri Lankan Women's Movement", in *Women & Nation's Narratives: Gender and Nationalism Twentieth Century Sri Lanka*, New Delhi: Kali for Women.

——— (2004) "Body Politics: (Re)Cognising the Female Suicide Bomber in Sri Lanka", *Indian Journal of Gender Studies*, Vol. 11, No. 1, pp. 75–92.

——— (2007) *Militarizing Sri Lanka: Popular Culture, Memory and Narrative in the Armed Conflict*, LA, London, New Delhi: Sage

De Silva, Mangalika (2007) "The Other Body and the Body Politic: Contingency and Dissonance in Narratives of Violence", in Monique Skidmore and Patrician Lawrence (Eds.) *Women and the Contested State: Religion, Violence, and Agency in South and Southeast Asia*, Notre Dame, IN: University of Notre Dame Press.

De Silva, Nirekha (2006) *Transnational Justice for Women Ex-combatants in Sri Lanka*, New Delhi: WISCOMP.

DeVotta (2009b) "The Liberation Tigers of Tamil Eelam and the Lost Quest for Separatism in Sri Lanka", *Asian Survey*,Vol. 49, No. 6, pp. 1021–51. 2009b

Eisenstein, Zillah. "Resexism Militarism for the Globe." *Feminism and War: Confronting US Imperialism.* Eds. Robin L. Riley, Chandra Talpade Mohanty, and Minnie Bruce Pratt. London and New York: Zed Books, 2008.

Espinoza, Julio Garcia. "For an Imperfect Cinema." *Twenty Five Years of the New Latin American Cinema.* Ed. Michael Chanan. UW: BFI Books, 1983.

Gautam, Shoba, Amrita Banskota, and Rita Manchanda. "Where There Are No Men: Women in the Maoist Insurgency in Nepal." *Understanding the Maoist Movement in Nepal.* Eds. Deepak Thapa. London and New Delhi: Sage, 2003. 214–251.

Geetha, V. *Undoing Impunity: Speech after Sexual Violence.* New Delhi: Zubaan, 2016.

Hoole, RajanDayaSomasunderam, K. Sritharan, RajaniThiranagama (1990) *The Broken Palmyrah: The Tamil Crisis in Sri Lanka—An Inside Account*, Claremont: The Sri Lankan Studies Institute.

Jayaskankar, K. P., and Anjali Monteiro. *A Fly in the Curry: Independent Documentary Film in India.* New Delhi: Sage, 2016. 322–343.

Joshi, Namrata. "Are they Dead, Alive, or have They Turned into Ether?" *The Hindu* 13 February 2016.

Kak, Sanjay. "The Last Option: A Stone in Her Hand". *The Times of India* 8 August 2010. http://timesofindia.indiatimes.com/home/sunday-times/deep-focus/The-last-option-A-stone-in-her-hand/articleshow/6272689.cms. Accessed 15 December 2016.

Khan, Rahat. *Activist Documentary Film in Pakistan: The Emergence of a Cinema of Accountability.* New York: Routledge, 2016.

Kirby, Paul. "How Is Rape a Weapon of War? Feminist International Relations, Modes of Critical Explanation and the Study of Wartime Sexual Violence." *European Journal of International Relations* 19.4 (2012): 797–821.

Kleinhans, Chuck. "Forms, Politics, Makers and Contexts: Basic Issues for a Theory of Radical Political Documentary." *"Show us Life": Toward a History and Aesthetics of the Committed Documentary,* 9th ed. Ed. Thomas Waugh. Metuchen, NJ and London: The Scarecrow Press, 1984. 318–344.

Lamakaran: An Open Cultural Space. An Evening with Iffat Fatima and Screening of Khoon Diy Baarav. International Association of Women in Radio and Television. December 4, 2015.

Leve, Lauren. "'Failed Development' and Rural revolution in Nepal: Rethinking Subaltern Consciousness and Women's Empowerment". *Anthropological Quarterly* 80.1 (Winter 2007): 127–72.

Manchanda, Rita. "Empowerment with a Twist." *The Hindu* 21 November 1999.

Manecksha, F. "Autonomy under Siege." *Himal Magazine* 7 January 2014. http://old.himalmag.com/component/content/article/5218-autonomy-under-siege.html. Accessed 15 December 2016.

Minh-ha, Trinh T. "An All-Owning Spectatorship." *When the Moon Waxes Red: Representation, Gender, and Cultural Politics.* New York: Routledge, 1991.

Misri, Deepti. 2014. *Beyond Partition: Gender, Violence, and representation in Postcolonial India.* Champaign: U of Illinois P.

Murthy, Laxmi. "Mandira Sharma: Court Martials and the Impossibility of Justice." *A Difficult Transition: The Nepal Papers.* Ed. Mandira Sharma and Seira Tamang. New Delhi: Zubaan, 2016. 322–343.

Ranjan, Amit. "A Gender Critique of AFSPA: Security for Whom?" *Social Change* 45.3 (2015): 440–57.

Shohat, Ella. "Post-Third Worldist Culture: Gender, Nation, and the Cinema." *Rethinking Third Cinema.* Ed. Anthony R. Guneratne and Wimal Dissanayak. New York: Routledge, 2003. 51–78.

Skaine, Rosemarie (2006) *Female Suicide Bombers,* Jefferson, SC.: McFarland.

Sorel, Georges (1961) *Reflections on Violence,* New York: Collier.

Sunder Rajan, Rajeswari. *Real and Imagined Woman: Gender, Culture and Postcolonialism.* London and New York: Routledge, 1993.

Tamang, Siera. "The Hindu State, Women's Activism and the Cultural Coding of Sexuality." *A Difficult Transition: The Nepal Papers.* Ed. Mandira Sharma and Seira Tamang. New Delhi: Zubaan, 2016. 54–97.

10 Queering South Asia? Deviant Sexualities and the Role of the Indian Media in Shaping Perceptions

Shoba Sharad Rajgopal

If women's physical needs get fulfilled though lesbian acts, the institution of marriage will collapse.
—Petition by the Shiv Sena to ban the film *Fire* (1995), Vanita and Kidwai 2008

We are no longer the castrated men who guarded royal harems of Arab kings
—Venkat, "From the Shadows," *Frontline*, February 29, 2008

In this article I examine the representation of alternate sexualities in South Asia in both the precolonial and the postcolonial eras and its repercussions on the body politic of the nation state. One of the main

Figure 10.1 Folk theater representation of the Hindu deity Shiva as Ardhanareeswara, half male and half female.
Credit: Shoba Rajgopal.

questions examined is, the role of the media as well as feminist organizations in this controversy, through an analysis of the major Indian films that have dealt with "deviant" sexualities. Among the films examined are *Sancharam* (The Journey, 2004) by Liji J. Pullappally, *Navarasa* (Nine Emotions, 2005) by Santosh Sivan, and *Ajeeb Dastaan Hai Yeh* (Strange Story, 2013) by Karan Johar. This article is more of a continuing study rather than a project that is complete, as this is an era of great change and political ferment in South Asia. It is also a study of the responses and reactions of students in the West, who have been mired in colonialist perspectives of the developing world and a Huntington inspired mindset of "the clash of civilizations" (Huntington 1996). US based students are often horrified by the alleged outmoded and uncivilized attitudes of non-western cultures with regard to gender and sexuality. From this perspective, gender issues like the enforcing of the burqa, and attacks on queer communities are perceived as examples of the essential lack of progress of non-Western societies. I encourage my students to look beyond their own prejudices to comprehend the time period in which these attitudes toward gender and sexuality came to be developed and the role of West too, through colonialism and imperialism, in developing this mindset. In this case, my students would be learning about South Asian cultures, their politics and colonial histories, all of which are imbricated in attitudes towards sex and gender, learning not only the current position of queer communities in South Asia, but the colonial policies instituted there, transforming some of those regions into dangerously sexist and homophobic regions.

Colonial Mores, Postcolonial Realities

India has undergone a sea change in attitudes towards sexuality in recent decades, thanks to the resurgence of feminist energy, coinciding with the third wave of feminism in the West, even if some of the participants of the diverse movements do not necessarily identify as feminists. For the first time in its history, India has seen gay parades organized across the length and breadth of the country, even in small towns in the deep south of India. However, it has simultaneously also seen a rise in homophobic attacks on films and groups that support liberal attitudes regarding sexual orientation, seen in the fact that both the quotes with which I start this article occur within the same time period, one expressing a fear of same-sex desire while the other quote expresses the new feeling of empowerment within formerly stigmatized transgender communities. Indeed, after an epic battle that lasted nearly two decades, Section 377 of the Indian Penal Code that criminalized queer relationships was struck down, but that judgment was overturned by the Supreme Court of India on December 12, 2013, with the Court holding that amending or repealing Section 377 should be a matter left to Parliament, not the judiciary.

Newspaper editorials have denounced the move, with papers like the venerable Madras based newspaper, *The Hindu* leading the charge. "In an age where there is growing acceptance of the idea that LGBTs must be allowed to live in dignity and respect, it is a shame that India cannot bring itself to legalize gay behavior" (Ram 2009). How far have these actions helped raise awareness of these issues in the country? I examine this central query in this article through a specific study of some path-breaking Indian films over the past few decades.

Cinema and Queer Representation

Back in the colonial era, queer identities were actively looked down upon and represented as deviant sexuality, but how much have things changed today, especially in the light of a growing movement for queer empowerment? I argue that for a long time they were not even clearly articulated within the public sphere of much of Indian cinema, but merely hinted at, if at all. This was the case even in Hollywood for several decades, due to the infamous Hays Code of 1930. For over a half century, under pressure from the Church, Hollywood cinema marginalized homosexuality, forcing gay actors to lead closeted lives. If homosexual characters in Hollywood have been drawn as darkly alien and monstrous in a twilight world of horror and dread (Russo 1985), with menacing figures like the lesbian housekeeper Mrs. Danvers in *Rebecca* (1940), they were not even represented in much of Bollywood cinema. Indeed, Bollywood cinema had until fairly recently, not even dared to venture into this arena of queer relationships, for fear of arousing the ire of the Hindutva brigade, which had created havoc in Bombay at the initial screening of the independent film *Fire* (Deepa Mehta 1995). The Far Right Shiv Sena party's demand that the film be banned was on the basis that the depiction of two Hindu women engaged in a lesbian relationship was against Hindu culture and tradition, especially considering the fact that the principal character in the film had the name of the Hindu Goddess, Sita, famed for her purity, and hence the name had to be changed to Nita before the film could be released once more in northern India (Lal 2014). This incident led to widespread protests and sparked a debate across the country about culture, sexual identities, and freedom of expression. However, what must be noted in this context is not just the brouhaha caused by the Right Wing hooligans about the film, but the role of activists supporting freedom of expression within the media. Indeed, at a public rally for freedom of expression, some women's groups tried to dissuade lesbian activists from carrying placards and speaking about lesbianism, so as not to 'dilute' the issue (Chandiramani and Misra 2005).

There have been numerous instances where Bollywood films have showed a glimpse of queer relationships, only to step back quickly. Many

such instances involve male relationships wherein the two male protagonists appear to have far more chemistry with each other than with their
female counterparts. This paradigm has in fact led to the discussion of
the "buddy film" where the two male buddies spend a lot of time engage
in playful banter with each other, which can be coded very differently
by queer audiences.

The most notable of these is the famous duet "Yeh dosti" in *Sholay*
(Flames 1975). Translated loosely as "This friendship," the song
sequence pictures the two comrades Jai and Veeru, riding on motorcy-
cles, singing of their love for each other. But lest you wonder whether
there was anything more to their relationship, the film quickly has them
getting into heterosexual relationships, establishing heterosexuality as
the norm, with queer as being outside that parameter. Other more recent
films such as *Kal Ho Na Ho* (If Tomorrow Comes, 2001) also depict a
very close male bonding between the two male protagonists which ends
only when one dies and literally hands his lover into the arms of the
other male. But what endeared it to many queer viewers is the fact that
the two main male leads pretend to be gay throughout the film, much to
the disapproval of Kantaben, the housekeeper. They constantly caress
each other and spout double- entendre dialogue to shock the conservative elderly woman, but of course in the end they turn out to be straight
after all. The buddy relationship is reprised in other recent films like
Lage Raho Munna Bhai (Carry on, Brother Munna, 2006).

If such interludes which could be interpreted as gay interludes are fairly
frequent, lesbian moments are few and far between, one of the most
notable ones being the famous "*Choli ke peeche*" duet in *Khalnayak*
(Villain, 1993) between two women, the police officer incognito, Ganga,
and the dancer, Champa Didi, with the voyeuristic gangster covertly
ogling the two women. But, although the male gazes at the women, it
is hardly the Mulvean "male gaze," (Mulvey 2006), as the male figure
becomes peripheral to the scene of desire, with the scene shifting to the
two women, who are clearly more engaged with each other than with
him. As such it is hardly surprising that the song became a staple in
drag performances in South Asian queer spaces within multiple diasporic locations (Gopinath 2006). The song's chorus translates loosely as
"What's under your blouse? What's under your scarf?" while the camera
zooms in on the heaving bosoms of the dancers. But the scene ends with
the undercover cop Ganga demurely confessing that what lies beneath
her blouse is only her heart, and then, disappointingly, moving away
from the other female dancer rather than taking up where the song ends.

Another iconic moment is depicted in the only feature film to have
ventured to depict the famous Mughal Empress Razia Sultan, who had
been a ruler in her own right rather than the mere consort of one. The
film *Razia Sultan* (1983), discussed the possibility of the Empress having been in a relationship with another woman. Considering that she

was a very unusual figure in Indian history, as the only female ruler of both the Sultanate and the Mughal period, although other women had ruled from behind the scenes, it is surprising that there have been no other films about her. But its daring in depicting this sexual deviance has been celebrated by queer filmmakers like Pratibha Parmar who in fact depicts a scene in her film *Khush* (Pleasure, 1991) wherein two South Asian lesbians languidly recline on pillows and watch old Bollywood films together. In direct homage to *Razia Sultan*, the final shot of *Khush* is of one woman bending over the other to bestow a kiss upon her lips against the backdrop of the Bolllywood film. As Gayatri Gopinath points out, Parmar cleverly reframes the kiss between Parveen Babi and Hema Malini, and her translation of the scene into a queer diasporic context refuses to block our spectatorial gaze, and instead "acknowledges the pleasures afforded by dominant representations of hyperbolic femininity and female homosociality to queer viewers, while rendering explicit their homoeroticism" (Gopinath 2006: 112).

The topic was taken up with greater sincerity by diasporic South Asian film maker Deepa Mehta in *Fire* (1995) but became mired in conflicts with Right Wing Hindu militants over the role of women in society. Brinda Bose argues that *Fire* primarily evokes female homoeroticism in order to define a "feminist" resistance to patriarchal constructions of female sexuality (Bose 2000). Indeed, contrary to the representation of cultural nationalists of the home as a space of heterosexual normalcy, Radha and Sita, as queer subjects, rework notions of the 'home' within the interstices of 'queered' domestic spaces. In doing so, they challenge the assumption behind hegemonic forms of Indian nationalism that suggest that the queer subject is alien, inauthentic or outside the community (Raj 2012). In the face of a concerted campaign by the Hindutva forces to stop the screening of the film across the country, claiming that it would corrupt Indian (Hindu) culture, Mehta defended herself by claiming that the film was about choice and not about lesbian sexuality per se (Desai 2004; Lal 2014), a fact that was castigated by the Indian lesbian community that had defended her film from the onslaughts of the forces of the Hindu Far Right. Mehta's defense appears to hold some truth, for female same-sex desire appears to develop in the film more from a failure of patriarchal heterosexuality than from a true relationship of lesbian desire. Nevertheless, the conclusion of the film, with the two lovers fleeing their marital homes and seeking refuge in the Sufi shrine denotes their outsider position within the hegemony of the postcolonial nation state. Small wonder that the Hindutva forces were so outraged by its message, which appears to be as much the failure of the family within the nation state as a rejection of its patriarchal heterosexual codes.

Other Indian films that have dared to represent queer relationships in a positive light are less well known to mass audiences in India, but have definitely struck a chord among non-mainstream audiences. *Bombay*

Boys (1997) startled Indian audiences with its buoyant insouciance as it presented its sardonic take on Indian sexual mores. Another noteworthy film is *My Brother Nikhil* (2005), based on the real life story of the trials and tribulations of a famous gay athlete Dominic D'Souza. A less well known film is *Honeymoon Travels Pvt. Ltd.* (2007), about six couples on a honeymoon package tour vacation in Goa, which dares to delve into dangerous territory that is not common even in much of Hollywood cinema. During the course of the vacation, two of the men on the trip get attracted to each other. One comes out to his wife, who is furious about the deception, but they eventually become friends, while the other one gets back in the closet and says nothing to his newly married wife. It is no surprise that it received the Best Film award at the inaugural Indian Queer Media Awards in 2007 that honor sensitive media representations of LBGT characters.

Even more clearly focused attempts are Ligi J. Pullappally's independent film *Sancharam* (The Journey, 2004), located in Kerala, and Karan Johar's *Yeh Ajeeb Dastaan Hai Yeh* (2013) set in Bombay. In both these films, the protagonists are queer from the get go, not forced into it through neglect or circumstance, as with Mehta's *Fire*. Both films are set partly within the domestic arena, a space that has often been characterized in both feminist and queer theory as a site of repression with regard to gender and sexuality, where women are afflicted with "the problem that has no name" (Friedan 1963). In *The Journey*, as was the case in *Fire*, the protagonists, Kiran and Delilah, as was the case with Sita and Radha before them, are located within the domestic setting of the home. But the difference between the reception of the films is telling. Whereas Mehta's film was attacked viciously by the Hindu Far Right Shiv Sena cadre, which was in fact the ruling party at the time in Bombay, Pullappally's film was not only not attacked by agents from the ruling party of the state, but was actually partly financed by the Left leaning Kerala state government in a very progressive move to support lesbian communities as the state had been rocked by the high rate of lesbian suicides in recent times. Such incidents are so frequent that there is even a watchdog organization in Kerala that keeps track of them and offers counselling sessions. These tragedies inspired Pullappally to offer a positive representation of queer identity through a popular medium that has the potential to reach a wide audience. Hence the film was intended as much to help parents and teachers to recognize queer identities as being valid identities as it was to support the lesbians themselves.

The story of two women, Kiran and Delilah, who are close friends who slowly over time fall in love with each other is markedly different from the portrayal of same sex desire in Mehta's *Fire* (1995), where the lovers turn to each other only out of frustration as they are ignored by their male partners. In this Malayalam film, on the contrary, although Rajan, a male classmate of theirs, falls in love with Delilah, she rejects him for her beloved female friend, Kiran. Unlike an earlier Kerala film on female romantic relationships, namely P. Padmarajan's film *Desadanikilli karayarilla*, (The Migratory Bird Never Cries, 1986), this film ends on a more hopeful note. Whereas the previous film had the two protagonists, Sally and Nirmala commit suicide when they cannot be together, this film ends with Kiran, the poet deciding to leave her home and carve a new path for herself even after her lover Delilah has been forcibly married to a man upon their discovery of the illicit lesbian relationship.

The director, interestingly a human rights attorney, who had won a major award for her work on women's issues, had wanted her film to be a counterpoint to the popular tendency to pathologize homosexuality in Indian films. In an interview with the US based queer activist and media personality Ellen Degeneris, Pullapally discusses her determination to make the film as having been inspired by the rash of lesbian suicides in the region. It is not that the families themselves literally attack the women, but they persecute them by forcing them into heterosexual marriages in order to "cure" them, much as was the case in the West for many years. "These stories are sometimes reported in newspapers," she explains, "but most go unreported, as the surviving family members have an interest in keeping the shame and scandal fallout to a minimum" (Warn 2005). The interview with the film maker reveals that an additional factor that was important to Pullappally was that her film be located in a rural setting. Whereas Mehta's much better known film features urban women who have available to them the resources that metropolitan life offers, Pullappally wanted to portray life in rural areas far from the city and the isolation that often comes with it. This fact adds to the film's importance as *Fire* is located in a modern city that is the nation's capital, whereas *Sancharam* is located in the rural hinterlands of India's southwest. As the most literate state in the country, Kerala is noted for having an emerging queer community, but many young people have no access to anything that supports a queer community that is neither male nor urban. As such, the film plays an important role in revealing the struggles of lesbians in small town India, *Sancharam* has won several awards, and has been screened throughout the US and in many parts of India and continues to tour the festival circuit, but what I found especially important about the film is its message which is in keeping with the alternate cinema tradition in a state with a Marxist history. Moreover, as a lawyer with a background in fighting for women's rights issues, this promising filmmaker brings a unique sensibility to her work.

Karan Johar occupies a very different position from Pullappally in that he is one of the best known directors of mainstream cinema in today's Bollywood, who had been invited to contribute a film to celebrate the centenary of Indian cinema. His short film, *Ajeeb Dastaan Hai Yeh* is thus a part of the four film anthology, *Bombay Talkies*, 2013, brought out to celebrate a century of Bollywood cinema, from its first triumphant moment with Dadasaheb Phalke's maiden venture, *Raja Harischandra* (1913). However, this director, who had been celebrated for his commercial films for well over a decade now shocked audiences with his gritty tale of a homosexual trapped in a heterosexual marriage and yearning to break free. Sparks fly between the two men, the rebellious intern, Avinash and the handsome closeted television news anchor, Dev, who ignores his attractive wife, Rani to turn his attentions on her young male intern, thereby stunning the audience. The film employs old Bollywood traditions such as reusing famous songs from a Bollywood of an earlier era such as the Lata Mangeshkar song *"Ajeeb Dastaan Hai Yeh."* The song, sung by a forlorn waif at a train station, is the backdrop to the outing of the successful anchor, who loses his home and reputation and is eventually found seated dejectedly at the station as the score plays on.

> Ajeeb daastaan hai yeh
> Strange story it is indeed,
> Kahan shuru kahan khatam
> Where it started and where it ended
> Yeh manzile hai koun se
> What kind of destiny is this?
> Na who samjh sake na hum
> Neither he understood nor I.
>
> (My translation)

Some very poignant scenes may well have resonated with modern audiences, such as the one where Rani, after finding out that her husband of so many years is gay, pushes him away and sits at her make up table, wiping off her stale makeup and reapplying her lipstick as she states flatly, "I am finally free!" Indeed, we have come a long way from the original film the anthology was meant to celebrate. In that film of 1913, Raja Harishchandra left his devoted wife because of his promise to the irascible sage Vishwamitra, while in the 2013 Karan Johar film from *Bombay Talkies*, the devoted wife Rani leaves her husband because of his affair with another man. However, critics like Sandip Roy in the *First Post* Indian news site add this diatribe,

> Didn't it occur to you that this opportunity also came with some measure of responsibility? For the thousands for whom your film might be the first exposure to real gay characters (after the faux-gay jokes of *Dostana*), gay will now mean the guy who comes to dinner and steals his hostess' (and best friend's) husband on the way out without any moral qualms at all, not even a moment's misgiving.
>
> (Roy 2013)

To this criticism I add, when specific sexual orientations have been not just marginalized, but actively persecuted, the individuals concerned may sometimes hit back in ways that heterosexual society may find appalling, at a society they find oppressive and homophobic. It is easy to talk about supporting queer identities, but how many people would dare to actually do that in societies where heterosexual marriage and procreation are the be all and end all of existence?

The alternative sexualities website Gaylaxymag.com has a very different take on the film, where the author discusses how the film is a lot about breaking social norms as well as gender roles. In one scene Avinash kisses Dev on his neck in front of his office colleagues. This crucial gesture is all about claiming legitimacy of being gay and to be cool about it in public, and with it, the strict structure of heterosexuality is already dismantled (Davidson, K 2013). Interestingly, the scene reprised for me a scene from the famous Hanif Kureishi-Steven Frears film, *My Beautiful Laundrette* of the mid 1980s, where the white punk character Johnny played by Daniel Day Lewis licks the ear of his Asian lover Omar Ali in a public act of outing, shocking his heterosexual gang of racist punks. The film is important in that it addresses key issues of the Thatcherite era, including racism, unemployment and homosexuality. One could argue that these are key issues in today's India as well. Another interesting point to keep in mind is that, unlike in the case of the first feature film to deal with gay male identities, *My Brother Nikhil*, 2005, which was an independent film, this is very much a commercial film produced and directed by one of the top directors of the Bollywood establishment, and as such, carries an important message: gay liberation has finally arrived in Indian cinema. We have indeed come a very long way from the buddy films of Bollywood where despite a hidden gay subtext, the main plot is very much a heterosexual love story, which often ends with one of the men dying, as in *Sangam* (1964) or *Sholay* (1975) a decade later, or more recently, in *Kal Ho Na Ho* (2001), with the heterosexual unit in place with a happily ever after narrative.

If gay and lesbian identities are beyond the pale in mainstream cinema, transgender identities are even further off the map. Transfeminism insists that transsexuality is not an illness or disorder, but is as much a part of the wide spectrum of ordinary human experience as pregnancy (Emi 2003). The first and to date only major Bollywood film to represent a Transgender person as the protagonist of a film and represent the Transgender community in a humane light is Mahesh Bhatt's *Tamanna* (1997), which portrays two of those most "unwanted" within patriarchal society, the girl child and the hermaphrodite. The infant is rescued from certain death by Tinku, a lonely queer person who picks her up in a garbage bin where she has been abandoned and cares for her. The compassion of the transgender woman is in stark contrast to the callousness of the child's father who berates his wife for giving birth only to girls and then sends the child away to be killed. It took a decade before cinema ventured into this arena again in order to represent transgender individuals in a more humane light, with Santosh Sivan's Tamil film *Navarasa* (2004), but here again, it is important to note that this is alternate cinema and not mainstream cinema. The director brings in his previous background as cinematographer to play with concepts of light and dark, shadow and sunlight to depict the ambiguities that underline human sexuality (Figure 10.1).

Sivan's film, along with other important moves by activist organizations to effect change in society has definitely yielded fruit. Through the eyes of the young female narrator, Shweta, we perceive the conflict between giving up a beloved uncle figure and learning to understand and accept his/her very different gender orientation. She starts off being shocked and bewildered by her uncle's gender deviance, and, although sympathetic that he is cowed by his older brother who keeps him in rein with threats of violence, she sees only that he needs to be cured, the infamous conversion therapy so loved by the Christian Far Right. However, this attitude gradually changes as she begins to comprehend the depths of suffering that the differently gendered go through, though the person both of her own uncle and the irrepressible Dolly, a transgender activist and actress who waltzes into her life as Shweta pursues her uncle in the recesses of rural Tamil Nadu during the famous transgender festival of Koovagam. The fact that the transgender actress Dolly has in reality assumed some measure of success in Bollywood circles is proof too of the changing scene in Indian cinema. The cinema indeed mirrors real life, for transgender politicians have become immensely successful in India, and one of them now even heads her own political party as an openly trans person.

Shweta represents the mainstream societal perspective on the transgendered, and through her own journey from disgust and revulsion to understanding and acceptance of her uncle's sexual orientation lies the film's integrity and sensitivity. It accomplishes this not by castigating Indian society but by reminding Indians of their own mythology, of a time when gender identities were more fluid. In his film on the ambiguities of the third gender, Santosh Sivan takes us into the shadowy world of the transgendered community as they gather to celebrate their identities at their annual festival in Koovagam in Tamil Nadu. This unusual coming of age story features two gender related ceremonies, on the one hand a traditional puberty ceremony in her home for the young girl, Shweta, the other of the transitioning of her uncle Gautam into his feminine identity, as Gautami. The second ceremony is invested with even more mythological significance in that it is actually located within a temple in the rural environs of Koovagam, in the heart of Tamil Nadu. The Koovagam festival, in addition to being a common gathering point for *Aravanis*, also serves as an empowering space in which to publicly worship and re-write the framing of religious texts from a gender-queer perspective and as a subaltern re-reading of an episode from the *Mahabharata*. Every year, for hundreds of years, according to their narrative, during the first full moon of the Tamil month of *Chittirai* (April–May) *Aravanis* have converged at Koovagam to commemorate this ancient mythological event. The Koovagam festival serves to validate the *Aravanis'* place within a traditional social structure and has, over the years, morphed into a unique space for transgenders in Southern India to bond, share experiences, and coordinate their campaign for recognition (Mitra 2010).

Tamil Nadu has the distinction of being the first state in India to grant transgendered people special rights and protection, followed shortly by Kerala, and the role of the media in bringing this about must be noted. They have brought in legislation to include the third gender in ration cards, a factor that has effected a mini revolution in the state because now there is an actual official space for them to exist, as they are now able to write 'T' within the gender column while applying for admission to educational institutions or government hospitals. The State Directorate of Collegiate Education in its newly-designed application form for the degree courses in all its colleges has included the transgender as a separate category. Under the column "Sex," the application forms now provide three options: Male, Female and *"Thiru Nangai"* (the Tamil name for transgender). The two southern state governments have been the first to create a transgender policy aimed at ending societal stigma attached to this sexual minority. The policy covers all categories of transgenders, including male to female transgenders and intersex people. It also stresses on the rights of the minority community to self-identify as man, woman, or transgender, as stated in the Supreme Court judgement of 2014 (Malhotra 2015).

However we also see a critique of such state based intervention into social inequality by theorists like Govindan and Vasudevan, who claim that the use of a Spivakean (2006) strategic essentialism certainly has its political uses by presenting the *Aravani* identity as homogenous across the population, part of a supposedly blameless and glorious Indian past, and thus deserving of civil rights and social acceptance. However, this technique of visibility has the effect of denaturing all that is subversive, sexual, and liberatory about the traditional *jamaat* practice—preventing an honest community appraisal of what is both an oppositional and oppressive alternative social system, while giving it the sheen of nonthreatening tradition. Indeed, official change and accommodation of any sort bring with them dangers of complacency and the state-led co-opting of oppositional politics, blunting its edges, as it were. In other words, with the creation of categories for welfare and rights, the state could potentially set in motion a politics of appeasement where the hidden aim would be the deferral of true reform (Govindan and Vasudevan 2008).

This position is supported by Judith Butler who asserts,

> I want to maintain that legitimation is double-edged: it is crucial that, politically, we lay claim to intelligibility and recognizability; and it is crucial, politically, that we maintain a critical and transformative relation to the norms that govern what will and will not count. This latter would also involve a critical relation to the desire for legitimation as such. It is also crucial that we question the assumption that the state furnishes those norms.
>
> (Butler 2004: 117)

What the *Aravani* experience as well as that of other gender deviant communities in South Asia goes to show is that while the state's legitimation of queer identities can be supportive to marginalized groups, it is important not to rely on that alone as a means of asserting queer power. Rather, as articulated by Arvind Narain, any law reform which does not take into account a simultaneous change in the homophobic attitudes of people which are constantly reinforced by existing societal structures such as family, religion, and media is bound to be fruitless as legal change can only be part of a wider process of social change (Narain 2004).

The Role of History in Shaping the Postcolonial Nation

It must be noted here that societal attitudes in India toward queer identity have been shaped not through the lens of religion but rather through that of British colonialism. South Asian scholars have noted that queer identities, far from being looked down upon were in fact celebrated in ancient times. As mythologist Devadutt Pattanaik reminds us, on Krishna's chariot stands the transgendered warrior, Shikandi. Indeed, westernization has not changed bedroom habits, it has simply led to an embarrassed denial of our sacred scriptures. Those who want to see hijras as 'alien to Indian culture' claim they came as slaves and servants alongside Central Asian warlords who invaded India around a thousand years ago. However, the story of Brihanalla (Arjuna being cursed to live as "a eunuch dancer" in King Virata's court) in the *Mahabharata* dated to 300 BCE, indicates they were known in India even before the Central Asian invaders. Moreover, the Sanskrit *Kama Sutra* dated to CE 300, refers to *trittiya prakriti*, or the third nature of people who cannot be classified as men or women (Pattanaik 2014).

Indeed, the hijra community was patronized in medieval times by the Muslim and Hindu rulers of the land, as singers and dancers, invited during wedding and childbirths to bless, usher in fertility and ward away malevolent spirits. But things changed with the arrival of the colonizers from the West, and not just the subcontinent, but all the territories annexed by the British worldwide, with their repressed Victorian notions of sexuality and morals. "Buggery" had become a criminal offence in England under King Henry VIII in 1533, and they bequeathed their buggery laws to all the dominions ruled by the crown. Indeed, of the seventy-six countries that still criminalize sodomy around the world, most do so as a holdover from British colonial rule (Scott 2015). This dark side of British law has hardly been represented in cinema, with the exception of recent films like *The Imitation Game*, 2014, where the brilliant cryptanalyst and war hero Alan Turing, is subjected to chemically-induced castration in lieu of jail time. Since many of the details were kept classified for a good half century, few knew of the extent of his wartime feats, even though he was awarded the Order of the British Empire for his services in 1945. Dr. Turing was eventually officially pardoned posthumously by Queen Elizabeth in 2013, close to a half century after his suicide. Ironically, Britain has itself repealed its buggery laws in 1967, followed by several other Commonwealth countries or former territories, including New Zealand, Hong Kong, Australia, and Fiji, but they still exist in the statute books of its former dominions such as Belize, Jamaica, Nigeria, Uganda, Indonesia and India (Scott 2015).

Elsewhere too, religious conservatives, be it the Christian Right or the Islamic Right, have actively lobbied to prevent changes to these outdated colonial laws. In Jamaica, for instance, activists from the United States and United Kingdom opposed to LGBT rights have urged local Christian conservatives to resist repealing the law, arguing that homosexuality is a choice and connected to pedophilia. In Uganda, the government has gained a reputation as one of the most dangerous countries for LGBT rights, in part because of recent moves to strengthen its already restrictive anti-homosexuality laws. Under the current law, gay people face fourteen years to life, but since 2009, some Ugandan lawmakers have been pushing to enact an "Anti-Homosexuality Bill" that would impose even harsher penalties and potentially even the death sentence. Their position is strengthened by funding from Evangelical groups from the US Likewise, a bill passed by Nigeria's National Assembly in 2013 severely raised the stakes by criminalizing gay marriage, same-sex "amorous relationships" and even membership in gay rights groups, carrying penalties of up to fourteen years in prison. Several states in northern Nigeria also operate under a form of Sharia law in which homosexuality is punishable by death for men and whipping and/or imprisonment for women. Yet, in all these cases, few human rights groups connect the dots to the impact of colonization on the cultural values and mores of a subject people.

It is important to examine the conditions in precolonial days as it reveals surprising facts. Indeed, far from being an alien concept, ancient Indian texts from the Vedic period and the *Kama Sutra* indicate that ancient Hinduism did in fact permit both alternate sexuality and gender deviance (Butler 2004; Vanita and Kidwai 2008). In this sense, the concept of heteronormativity coined by queer theorists as the binary gender system wherein only a physical relationship with the opposite gender is perceived as "normal," was not as common in precolonial India as we might imagine. Anthropologists have gone so far as to claim that Hinduism, as it was practiced in precolonial times, was more open to alternate sexualities and gender roles which did not fall into rigid binary oppositions, as in much of western mainstream culture, which accepts only two sexes and genders (Garfinkel 1984; Nanda 1990). But in 1861, the British legal system was imposed on India as the Indian Penal Code, with Section 377 of this Code being an offshoot of the homophobic British 1860 anti sodomy law, and thus male same sex acts were criminalized. This draconian legislation states, "Whoever voluntarily has carnal intercourse against the order of nature with any man, woman, or animal shall be punished with imprisonment for life, or with imprisonment for a term which may extend to ten years, and shall be liable to a fine" (Kakar and Kakar 2007).

In recent years however, the law has been challenged in the courts by gay rights organizations, with Gay Pride marches held across the length and breadth of the nation. The Indian media have been surprisingly supportive of queer rights and a plethora of websites have challenged this homophobic perspective, with eloquent declamations such as this Editorial in the website, *India Opines*:

> The LGBT community in India has been persecuted, harassed, discriminated against, often molested and beaten for their apparent 'sexual deviance.' Their Right to Life, one of the seven Fundamental Rights of the Indian Constitution, has been violated and snatched away from them. For many, this is not their first fight, possibly not even their hardest battle; that would be when they have had to come out of the metaphorical dark and suffocating closet to face society.
>
> (Maheshwari 2014)

But the reach of the colonial imaginary can be seen in the fact that this piece of British legislation is still on the statute books. The British also collected, translated, rearranged and sometimes rewrote Indian history as part of their 'Orientalist' agenda during the two centuries of their rule and part of their rearrangement included eliminating or marginalizing all traces of positive same-sex references. Ashish Nandy and Uma Chakravarty have discussed the manner in which British Orientalism worked to emphasize "Great Tradition" works and delegitimize "Little Tradition" works by focusing on texts which supported British notions of masculine virility, and where femininity and women could be marginalized, thereby putting in place forms of misogyny that would underlie what Paola Bacchetta calls postcolonial queerphobia (Bacchetta 1999). This has been the subject of numerous books and films of more recent times by British writers and film makers such as E.M. Forster and his film counterpart, David Lean in the film version of his book, *A Passage to India* (1982). The scene which presages the young English-woman Adela Quested's descent into delirium in the famous Marabar caves where she later accuses the hapless Dr, Aziz of rape can in fact be read as her own emotions and hormones running riot when placed within close proximity to forbidden fruit, namely the virile young native. Thus, well before the incident in the caves, Lean presents the young woman faced with her own sexual fears and desires, when con-fronted with the erotic carvings of Hindu gods and goddesses in an abandoned temple (Sharpe 1994).

In fact, the paintings and sculptures at ancient Hindu temples like those of Khajuraho bring to focus that ancient India had far more lib-eral attitudes toward sexual relations and gender mores. This fact has been enshrined in documents like the *Kama Sutra*, which, contrary to common lore, is more of a treatise on gender mores and cultural values than a smutty book on sexual positions. Indeed, as clarified by psy-choanalyst Sudhir Kakar and anthropologist Katharina Kakar in their analysis of Indian sexuality, homosexual activity itself was ignored or stigmatized as inferior in ancient India, but never actively persecuted, and this did not change materially in spite of the advent of Islam which unequivocally condemns homosexuality as a serious crime. Interest-ingly, however, Islamic culture in India also had a Persian influence, wherein homoeroticism is celebrated in literature, as in Sufi mystical poetry where the relationship between the divine and the human was expressed in homoerotic metaphors (Kakar and Kakar 2007). Going back even further, a Bengali story from the Hindu scriptures ascribes the birth of one of the greatest sages of ancient India, Bhagiratha, whose spiritual devotions earned him the ability to bring the River Goddess, Ganga, down from the Heavens to the earth, to two women, with his very name meaning "One born of two vulvas" (Pattanaik 2014). Queer theorist Ruth Vanita too ascribes this legend to the renowned fourteenth century Bengali poet, Krittivasa in his version of *The Ramayana* (Vanita and Kidwai 2008).

It is interesting too to examine the position of the most marginalized of queer communities in most parts of the world, namely transgender communities, and how they have transformed their position in South Asia. The Transfeminist Manifesto articulated by third wave feminist, Koyama Emi defines "Trans" as an inclusive term encompassing a wide range of gender norm violations that involve some discontinuity between the sex a person is assigned at birth and his or her gender expression. The phrase "Trans women" is used to refer to those individuals who identify, present, or live more or less as women, despite their sex assignment at birth. "Trans men," likewise, is used to describe those who identify, present, or live as men despite the fact that they were perceived otherwise at birth. (Emi 2003). The Transfeminist movement therefore, has been described as primarily a movement by and for trans women who view their liberation to be linked to the liberation of all women. It embodies feminist coalition politics in which women from different backgrounds stand up for each other, "because if we do not stand up for each other, nobody will" (Koyama 2003).

This statement is especially important in the context of human rights activism in the subcontinent, where women's rights organizations have often turned their backs to the struggles of queer communities. This troubled history mirrors that of the US women's movement of the 1970s, where second wave feminism tended initially to marginalize lesbian struggles, with even Betty Friedan (1963) denigrating lesbians as "the lavender menace." Ms. Friedan did eventually come round and accept the lesbian struggle as a part of women's rights activism, but it was not without a struggle that pitted straight activists against lesbian activists, including a separatist movement within radical feminist circles. In her seminal essay, queer theorist Adrienne Rich used the phrase "compulsory heterosexuality" (Rich 1980), to describe the acceptance within mainstream society of heterosexuality as the norm, effectively erasing lesbian experience or making it appear outside the norm. If that was the case in the far more liberal West, at the height of the second wave of the feminist movement, how much more would that be the case in the developing world, where feminists were already struggling to hold their heads above water due to the avalanche of patriarchal onslaughts against them?

Historian and co-founder of the renowned Indian women's rights journal, *Manushi*, Ruth Vanita castigates this homophobic mindset as one that has divided even progressive groups in India. One example of that is the one where in 1994 the Communist Party of India's women's front opposed a gay men's conference in Bombay, claiming that homosexuality is the result of decadent Western influences, while just a year later, the Hindu rightwing organization, the Shiv Sena, attacked cinema halls that were screening the lesbian film *Fire*, with its chief Bal Thackeray claiming that lesbianism was not a part of Indian culture (Vanita and Kidwai 2008). It is a truly ironic moment when the Left and the Right come together to attack marginalized groups as being non-representative of the home culture. This attitude has been described by Paola Bacchetta as xenophobic queerphobia which justifies itself by constructing the self-identified Indian queer as originating outside the nation, or a foreign import (Bacchetta 1999).

The third wave of feminism, as coined in the 1990s by Rebecca Walker, has taken sexuality as one of the central planks of its movement, with a renewed focus on the ties between patriarchy and heteronormativity.

Indeed, the suppression of sexual agency and exploration is often used as a method of sexual control and domination, seen in the homophobia that mandates heterosexuality (Walker 2001). It has been used by devout Christian communities in even the alleged liberal West of the last century to commit female genital cutting on women who masturbated, or worse, had intimate relations with other women, in order "to cure them" of their unnatural desires. In the India of recent times, the Indian third wave has taken a keen interest in the assertion of Hindutva that queer identity is an example of Mother India having been tainted by western civilization. Scholars like Chandra Talpade Mohanty, Inderpal Grewal, Gayatri Gopinath, et al., have examined the role of national and nationalism in developing and indeed, creating, the psyche of the heteropatriarchal postcolonial state. It is hardly a surprise that violent debates over national identity have taken place outside the home country, a factor that Gayatri Gopinath hones in on as the manner in which the diaspora attempts to assert its true Indianness by reverting to an imaginary authenticity. Thus we see its appearance in the South Asian diaspora at special public representations such as the Indian Republic Day Parade in New York City, where the South Asian Gay and Lesbian Association (SALGA) waged an ongoing battle throughout the 1990s over their right to march in the annual India Day Parade. The group that challenged SALGA's right to participate in this demonstration of diasporic unity was made up of a group of Indian businessmen known as the National Federation of Indian Associations (NFTA), which had taken it upon themselves to be the voice of the diaspora (Gopinath 2006).

Ruth Vanita and Salim Kidwai denounce this delusional perspective as the myth that same-sex love is a disease imported into India which contributes to an atmosphere of ignorance that has led to much suffering among these already marginalized groups. Furthermore, what is even more shameful is that all of this oppression has been completely ignored by most political parties and social activists, including those who are supposedly radical. Indeed, Vanita and Kidwai add further that the editor of a prominent women's rights journal told them that "such issues" are not important, since Indians face "life and death issues." They add that for many homosexually inclined Indians, their sexuality does become a life and death issue (Vanita and Kidwai 2008). In fact, the authors go on to assert that labels like "abnormal," "unnatural," and "unhealthy" are of relatively recent origin in India and their exhaustive anthology on same-sex love in India is a part of their mission to educate the Indian public into recognizing that alternate sexualities, far from being an anomaly, have in fact been very much a part of the history of the Subcontinent.

Indeed, alternate sexualities were regarded, if not with acceptance, at least without abhorrence in ancient Hindu society. In the ancient Hindu epics, in fact, one often comes across explicitly sexual interactions between men and women, one example being the description in the Valmiki Ramayana of the women Hanuman perceives in the Sri Lankan King Ravana's palace and in other houses in the island kingdom. They are described as lying half nude in each other's arms, as if with male lovers. Hanuman even admits that he feels guilty about having violated their privacy, but concluded that since his voyeurism happened accidentally, it is pardonable (Vanita and Kidwai 2008). Under the circumstances, one would have to conclude that the modern day right wing Hindu morality police are actually guilty of ignorance of the content of the epics they supposedly hold in such high regard. Bacchetta traces this ignorance to the deliberate manipulation of knowledge by Orientalists of past eras who ignored the vast array of sources that celebrate queerdom, such as not merely the *Kama Sutra* but even common practices such as *Naitri karar*, meaning friendship agreement, a form of marriage between women, and the exquisite same-sex iconography in the Tara-Taratini temple of Orissa (Bacchetta 1999).

Transgendered individuals too had an accepted place in Indian society, much as was the case in indigenous communities in many other parts of the world, such as the two-spirit or *Berdache* in Native American communities, which were in fact held in much reverence in the precolonial Americas. Priya Babu, a famous transgender activist and writer based in Madras discusses in her study of *Aravani* musical traditions how the Tamil epic *Shilappadikaram* refers to the unique art practices of the *Aravani* community (Babu 2007). The Transgenders of Tamil Nadu identify themselves with the female form Lord Krishna assumed for his night with Prince Aravan, hence they call themselves *Aravanis*—wives of Aravan, as opposed to *Hijras*, the more pejorative term common to the rest of India (Mitra 2010). In this mythological tale from the annals of the ancient Hindu epic, the *Mahabharata*, when the Goddess of war, Kali, is approached by her devotees, the Pandavas, seeking victory over their dreaded foes, the Kauravas, the Goddess grants it to them on one condition, that they sacrifice one of their purest souls. The young prince who offers himself as a human sacrifice is none other than Aravan, son of the great warrior prince, Arjuna. But he has a condition too, that he does not want to go into the arms of death as a *brahmachari* or single man, he desires at least one night of connubial bliss. Perceiving the fact that no woman would opt to wed a man who was destined for death the very next morning, God himself, through the deity Krishna, turns himself into a woman, Mohini the enchantress.

Thus the transgender community in Southern India claims a link of more than 4,000 years of recorded history to one of the most ancient and sacred of epics of Hinduism, the *Mahabharata*, with Lord Krishna himself as their initiator. However, mythologist Devdutt Pattanaik reminds us that many stories from Tamil folklore and even the Tamil version of the *Mahabharata* are relatively unknown in much of Northern

India, where a more patriarchal version of the myth holds centerstage (Pattanaik 2014). Another link to Hinduism lies in the fact that as per Hindu mythology, *Hijras* represent the *Ardhanareeswara*, the half-male, half-female image of Shiva—an image symbolic of a being that is ageless and sexless. The hijras' third sex dimension is said to infuse them with 'Shiva Shakti,' the power of both male and female deities, and give them supernatural powers to bless or curse, a belief that has helped them in northern India to occupy a niche in society (Nanda 1990; Narain 2004), wherein they have the authority to venture into a neighborhood with a newborn child and demand a ritual amount for blessing the infant.

However, mythological associations aside, hijras have for many years been a fringe group in Hindu society; feared and despised for their gender bending and sexual non-conformity far more than they are revered for any spiritual powers. Segregated and excluded from most occupations, they had earned a living for many years through begging and sex work, an existence fraught with danger; wherein they are often victimized and degraded by both clients and the police. Santosh Gupta points out that the intersex individual occupies the lowest rung of society within patriarchy because s/he is unable to reproduce and when such children are born, they are usually abandoned and disowned by their families, and usually go away to live within other such communities where they live on the margins of society (Gupta 2002). But this marginalized position has been changing in recent years, as seen especially in the case of the *Aravanis* of Tamil Nadu. Indeed, considering how far back this record of the community goes, it is ironical that the Hindu Far Right now puts forth its doctrine of *Hindutva* as an atavistic homophobic credo, a stance which, ironically enough considering its stated antipathy to other faiths, has a lot more in common with the Christian Far Right and the Islamic Taliban than with its own ancient treatises on sexuality. Indeed, the idea of "Hinduism" was reinvented by the Hindu militants as an instrument of exclusiveness, and what had been a rich, varied cluster of religious and cultural traditions was grossly simplified. This re-invention of India through the lens of Hindutva is perceived as a threat by all minorities and underprivileged groups who fear its implications, and rightly so, for it serves to undermine the very idea of India, as envisaged by its first Prime Minister, Jawaharlal Nehru and his colleagues in the first Indian parliament who visualized it as an inclusive democracy, respectful of the rights of all its minorities. In his incisive analysis of this vision of a new nation, cultural theorist Sunil Khilnani points out that India's vision of itself has been created out of cultural collisions and interactions with a wider world. In fact, Prime Minister Nehru, during his long tenure of close to two decades had envisaged India as a composite, secular nation that included a great diversity of peoples and reflected a many-layered sense of "being Indian" that grew out of the subcontinent's long history of dealing with outsiders who lived there, both as rulers and the ruled (Khilnani 1997).

I conclude with a statement from one of my own students in my Indian Cinema, Gender and Cultural Identity course, as it brings in a wider perspective.

> It is wonderful to know that even part of a country can accept alternate sexualities, considering the amount of violence and hatred directed towards transgendered people. It gives me hope that perhaps, at some point, all across the US too, as well as in other countries, people will begin to accept people of alternate sexual orientations and genders without judgment.
>
> (Morgan Foley 2012)

For even in the allegedly liberal US, although they are not openly discriminated against in schools or jobs, an immense amount of hatred and distrust is still directed towards them in many parts of the country, including open violence, as depicted in films like Kimberley Pierce's *Boys don't Cry* (1999) and Ang Lee's award winning drama, *Brokeback Mountain* (2005). Bollywood's venture into the realm of depicting alternate sexualities have been few and far between, but there is hope on the horizon through more recent films which have received a surprisingly positive reception from audiences and without the accompanying backlash from the right wing, unlike the case just two decades before with *Fire* (Mehta, 1995). In this sense, truly, the idea of India, as envisaged by Khilnani, may yet buck the onslaught of the conservative forces and grow closer to the mindset of previous, precolonial eras, as a true space of diversity in all its myriad shapes and forms.

References

Babu, Priya. *Aravanigal samugya varaiviyal*. Chennai: Thenthisai, 2007.

Bacchetta, Paola. "When the Hindu Nation Exiles Its Queers." *Social Text: Out Front: Lesbians, Gays, and the Struggle for Workplace Rights*. Durham: Duke University Press, Winter 1999. 141–66.

Bose, Brinda. "The Desiring Subject: Female Pleasures and Feminist Resistance in Deepa Mehta's *Fire*." *Indian Journal of Gender Studies* 7 (2000): 249–62.

Burton, Richard F. *The Kama Sutra of Vatsyayana*. New York: E.P. Dutton, 1964.

Butler, Judith. *Undoing Gender*. New York: Routledge, 2004.

Chandiramani, Radhika, and Geetanjali Misra. "Unlearning and Learning: The Sexuality and Rights Institute in India." *Sexuality, Gender and Rights: Exploring Theory and Practice in South and Southeast Asia*. New Delhi: Sage Publications, 2005.

Davidson, K. 2013. www.gaylaxymag.com/articles/entertainment/ajeeb-dastaan-hai-yeh.

Desai, Jigna. *Beyond Bollywood: The Cultural Politics of South Asian Diasporic Film*. New York: Routledge, 2004.

Doniger, Wendy. *Siva: The Erotic Ascetic.* New York: Oxford University Press, 1973.

Dudrah, Rajinder. *Bollywood: Sociology Goes to the Movies.* New Delhi: Sage, 2006.

Emi, Koyama. "The Transfeminist Manifesto." *Catching a Wave: Reclaiming Feminism for the 21st Century.* Eds. Rory Dicker and Alison Peipmeier. Boston, MA: Northeastern University Press, 2003.

Foley, Morgan. Class Discussion. Westfield State University, 2012.

Friedan, Betty. *The Feminine Mystique.* New York: Norton, 1963.

Garfinkel, Harold. *Studies in Ethnomethodology.* Cambridge: Polity Press, 1984.

Gopinath, Gayatri. *Impossible Desires: Queer Diasporas and South Asian Public Cultures.* Durham, NC: Duke University Press, 2006.

Govindan, P., and A. Vasudevan. *The Razor's Edge of Oppositionality: Exploring the Politics of Rights-Based Activism by Transgender Women in Tamil Nadu.* 2008. www.lassnet.org/2009/readings/govindanvasudevan2008 razors-edge.pdf.

Gupta, S. "*Tamanna*: Desiring the Undesired." *Films and Feminism, Essays in Indian Cinema.* Eds. Jasbir Jain and Sudha Rai. Jaipur: Rawat Publications, 2002.

Huntington, Samuel. *The Clash of Civilizations and the Remaking of World Order.* New York: Simon and Schuster, 1996.

Kakar, Sudhir, and Katharina Kakar. *The Indians: Portrait of a People.* New Delhi: Viking, 2007.

Khilnani, Sunil. *The Idea of India.* New York: Farrar, Strauss and Giroux, 1997.

Kumar, Nirnimesh. "Delhi High Court strikes down Section 377 of IPC." *The Hindu,* July 3, 2009. www.thehindu.com/todays-paper/delhi-high-court-strikes-down-section-377-of-ipc/article219269.ece.

Lal, Malashri. *In Search of Sita: Revisiting Mythology.* Gurgaon: Penguin Books, 2014.

Malhotra, N. Accessed March 12, 2015. www.thebetterindia.com/38398/kerala-writes-history-with-indias-first-transgender-policy/.

Maheshwari, A. "On Section 377." *India Opines,* 2014. http://indiaopines.com/section-377/.

Mitra, M. N. "Brides of Aravan." *Caravan: A Journal of Politics and Culture.* 2010. Accessed October 12, 2012. www.caravanmagazine.in/print/1414.

Mulvey, Laura, "Visual Pleasure and Narrative Cinema." *Media and Cultural Studies.* Eds. Meenakshi Gigi Durham and Douglas M. Kellner. Malden, MA: Blackwell, 2006.

Nanda, Serena. *Neither Man nor Woman: The Hijras of India.* California: Wadsworth Publising Company, 1990.

Nandy, Ashis. *The Intimate Enemy: Loss and Recovery of Self under Colonialism.* Oxford: Oxford University Press, 1983.

Narain, Arvind. *Queer: Despised Sexuality, Law, and Social Change.* Bangalore: Books for Change, 2004.

Patel, Geeta. "Trial by Fire: A Local/Global View." *Gay Community News* 24.2 (1998): 10–17.

Pattanaik, Devdutt. *Shikandi and Other Tales They Don't Tell You.* New Delhi: Zubaan, 2014.

Raj, Senthorun. "Igniting Desires: Politicising Queer Female Subjectivites in *Fire*." *Intersections: Gender and sexuality in Asia and the Pacific*. Ed. Carolyn Bower, Issue 28, March 2012.

Ram, N., Ed. "Don't Dither on Section 377." *The Hindu*, July 1, 2009.

Rich, Adrienne. "Compulsory Heterosexuality and Lesbian Experience." *Signs: Journal of Women in Culture and Society* 5.4 (1980): 631–60.

Roy, Sandip. 2013. "Dear Karan Johar, Do You Really Think Gay Men are Like This?" Accessed May 25, 2015. www.firstpost.com.

Russo, Vito. *The Celluloid Closet: Homosexuality in the Movies*. New York: Harper and Row, 1985.

Scott, J. "Don't Tell: The Lonely Fight to Overturn Antigay Laws in Belize." *The New York Times Magazine*, May 24, 2015.

Sharpe, Jenny. "The Unspeakable Limits of Rape: Colonial Violence and Counter-Insurgency." *Colonial discourse and postcolonial theory, A Reader*. Eds. Patrick Williams and Laura Chrisman. New York: Columbia University Press, 1994.

Vanita, Ruth, and Salim Kidwai. *Same-Sex Love in India: A Literary History*. New Delhi: Penguin Books, 2008.

Venkat, V. "From the Shadows." *Frontline* 25.4 (February 29, 2008): 100–104. www.flonnet.com/fl2504/stories/20080229607610000.htm.

Walker, Rebecca. "Lusting for Freedom." *Listen Up: Voices from the Next Feminist Generation*. Ed. B. Findlen. New York: Seal Press, 2001.

Warn, S. Review of *The Journey*, July 12, 2005. www.afterellen.com/movies/4756-review-of-the-journey.

11 The Complexities of Transnational Female Solidarity in "Driving with Selvi"

Rajini Srikanth

"Driving with Selvi" is a documentary film released in October 2015, made by the Canadian filmmaker Elisa Paloschi. The film's eponymous protagonist is a woman from the South Indian state of Karnataka, a feisty individual who rejected the life that was forced on her and chose to follow her own ambitions. Her journey from child bride to first female taxi driver in South India and now a happy mother and wife with a partner of her choice is the story that Paloschi's film tells. This essay examines the complex terrain of transnational feminist solidarity that is the backdrop of the film's production, and it addresses the politics of feminist connections between the global North and the global South.

The film opens with the following statistics culled from UNICEF data: 700 million women alive today were married before the age of eighteen; of this number, 250 million were married before fifteen. One-third of child brides around the world are in India.[1] The larger framework in which we are urged to view the film is thus presented, and the filmmaker attempts to steer our reception of Selvi's story as a challenge to and triumph over the system of child marriage. However, the film escapes its own frame and becomes the portrait of an ebullient and complex individual who seizes our attention from early in the film, when she speaks of the decision to run away from her abusive marriage, intending to throw herself in front of a bus, but, instead, when the bus approached, she raised her arm to flag it down and then boarded it. This is a woman with courage and resolve who is bold enough to flee her circumstances and confront the uncertainties of the world out there.

As a tribute to Selvi, the film succeeds admirably. It is impossible not to admire her perseverance, her adaptability, her continuous curiosity of what life holds. But there are at least three instances in the film that could have been developed further in order to illuminate the context in which Selvi takes advantage of opportunities that present themselves to transform her situation. All three involve men who enter Selvi's life at various moments, and the supportive nature of their relationship to her. Let me be clear: I am not advocating for a shift in the focus of the film— it is and should remain Selvi's film, rightly featuring her extraordinary determination and resilience. But, as Selvi herself says, there were crucial circumstances that enabled her to take advantage of expanded possibilities, and some of these circumstances came about through the support of men. Particularly because the filmmaker intends to screen the film to one million viewers in India in an attempt to initiate change and open up the possibility of non-traditional employment opportunities (such as taxicab driving) for women, minimizing the role of men in their capacity as helpers runs the risk of making Selvi's changed life seem unrealistic and confined to the miracle of her impressive personality and good luck. Robert Connell's observation that men typically hold the political and cultural "authority" to facilitate change and, therefore, function as "gatekeepers for gender equality"[2] applies with particular force in rural communities. In villages, initiatives for change must necessarily engage men. "Driving with Selvi" is most definitely inspirational for women, but the women who view her as a possible role model also need to understand why and how the men and other individuals in her life who were instrumental in facilitating her changed opportunities came to hold the supportive attitudes they did. In exploring the context of Selvi's change from child bride to taxi driver, this essay addresses the interplay among masculinities, South Asian feminisms, and friendship.[3]

During the post-screening discussion of the film in Macedon, NY's India Community Center,[4] an audience member asked Paloschi why the men in the film are given little play and, in one instance, even kept off-camera (when Selvi urges the husband of her former taxicab driving companion to "allow" his wife to drive a cab and make money that the family needs). Paloschi's response did not adequately address the issue of the minimal attention that the men in Selvi's life receive. Her answer was that she made an artistic choice to focus exclusively on Selvi and, therefore, to select accordingly from ten years of footage. One might see this response as warranted from a filmmaker who wished to foreground her female protagonist and bring her center stage. But, as I argue throughout, in choosing to sidestep the complicated relational intricacies between Selvi's confident assertions of autonomy and the diverse masculinities exhibited in the film, Paloschi misses the opportunity to enrich and deepen understanding of how Selvi's changed circumstances occurred. Karen Lindo's observation of the difference between patriarchy and masculinity are important to recall:

> Patriarchy must... be distinguished from masculinities since the former lays claims to an immutable atemporal naturalized male domination. Masculinity like femininity, on the other hand, is concerned with behavioral patterns *that are local and fluctuate over time*. This distinction between patriarchies and plural masculinities and femininities opens up new avenues by which to more subtly interpret the male characters.[5]
>
> (emphasis added)

Paloschi first made Selvi's acquaintance in 2004; the film was completed in the Fall of 2015. The film is a paean to Selvi, and it presents her as the author of her own destiny, almost as if her extraordinary courage and determination originate in a vacuum. The focus on the individual—Paloschi characterizes Selvi as "unique" and "powerful"[6]—and on her achievement as an individual is both laudable and problematic: laudable, because it emphasizes the extraordinary qualities of resilience and boldness in Selvi and underscores how change is significantly driven by internal ambitions, but it is problematic because it minimizes the influence of factors outside the self that are often crucial to enabling and sustaining individual resolve. Fawzia Afzal Khan makes a similar point in her critique of "the politics of pity" and the emphasis on the courage of individual women that is the preoccupation of the West, as it seeks to cast itself in the role of rescuing oppressed women in the global South. The efforts of women and supportive men in these locations who create the conditions that stimulate change are frequently ignored and the focus is exclusively on the individual. Khan's essay concerns itself with two women from Pakistan, Mukhtaran Mai and Malala Yousafzai, who have become poster examples in the West to both illustrate the oppression of women in the third world and to celebrate their extraordinary courage in challenging oppression. Her point is that the "very real challenges to Pakistan's patriarchal, misogynist culture organized and led by Pakistani feminist and women's rights activists, even when not fully successful, are *not* what mainstream American media has focused on in its coverage" of women in South Asia.[7] Like bell hooks, she argues that this misplaced exclusive attention on the individual celebrates a "faux feminism," which obscures collective efforts that create the conditions for long-standing gender equality.[8]

A lengthy *New York Times* article details the enormous obstacles faced by women in one region of India in their quest for employment at a meat-processing site; they are blocked in their efforts by the stranglehold of male elders, even though the women display extraordinary strength and courage to defy tradition.[9] Despite the support of the state, lackluster though it is, and the existence of laws on the books that call for equal employment opportunities for women and men, unless the male elders' cooperation is enlisted, the number of women who can resist obstructions is small, and their victories may be temporary. Therefore, the conversation about women and employment, particularly at the rural level, has to bring in the voices of village leaders. Exemplary women are powerful paradigms, and it is tempting to hold them up as independent and autonomous agents of change. But even exemplary women operate within the framework of political, economic, and social forces that intersect in specific ways at particular moments of time, and these intersections create the disruptions that facilitate change and the dismantling of oppressive structures.

Involving men in women's empowerment is not a new idea. In the last ten years, there has been "a shift in development institutions' focus from 'women' to 'gender' that has sparked an explosion of interest in working with men to establish gender equitable societies."[10] Shukria Dini, writing specifically of the Somali context, notes the success from involving men in issues that affect women's wellbeing—issues such as literacy and anti-Female Genital Mutilation campaigns:

> While the war in Somalia has presented women with an opportunity to exercise their activism and address their vulnerabilities, it has also taught them that the success of programs designed to empower women depends in part on negotiations with their countrymen, particularly those who may feel emasculated by the war and threatened by the heightened visibility of women in their communities.[11]

Those who recognize the importance of involving men in empowering women are clear that such involvement cannot shift the focus from the ultimate objective at hand—the creation of an environment in which there is access to opportunity for women in the same measure as for men, and conditions in which both men and women can together work to build safe and sustainable communities for all. In a similar vein, Fauzia Ahmed argues that microcredit schemes that are focused on women in Bangladesh can actually place women in situations of great vulnerability if they do not engage the men in their lives.[12] Likewise, in South Africa, men's groups engage in discussions of anti-hegemonic masculinities in the context of living with HIV and constructing meaningful lives with female partners. These "responsibilised" subjects are keenly attentive to the influences of community, political, public health, and economic forces in crafting "responsible masculinities." As Steven Robins notes, "Rationalist and liberal individualist conceptions of the modern subject and the rights-bearing citizen are inadequate for understanding the transformative character of these new biosocial processes and identities."[13]

Odanadi Girls' Home, the place to which Selvi fled when she left her abusive marriage, was started by two men, former newspaper reporters, who tell the story of how they were shamed into setting up the rescue home by a woman, Radhamma, who taunted them with profiting from other people's misery. More than twenty years ago, they were interviewing taxi drivers when they came across Radhamma; she was openly critical of their work and accused them of advancing their own careers. Radhamma's story of having been a child bride, who was sold to a brothel by her husband, prompted Stanly Varghese and Parashuram Lingegowda to start Odanadi. "[W]e were challenged to do more than just report what we'd heard," they say.[14]

Selvi calls Stanly and Parashuram her brothers, and she finds in them the love and support that she had expected in her own brother, who, instead, forced her into marriage at the age of fourteen. She feels a deep sense of betrayal at this act by her biological brother, and she is also extremely resentful of her mother from whom she received no love and support. In Odanadi Girls' Home, she finds her group of friends and her new avocation—learning to drive.

The film offers us a minimal view of Varghese and Lingegowda, Odanadi's founders. These men and the residence they established is crucial in enabling girls in abusive situations to become confident women who make choices about the future trajectories of their life. It would be helpful to know how Varghese and Lingegowda view the interventions they have been able to make—do they feel that they are having an impact on long-established institutions and facilitating fundamental changes of attitude, or do they see their work as largely a rescue effort whose focus is less on institutional change and more on providing a place for the psychological and emotional healing of deeply injured girls? What is their relationship to other organizations and individuals working in the same arena? The little that I was able to find out about them I gleaned from an interview published in *The Guardian* newspaper and from the Odanadi website.[15]

Varghese and Lingegowda are not focused only on the girls and women in Odanadi. What is significant about their approach is that they understand the degree to which they have to work with community members in order to have the type of impact they seek. They note: "The focus is very much on raising awareness and changing the mindset of men towards gender equality, through training, education and sensitizing the entire community."[16] The Odanadi website explains: "We have adopted a holistic approach to combat sexual violence through prevention, rescue, rehabilitation, awareness and training programmes." Varghese and Lingegowda stress the importance of working with a wide range of individuals and groups in order to bring about change at the level of the village: "Odanadi has a long history of encouraging stake holdership to create social responsibility in the society. Advocates, painters, writers, students, media persons, police, doctors, ngos and community organisations have become a part of this people's movement."[17] Those who work in the realm of transforming gender relations underscore the importance of making these changes through community involvement in order to sustain the changed attitudes and actions. The United Nations' Committee on the Status of Women made as one of its priority themes for 2004 "the role of men and boys in achieving gender equality" and, in 2006, undertook an assessment by member states of the recommendations that were articulated in 2004.[18]

One could argue that Paloschi's decision not to give the Odanadi founders more time in her film comes from knowing that there are other avenues online from which one can get the necessary information about them. Indeed, this is true, but while these online sources (*The Guardian*

interview and the Odanadi website) give us details of what the organization does and the holistic approach that it employs, they do not offer us
insight into the challenges that the two founders experience(d) in changing attitudes in the wider community about girl children, or the inroads
they have made in the years since the founding of Odanadi. What makes
them persevere? Who are their allies? Who their adversaries? Given
Paloschi's ten-year connection with Mysore during the years that the
film slowly came into being, she had ample opportunity to procure such
information from Varghese and Lingegowda. As those who work in the
realm of women's empowerment know, there are numerous organizations in India that provide essential support and crucial interventions
for girls and women in abusive situations. The issue, as I discuss later,
is not that "outsiders" catalogue the extent of India's social ills, but that
outsiders seldom communicate the extraordinary work of local organizations or individuals who labor everyday under relentless challenges
and significant danger to themselves. In not providing viewers with a
window into these efforts through a strategic engagement with Varghese
and Lingegowda, Paloschi diminishes not only the significance of the
two founders' work but also the robust efforts of local groups working
in the area of women's empowerment and gender equality. I would call
Varghese and Lingegowda "womanist" in their worldview and actions,
because they understand the importance of involving the community,
the entire ecosystem of local, regional, and national life that enables
egalitarian masculinities and confident feminisms. They exemplify Alice
Walker's definition of womanist: "Committed to survival and wholeness
of an entire people, male and female."[19] Also, it is crucial to acknowledge the "everyday heroism" of these two men. Karen Lindo draws on
Jude Akidinobi's conception of this type of practice as "bring[ing] together the familiar, regular and even the banal with the 'remarkably
exceptional.'"[20]

A second missed moment for deepened understanding of the circumstances leading to Selvi's success as a taxi driver is when she asserts
that the male taxi drivers did not resent her presence but in fact respected and welcomed her, though they joked that she had come to take
away their jobs. We witness one scene in which they are full of smiles
and camaraderie for Selvi. There is an entire unexamined world that
this scene rests on, but Paloschi simply glides over the surface of this
visual without probing it for its crucial revelations. If, as the film implies,
the prevailing norms of rural India devalue girls and women, and if a
combination of centuries-old cultural traditions and current-day economic pressures compels families to marry off their girl children early,
what makes these male taxi drivers so willing to accept Selvi into their
midst? How have they come to adopt this enlarged attitude toward Selvi,
though she has entered into a non-traditional workspace for women and
is in direct economic competition with them? Did Odanadi work with

the taxi cab drivers of the region to train them and help them understand how they could benefit from Selvi's and other female taxi drivers' presence? Paloschi speaks of "the dignity that comes with driving" and the compelling persona of Selvi as the principal reasons for the male drivers' respect of her.[21] Yet, these factors alone cannot explain the total absence of tension and hostility in the men's reception of her. The scene that we view cries out for further examination.

In my research about female taxi drivers in India—and there are many taxi companies in India that employ female drivers, in cities like Trivandrum, Mumbai, Delhi, Kolkata, Pune, Chennai, Hyderabad, and Bangalore, to name some—I learned that the demand for them stems from the lack of safety that female passengers feel with male taxi drivers. Female taxi drivers offer a safe alternative for women and children and provide an important avenue for economic self-sufficiency for women. Men are allowed as passengers only if they are accompanied by women.[22] It would have been very important to find out whether the male taxi drivers' acceptance of Selvi was in part facilitated by their view of her as serving primarily a female passenger market (and therefore not as intense a competitive threat to them), or whether they were welcoming of her participation as an equal—as her entitlement to pursue any vocation she desired. An inquiry that engaged these types of issues would have strengthened the significance of the scene in the film in which we see Selvi's warm and easy interaction with her male driver colleagues. As it stands now, the scene adds to the aura of Selvi's uniqueness and conveys the impression that it is something about her that leads male taxi drivers to see her as a friend and not as an unwelcome intruder. There is no doubt that Selvi is a compelling person, but her strength of character alone cannot explain the respectful attitudes of the men to her. She is not the only female taxi driver that Odanadi produced; what made it possible for the other female taxi drivers to pursue their trade?

The third area of insufficient development in the film is the character of Viji, Selvi's second husband, the person she marries for love. We get but a mere glimpse of Viji and no understanding of why he pursues Selvi and so obviously admires her. He is in awe of her courage and is extremely supportive of her, but even so we sense that he, too, can fall into obstructionist ways of thinking, as he does, when he does not wish her to go back to work (driving a taxi) after the birth of their first daughter. Selvi tearfully intones, "This is my fate." But the trajectory of her life changes again, because we see her going to a school for truck drivers to determine whether she is eligible to apply for training. How did this opening of possibility come about? What transpired in her home that Viji is no longer an obstacle? Was it simply that her daughter reached an age at which both she and Viji felt comfortable that she could return to work? We know that she and Viji both drive trucks, and their dream is to own a fleet of trucks, so was it an aspiration for economic autonomy

that led Viji to realize the advantages of having Selvi as a business partner in addition to her being his life partner? The complexities of their
relationship are left entirely to the imagination—not that such an editorial move is always problematic. In fact, when there is a stereotypical
script that tends to play out in the viewers' mind, a cinematic decision
that withholds easy confirmation of that script and introduces the possibility of a disruptive narrative through gaps in the unfolding of events
can perform a salutary and transformative function. But in this instance,
Viji's own journey is as important as Selvi's, if only because it offers one
possible way in which other men can be enlisted in the cause of wom-
en's empowerment. Surely Viji is not so unusual that other men cannot
see themselves in him. Could Viji have understood the sentiment that
Connell articulates:

> Gender equality is an undertaking for men that can be creative and
> joyful. It is a project that realizes high principles of social justice,
> produces better lives for the women whom men care about, and will
> produce better lives for the majority of men in the long run?[23]

One other scene bears mentioning for its simultaneous limitations and
possibilities. Selvi has gone to visit her friend and former Odanadi
resident who, like her, became a taxi driver. The friend is now married
and a mother, and she no longer drives a taxi. However, she wants
to return to being a driver in order to help out with the household
finances, but her husband will not allow her. Selvi decides to speak
with the husband and to persuade him of the advantages of his wife's
being a driver. The conversation takes place with the friend's husband
literally off camera, outside the cinematic frame. Selvi is seated with
her friend and she projects her voice so that the husband can hear
her in the interior of the house. His responses to her come as muffled mumblings (in an interesting reversal of the typical relegation of
women to inner spaces while men occupy public spaces). We never
see him, we don't know what his facial expressions or body language
are, and we are never told why he will not or cannot reveal himself.
Is he unwell at the time of Selvi's visit? Is he too embarrassed to show
himself to a foreign filmmaker? The film's portrayal of this exchange
between him and Selvi, with him off-screen, suggests several possibilities, including (1) his extreme arrogance and therefore his refusal to
deign to be present for the camera; (2) his extreme shyness and therefore his anxiety at being present for the camera; and/or (3) his refusal
to participate in a public airing of the disagreements he has with his
wife. Keeping him off screen is perhaps a way of underscoring that
Selvi, unlike her friend, will not allow her husband to loom large in her
life. His off-screen voice, in contrast to her confident and courageously
posed questions and strong assertions, is only just audible. The film's

message could be seen as both that men can exert a powerful influence even when they are not physically present *and* that women should confine men to the sidelines if they prove obstructionist. But while this decision to keep him off camera is a not unusual cinematographic decision by a filmmaker who is clear about spotlighting her female protagonist, and one that provokes many questions about the role of men in the lives of their wives' futures, the artistic implications are beside the point here. What is important is the necessity of realizing that if rural women are to sustain their ambitions to work outside the home even after being married and becoming mothers, then their husbands must become fully involved in the process of making such an outcome possible and sustainable.

In preparation for screening the film to one million viewers in villages around India, Paloschi has, so far, had it translated into Hindi, Marathi, and Odiya (Selvi lives in the state of Karnataka, so the original languages of the film are Kannada, Tamil, and English). For the screenings to engage the diverse traditions and priorities of the audiences in different regions in India, Paloschi knows that she will have to work with local civil society organizations, community social workers, and individuals who are tuned in to the likely reactions of the viewers in each screening location. There are wide regional variations of culture and practice in India. Historian Ramachandra Guha observes that India is unique in its ability to cohere as a nation of multiple and innumerable languages, ethnicities, and cultures. It is "simply sui generis," he declares, and defies all paradigms of nationalism.[24] There is also no uniformity of gender relations among different parts of the country. Therefore, each region will require its own tailored post-screening discussion. Unless Paloschi can engage the issue of the role for men in the kind of future she portrays for Selvi and others like her, the film will remain a celebration of one individual rather than a catalyst for institutional and systemic change in how girl children are viewed.

That Paloschi is ready to do the hard work of such engagement is signaled by the ten plus years that she took to make the film. Her comment at the discussion in Macedon about Selvi's gradual healing (every time she returned to India, she found that Selvi had healed some more and was in a different place emotionally and psychologically than on the previous visit) indicates that she is comfortable with slow-moving and protracted narratives and is not seeking a quick outcome. But where Paloschi may have to be willing to invest more time and effort than she currently has is in finding effective ways to draw men into the discussion alongside the women in their lives.

Selvi echoes the language of "self-reliance" that the film champions through Paloschi's predominant focus on her. In an appearance on a panel in New York during the week of January 23, 2016 at a symposium on the impact of media on gender equality—organized by ITVS

Independent Television Service, Women and Girls Lead Global, The Ford Foundation and USAID—Selvi declared,

> If you think that anyone, like your brother or your mother or anyone else, is going to come to your rescue, that's never going to happen... You need to figure out what you need for yourself and you have to find the confidence in yourself that you can achieve something. Then you can do whatever you want.[25]

These are inspirational words, and they are a necessary and crucial stimulus to girls and women in abusive situations; but Selvi's understandable pride in herself and her rightful anger at her brother and mother for their betrayal of her obscures the importance of other men and women who supported her in her dreams and recognized the qualities in her that would enable her to forge through constraints. It is easy to take pride in oneself as a lone actor, particularly when the international audience to whom one is being presented celebrates you for the display of individual courage. Fawzia Afzal Khan notes that when Mai and Yousafzai speak of the challenges they have overcome to a Western audience, the collective "we" that permeates their articulation, in Pakistan, of how these advances for justice for women are made is replaced by the "I." Solidarity fades into the background and the individualized subject emerges.[26] Post-screening discussions in rural India, if they are to have the intended effect of opening up non-traditional avenues of employment for women that take them outside domestic spaces and provide mobility and physical independence, must draw into the conversation men and other actors (patriarchal and matriarchal elders) who are typically seen as obstacles to gender equality. The screenings and discussions will have to mobilize local ecosystems in order to guarantee audience turnout and effective participation leading to concrete next steps that create necessary opportunities for women.

To Paloschi's credit, she did not come to India to make a film about abused girls or to kick start her own suspended career as a filmmaker. She cannot be accused of using India as the stage for her own revival or of harboring a grand desire to ride in as a champion to save disenfranchised girls and women (the literature critiquing such sentiments is voluminous and rich in its analysis).[27] The global South is considered to be fertile territory for the discovery of "purpose" in one's life; the deprivations and injustices are perceived to be so blatant that any kind of intervention, however small, can leave one feeling that one has made a meaningful contribution to "better" the life of a single person. Institutions and philanthropies in the global North (e.g., the Ford Foundation, the Bill and Melinda Gates Foundation, Global Fund for Women, Channel Foundation, Levi Strauss Foundation, The International Development Centre, The McCormick Foundation, and

Independent Television Service—ITVS) provide opportunities to insert oneself in the fight against the victimization of women and illuminate deplorable practices like child marriage and human trafficking. These interventions are largely in the realm of bringing to the awareness of viewers in the global North the everyday conditions of life for their "less fortunate" sisters in the global South. The expectation is that once one becomes aware, one will then engage in the next step and become involved in ending this injustice in the manner that is realistic given one's own life circumstances.

This type of awareness-raising work is fraught with problems and can lead to exacerbating the types of exploitation of vulnerable groups that it seeks to end. The complexities of such interventions are the subject of James Dawes 2007 book *That the World May Know*. He focuses on the efforts of humanitarian workers and human rights reporters, photographers, and creative artists in recording and portraying abuses of human rights around the world. The authors' and visual artists' awareness of the complicated politics enmeshing their work—questions such as, to what extent they exploit their subjects' suffering, how do they re-evoke traumas by pressing their subjects to describe what they have been through, how much of their subjects' complex narratives can they realistically embed in newspaper stories, how can they fulfill the trust that their subjects place in them when they bare their souls to speak of unimaginable suffering, how can an "opening night" exhibition (replete with wine and cheese and tasteful music) of photographs of torture or other human rights abuses convey to the attendees the moral responsibility they carry for addressing these atrocities?—form the subject of Dawes analysis.[28] Paloschi appears to have asked herself these questions: she returned every year for ten years to spend time with Selvi and to chart the course of her healing; there is a definite intimacy that develops between them that prevents the film from becoming an exploitative tool through which Paloschi enriches herself; and she and Selvi plan to tour the villages of India to screen the film and stimulate the setting up of infrastructures that will enable women to learn to become taxicab drivers.

In addition, Paloschi, it would appear, is not unaware of the politics of representation—of her being a woman from Canada presenting to Indian audiences a film about the institution of child marriage and its impact on girls and women. At the India Community Center in Macedon, she was asked how the first Indian screening—in Mumbai in October, 2015—was received. She responded that she had been very nervous, particularly as an outsider depicting a social ill in a country that is not one's own. But, she observed, she was very surprised by the positive and warm response she received. She attributed the favorable reception to the intimacy that the audience sensed between Selvi and her and to the length of her association with Selvi and the continued connection between them.

The friendship between them appears to be complex, and it spans multiple "borders and boundaries, including… race, class, ethnicity, and nation." Chowdhury's textured analysis of "dissident" friendship—the type of intimacy "which requires us to unravel our assumptions and to clear the colonial, sexist, ableist, and racial debris from our perceptual apparatus to truly see one another"—provides a rich lens through which to understand the bond that exists both on and off screen between Paloschi and Selvi.[29]

However, Paloschi's making of the film cannot be divorced from the complicated terrain of the global South's being an object of orientalist and imperialistic inquiry and examination by the global North. In her interviews with media outlets, the questions posed to her focus on the horror of child marriage and the unfortunate coercions and constraints faced by women in India. Though these are legitimate issues, what is problematic about the manner in which they are posed is that Paloschi seems to be regarded as an expert commentator on the conditions of Indian women. One exchange in particular stands out: the interviewer begins by lamenting the institution of child marriage, then moves quickly to probing Paloschi about women's opportunities to drive in India (wondering why women don't drive in India—"women are meant to be contained inside the house with the husband," Paloschi explains, but, fortunately, she does clarify that she is speaking about women in small rural communities; women in cities definitely drive!). From this topic, the interviewer shifts to a question about the likelihood of there being female engineers in India. Paloschi observes that the numbers are small, as though she has studied the percentage of women engineers in India and can provide expert insight on the situation.[30] Not only does Paloschi fail to disabuse the interviewer of her insufficient knowledge, but also neither she nor the interviewer is aware of the irony that India's probe to Mars, launched in 2013 but settling into orbit around Mars in September 2014, was made possible as much by female scientists as by male scientists. In fact, one physicist in the United States, a person of Indian origin, marveled at the Indian Space Research Organization (ISRO) photograph[31] capturing the celebration by ISRO's female scientists and engineers and asked, "When will we see anything like this in the US?" The point he was making is that for all the rhetoric about feminism and equal opportunity for males and females, there are forces at work in the United States that have led to a noticeable paucity of women engineers and scientists in the US. There are most certainly factors that concentrate the female scientists and engineers in India in particular socioeconomic class categories and caste groups, but these are criticisms that are of a different nature, not that the system does not encourage women to become engineers.

One cannot fault Paloschi for the curiosities of her interviewers or for their echoing familiar orientalist stereotypes of Indian women.

However, she can impress upon them that her knowledge of India and its women is limited and specific to her association with Selvi, and that she is a filmmaker primarily, not a scholar of transnational feminism or India. Though her brief sojourns in southern India over the past ten years give her a far deeper insight into a certain part of the country than a casual tourist might acquire, she has not made a serious study of the country nor reached out to local scholars and activists to construct the framework for her film. Like the film's underdeveloped narratives of the men who encourage Selvi to pursue her dreams, the absence of information about the efforts of local activists in the area of women's rights is an unfortunate gap that perpetuates the image of a country that is irretrievably caught in highly problematic practices. Elisa Paloschi becomes the spokesperson for details about child marriages in India. She is one more conduit through which the western world understands this deplorable practice that, unfortunately, still continues.

In recent years, there have been several films that focus on the practice of child marriage in India—some made by filmmakers from outside India and others by those within. The films by US-based filmmakers include "After My Garden Grows" (2014), a short film by Megan Mylan made in collaboration with the Sundance film organization and the Bill and Melinda Gates Foundation; the PBS "Now" series special "Child Brides: Stolen Lives" (2007), which begins near Jodhpur in Rajasthan and covers the practice of child marriage in India, Niger, and Guatemala; and Neeraj Kumar's film "Child Marriage" (2005). Indian-made films include Nandita Roy and Shiboprosad Mukherjee's "Joyee" (2015), which will be shown in villages across West Bengal, and Payal Sethi's film "Leeches" (2016).

The relevant question to ask about these films is the purpose for which they are made and screened and the positionality the filmmaker assumes with regard to the practice being portrayed. Sethi's film exposes a practice in Hyderabad where young girls from desperately impoverished families are contracted in marriage, sometimes just for a day, to much older men for a price. Sethi's film both honors the courage of an older sister who is determined to prevent her fourteen-year-old sibling from being traded in such a contract marriage to be a one-day bride and the activist Jameela Nishat, "whose NGO in Hyderabad works tirelessly, and often under threat, to empower and educate women and girls from poor Muslim communities in over twenty slums in the old city of Hyderabad." Sethi insists that her film is:

> …neither a documentary nor a serious social-issue film. I am not here to preach or provide propaganda; I'm merely trying to tell a story that has gotten under my skin, and the hope is, if I do this well, it will at least affect a handful of other people who may be similarly unaware of this ongoing practice.[32]

Presumably, the awareness will lead viewers to support local activists if they themselves cannot personally get involved in the efforts to stop the practice (Sethi now lives in India, but she was trained in the United States by the famous filmmaker Mira Nair).

Roy and Mukherjee were commissioned to make the film by the West Bengal State Legal Services Authority to show how the state government's efforts to "create an enabling environment for elevating the education, health, and nutrition status women and children"[33] were bearing fruit. The government intends to use the film to start a conversation about why the practice of child marriage persists and to ask how it can be ended. The inspirational figures in it are the young girls who resisted the practice of child marriages in their villages and succeeded in convincing their elders to permit them to continue with their studies. The film is part of a governmental effort to persuade village communities to stop a practice that has been legally outlawed in 1929. Mukherjee and Roy are well-known filmmakers, so they were commissioned to make the film.

The ineffectiveness of the state in preventing child marriage also comes through in the PBS Now documentary. Here we see the extraordinary courage of an activist on the frontlines, a woman who visits villages and attempts to prevent mass child marriages. She is beaten, her hand cut off, and left for dead. We learn that law enforcement officers and government bureaucrats seemed unable to exercise their power in her behalf. Yet, she perseveres, because she considers her work incomplete. What is striking about this woman's quiet courage is the contrast with the PBS reporter Maria Inahosa's intrusive insertion of herself and her film crew into the situation she is covering: one of the women she interviews has accused her husband and his family of abuse, and she refuses to return to her husband. The woman's family seeks a formal divorce, and Inahosa takes it upon herself to go to the husband and ask for his perspective on the accusation and what he proposes to do. It is as if Inahosa wishes to push the individuals involved toward an agonistic climax that she can capture on screen. There is too much Inahosa on the screen.

The PBS documentary begins with this assertion by Inahosa:

> As the mother of a nine year old girl, I wanted to find out about the cultural and economic pressures that could lead parents to marry off their young daughters and see what's being done from the grassroots to change that.[34]

This desire to understand the complexities in various parts of the world is commendable, but the question still remains whether such knowledge leads to more than just a feeling of self-congratulation that one has become better informed, empathetic, and cross-culturally aware. Does such inquiry result in a corresponding interrogation of practices within one's own country—whether the United States, Canada, the United Kingdom, or Germany—that might need similar analysis.

In this context, a report by three women charged by the United Nations to assess gender equality in the United States offers a fascinating intervention in the domain of feminist discourse. The women were from Poland, the United Kingdom, and Costa Rica, and their task was to "evaluate a wide range of U.S. policies and attitudes, as well as school, health, and prison systems."[35] In advance of the release of the full report, the delegates shared some of their reactions: They were "appalled" by the lack of gender equality, particularly the hostility to women's reproductive rights, which they experienced during a visit to an abortion clinic in Alabama. One of the delegates characterized the harassment they were subjected to as they neared the clinic as "a kind of terrorism." They deplored, as well, the absence of paid maternity leave for many women and said they found "shocking" the lack of accommodation in the workplace to women's "pregnancy, birth, and post-natal needs." Another significant danger to US women that the delegation observed is that "Women are 11 times more likely to be killed by a gun in the United States than in other high-income countries." But perhaps one of the most telling insights the delegates gained is that women in the United States "don't seem to know what they are missing." They believe themselves to "be better off with respect to rights than any woman in the world" and could not believe that women elsewhere have paid maternity leave, for example. (The full report will likely reveal that such surprise is exhibited predominantly by white middle- and upper-middle class women. Most women of color and working class women recognize "what they are missing" with respect to basic rights). It is in this context of US-centric solipsism that efforts by white US feminists to educate oneself about the problematic practices of other nations—particularly developing nations—often meets fierce resistance and criticism in countries of the global South. A similar distrust greets European feminists as well.

The year 2015 saw the release of a highly controversial film about India and the dangers to women there. British filmmaker Leslee Udwin's film "India's Daughter" takes as its starting point the gang rape by six men on a bus on December 16, 2012 of twenty-three-year-old Jyoti Singh in Delhi and the outrage that ensued nationally, with women and men of all classes marching the streets of Delhi and other cities demanding fundamental changes in attitudes to women and police response to reports of rape. In an impassioned TEDex talk, Udwin declares that she was "At the end of my patience as a woman waiting to be accorded equal status to men." She says that she saw in the grassroots mobilization in India the beginning of a journey of hope that led her to believe that "we are at a time on the cusp of change." Inspired by the extraordinary protests that erupted in India, she left her family and children in England and went to India, determined to:

> ...amplify these voices that cried 'Enough is enough.' There was something absolutely tremendous about these protests. Braving the December freeze, the ferocious government crackdown. India was leading the world by example. In gratitude to these protestors, I gathered my family and told them why I needed to go.[36]

Udwin's remarks are worthy of careful analysis; it is important to understand her *desire* to travel to India and the provocation that the rape and the response to it constituted for her as a woman and a filmmaker. Is she being sincere, or are her declarations of admiration for the men and women who turned out in thousands to demand accountability disingenuous? The complicated motivations that brought her to India and the process by which she makes the film invite close study within the context of global feminism. Udwin's presentation of herself as the person who understands what the rape and the protests it sparked really mean, or her surprise that her "gift" to the Indian people would be so ungraciously rejected by the Indian government could be seen as one more instance of the dangerous fault lines in the terrain of global feminism and transnational feminist solidarity.

The Indian government banned the film, claiming that its footage of the rapists' unrepentant remarks and the justification for rape by one of the defense lawyers was "incendiary" and likely to cause riots and disturbance. The parliamentary affairs minister called the film an "international conspiracy to defame India."[37] The banning has provoked a surge of interest in the film, which in today's technological age, is available on the internet. It's an unfortunate and wrong-headed move by the government, whose ban had precisely the opposite effect than the one intended: Indian officials are seen as unwilling to engage rape in a meaningful way, and there is further confirmation of the impression that India tolerates a culture of rape and the devaluing of women.

It is worth underscoring what Ania Loomba and Rita Lukose observe about South Asia (of which India is a part) and feminisms: as a "'location' produced by the crisscrossing of geopolitics, history, and culture, South Asia is less a static place and more a dynamic crossroads of various regional, national, and global forces."[38] The robust networks of feminist praxis cannot be reduced to simplistic framings. They note that South Asian feminists "understand the nationalistic forces that interrupt their solidarity work, but they also actively resist these impediments to forging alliances." They persevere in the "sustained focus on the dense histories, interconnections, and dynamic complexities of South Asia" and they challenge the "reductive ways in which Western feminist frameworks incorporate their others."[39]

In contrast to Udwin's film, "Driving with Selvi" is both an indictment of India and an optimistic portrait of the "redemption" that is possible even in an environment that appears to be unrelentingly hostile to women. Selvi is an engaging protagonist, and Paloschi's close friendship with her emerges in the cinematic technique of the film—there is a genuine comfort in Selvi's answers, and we sense a deep affection between filmmaker and subject. Paloschi has received favorable reviews in screenings, which have covered a broad geographical terrain, including Europe, the United States, Canada, Jordan, Peru, and Kenya. However, the journey of the film within the Indian context has only just begun. Paloschi has spoken of the obligation she felt to Selvi to complete the film, though it took her ten years to do so.[40] I would argue that, while Paloschi is absolutely right to recognize what she "owes" Selvi, it is also equally important that she recognize what she owes the millions of women and men of India as she takes the film on the road. The film cannot be a celebration of one woman's triumph; it must clear the space for a meaningful discussion between women and men in countless rural communities so that they can all work together for a future in which both genders are equally empowered.

Rajini Srikanth
University of Massachusetts Boston

Notes

1 See the UNICEF website on "Child protection from violence, exploitation, and abuse" at www.unicef.org/protection/57929_58008.html (last accessed on February 10, 2016).
2 R. W. Connell. "Change among the Gatekeepers: Men, Masculinities, and Gender Equality in the Gender Arena." *Signs* 30, no. 3 (Spring 2005): 1802.
3 See Elora Halim Chowdhury, "Friendship." In *Gender: Love* (Macmillan Interdisciplinary Handbooks), ed. Jennifer Nash (Farmington Hills, MI: Macmillan Reference USA, 2016), 17–26.
4 The screening was held on the afternoon of January 30, 2016.
5 Karen Lindo, "Ousmane Sembene's Hall of Men: (En)gendering Everyday Heroism." *Research in African Literatures* 41, no. 4 (Winter 2010): 112.
6 Comments made during a question and answer session with the filmmaker at the Edmonton Film Festival on October 2–3, 2015; www.youtube.com/watch?v=15f0kT-mdzA (last accessed on February 10, 2016).
7 Fawzia Afzal Khan, "The Politics of Pity and the Individual Heroine Syndrome: Mukhtaran Mai and Malala Yousafzai of Pakistan." *Performing Islam* 4, no. 2 (2015): 157.
8 bell hooks, "Dig Deep: Beyond Lean In." *The Feminist Wire* (October 28, 2013): http://thefeministwire.com/2013/10/17973/ (last accessed on November 10, 2016).
9 Ellen Barry, "Battling Tradition with Defiance: Indian Women Seeking to Work Confront Taboos and Threats." *The New York Times* (Sunday, January 31, 2016): 1/10–12.
10 Alan Greig, "Reflections from the Board of Editors." *Critical Half: Bi-Annual Journal of Women for Women International* 5, no. 1 (Winter 2007): 5.

11 Shukria Dini, "Negotiating with Men to Help Women: The Success of Somali Women Activists." *Critical Half: Bi-Annual Journal of Women for Women International* 5, no. 1 (Winter 2007): 36. Volume available online at http://wfwmarketingimages.womenforwomen.org/news-women-for-women/assets/files/critical-half/CriticalHalf.pdf (last accessed on February 10, 2016).

12 Fauzia Ahmed, "Microcredit, Men, and Masculinity." *NWSA Journal* 20, no. 2 (Summer 2008): 122–55.

13 Steven L. Robins, *From Revolution to Rights in South Africa: Social Movements, NGOs, and Popular Politics after Apartheid* (Boydell and Brewer, 2008), 164.

14 Natricia Duncan, "Human Trafficking: 'We are Haunted by the Horror that We have Witnessed." *The Guardian* (March 14, 2014) www.theguardian.com/global-development-professionals-network/2014/mar/14/human-trafficking-slavery-india (last accessed on February 10, 2016).

15 See www.odanadi.org.

16 See Duncan, "Human Trafficking."

17 See the Odanadi website at www.odanadi.org/?page_id=10 and www.odanadi.org/?page_id=2001 (last accessed on February 10, 2016).

18 See *Women 2000 and Beyond: The Role of Men and Boys in Achieving Gender Equality.* United Nations Division for the Advancement of Women (December, 2008). See especially pages 1–7. www.un.org/womenwatch/daw/public/w2000/W2000%20Men%20and%20Boys%20E%20web.pdf (last accessed on February 10, 2016).

19 Alice Walker, *In Search of Our Mothers' Gardens: Womanist Prose* (Harcourt, 1983), xi.

20 See Lindo, 111.

21 Paloschi at the Edmonton Film Festival in October, 2015. Available at www.youtube.com/watch?v=15f0kT-mdzA (last accessed on February 10, 2016).

22 Poulomi Banerjee, "Women at the Wheel: How They Handle Bias and Threats on the Road." *Hindustan Times* (February 15, 2025): www.hindustantimes.com/india/women-at-the-wheel-how-they-handle-bias-and-threats-on-road/story-qSqJuITVfUBFItgGXJjgYN.html (last accessed on February 10, 2016).

23 Connell, 1819.

24 Ramachandra Guha, *India after Gandhi: The History of the World's Largest Democracy* (Ecco, 2007), 758.

25 Gant News, "Former child bride becomes India's 'first female taxi driver.'" Available at http://gantdaily.com/2016/01/27/former-child-bride-becomes-indias-first-female-taxi-driver/ (last accessed on February 10, 2016).

26 Fawzi Afzal Khan, "The Politics of Pity," 159–67.

27 Lila Abu-Lughod, *Do Muslim Women Really Need Saving?* (Cambridge, MA: Harvard University Press, 2015); Rogaia Mustafa Abusharaf's edited collection, *Female Circumcision: Multicultural Perspectives* (Philadelphia: University of Pennsylvania Press, 2006); Obioma Nnaemeka's edited collection *Female circumcision and the politics of knowledge: African women in imperialist discourses* (Westport, CT: Praeger Publishers, 2005); Chandra Talpade Mohanty, *Feminism Without Borders: Decolonizing Theory, Practicing Solidarity*, 5th edition (Durham, NC: Duke University Press, 2003); Elora Chowdhury, "Development Paradoxes: Feminist Solidarities, Alternative Imaginaries and New Spaces," *Journal of International Women's Studies* 17, no. 1 (January 2016): 117–32 are a handful of the many publications that critique the practice of framing women in the global South as needing to be rescued from the clutches of their traditions and cultural practices.

28 James Dawes, *That the World May Know: Bearing Witness to Atrocity* (Cambridge: Harvard University Press, 2007).

29 Elora Halim Chowdhury, "Friendship," 17–18. I saw Paloschi and Selvi together at a screening in Salem, MA in March 2016.

30 "Daniel Garber talks to Elisa Paloschi about her new documentary Driving with Selvi premiering at the ReelAsian Film Festival." Available at https://danielgarber.wordpress.com/2015/10/27/daniel-garber-talks-to-elisa-paloschi-about-her-new-documentary-driving-with-selvi-premiering-at-the-reelasian-film-festival/ (last accessed on February 10, 2016).

31 Soutik Biswas, "India's Mars Mission: Picture that spoke 1,000 words." *BBC News* (September 25, 2014): www.bbc.com/news/world-asia-india-29357472 (last accessed on February 10, 2016).

32 Bollywooddirect, "Not just another 'One Day Bride'—An Interview with Payal Sethi." Available at www.bollywoodirect.com/not-just-another-one-day-bride-interview-payal-sethi/ (last accessed on February 10, 2016).

33 Shoma A. Chatterji, "A Crusader Inspires a Film against Child Marriage." *Press Institute of India* (June 2015). www.pressinstitute.in/a-crusader-inspires-a-film-against-child-marriage/ (last accessed on February 10, 2016).

34 PBS NOW, the weekly news magazine; www.pbs.org/now/shows/341/video.html (time signature 2:47–2:56).

35 Laura Bassett, "The U.N. Sent 3 Foreign Women to the U.S. to Assess Gender Equality. They were Horrified." *HuffPost Politics* (December 15, 2015): www.huffingtonpost.com/entry/foreign-women-assess-us-gender-equality_us_566ef77de4b0e292150e92f0 (last accessed on February 10, 2016).

36 Leslee Udwin, TEDex Janpath talk. February 28, 2015. www.youtube.com/watch?v=b2lrzgVZzas (last accessed on February 10, 2016).

37 Anoosh Chakelian, "Silencing India's Daughter: Why Has the Indian Government Banned the Delhi Rape Film?" *New Statesman* (March 5, 2015): www.newstatesman.com/world-affairs/2015/03/silencing-india-s-daughter-why-has-indian-government-banned-delhi-rape-film (last accessed on February 10, 2016).

38 Ania Loomba and Ritty A. Lukose, "South Asian Feminisms: Contemporary Interventions." In *South Asian Feminisms*, ed. Loomba and Lukose (Duke University Press, 2012), 25.

39 *Ibid.*, p. 24.

40 Comment made at the discussion in Macedon, NY on January 30, 2016.

12 Ethical Encounters

Friendship, Reckoning and Healing in Shameem Akhtar's Daughters of History (1999)

Elora Halim Chowdhury

This chapter is an exploration of the idea of friendship between women across nations as a basis for social and political transformation. Friendship as defined by feminist scholar Richa Nagar (2006) is a collective journey among women across differences involving personal transformation and political struggle and striving toward solidarity, reciprocity and accountability. Deploying a transnational feminist analysis (Stone-Mediatore 2003), that is, paying attention to the ways in which far-reaching relations of domination shape and influence the lived realities of communities and individuals across borders, I weave Bangladeshi feminist director Shameem Akhtar's film, *Itihaash Konna* (*Daughters of History*: 1999) with women of color theories of friendship politics and transnational film feminism to further a discussion on solidarity among women. *Itihaash Konna*, I argue, is an important film that helps illuminate the complicated histories and politics of nation-states, war, and gender as they impinge upon interpersonal relationships across time and space. The politics of marginal friendship is taken up by Leela Gandhi in her book *Affective Communities* where she draws attention to hitherto ignored individuals and groups who renounced the privileges of imperialism and allied with victims of their own expansionist cultures. Devoting attention to these presumed "nonplayers," Gandhi's work seeks to illuminate some "minor" forms of anti-imperialism that emerged in Europe, specifically in Britain at the end of the nineteenth century, which took the form of what she calls "dissident friendships." Akhtar's film, I argue, helps us draw attention to similarly presumed minor relationships between women, which defy the logic of colonial and nationalist hierarchies. Relationships between women can be seen in a context much more complex than a mere separation of colonized and colonizer, particularly for women who are part of either side of nationalist projects.

While Gandhi's purpose is in part historical redress, I am inspired by her impulse to unpack the politics of "dissident friendship" in order to think through relationships between women across differences, or more specifically between a lesser colonizer and colonized. By "lesser colonizer" I mean those who were in some ways on the fringes of imperial society—women, LGBTs, and people of color. For example, Jan Jindy

Pettman (2006) elucidates the intersection of privilege and oppression of white European women in settler colonial societies. They were at once marginalized because of their gender yet privileged by their racial identity. Even in colonial societies, hierarchical class structures put certain native groups closer to center of power. Uma Narayan has demonstrated the similarities between the ideology of sexism and colonial racism where physical and moral attributes were used to define women (of the colonizer society) and the colonized (men and women) as the weaker sex/race (Narayan 1995).

Yet, despite being of the "weaker sex," colonizer women played vital roles in maintaining the colonial project and taking on the "white man's burden" that put them in paternalistic positions in relation to the colonized. Like their male counterparts, they replicated the colonial structure of at once oppressing the natives while at the same time couching that subjugation in the ethic of care. This system, that robbed the colonized of full humanity and rights, was justified by an ethic of responsibility and obligation of the oppressor to provide moral and cultural guidance to the "less enlightened." Even within these hierarchical conditions, relationships emerged to varying degrees that hinted at affinity and friendship. Forged whether accidentally or purposefully, friendship is a vehicle for furthering political and social goals within intimate spaces. In another essay, Narayan takes up the idea of dialogue between members of heterogeneous groups in encounters that can take the form of friendship or politics. She states that it is important to understand:

> Working across differences is a morally and politically important enterprise in either context. Both in political contexts and in the context of friendship, such differences in elements of background and identity can be enriching resources, epistemologically, politically and personally. Learning to understand and respect these differences can make more complex our understanding of ourselves and our societies, can broaden the range of our politics and enrich the variety of connections we have as persons.
>
> (Narayan 1988: 32)

In this paper, I join Gandhi's insistence of paying attention to dissident friendships with Narayan's urging that relationships between individuals of heterogeneous backgrounds with discrepant power positions in society can elicit a deeper understanding of human connection.

I find Akhtar's film a significant contemporary text to engage the ideal of lasting social and political change through the practice of female friendship between women of differential gender positionality—however fleeting and difficult that may be. The film focuses on friendships between women in the context of the ruins of a devastating war that "liberated" and established Bangladesh as an independent nation from its "colonial occupier," West Pakistan. The Partition of British India in 1947 created two new nation states of India and Pakistan. Pakistan was formed along religious lines with the two most populous Muslim regions of the sub-continent becoming its western and eastern wings. The eastern wing of the new Islamic state of Pakistan suffered under the political, cultural, and economic domination of West Pakistan until March 1971, when po-litical discontent and cultural nationalism led to a military assault by the West Pakistan army, and the declaration of East Pakistan's independence and renaming as Bangladesh. The independence war of Bangladesh was ultimately supported by India. In December 1971, Bangladesh became an independent nation after a nine-month long war.

I argue that the film, *Itihaash Konna*, offers an example of a dissi-dent friendship between Lalarukh (Sara Zaker), a Pakistani researcher working on war crimes committed by Pakistani military on Bengalis in 1971, and Monika (Rahnuma Ahmed), her Bengali activist friend whose family is a survivor of the violence as both women experience trans-formations of consciousness through their intertwined struggles. As a Pakistani, Lalarukh bears the burden of the genocide unleashed in 1971 on the Bengali population by her own government and military forces. Yet, with deep roots in East Pakistan, having been born in the Eastern wing and to a Bengali mother, and as a woman, she finds herself in the conflicted position where on the one hand she is empathetic towards the war affected families of Bangladesh, particularly her childhood friend Monika, yet on the other, she must make sense of the silence and sanc-tioned ignorance of her own family during the war. The two women's contrapuntal trajectories of the war and its consequences—as part of the oppressor and oppressed nations—form the premise of a dissident alliance.

The colonial dynamic between West and East Pakistan following the Partition of the Indian subcontinent summarily inherited the legacy of British colonial rule in the region. Akhtar's film set in post-independent Bangladesh offers an opportunity to probe the violent inheritance es-pecially because the relationship between the two women in question is indelibly framed as a colonial one. Even though Lalarukh had family ties in East Pakistan, and Monika in West, the war severed these phys-ical ties locating Lalarukh squarely as an agent of the oppressor nation and Monika seeking to document and mobilize a response to the 1971 genocide. While numbers are contested with regards to the killings in East Pakistan in 1971, reportedly, 1–3 million lives were lost, 200,000 women were victims of sexual violence, and 25,000 forced pregnan-cies occurred during the war. The dynamic between the women allows readers to consider the underside of the perhaps "incomplete liberation" of a specifically post-colonial national context, and the kinds of social alliances possible within it, which are nevertheless deeply imbricated in older colonial histories. Intimate bonding of women is tested by the power of an idealized nationalism that is elusive in providing protection and security to women, and fostering trust between women. Further, national independence did not necessarily "liberate" the women of the nation from patriarchal oppression in war and peacetime.

While these alliances may be minor narratives, I believe they are significant for three reasons: first, they offer another instance of understanding the colonial encounter beyond its categorical West/non-West binary; second, they illuminate ways in which the colonial power structure replicates itself even in marginal sites and relationships, and allow us to think of friendship—at times clandestine, conflictual, even unacknowledged—as a mode for social and potentially political transformation for diffused groups and individuals; and third, it takes as the premise of such transformation the desire to recognize a mutual humanity based on compassion and empathy. I use these terms with some caution here and do not mean to evoke romanticized nor cultural relativist notions of unity within diversity. Again, I refer to Uma Narayan who unequivocally states that empathic sensitivity in unions across differences do not simply hinge on "good will" (1988). Similarly, feminist theorist Jane Mansbridge defines empathy against such emotions as pity, condescension, or self-righteousness and instead as a gesture towards human connection. It is that which Adrienne Rich calls furthering "the conscious work of turning Otherness into a keen lens of empathy, that we can bring into being a politics based on concrete heartfelt understanding of what it means to be Other" (1995: 400). Alliance across differences for the purpose of this project, then, is a connection based on shared humanity across differences that has to be strived for. I would like to explore whether such alliances are inevitably crushed within dominant patriarchal colonial relations or whether they can cause a change in self-and-other-perception and potentially contribute to social and political transformation, and, in the process, become transgressive.

In this paper, I have largely used the terms alliance, friendship, community, and solidarity interchangeably. While alliance, community, and solidarity are generously discussed in literature dealing with social change, friendship is often believed to be outside the realm of social and political transformation. I intend to trouble that assumption to convince readers that friendship revisioned can be the basis of (potentially transformative) solidarity precisely because it is premised on a kind of human connection that other types of unions may not contain as explicitly. What makes friendship an interesting medium to discuss is that it allows for the expression of emotion, which in more formal political unions is more often than not dismissed. Instead of rejecting emotions, Narayan, in "Working Together Across Differences," proposes that emotions can infuse our experiences and knowledge of reality in a way to expose the subtle workings of power more insightfully and intensely; hence, their role in explaining human connection should not be presumed to be outside of politics. An exploration of friendship allows us an understanding of power and oppression that is more immediate, complex, and subtle. In addition, following Gandhi's cue, friendship in this project refers to a collaboration between the "most unlikely of associates" (2006: 10). It may take the form of minor or seemingly insignificant gestures of affinity to the other at the risk of endangering the self's security in her own community. I am particularly interested in exploring when and whether "dissident crosscultural friendship"— sometimes between these unlikely associates of oppressor and oppressed communities—trumps, or is trumped by, other kinds of loyalties women might have, to family, community, or nation in the pursuit of social justice (Chowdhury 2016).

Feminist theorist Maria Lugones has also talked about friendship as "bonding among women across differences." Such bonding does not presuppose unconditionality but does recognize the situationality of each person while being cognizant of their plural realities. According to Lugones, friendship can be based on "practical love" and knowledge of and commitment to the other person. She says,

> Because I think a commitment to perceptual changes is central to the possibility of bonding across differences and the commitment is part of friendship, I think that friendship is a good concept to start the radical theoretical and practical reconstruction of the relations among women.
>
> (Lugones 1995: 141)

Understood as such, friendship recognizes the logic of plural realities, and remains open to the possibility of self-reflexivity and transformation in perception. That is, instead of the impulse to make the other in to an image of one's own, in friendship "...one comes to see oneself as constructed in that reality [other's realities] in ways different from the ways one is constructed in the reality one started from. Thus pluralist friendship enhances self knowledge" (143). This enhancement is not merely a cooptation of the other in the service of self-actualization but involves a mutually meaningful and empathetic relationship with the other. It is an epistemically demanding position because one dislodges one's own centrality and strives to work across inequalities rather than simply acknowledging them.

This study employs a combination of filmic and transnational feminist analysis. I share Shari Stone-Mediatore's definition of transnational feminism, which is an analytical and a political project that goes beyond unpacking gender ideologies to confronting far reaching relations of domination spanning but not limited to political, economic, and cultural spheres. These relations of domination "cross over national boundaries and produce historically specific cooperative as well as hierarchical relations among women of different nations, races and classes" (Stone-Mediatore 2003: 129). This mode of analysis is also exemplified in Ella Shohat's (2003) work, which I will discuss in further detail in the conclusion, where she points out the multiple oppressive structures of colonialism and nationalism, spanning across geographic borders of the nation and shaping women's experience. A transnational feminist approach elucidates that women are part of various groups across communities and nations and thereby part of different, yet sometimes converging, struggles. Additionally, this approach suggests that women's myriad struggles, whether individual or collective, are often inseparable from structural oppressions shaping their and their communities' lives such as colonization, patriarchy, and poverty. A transnational feminist lens in this paper provides a way to understand the paradoxical dynamic of conflict and cooperation that shape women's relations with one another. This paper is an exploration of the idea of friendship between women across cultures as a mode for enacting social responsibility and care for the other. Through an investigation of the conflictual yet cooperative alliance between Lalarukh and Monika, women representing either side of a historical conflict, I reflect on the idea of dissident friendship, and argue that relationships between individuals of heterogeneous backgrounds with discrepant power positions in society can elicit a deeper understanding of human connection. I discuss how, despite being located on oppositional sides of the Bengali nationalist struggle and having suffered tremendous violence and loss that render their friendship to betrayal, both women have singular goals of realizing a historical acknowledgment of war crimes through documentation of its victims' experiences and mobilizing awareness and support to elicit an apology from the Pakistani state. In the process, however, both must confront their own silences and complicities and engage in critical self-reflection if not transformation.

Personal and collective challenges women must engage in the process of forging political and social alliance and solidarity are explored in the landmark feminist collection *This Bridge Called My Back*. In its foreword, Cherríe Moraga expresses the book's unique intention to create a space for dialogue among women as opposed to between men and women. She argued that understanding the specific conditions of oppression of women, be it for marginalized communities in the US or outside, is key to building a more effective "Third World feminism," which she described as follows:

> In the last three years I have learned that Third World feminism does not provide the kind of easy political framework that women of color are running to in droves. We are not so much a "natural" affinity group, as women who have come together out of political necessity. The idea of Third World feminism has proved to be much

easier between the covers of a book than between real live women. There are many issues that divide us; and, recognizing that fact can make that dream at times seem quite remote.

(Moraga 1983: no page number)

Together with Stone-Mediatore, Moraga's vision is an effective medium to both illuminate and analyze the "internal differences" within groups, even women's groups, which feminist debates have shown are never coherent. When thinking about and organizing around women's oppression, the cooperative yet conflictual lens that transnational feminism provides is a medium that humanizes the suffering of others different from "us" even as it recognizes friendship, community and solidarity not as natural alliances but as being sought for through active engagement and reflection. Such alliances can take on dissident forms across cultures and are steps to the realization of that remote dream Moraga talks about for feminism—human connection that nourishes self-growth as well as fosters community.

Woman, Nation, Conflict

Daughters of History, arguably, revolves around the challenges to and potentials of dissident friendship. In the last two decades, key texts and films have appeared that disturb a silence in Bangladesh around women's varied experiences of the 1971 War of Liberation. The relatively unknown history of the Liberation War of Bangladesh, or the second Partition of the subcontinent, has been the subject of a number of critical fiction and filmic representations in recent decades. Tahmima Anam's novels, *A Golden Age* (2007), and its sequel, *The Good Muslim* (2011); Shaheen Akhtar's novel, *The Search*; Bina D'Costa's *Nationbuilding, Gender and War Crimes in South Asia* (2010); Nayanika Mookherjee's *The Spectral Wound: Sexual Violence, Public Memories and the Bangladesh war of 1971 (2015)*; Yasmin Saikia's *Women, War, and the Making of Bangladesh: Remembering 1971* (2011); Tareque and Catherine Masud's film, *The Clay Bird* (2002); Nasiruddin Youssuf's film *Guerilla* (2011); *Itihaash Konna* (1999); and the film, *Meherjaan (2011)* are contributing to a new genre of cultural production that seeks to illuminate internal and external tensions surrounding the representation of war, gender, memory, and justice for a wider regional and global audience. There is a robust tradition of writing, filmmaking, theater, and television dramas in mainstream media in Bangladesh on the topic of the Liberation War. Yet, these newer efforts together have departed from conventional norms of representations and launched a crucial and critical discussion of war, genocide, and gender justice on a transnational scale. While it is beyond the scope of this paper to explore a multi-genre investigation of gendered experiences of 1971 that these texts—including *Itihaash Konna*—initiate, I would like to suggest that together they are attempts to restore an ethical dimension to history and in the decolonization of subjectivity and personal identity (Saikia 2011: 9) and to intimate/inter-personal encounters of healing. Like other texts I mentioned in this genre, the films challenge a number of cherished, and inherited 'truths' regarding the Bangladesh War of Liberation in 1971 (Chowdhury 2012). These texts in different degrees are groundbreaking. Their scope is more global as they shed light on a forgotten [outside of Bangladesh that is] conflict in the history of modern South Asia. There is, indeed, a global and regional silence about 1971. In the subcontinent, the Bangladesh Liberation War is either erased as a shameful past, as is the case in Pakistan, or is subsumed under the better known "Indo-Pak" war in which India plays the heroic role in bringing liberation to Bengalis, as is the case in India. In the fields of genocide and trauma studies, very few know or discuss this history.

Some of these texts are also provocative because they debunk a number of national myths that have shaped the consciousness of the post-1971 nation of Bangladesh. The abundance of literature generated in Bangladesh about the war, published as memoirs, novels, district level reports, and accounts of war crimes together have re-membered the war as a triumphant narrative of masculinist liberation [by and large stories of male valor and female victimization—often represented as the plunder of nation and its women]. War time films—commercial films— frequently depict women characters as the sacrificing mother, the rape victim who are absent-present and often silent about their experience, commit suicide, or otherwise killed off. Thus, women's wartime experiences and struggles in these narratives have not only been made invisible but also reduced to sexual victimization in "the private sphere and ... dealt with as private matters by the victims' families often solely by the victim who hides in shame" (Saikia 2011: 54). In contrast, these texts prioritize women's narratives as the primary vehicle for reconstructing this forgotten history. Unlike predominant masculinist narratives, the female characters of *Itihaash Konna* are agentic and project what Janelle Hobson calls "embodied resistance" even as none of them are representative of the "emblematic survivor" (Rothe 2011: 36) of 1971. Emblematic survivors are recognizable in the genre of war films in Bangladesh as iconic representatives of victimized women—the rape victim, who is disheveled in appearance, is mentally unstable, and exits the narrative by suicide or homicide. Countering reductive renditions, Akhtar's film urges an ethical memorialization and initiates multiple tellings of 1971. Akhtar emphasizes a "reckoning" with the "Other", not necessarily at the state or juridical level, but through interpersonal relationships. Akhtar's film deploys an affective lens of shared vulnerability and humanity toward an Other. Bypassing recognizable visual representation of atrocities committed by the Pakistani army and averting retributive violence, it is more interested in human encounter where the self-Other relation is not generative of hostility but an obligation of care and reconciliation. In doing so the film opens up a conversation about a different self-Other relationship between the divided people of South Asia. *Itihaash Konna* consciously attempts to broaden the scope of reconstructing and remembering 1971 beyond the borders of Bangladesh and to reestablish an intertwined history of the region.

One of the few films about the Liberation War directed by a woman, and foregrounding the standpoint of women, *Itihaash Konna* deals with genocide, rape, and war children through the lens of a moral reckoning ("separation vs. liberation" of East Pakistan in 1971) and responsibility on either side. The reckoning is explored through a long and beleaguered friendship between a Bengali and a Pakistani women. The intertwined histories of the two nations are reflected in the intimate relationship—though severed at the bloody birth of Bangladesh—between the characters. Monika was born in Rawalpindi, West Pakistan and Lalarukh in Dhaka, East Pakistan. They studied together in Dhaka until Lalarukh's family left for West Pakistan in March of 1971 days prior to Operation Searchlight, the first massive and brutal strike by the West Pakistan army against Bengali civilians in its then eastern wing including on the campus of Dhaka University. The campus of the largest public university in Bangladesh was especially affected by these strikes, which targeted academics and students, particularly from the Hindu minority. The film depicts many scenes where Lalarukh visits the various sites on the campus commemorating this massacre.

Many years after the independence of Bangladesh, the two friends reacquaint as adults and activists in a seminar on genocide in London. Thereafter, Lalarukh comes to Dhaka to conduct research and is hosted by Monika, who is engaged in archiving an Oral History Project about the women survivors of the war. Lalarukh's return to Dhaka, twenty-eight years after her family left at the cusp of the war, is bittersweet. She expresses her noble objective to Monika, "I intend to work for an apology [at the state level]." Monika is skeptical of Lalarukh's intentions to learn about war affected families in her brief one week visit. At the same time, she is hesitant to rekindle their own personal friendship, given Lalarukh's long absence and silence about the war. One scene depicts the two as seated on Monika's bed. Monika looks fatigued, bearing the weight of the war's devastation. Lalarukh probes, "I want to know everything. I have a personal stake in this." The viewer is reminded of an earlier scene when Lalarukh insists that she has a right to return to this land, as her mother was Bengali. A stubborn Monika responds, "Two people can have totally different experiences of a war. These distinct experiences can change a relationship forever." Monika presses her friend about the silence from Pakistanis about the atrocities committed during 1971. Lalarukh tries to defend her position by touting the then-government propaganda about Bengalis dancing to the tune of India and acting as separatists. Her family was in the dark, says Lalarukh in defense, given the news blackout about what was happening in East Pakistan. Monika reminds her of the international movement on behalf of Bangladesh liberation, the concert in Madison Square Garden, and the statements by Tariq Ali—a Pakistani intellectual who criticized the military repression. She admonishes Lalarukh about her silence and complicity.

Lalarukh is further confounded by the coldness from her friend's family members. The once lively house she used to visit in her childhood seems to be shrouded in damp and gloom. Ananya's grandfather and Monika's father, Nanu (affectionate term for maternal grandfather), refuses to meet Lalarukh face to face even though he ensures proper hospitality for the guest. The silence is finally broken as the family sits down together for a feast on the day of Lalarukh's departure for Pakistan. Once again, Monika and Lalarukh, seated across from each other at the table, debate the merit of an apology from the Pakistan state, and acknowledgment of war crimes when Monika's father, seated at the head of the table, directly confronts Lalarukh. He asks whether she would forgive the rape of her own sixteen-year-old daughter. "If she is raped, would you be able to forgive [the rapist]?" Lalarukh lowers her glance and admits, "No." She adds, "But, I would want a trial and punishment for the perpetrator." Nanu (Abul Khair) responds, "What about the victim? How would justice be served for them?" The confrontation leads to the revelation by Nanu that Ananya (Nasrin Siraj), daughter of his younger daughter Konika, is a child of rape. Konika committed suicide months after the birth of Ananya. Konok Khala, who quietly exits the frame, during this encounter, and who raised Ananya, was held captive in the same rape camp as Konika. A member of the Hindu community, Konok's entire family was massacred in 1971. The exit from the gathering and the frame of the *birangona* at this critical scene reemphasizes the question of acceptance and justice for the victims of sexual violence, a question that remains largely unresolved if not unattended in the postwar social and political discourses. The word *birangona* means brave woman or war heroine. During the war, thousands of women and girls were tortured in rape camps and army barracks. Rape as a weapon of war was deployed to terrorize the Bengali-speaking Muslim majority and the Hindu minority of Bangladesh. Following independence, the term *birangona* was bestowed on the survivors of sexual violence by the government of Bangladesh in order to honor the women for their role in the freedom struggle. The label frequently served to further ostracize the women, as their reintegration into society remained incomplete.

Shameem Akhtar's *Itihaash Konna* emphasizes a "reckoning" with the 'Other', not necessarily at the state or juridical level, but through suturing torn interpersonal relationships. Namely, an irreconcilable conflict was institutionalized at the moment of original trauma, that is, when "war babies" were declared tainted and ejected from the nation (the womb) by state-sponsored post war policies of abortion or foreign adoption. It is Lalarukh's arrival that opens up the conversation about Ananya, the war child, and Konika, her mother who committed suicide following her birth. Unlike the state, however, the family unquestion-ingly accepts Ananya as their own. Lalarukh's mission is to write about the genocide and mobilize a movement for a national apology. Monika finds common ground in that objective as it would imply recognition of war crimes—even though her father, the elder survivor of war is not so sure if that would be meaningful for victims. In the scene where this reckoning takes place, Konok (Bonna Lohani), a Hindu woman who was at the same rape camp as Konika and helped raise Ananya, quietly leaves the room. Even though Konok's departure from the frame might be read as a kind of "exit narrative" that has been critiqued by feminist scholars with regard to categorical disappearances of *birangonas*, at the same time it can also be read as a way to signal an "ethical reckoning" where the war child (Ananya) is center-stage along with the feminist activists (Monika and Lalarukh). This scene and encounter is a critical conjuncture where the past, present and future questions around healing and reconciliation are on the table and set in motion.

Ananya (whose name means exceptional in Bengali)—Monika's now adult niece, daughter of Konika, Monika's sister—is then revealed to be a war child. At their first meeting, when Lalarukh introduces herself as a foreigner (bideshi), Ananya corrects her by saying "Not a foreigner, a Pakistani"—hinting at the intimacy of her identity that is like no other. Ananya becomes Lalarukh's guide and research assistant during her stay taking her on a tour of the various war memorials and museums in the city. Lalarukh is left overwhelmed by the intensity and enormity of the atrocities and consequent losses. Ananya comforts her and in turn Lalarukh urges her to address her as "tumi"—the less formal version of the pronoun "you" reserved for friends. Ananya ponders over the request and says, "It will take time."

Ananya's brief association with Lalarukh leads to a different kind of reckoning between the younger woman and her older aunt, Monika. It is as though the latter comes to see the former in a new light, transformed into her own person. "You've grown up; I've never heard you speak like this," says Lalarukh when Ananya raises the question of the somber household and lack of festivities there. Ananya says, not without a hint of reproach, "You did not want to realize it." She asks her aunt about her childhood friendship with Lalarukh when everything was different and more exuberant—the house, Nanu, Monika. The film raises the ques-tion of a possible (or impossible) union between Monika and Ananya; and, Ananya with Lalarukh. Their union breaks down the seemingly irreconcilable conflict that was institutionalized at the moment of original trauma when "war babies" were declared tainted. It is noteworthy that Lalarukh's arrival leads to the opening of the Pandora's box of memories, breaking the silence in the house, and taking steps towards healing. Ananya's full story can only be sensible if coevally developed with Lalarukh's and Monika's (im)possible union. Rather than assigning Ananya to the periphery, the film simultaneously develops the conflicted relationships between the three women as representative of the historical conflict between woman and nation. The source of the hatred hinges on the original trauma of the rape of Bengali women and forced impregnation as a war strategy. The desire to 'flush out' the enemy through state-led policies of abortion and foreign adoption institutionalized the hatred of the Other. In that sense, Ananya's union with Lalarukh (and Monika) is a feminine revisioning of history that includes the acceptance of the war child and a rejection of masculinist war narratives. Feminist scholar Kavita Daiya (2008) has illustrated how within Partition narratives, the female body comes to be symbolically overlaid with the project of nationalism to the extent that it serves as metaphor for their perceived otherness. In Bangladeshi films, the methodical reproduction of the "authentic Birangona" reifies the otherness through similar iconic imagery (Mookherjee 2015). The regulation of the *birangonas* by the state rendered women's bodies as a public site onto which "social debates and collective anxieties about morality, religion, policy and the state are inscribed" (Nash 2008: 57).

Lalarukh's return to Bangladesh stirs up repressed emotions, opens old wounds and instigates an intimate as well as political reckoning across time, space and history. Ananya comes to know the truth about her birth and the identity of Konok Khala, her surrogate mother. Nanu confronts Lalarukh about her quest for "justice" and asks whether the victims of 1971 will be appeased by it. Following this encounter, he takes out a dusty old picture of his daughter and places it on the bureau. He is finally able to place in the open the photo of his dead daughter and face that painful history. Ananya comes to terms with the story of her birth, and the realization that it is inextricably interwoven with the individual and collective journeys of Monika and Lalarukh. Following her departure from Bangladesh, Lalarukh writes a letter to Monika from Pakistan admitting her—and her family's—complicity by not speaking up against the atrocities of 1971. The question of women survivors may remain incomplete; yet the healing begins with them. Ananya continues to work on the Oral History Project with Lalarukh and Monika, becoming the bridge between the women separated by the burden of historical conflict. Monika begins to look at Ananya in a new light and both women come to the realization of their shared struggle. Lalarukh leaves with a heavy heart asking Monika and her family "to take care of Ananya." The soundtrack by Shimul Yusuf plays, "Tears of yester years as life goes on..."

Akhtar's film provides an opportunity to read the complex machinations of gender, nation, and patriarchy, particularly as they operate between women of opposing national contexts, while exploring both the limits and possibilities of solidarity in spite of these forces. More specifically, it enables a discussion of circumstances where women's loyalty to family, nation, and the community's specific structures is disrupted by the possibility of an alliance shaped by gender-based oppression. It is an instance to test the ideas of contrapuntal histories of the oppressor-oppressed and the possibilities of cross-cultural dissident friendship within that context.

Transnational Feminism, Film, and Ethical Encounters

Feminist filmmakers and scholars have long engaged in their work the anomalous relationship of woman to nation. Kathleen McHugh (2009), one such scholar states,

> Notably, women's worldly space was not independent of country, of the national, but based on spatial paradox: they were at once inside, marginal, in the private sphere of the nation-state (within patriarchal ideas, institutions, and histories in which women have no place) and, at the same time, not contained by, in excess of that state by reason of these internal and internalized exclusions and difference.
>
> (112)

McHugh's claim shines light on how women are both insider and outsider to nationalist and colonialist struggles, and that to mount a deeper understanding of this complex and contradictory location women occupy, a layered perspective is necessary. McHugh locates "women's place in cinema within transnational influences and relationships" in order to generate a broader understanding of "structures of opportunity," ideological underpinnings, production, reception, and circulation of films that are feminist (126). This allows for a deeper understanding of the "worldly space" women occupy, and of the "internal" exclusions and difference that are particularly critical to feminist film-making. Similarly, Ella Shohat (2003) locates "transnational film feminisms" as a distinctive historical modality advancing a decisive political project that critiques both nationalism and colonialism in relation to feminism. Here, the transnational is defined as "...spaces and practices acted upon by border-crossing agents, be they dominant or marginal" (citing Francoise Lionnet and Shu-mei Shih, 119)—a definition that takes into consideration cinematic approach as well as the location of the work within a broader framework beyond the national in an age of rising global mass culture. The transnational analytic lens, and agents—filmmakers and financiers—offer the scope to historicize women's struggles within the broader legacy of colonial processes and realities of nationalist struggles and sheds light on cross-border connections in feminist filmic representations and interpretations. Seen within a transnational framework where women's wartime experiences can be placed within a global movement for justice, Akhtar's sensitive treatment of war's consequences on women is instrumental in mobilizing awareness and action while developing collective critique and resistance. The film can be seen as transformative in launching a dialogue about women's 1971 within and beyond a nationalist and national framework and beyond a narrowly constructed notion of liberation.

The film is also instrumental in opening a conversation about the necessity of an 'ethical reckoning' of genocide in 1971. Such a reckoning stands the chance to recuperate—even if only partially—forgotten histories, particularly for women. It is important to situate *Itihaash Konna* within the new genre of cultural production centered on gendered experiences of the nation and the larger transnational movement of healing and reconciliation where femininity is the location of caring and nurturing. Instead of retribution, the focus of much political discourse in post-Independent Bangladesh, the film looks at internal tensions, interpersonal healing, and gendered justice. This shift hints at an emerging new direction in feminist scholarship about women's experiences of 1971.

I would like to return here to the question of dissident friendship, community, and solidarity between women and explore further the circumstances in which these are or not trumped by loyalties women have to their families, communities or nations. Of course, the idea of friendship and community in feminist discourses are contested. In the collection of essays *Feminism and Community* (Weiss and Friedman 1995), the contributors make the distinction between "traditional" and feminist communities. They argue that, in traditional settings, significant relationships of female support and acts of resistance can co-exist with hierarchical and exploitative ones, whereas internal struggles can also inhibit feminist communities from achieving the desired political transformation on behalf of women. The point is that these two settings are neither mutually exclusive nor completely antithetical to one another. Rather, the authors suggest that, "Both can be the sites of genuine friendship, social support, and collaborative political activism among women" (Weiss and Friedman 1995: xii). The arenas Akhtar highlights in *Daughters of History* are conflictual—the Bengali nationalist, and the naïve Pakistani researcher—reflect these dual settings—where both women are motivated by political activism and a certain reconciliation. Within these settings also exist collaborative relationships among women who come from opposite ends of the spectrum forming unexpected alliances. At the same time, it is useful to keep in mind Penny Weiss' cautionary note to not engage in uncritical celebration of women's agency and resistance within traditional communities, but instead to listen carefully to women in all of these contexts in order to learn the specific insights women as women have to offer in the larger struggle for social transformation (1995: 162). While Lalarukh and Monika may not have achieved much—in the sense of official or lasting peace between the two nations in question—through their sometimes dissident, always conflicted alliance, viewers come to learn how the identities—or positionalities—of each are constituted through their specific national and gender locations. These positionalities dictate the limits of their agency and the risks each can take on behalf of women's freedom. In the final reckoning, even Monika admits to the value in Lalarukh's work which aims to raise awareness in Pakistan and globally so that the state moves towards an acknowledgment and ultimately apology for war crimes.

Feminist political theorist Iris Marion Young (1995) has argued for the need to broaden an understanding of individuality and community that does not pit one in a negative relation to the other. *Daughters of History* then allows us to expand this debate, and to recognize when striving for solidarity that women's relationships are heterogeneous, complex, and conflicting. Solidarity is a demanding ideal to strive for. Moreover, the attainment of it can be ambiguous and fleeting. These ephemeral moments nevertheless allude to "disruptive possibilities" (Friedman 1995: 200) and can lead to important transformations in female consciousness in the broader and ongoing struggle to create more enabling conditions of care.

References

Akhtar, Shameem (Director). *Itihaash Konna* (Motion picture). Dhaka, Bangladesh: Laser Vision Limited, 1999.

Chowdhury, Elora Halim. "Debunking 'Truths' Claiming Justice: Reflections on Yasmin Saikia's Women War and the Making of Bangladesh: Remembering 1971." *Human Rights Quarterly* 34.4 (2012):1201–11.

Chowdhury, Elora Halim. "The Space between Us: Reading Umrigar and Sangari in the Quest for Female Friendship." *Dissident Friendships: Feminism Imperialism and Transnational Solidarity.* Ed. Elora H. Chowdhury and Liz Philipose. Urbana: U of Illinois P, 2016. 160–181.

Daiya, Kavita. *Violent Belongings: Partition, Gender, and National Culture in Postcolonial India.* Philadelphia, PA: Temple U P, 2008.

D'Costa, Bina. *Nationbuilding, Gender and War Crimes in South Asia.* New York: Routledge, 2010.

Friedman, Marilyn. "Feminism and Modern Friendship: Dislocating the Community." *Feminism and Community.* Ed. Penny E. Weiss and Marilyn Friedman. Philadelphia, PA: Temple U P, 1995. 187–208.

Gandhi, Leela. *Affective Communities: Anticolonial Thought, Fin-de-Siecle Radicalism, and the Politics of Friendship.* Durham, NC: Duke U P, 2006.

Hobson, Janelle. "Militarizing Women in Film: Toward a Cinematic Framing of War and Terror." *Security Disarmed: Perspectives on Gender, Race, and*

Militarization. Ed. Barbara Sutton, Sandra Morgen, and Julie Novkov. New Brunswick, NJ: Rutgers U P, 2008. 231–43.

Lugones, Maria in collaboration with Pat Alake Rosezelle. "Sisterhood and Friendship as Feminist Models." *Feminism and Community*. Ed. Penny E. Weiss and Marilyn Friedman. Philadelphia, PA: Temple U P, 1995. 135–46.

Mansbridge, Jane. "Feminism and Democratic Community." *Feminism and Community*. Ed. Penny E. Weiss and Marilyn Friedman. Philadelphia, PA: Temple U P, 1995. 341–66.

McHugh, Kathleen. "The World and the Soup: Historicizing Media Feminisms in Transnational Contexts." *Camera Obscura* 24.3 (2009): 111–50.

Mookherjee, Nayanika. *The Spectral Wound: Sexual Violence, Public Memories, and the Bangladesh War of 1971*. Durham: Duke University Press, 2015.

Moraga, Cherrie. "Refugees of a World on Fire: Foreword to the Second Edition." *This Bridge Called My Back: Writings by Radical Women of Color*. 2d ed. Ed. Cherrie Moraga and Gloria Anzaldúa. New York: Kitchen Table: Women of Color Press, 1983.

Narayan, Uma. "Colonialism and Its Others: Considerations on Rights and Care Discourses." *Hypatia* 10.2 (1995): 31–47.

———. "Working Together across Difference: Some Considerations on Emotions and Political Practice." *Hypatia* 3.2 (1988): 133–40.

Nash, Jennifer. "Strange Bedfellows: Black Feminism and Antipornography Feminism." *Social Text* 97 26.4 (2008): 51–76.

Pettman, Jan Jindy. "Women, Colonisation, and Racism." *Beyond Borders: Thinking Critically about Global Issues*. Ed. Paula S. Rothenberg. New York: Worth Publishers, 2006. 142–49.

Rich, Adrienne. "If Not With Others, How?" *Feminism and Community*. Ed. Penny E. Weiss and Marilyn Friedman. Philadelphia, PA: Temple U P, 1995. 399–406.

Rothe, Anne. *Popular Trauma Culture: Selling the Pain of Others in the Mass Media*. Newark: Rutgers U P, 2011.

Saikia, Yasmin. *Women, War, and the Making of Bangladesh: Remembering 1971*. Durham, NC: Duke U P, 2011.

Sangtin, Writers and Richa Nagar. *Playing with Fire: Feminist Thought and Activism through Seven Lives in India*. Minneapolis: U of Minnesota P, 2006.

Shohat, Ella. "Post-Third-Worldist Culture: Gender, Nation, and the Cinema." *Rethinking Third Cinema*. Ed. Anthony Guneratne and Wimal Dissanayake. London: Routledge, 2003. 51–78.

Stone-Mediatore, Shari. *Reading across Borders: Storytelling and Knowledges of Resistance*. New York: Palgrave Macmillan, 2003.

Weiss, Penny, and Marilyn Friedman, eds. *Feminism and Community*. Philadelphia, PA: Temple U P, 1995.

Young, Iris Marion. "The Ideal of Community and the Politics of Difference." *Feminism and Community*. Ed. Penny E. Weiss and Marilyn Friedman. Philadelphia: Temple University Press, 1995. 233–58.

Part IV
Literature

13 Beyond Violence

South Asian American Feminism in Jhumpa Lahiri's *The Lowland*

Nalini Iyer

Any examination of South Asian feminisms must examine what Inderpal Grewal calls "transnational connectivities as the means through which subjects and identities were created."[1] As Grewal notes: "Connectivities enabled communication across boundaries and borders through articulations and translations of discourses that circulated within networks."[2] Although particular acts of gendered violence or feminist activism might seem confined to national boundaries or local communities, the discourses of gender circulate within transnational networks. In the twenty-first century, the connectivities between people living in South Asian nations and their diasporic subjects located in the West, especially North America, is particularly strong. South Asian diasporic communities are significant agents in the flow of information to and from South Asia. Postcolonial South Asian nations in the late twentieth century have seen significant connectivity with their diasporic subjects located in the West and in North America in particular through both kinship networks as well as through state sponsored initiatives such as India's OCI card or celebrations of Pravasi Bharatiya Diwas. Unlike the diasporas of the late nineteenth century that took indentured laborers to Mauritius, Fiji, and the Caribbean, for whom return was not always easy, the twenty-first-century South Asian diasporic subject in North America is highly mobile, often an upper middle-class professional, and frequently one who operates in transnational networks in cyber space as well as in the world of multi-national corporations. South Asians in diaspora actively engage in debates and discussions on social and political happenings, including instances of gender violence, in South Asia. Thus, the Delhi gang rape of a student and her subsequent death in 2012, the lynching of a Muslim family in Dadri in 2015, the student uprisings in Hyderabad and Delhi, and the murder of social media star Qandeel Baloch by her brother are some of the major events that have recently resonated beyond national borders. These high profile incidents make an impact beyond South Asian media, thus perpetrating a narrow and skewed understanding of South Asian women as victims who are constantly subject to violence.[3] Despite the numerous and heterogeneous feminist organizations and activists doing extraordinary work for gender justice in South Asia, the predominant media narrative in the West is that of South Asian women as oppressed.

Feminism thrives in South Asian diasporic communities as well. South Asian feminist organizations do anti-racism work, support victims of domestic violence, fight for immigrant rights, and many academic programs in women and gender studies in North America have feminist activists and scholars engaged in transnational feminist work. Although there is no comprehensive study of South Asian feminisms in North America, cultural works such as literary texts or films, contribute significantly to how people perceive gender issues and feminisms in South Asia and the South Asian diaspora. Women writers are major contributors to the South Asian diasporic literary canon in North America, and some of these writers like Chitra Divakaruni or Meena Alexander identify as feminists.[4] The explosive growth of the Indian immigrant community in the US after 1965 has made South Asian people and culture familiar in the US and particularly in the urban areas. According to the 2010 census, South Asians number 3.4 million in the US and are the second fastest growing immigrant community in the US. The literary works of South Asian American writers such as Bharati Mukherjee, Chitra Divakaruni, Jhumpa Lahiri, Meena Alexander, and Tahira Naqvi and films by Mira Nair and Deepa Mehta among others have contributed to perceptions of gender issues both within and beyond the South Asian American community.

This essay examines the evolution of South Asian feminism within the South Asian American community by exploring Jhumpa Lahiri's novel *The Lowland* (2013).[5] I propose that the narrative trajectory of the novel focused on two feminist women, a mother and daughter, offers a nuanced perspective on South Asian diasporic women; the impact of family, community, and state(s) on their lives; their evolving feminist views which shapes their lives against dominant perceptions of race, class, and culture; and the transnational connectivities in their perception of feminist politics and praxis. By delving deeply into the lived experiences of a pair of South Asian diasporic women, Lahiri counter balances the prevailing stereotype of South Asian countries as nations that victimize women that dominate news cycles when high profile incidents of gender violence occur. Lahiri's narrative focuses on the experiences of particular individuals without rendering them as representing the whole community or nation.

The winner of a Pulitzer for her debut short story collection and the runaway success of her first novel *The Namesake* and Mira Nair's cinematic version of the novel have made Lahiri's work emblematic of the South Asian American[6] experience. Whereas South Asian authors such as Bharati Mukherjee and Chitra Divakaruni had been writing about the Indian immigrant experience, theirs was a first- generation perspective. Lahiri voiced the experiences of the children of Indian immigrants[7] who had come of age in the United States and had to navigate the politics of race and class in the country of their birth while simultaneously understanding the cultural expectations of the homeland carried by their parents. Although Lahiri's earlier work, in particular her *Interpreter of Maladies* and *The Namesake*, had characterized her as a South Asian American writer with a finely tuned focus on the hardships experienced by the immigrant community with issues of assimilation, culture, and belonging, her most recent novel *The Lowland* examines the India of the 1960s, particularly the politics of West Bengal and Calcutta (now Kolkata). As many critics have noted, *The Lowland*, marks a shift in Lahiri's oeuvre from the predominant emphasis on the interior lives of her characters to the larger exterior issues of national politics and culture in India that impact their lives.[8]

This novel links postcolonial India and its tribulations very strongly with the narrative of immigration. What happens in India does not stay in India and bleeds into the lives of immigrants. India in *The Lowland* is not just an exotic, distant homeland nor a nostalgic backdrop for stories of New England Bengali immigrants.[9] Whereas the majority of the reviewers of the novel have seen it as the story of two brothers separated by immigration and politics, this essay examines the novel as one that explores South Asian diasporic feminism by telling the story of a mother and daughter, Gauri and Bela, whose lives are irrevocably changed by what happened during the 1960s and 1970s in West Bengal and Calcutta in particular. Lahiri's novel deftly and carefully traces the emergence of a diasporic feminism which is shaped by both political events in postcolonial India and by the experience of immigration. The violence at the heart of the novel is state sponsored police brutality against a radical student activist. The narrative traces the impact of this violence on a woman; how family, community, and nation construct a woman's identity; and how migration disrupts and reshapes these same elements. Lahiri recognizes that feminism in the twenty-first century for South Asians is more than recirculating particular pre-determined notions of South Asian women as victims. In this novel, we see the evolution of transnational feminism across generations.

In following the story of Gauri, a first-generation immigrant, we see how South Asian American women must constantly negotiate home and homeland. Hers is a story that disrupts dominant narratives of motherhood, nation, and sexuality that inform South Asian American culture. In tracing the daughter Bela's evolution, Lahiri reverts to a theme familiar to her readers—the experiences of the children of immigrants who must work their way through their parents' stories of home, nation, and family. Unlike *The Namesake* where the heteronormative, middle-class, professional family forms the familiar context of the drama of identity for Gogol, in *The Lowland*, Bela's story breaks away from the oft repeated struggles of assimilation narrative of a bourgeois Indian family.

Through Gauri and Bela, Lahiri offers an alternative and complex narrative of gender politics than what has captured the imaginations of the global community about India and the South Asian American community in particular.

The Lowland tells the story of two brothers Udayan and Subhash who grew up in lower middle-class Calcutta in the 1960s surrounded by reminders of the recently defunct British Raj. As the new nation grapples with political and economic issues, a radical Maoist movement emerges in West Bengal to redress economic injustices and to secure peasant and workers' rights. This movement is referred to as the Naxalite movement after the village of Naxalbari where Charu Mazumdar and Kanu Sanyal of the Communist Party of India, Marxist (CPI-M) initiated a violent uprising to redistribute land to the landless. The movement soon spread amongst college students in West Bengal. In the novel, the two brothers, Udayan and Subhash, who are college students at this historical juncture, are impacted differently by the political movement. Subhash goes to the US to study and Udayan becomes a Naxalite revolutionary who is caught by the police and brutally murdered in front of his parents and his pregnant new wife, Gauri. Gauri is traumatized by the death of her beloved husband and further abused by her mother-in-law's orthodox practices regarding Hindu widows. Subhash, who is visiting India to support his family during the tragic time, is moved by Gauri's precarious situation and marries her. He provides her the opportunity to reinvent herself in the United States. Udayan and Gauri's child is born in the US and raised by her biological uncle and adoptive father and is not told her story until she is an adult. At this point in the narrative, the martyred Udayan is a presence that haunts both Gauri and her new husband and the narrative shifts its focus to examine the impact of the political tragedy on the lives of Gauri, Subhash, and their child, Bela. Udayan represents more than a family secret; he also represents how families repress traumatic events by not speaking of them to their children as they strive to make a new life in a new country.

In Gauri's journey of self-discovery and Bela's emergence as a young Indo-American woman with a passion for environmental issues, we see Lahiri tracing the evolution of diasporic feminism. While Lahiri recognizes generational and historical differences as shaping the mother-daughter duo's growth, it is important to note that this diasporic feminism is largely middle class (and uncritically so) and is shaped significantly by the fraught sense of home that pervades much of diasporic culture. Although the Naxalite movement with its awareness of class issues is an element of plot, the narrative steadfastly focuses on the tribulations of the middle classes—how the family was affected by the actions of the student radical, the trauma of witnessing a brutal murder, the relationship between mother-in-law and daughter-in-law, and the impact of emigration to the US, stimulated by the Immigration and Nationality Act of 1965, on familial and gender roles.

Gauri's narrative begins in Calcutta of the 1960s where as a college student drawn to philosophy, notably Western philosophy, she becomes involved with a radical friend of her brother's, Udayan. Moved by the student revolution that swept the state, Udayan joins other college students influenced by the peasant uprising in Naxalbari. His solidarity with peasants and workers to effect socio-economic change is based on the philosophy of Mao[10] filtered through the work of radical intellectuals in Calcutta, Charu Majumdar, and Kanu Sanyal. What marked the Naxalite movement was the violence against agents and institutions of the state that was vastly different from the Satyagraha movement that had grabbed the national imaginary only two decades previously under Gandhi. When we hear the story of Gauri and Udayan, it becomes clear that Lahiri views the Naxalite movement as dominated by male activists although they focused on class based revolution. Lahiri presents women Naxalites as ancillaries to the work of men, often acting as informants and covert operatives because of their ability to move undetected in certain facets of society.[11] The couple elopes, much to the chagrin of Udayan's bourgeois parents, and despite his radical ideas about social change, Udayan choses to move into his parents' home with his new bride in a rather conventional multi-generational family set up.[12] Gauri is not welcomed by her in-laws because of the non-traditional marriage and she settles into domestic chores as a daughter-in-law while her husband leads a dual life—teacher in the public eye and radical activist in secret. Gauri spends her days immersed in her study of philosophy—mostly Western philosophical texts. She does not question her husband's secret activities and acquiesces to tutoring a child in another neighborhood while reporting on the daily routine of a policeman, Nirmal Dey. At the end of the novel, we learn that Gauri's report on the policeman facilitates his death and that Udayan was likely the bomb maker who master minded the murder. When the police crackdown on the radicals and come to arrest Udayan, he escapes into the Lowland, the nearby marsh, only to be caught and arrested. He is later shot in the back as he is "freed" by the police and his body is never recovered by the family.

Gauri's role in this revolutionary movement is mostly passive and motivated by her love for Udayan. She leads her everyday life as daughter, sister, wife, daughter-in-law, and widow in a passive, acquiescent fashion and her primary rebellion is in her retreat into philosophical tomes, which she seems to mostly consume passively. She agrees to marry Subhash also in response to his proposal and to give her a way out of the crushing domesticity and repression in middle-class Calcutta. Overall, the section of the novel set in Calcutta provides an outline of the Naxalite movement and the contrasting approaches of the two brothers to the political problems of the day. Udayan is romanticized as the revolutionary and Subhash as the staid brother who leaves in search of personal and professional opportunities. The women in Calcutta are shadowy creatures and the only women characters are Gauri and her mother-in-law. The former is passive and for all her study of philosophy offers little or no critique of gender issues in her time. She seems content surviving the status quo and attaching herself to the glamor of her husband. Udayan's mother becomes a stereotype of all that is "traditional," a gendered notion of continuity and status quo manifested as support of repressive domestic practices. For all of his revolutionary thinking, Udayan has nary a word to say about the position of women.[13] Lahiri's depiction of women's issues in Calcutta through Gauri and her mother-in-law underscores the domestic realm as the space of oppression. Neither Lahiri nor her protagonist Gauri connect the class and caste issues raised by the Naxalite movement as being related in any way to the gendered domestic realm. The women—Gauri and her mother-in-law—are both victims of an undifferentiated patriarchy. In this narrative, it is the radicals and the state who perpetrate physical violence; the oppression in the middle-class domestic sphere is largely psychological and chronic and carried out in the name of preserving cultural practices.

The victim of the patriarchal system gets her opportunity to escape when Subhash marries her. Going away to America, then, becomes a moment for Gauri to re-invent herself. Thus, the US offers greater agency for a woman than India—a theme that persists in the fiction of other South Asian American women writers as well. As in her earlier works, Lahiri sees emigration as a personal choice rather than one that might be shaped by the push-pull factors of economic policies, labor markets, and immigration legislation of both the US and India.[14] She depicts the South Asian American community as a largely professional and middle-class group of immigrants. Although there are significant numbers of working class migrants, it is the middle class that dominates South Asian American literary works, and this reinforces the model minority image. As Annanya Bhattacharjee, Margaret Abraham,[15] and others have noted, the woman is seen as the bearer, preserver, and transmitter of Indian culture within the South Asian immigrant community. Thus, when Gauri marries Subhash to escape the oppressions of the middle-class Bengali home, she cannot fully escape those practices unless she shrouds her past in secrecy. By mutual agreement, neither she nor Subhash share their story with anyone, including their daughter. From the outside, they are the typical middle-class Indian family, the model minority, consisting of educated, professional parents, and a daughter. They progress through life in terms of work, home ownership, and education in a stereotypical manner. However, the only way they can manage the external is by never speaking of the past in Calcutta.

Once Gauri arrives in the US, Lahiri treads familiar ground in her fiction—the challenges of migration and the alienation experienced by immigrants in their new home. Where this novel differs from Lahiri's earlier works is that neither Subhash nor Gauri experience integration into a local South Asian community. There are no weekend potlucks, celebrations of Indian holidays, and bonding over shared history and culture as in *The Namesake*. Both Subhash and Gauri live fairly isolated lives in the Rhode Island college town they call home. The one Indian faculty member Subhash meets is only marginally engaged with them— they offer baby clothes and furniture to the new couple and the relationship does not progress beyond that. Instead the emphasis in the narrative is on the complex relationship between husband and wife. Both have to cope with the loss of Udayan and his haunting presence. They have to awkwardly find their way into a sexual relationship overcoming the barriers of their prior relationships. They have to preserve their secrets from their daughter who knows nothing about her biological father or his story. Neither does the narrative engage larger social issues in America such as race that might contribute to the isolation and alienation of the couple. In the logic of the narrative, everything stems from the brutal death of Udayan and the repression of that story.

Lahiri's sharp departure from the Indian family narratives she has previously written (short stories in *Interpreter of Maladies* and *Unaccustomed Earth* and the novel *The Namesake*) emerges in her depiction of Gauri and Subhash as parents once Bela is born. Subhash observes that:

> Though she cared for Bela capably, though she kept her clean and combed and fed, she seemed distracted. Rarely did Subhash see her smiling when she looked into Bela's face. Rarely did he see Gauri kissing Bela spontaneously. Instead, from the beginning, it was as if she'd reversed their roles, as if Bela were a relative's child and not her own.[16]

Subhash's observation has underlying assumptions about how a mother should respond to her child, about what is supposed to be "natural" for a mother. Such assumptions abound in Indian (and other) cultures about the inherent attitudes expected of mothers. As Jyoti Puri has noted in her study *Woman, Body, Desire in Post-colonial India*, "From a cultural standpoint, marriage and motherhood are considered the primary gender roles for women across social classes. Indeed, motherhood is seen as the essence of womanhood, and marriage, the context within which a woman should bear children."[17] Puri's study of middle-class women in India and their narratives of gender and sexuality demonstrates that this idea of marriage and motherhood continues to pervade most of middle-class India, and so Subhash's view of Gauri as a mother is deeply rooted in his cultural beliefs. Thus, Gauri's quest for an intellectual life, for solitude, and her rejection of parenthood mark her as an "unnatural" mother.[18] Gauri does not see mothering as inherent to her identity and her distance from Bela is not because of grief over Udayan, but because she never quite embraced the idea of having a child—Bela was conceived accidentally in a moment of careless passion with Udayan.

By depicting Gauri as an unhappy and reluctant mother, Lahiri re-inscribes the narrative of motherhood within Indian culture. Motherhood is venerated and fetishized in Indian culture including in literary depictions, film, and popular culture. During the anti-colonial nationalist movement, the nation was represented as Mother India, a goddess like figure to be venerated by her brave sons who fought for her freedom and dignity.[19] Thus, the figure of the mother is imbricated in forms of feminist nationalism as well as in right wing nationalism.[20] Not surprisingly, this idea of motherhood as the cornerstone of the family carries forward within diasporic culture as well. Gauri's transformation occurs after the birth of her daughter. She yearns to attend philosophy lectures, spend time in the library, and for solitary time when she is neither wife nor mother. Subhash is supportive of her academic interests only as long as it does not interfere with her obligations as a mother. He is unwilling to consider a nanny or a babysitter for the child and does adjust his work schedule to facilitate her studies. However, Gauri continues to struggle against the demands of motherhood and secretly leaves her young daughter alone for periods of time, much to Subhash's chagrin. Gauri manages to complete her doctoral degree in philosophy despite her growing frustration with motherhood. Eventually, when Subhash and Bela travel to India for his father's funeral rites, Gauri walks away from her marriage and her child and moves to California to pursue her life as an academic. That Lahiri recognizes that the quest for female autonomy may require negating the role of the mother is radical within the Indian context where motherhood is venerated. Such a move is only possible because of Gauri's education in the US, her financial independence as a consequence of that education, and the ability of Subhash to raise Bela as a single parent. Subhash and Gauri never divorce until much later in their lives when Subhash decides to marry another woman. Thus, they maintain the illusion of a middle-class nuclear family not just for the world outside but for themselves as well. Even as Gauri disrupts the narrative of motherhood, it is a stealthy disruption and one that is cloaked in secrecy. Exercising her autonomy is a private act of an individual and not intended for social change. Gauri thrives in her role as an academic in California:

> Her output apart from the teaching, was steady, esteemed by a handful of peers. She had published three books in her life: a feminist appraisal of Hegel, an analysis of interpretive methods in

Horkheimer, and the book that had been based on her dissertation, that had grown out of a blundering essay she'd written for Professor Weiss: *The Epistemology of Expectation in Schopenhauer.*[21]

Gauri's feminism is academic, focused on German philosophy, and strongly separates the personal from the political and the private from the public. As Lahiri continues her description of Gauri's life in California, she dwells briefly on her affair with Lorna, a graduate student from another university who is an admirer of Gauri's work. Aware that she has breached professional ethical boundaries, Gauri simply shrugs off that experience as yet another in her life. It seems to have a minimal influence on her. She notes that although she sees California as home, she has retained her Indian citizenship, and that her race will always cause some people to pause: "Her appearance and accent caused people to continue to ask her where she came from, to for certain assumption."[22] These are passing recognitions on her part—her race, her cultural identity, and her flirtation with a lesbian relationship. She does not recognize the orientalist underpinnings of her education in Western philosophy starting with Calcutta and continuing in Rhode Island where her mentor, Dr. Weiss, is described in the following way: "He'd read the Upanishads, talked about their influence on Schopenhauer. She felt a kinship with this man."[23]

Through Gauri's narrative Lahiri reconfigures the role of the Indian immigrant woman, she is not the bearer of Indian culture who will transmit ideas of nation, culture, and religion to her children. She is not a domestic goddess who will create a refuge at home for the family as they experience the travails of life in the United States in terms of race and class. She is not a victimized Indian woman who cannot escape patriarchal control. However, this South Asian American feminism is not about activism or social change. While many public conversations and debates on gender justice in the South Asian American community or the work of feminist organizations foreground the community and social change aspect of South Asian American feminism, Lahiri's female protagonist embodies small, personal revolutions.

In the latter part of the novel, Lahiri shifts the focus to Gauri and Subhash's daughter, Bela. A happy, curious child who enjoys time with her mother, she is abruptly separated from her mother upon her return from India when she discovers that her mother had left home. Bela's first and only trip to India happens when her grandfather (Subhash's father) passes away. She experiences middle-class Calcutta, hears about changes from Subhash, meets her grandmother, almost learns the secret of her biological father, and experiences life at a country club that had once been barred to her father and uncle due to race. Bela's childhood and adolescence are marked by her mother's absence. When Subhash shows his mother an album of photographs, she asks where Gauri is in the photos.

Bela realizes that there is no photographic evidence of the presence of her mother in her life except for one accidental appearance in the background of a Halloween picture. While Subhash cares for Bela's daily needs, he is unaware of her grief over her mother's departure. While he seeks the help of a therapist, he knows little about what affects the girl—he mostly drives her to the therapist and pays the bills. Lahiri narrates much of this in a distant manner chronicling Bela's growth from teenager to college student.

The adult Bela becomes increasingly interested in ecological issues and following college, she breaks the stereotype of the high-achieving professional that is common in South Asian American communities. She becomes an itinerant farm worker and works on growing organic foods and supporting cooperatives. While she retains her connection to Subhash with occasional visits home, she never discusses her mother. Bela returns to her father when she finds out she is pregnant. The narrative tells us nothing about the child's father or Bela's relationship with him; we know only that he is no longer in her life. Therefore, like her mother, Bela also disrupts the narrative of motherhood. However, unlike her mother, she chooses motherhood but eschews marriage. With Subhash's help, she raises her daughter Meghna. Toward the end of the novel, she cautiously enters a relationship with a white farmer who shares her views on organic, local, and sustainable foods. Bela's increasing connection to the land as that which offers her a sense of belonging, her move away from her Indian-ness, and a gradual deracination as she melds into "America" suggests that for twenty-first-century feminism, ecology and sustainability rather than race and origins are the most important issues. There is a romanticizing of the land and its connections to identity. Similarly, Subhash also becomes more American. He marries a teacher of American history, explores her Irish cultural roots with her, and moves away from Calcutta, Gauri, and all links to the past. While Gauri returns to India to confront her unwitting collusion in the death of Nirmal Dey and to reconcile herself with her past, Subhash and Bela embrace an assimilationist perspective.

The Lowland proffers an alternative view to the notion that often circulates in the media of South Asian women as victims of gender violence. However, even as Lahiri depicts the evolution of South Asian American feminism across generational lines through the story of Gauri and Bela, the conclusion of the narrative seems to suggest that Indo-Americans are best served by assimilation into the US and its culture. By leading local lives, focused on land and family, one can overcome barriers of race and gender. There is very little in this novel that recognizes systemic racism and gender justice issues in the US, or barriers to assimilation. The novel does not demonstrates cognizance of the idea that working class South Asian immigrants exist in the United States or that non-Hindu South Asian immigrants (such as Muslims and Sikhs) experience significant racial violence and discrimination. Apparently, it is simply a matter of the immigrant evolving to accepting his/her past and making peace with it.

In conclusion, it is necessary for any understanding of Indian feminism to recognize that gender justice issues must be framed transnationally while at the same time acknowledging the role of state(s) in legislating and/or perpetrating violence against dissidents. Such violence is perpetrated not just in South Asia but in North America as well. It is also important to note that women in India and Indian women in the US experience and understand gender issues differently and that any discussions of Indian feminism and representation must account for the diversity of perspectives and lived experiences within the diaspora.

Notes

1 Inderpal Grewal, *Transnational America: Feminisms, Diasporas, Neoliberalisms* (Durham, NC: Duke University Press, 2005): 36.
2 Ibid.
3 In her analysis of human rights discourse, Kamala Visweswaran has noted that culture is gendered such that particular countries are marked by their crimes against women so that they are recognized not as democracies or dictatorships but as "bride burners" and "honor killers." (Kamala Visweswaran, "Gendered States: Rethinking Culture as a Site of South Asian Human Rights Work," *Human Rights Quarterly* 26, no.2 (2004): 483.)
4 Ruvani Ranasinha's book *Contemporary Diasporic South Asian Women's Fiction: Gender, Narration, and Globalisation* (London: Palgrave, 2016) provides a substantive analysis of feminist diasporic fiction. Whereas Ranasinha examines diasporic writers residing in the UK, US, and other locations, this essay focuses on South Asian diasporic feminism within the United States since particular national cultures, social mores, and legal frameworks for immigration do impact women's lives differently.
5 Jhumpa Lahiri, *The Lowland* (New York: Knopf, 2013).
6 I use the terms "Indian-American" and "South Asian American" interchangeably in this essay while recognizing that both terms represent different but overlapping identity formations. The idea is not to render South Asian as synonymous with Indian but to recognize that Indian Americans respond differently to political and social occurrences in India and so often see themselves as both Indian American and South Asian American. The latter term suggests solidarity across people with histories rooted in the different nations of the region whose identity in the US is a collective one. Yet, the term "Indian-American" signals that specific Indian issues fragment the term South Asian American.
7 Jhumpa Lahiri, *The Interpreter of Maladies* (Boston: Mariner Books, 1999); Jhumpa Lahiri, *The Namesake* (Boston: Mariner Books, 2003).
8 See Ruvani Ranasinha for a deeper discussion of Lahiri's work see Chapter 5 in Ranasinha's book (175–234).
9 Whereas Lisa Lau lists Lahiri's *The Namesake* as one of the re-orientalist texts—those novels by South Asian women that reproduce orientalist discourse because they happen to be situated outside South Asia and are, therefore, in an unequal power relationship in producing discourse about

the orient—*The Lowland* is not a novel that can easily be classified as re-orientalist. See Lisa Lau, "Re-Orientalism: The Perception and Development of Orientalism by Orientals," *Modern Asian Studies* 43, no 2 (2009): 571–90.

10 It is important to note that this novel should also be read in the context of the resurgence of the Maoist movement in India in the last decade. The Naxals were declared to be the most significant threat to internal security by President Manmohan Singh in 2007, and the Indian state has been working to contain Maoist activity. Maoists claimed responsibility for 192 deaths in 2013. Although Lahiri's novel uses Calcutta of the late 1960s and early 1970s as its backdrop, the current situation points to the ongoing dispossession of large numbers of people by the state and the resulting violence aimed at state actors.

11 Lahiri's portrayal of middle-class women as ancillary to the Naxalite movement follows the predominant historiography of the Naxalite movement which only recently underwent a revision to look at female militancy and women's political agency according to Mallarika Sinha Roy's essay "Rethinking Female Militancy in Postcolonial Bengal," *Feminist Review* 101 (2012): 124–31.

12 Srila Roy in her essay on marriage and sexuality in the Naxalbari movement notes that marriage amongst middle-class Naxal revolutionaries faced a tension between revolutionary class politics and middle-class codes of sexual morality. While male and female activists often lived together or married by the 'red book,' some revolutionaries in the name of erasing class barriers often married subaltern tribal women and engaged in sexually exploitative relationships. According to Srila Roy, some other marriages idealized a revolutionary masculinity and a dependent femininity, and yet these relationships were framed in a narrative of rupture and revolution where the relationship sought to "erase power differentials to emphasize union and mutuality in aid of revolution" (111). See Srila Roy, "Revolutionary Marriage: On the Politics of Sexual Stories in Naxalbari," *Feminist Review* 83 (2006): 99–118.

13 It is important to note that the Maoist/Naxalite movement of the 1970s was primarily focused on peasants and student revolutions. For a discussion of the emergence of a women's movement in Calcutta, please see Chapter 3 of Raka Ray's *Fields of Protest: Women's Movements in India* (Minneapolis: University of Minnesota Press, 1999). For a discussion of the women's movement in India, see Indu Agnihotri and Vina Mazumdar's "Changing Terms of Political Discourse: Women's Movement in India, 1970s–1990s," *Economic and Political Weekly* 30, no. 29: 1869–78.

14 For a greater discussion of why South Asians left India in large numbers for North America in the 1960s and after, see Amy Bhatt and Nalini Iyer's *Roots and Reflections: South Asians in the Pacific Northwest* (Seattle: University of Washington Press, 2013).

15 Annanya Bhattacharjee, "The Habit of Ex-Nomination: Nation, Woman, and the Immigrant Bourgeoisie." *Public Culture* 5, no. 1 (1992): 19–44; Margaret Abraham, *Speaking the Unspeakable: Marital Violence Among South Asian Immigrants in the United States* (Princeton, NJ: Rutgers UP, 2000).

16 *The Lowland*, 150.

17 Jyoti Puri, *Woman, Body, Desire in Post-colonial India* (New York: Routledge, 1999): 136.

18 The rejection of motherhood as essential to a woman's identity was significant for second wave feminists in the West. Gauri's rejection of motherhood here echoes Doris Lessing's autobiographical novel *A Proper Marriage*, the second in her Children of Violence series, where Martha, the protagonist

leaves her husband and child because she finds marriage and motherhood suffocating. Martha's radical move mirrors that of her creator, Doris Lessing, who also left Rhodesia and her two children when she migrated to the UK. Lessing and her character were both critiqued for their abandonment of a "natural" role for women. See Doris Lessing, *A Proper Marriage*, (London: Michael Joseph, 1954). However, it would be simplistic to see Gauri as uncritically embracing a western feminist perspective as her rejection of motherhood is tied deeply to the trauma of losing Udayan. Both Udayan and Gauri, in theory at least, reject bourgeois family values—including parenting.

19 For a discussion on this issue, please see Sumathi Ramaswamy, *The Goddess and the Nation: Mapping Mother India* (Durham: Duke UP, 2009). See also Charu Gupta, "The Icon of Mother in Late Colonial North India: 'Bharat Mata', 'Matri Bhasha' and 'GauMata'," *Economic and Political Weekly* 36, no. 45 (November 10–16, 2001): 4291–9.

20 For a discussion of gendered ideas of nation see Nira Yuval-Davis, *Gender and Nation* (Thousand Oaks: Sage, 1997).

21 *The Lowland*, p. 234.

22 Ibid 236.

23 Ibid 165.

Bibliography

Abraham, Margaret. *Speaking the Unspeakable: Marital Violence among South Asian Immigrants in the United States*. Princeton, NJ: Rutgers U P, 2000.

Agnihotri, Indu, and Vina Mazumdar. "Changing Terms of Political Discourse: Women's Movement in India, 1970s–1990s." *Economic and Political Weekly* 30.29 (1995): 1869–78.

Basu, Srimathi. "The Public, the Familiar, and the Intimate in South Asia." *Journal of Women's History* 24.1 (2012): 180–7.

Bhatt, Amy, and Nalini Iyer. *Roots and Reflections: South Asians in the Pacific Northwest*. Seattle: U of Washington P, 2013.

Bhattacharjee, Annanya. "The Habit of Ex-Nomination: Nation, Woman, and the Immigrant Bourgeoisie." *Public Culture* 5.1 (1992): 19–44.

Grewal, Inderpal. *Transnational America: Feminisms, Diasporas, Neoliberalisms*. Durham, NC: Duke U P, 2005.

Gupta, Charu. "The Icon of Mother in Late Colonial North India: 'Bharat Mata', 'Matri Bhasha' and 'GauMata'." *Economic and Political Weekly* 36.45 (November 10–16, 2001): 4291–9.

Lahiri, Jhumpa. *The Interpreter of Maladies*. Boston, MA: Mariner Books, 1999.

Lahiri, Jhumpa. *The Namesake*. Boston, MA: Mariner, 2003.

Lahiri, Jhumpa. *The Lowland*. New York: Knopf, 2013.

Lau, Lisa. "Re-Orientalism: The Perception and Development of Orientalism by Orientals." *Modern Asian Studies* 43.2 (2009): 571–90.

Lessing, Doris. *A Proper Marriage*. London: Michael Joseph, 1954.

Puri, Jyoti. *Woman, Body, Desire in Post-colonial India: Narratives of Gender and Sexuality*. New York: Routledge, 1999.

Ramaswamy, Sumathi. *The Goddess and the Nation: Mapping Mother India*. Durham, NC: Duke U P, 2009.

Ranasinha, Ruvani. *Contemporary Diasporic South Asian Women's Fiction: Gender, Narration, and Globalisation.* London: Palgrave, 2016.

Ray, Raka. *Fields of Protest: Women's Movements in India.* Minneapolis: U of Minnesota P, 1999.

Roy, Mallarika Sinha. "Rethinking Female Militancy in Postcolonial Bengal." *Feminist Review* 101.1 (2012):124–31.

Roy, Srila. "Revolutionary Marriage: On the Politics of Sexual Stories in Naxalbari." *Feminist Review* 83 (2006): 99–118.

Visweswaran, Kamala. "Gendered States: Rethinking Culture as a Site of South Asian Human Rights Work." *Human Rights Quarterly* 26.2 (2004): 483–511.

Yuval-Davis, Nira. *Gender and Nation.* Thousand Oaks, CA: Sage, 1997.

14 The Whole Inside the Hole

Recent Telugu Dalit Women's Revolutionary Life Writing

Bonnie Zare

Telugu Dalit women's short stories and life writings have historically been derided for their blunt tone and lack of imagery. Stories written by marginalized writers are repeatedly dismissed as raw tales of protest. Recalling Stuart Hall's directive to attend to subaltern acts as a "historical-cultural force, [that] has constantly interrupted, limited and disrupted everything else" (1996: 140), critics should reject the idea of Dalit short stories as mere expressions of anger, and acknowledge their variety. This essay argues that recent stories by Telugu Dalit women writers deserve recognition for effectively revolutionizing form and content. Regarding form, in stories such as Jajula Gowri's "The Mud-Rice" (2004; English translation 2012), "Fence" (2004; English 2012), and "I am Like None Other" (2004; English 2012), Jupaka Subadra's "Horror in the Bathroom" (2003; English 2012), "Postcard from Rayakka" (year not available; English 2012), and Gogu Shyamala's "A Small Basket-like Mother is better than an Elephant-like Father" (2003; English 2012), to name just a few, writers deliberately use brevity and everyday language to contest a privileged, self-claimed "completeness" of the self. These writers step away from dominant major genres of Telugu literature, such as autobiography and the formal short story, and create a new aesthetic space, speaking out from a hole—created by deprivation of basic rights—to form a larger whole, a representation suggesting both the hole's depth but also the ability to imagine another way to live both as an individual and as part of a community.

Along with establishing the seriousness and appropriateness of the short form, these writers present new content: many women writers convey a noticeably expansive relationship to the body and honor bodily knowledge. For centuries philosophical traditions from both East and West have elevated men by claiming men represent the mind and women the body. These authors are having none of that. For example, Vinodini's "Block" (2008; English translation 2015), "The Parable of the Lost Daughter" (2008; English 2013), and Jupaka Subadra's "Horror in the Bathroom" (2003; 2013) establish the body as essential to, even indivisible from, the spirit and mind. To elaborate, whether readers are influenced by orthodox Brahminical philosophy or by Cartesian dualism

Figure 14.1 The writer M.M. Vinodini in 2014 (photographed by Bonnie Zare).

to see the body as inferior, these stories show the absurdity of strictly separating mind and body or keeping material, mental, and spiritual realms far apart. This work powerfully asserts that embodiment itself may be our most important teacher.

To better understand the context of the autobiographical stories discussed in this essay, some brief background on Telugu Dalit writing is in order. Because of their economic vulnerability, social marginalization and stigma, it was only at the time of India's Independence that Dalit people gained access to education, and even today literacy rates are low; merely 39% of Dalit women read and write, and there is a sharp economic divide between rural and urban populations. Yet, despite the small numbers, strong creative voices have emerged. Fueled by the example of the Maharashtra Dalit Panthers of the late 1970s and 1980s,[1] revolutionary thinkers from other language groups turned to poetry and story to push Ambedkar's message of equality, empowerment, and political representation. Aided by the Adi-Dravida and Adi-Andhra movements originating from 1917 to 1940 and the self-respect and reservation movements,[2] many groups formed in Andhra, not only to protest discriminatory acts but to articulate their identity via creative means.

By the 1990s Telugu Dalit women's writing had been appearing in many serial publications, and in 2003 *Nalla Poddu* [*Black Dawn*], the first volume to document the history of Telugu Dalit women's writing, was released by Hyderabad Book Press.[3] The ensuing debates about the literary quality of these fifty-four writers became a mobilizing point for a variety of writers and activists.[4] The first English anthology of Dalit Telugu women writers, translated by K. Suneetha Rani, appeared in 2012, thus expanding these authors' reach and further establishing Dalit writers' place on the literary landscape.

It is also important to mark three sources of overlapping oppression that Telugu Dalit women writers confront. First, canonical literature does not easily make room for stories by marginalized people. Second, writers do not necessarily feel unified amongst each other (and able to promote each other's work): Malas and Madigas instead cope with internal conflict between their sub-caste groups.[5] Finally, rigid ideas about gender potentially trouble a Dalit woman writer's identity construction. As their identity is whittled down by multiple external forces, it is no wonder that many of these writers choose to avoid speaking as the autonomous capital "I," an "I" that demonstrates mastery. Instead, many stories speak their truths in a small and collective "I," though their approaches differ.[6]

Much of Telugu Dalit writing draws on personal experience but defies the conventions of autobiography, particularly the Western tradition of tracing an honorable individual's chronological journey of development. Telugu Dalit women's recent life writings offer an alternative autobiographics, to use Leigh Gilmore's term; that is, they "follow a route of estrangement from dominant codes of meaning" (Gilmore, 1994: 6). As Telugu Madiga writer Vemula Yellaiah says, "[T]his is a life without embellishments, and characters with no halo" (Satyanarayana and Tharu 2013: 790). Jajula Gowri's "The Mud-Rice" illustrates this much larger pattern.

Gowri, who was born in 1967, is active in regional political movements in Andhra Pradesh and has a large body of short stories to her name. The four-page story "The Mud-Rice" tells of a childhood memory, beginning with "I have always seen quarrels at home from my childhood onwards." From further dialogue between the mother and father, the reader learns that the father's wages might as well be alcohol itself for all the family sees of his earnings. Often when father drinks, mother and the children get hit. Moreover, the mother and children live in constant physical hunger. All of this is reported in a matter-of-fact way that causes the reader to think beyond the speaking voice to all the voices who could repeat this story: many evenings ended, the speaker says, by lying in the dark feeling tears streaming down her face.

> Father beat her up and mother abused him. We felt like weeping on seeing this. I looked at my younger sister and lied down weeping. We didn't know when we fell asleep weeping. We didn't know if it was dawn by the time both of them went to sleep after those quarrels. We did not know.
>
> (Rani, *Flowering*: 201)

After a time, the father has difficulty obtaining work, and one morning, there is no breakfast. "My stomach was burning," the narrator states. Over the course of the morning, the daughter tries everything to get food—pleading with her mother, crying, drinking water, avoiding the sun's blistering rays. After a few more hours of non-stop hunger the girl gets dizzy; she sits down and weakly palms some mud as a distraction. A moment later she sees the pebbles have fallen away. "It had a fragrance about it. That's it; quickly I put it into my mouth. I kept eating until my hunger subsided" (205). Returning to the house, she finds her brother has arrived with a measure of rice, but the girl drinks a vessel of water quickly, lies down, and falls asleep. The story ends with the mother and siblings staring at the girl, stupefied at her contentment. Waking up later, in a bit of a daze, she says, "I didn't know what happened to me" (205). Because readers know just a bit about the girl and are so closely focused on her quest for one simple food item, the humble last words allow the reader to consider the girl, not solely as an individual, but as a stand-in for any struggling child in the world's community. The four-page story's brevity is the secret to its impact, carrying the reader so quickly to the girl's wonder at eating dirt. Hunger makes one vulnerable, yet the author consistently prevents readers from feeling distant or condescending. All of us are just a few steps away from seeing the foulest dirt as sustenance.

Although contemporary Dalit women writers have chosen to operate as outliers and are unafraid to redefine every genre, critics have seemed uncertain as to how to value a short sketch such as this one, which is only four pages. Short pieces are often passed over, and naming the genre becomes a challenge in itself. Susie Tharu has suggested the genre be called "little story" rather than "short story" (Scholars 2012): the word "little" is meant to acknowledge both the importance of the little magazine in which many of the stories first appear and the world of little, subaltern traditions. Some English readers, however, may hear "little story" as patronizing. To me, the phrase may dismiss what has spurred the stories: the enormity of the conditions of physical want and large-scale suffering. Because the stories often contain a high percentage of autobiographical material,[7] a more accurate classification is life writing.[8] These works follow the tendency in subcontinental autobiography to describe a worldview without emphasis on a separate and particular speaker. Instead, readers are immersed in a web of other lives, learning not mainly about one person but about their interconnection with "family, kin, caste, religion and gender" (Arnold and Blackburn 2004: 19). Indeed, in the context of full-scale Dalit autobiography, Raj Kumar says "that the autobiographical 'I' does not have an autonomous life outside the collective 'we'" (Kumar 2010: 232). Not having been raised to speak with public authority, women writers are even more likely to speak as a collective, transposing personal experiences to attest to a whole group's extreme suffering.

Unsurprisingly, Telugu Dalit women's stories also incorporate subversive subject matter, including what has formerly been seen as unmentionable in literature. Female authors, for example, are more likely to explore and question, rather than simply report, marital rape and physical violence against girls and women. Furthermore, as mentioned earlier, the authors do not accept the classic separation of mind and body. As Elizabeth Spelman's essay "Woman as Body: Ancient and Contemporary Views" reminds us, in the time of Plato, subjects marked as socially inferior were guilty by their association with the body. The grounds for women's lesser status were "similar to those given for the inferiority of slaves to masters, children to fathers, animals to humans" (Spelman 1982: 20). It is fair to say that Western philosophy, highly influenced by ancient Greek culture, has not celebrated the body. Somatophobia, which leads to both sexist and racist frames of reference, also operates forcefully in the context of simultaneous caste and gender discrimination. Stories such as Vinodini's "Block" and "The Parable of the Lost Daughter" and Jupaka Subadra's "Horror in the Bathroom" oppose somatophobia. They show the possibilities of a transpersonal lived body, a body that can be experienced as dominantly unitary and companionate with other bodies in the world.

To better highlight the philosophical stance in these stories, it is worthwhile to remind ourselves of traditional views. In the context of Brahminical Hindu thought, the school of philosophy known as yoga samkkya asserts that humanity's goal must be to transcend bodily attachment. In order to soar beyond materiality, one must subdue all sensory information and the workings of the mind itself. Patanjali, writing the definitive *Yoga Sutra* in the third century AD, clarifies:

Tranquility of thought comes...when the mind's activity,
arisen in the sense world, is held still....
...When concepts formed from knowledge
based on words and their meanings taint it, contemplative poise is
broken....

(Miller 1996: 35, 41–2)

As Barbara Miller elaborates, Patanjali fears seekers will welcome a
"false identification" "between material nature and spirit," an identification produced by the mind, which is inferior to the divine spirit
(Miller 1996: 78). All material, including things and processes of the
body come to seem impure, tainted by their ability to create attachment.
Sacred texts and stories about the god Siva, for instance, extol the high
spiritual quality to be gained from sexual abstinence. The containment
of semen is worshipped as a sign of strength, thereby denigrating any
bodily flow from inside to outside. In sum, attention to bodily knowledge and processes ultimately cannot coexist with an ideal inward focus.

This idea continues to be very pervasive today in ashrams and spiritual communities. A strong line is drawn between prakriti (or, matter
including mental matter or thoughts) and purusa (a sublime or transcen-
dent consciousness).[9] Notably, prakriti is a feminine word, a word for
generative fertility, and a carrier of energy but energy that is inextricably
earth-bound and therefore inferior and illusory. As long as prakriti and
purusha are separate, there is hierarchy: males look down upon females,
higher priestly castes (who can afford more time for introspection) look
down upon castes who labor in the soil. Significantly, however, some revered thinkers have questioned both caste divisions and bodily impurity.
For instance, two beloved low-caste saints or holy men of the fifteenth
century did not exactly embrace the body, but firmly defied the notion
that low-caste bodies were less pure than high caste ones. The poet Kabir
proclaimed we are all united by our bodily existence:

Says Kabir: No one is lowly born....

(KG pad 182, Hawley 1988: 54)

Why be so proud of this useless, used-up body?
One moment dead, and it's gone.
How nicely you adorn it with sugar and butter and milk:
Once the breath goes out, it's fit to burn.

(KG pad 62, Hawley 1988: 54)

Similarly, Ravidas, the cobbler-poet of Benares, felt lowly conditions
belonged to all: "No living being is spared the degradations of the
flesh, and whoever prefers to think otherwise is dwelling in a world of
make-believe" (Hawley 1988: 11). Moving to the early twentieth century, one should also remember the Ramnami tradition in central India,

based on the wandering monk Swami Ramdas.[10] Ramdas accepted the body as a vehicle for conveying kindness.[11]

> When we feed, clothe and attend on anybody, we feel like doing all these things to our own body, for which we do not expect any return or praise...because all bodies are our own; for, we as the all-pervading Atman or Spirit reside in all bodies.
>
> (Qtd. in Leder 1990: 163)

Despite the traditional Brahminical emphasis on body and thoughts as distractions from the highest spiritual realm, Kabir, Ravidas, and Ramdas affirm a Hindu acceptance of the body and a belief in human interdependence through bodily needs.

Dalit women authors tend to suggest a new understanding of the body as a spiritual teacher in itself. Though, of course, she would avoid such Brahminical words as purusa, authors such as the Telugu writer M. M. Vinodini expand the parameters for how purusa or divine consciousness may unfold: in this world, we grow more divine by accepting our existence as limited bodies. The story "Block" most powerfully conveys a rethinking of the body as teacher. "The Parable of the Lost Daughter" also emphasizes the essential contributions of the body.

M. M. Vinodini has become well-known as a Telugu writer with a bold tone who is unafraid to express the experiences of women in particular. As a young woman, she sought to abolish untouchability practices in Telangana villages and continues her activism while teaching Telugu literature at Yogi Vemana University. Three of her works have appeared in English anthologies: the poem "All Indians are My Brothers and Sisters" (2003), the story "Maria" (2012), and the story "The Parable of the Lost Daughter (2013)."[12]

In "Block," we are introduced to Jilakaramma, a collector of human waste, and we follow her on her rounds. She becomes synonymous with human waste and the tools she carries to scrape it up: we see her weaving her way between narrow alleys, carrying soil on her head, and when the rain brings it down in slops her body becomes a longer version of her broom. In the houses she serves, the people treat her the same as they treat material waste, forcing out two rupees to her while figuratively holding their noses. Beyond surviving on her meagre wages and braving daily stigma, we learn Jilakaramma is faced with a dilemma: her daughter's reputation is entwined with a man whose father is demanding one thousand rupees by the end of the month for her first instalment of dowry. Jilakaramma has no family to turn to for aid: her husband beat her right after she gave birth and left with another woman. Though she has worked for the local Brahmin households for the past twenty-five years, they will not give her an advance of any money. So she and her bosom friend hatch a plan: she will first block her regular households' toilets (with stones) so the area will become a huge stench, and then collect extra fees to repair the toilets. Readers will be aware of the recent Dalit protests in Gujarat (July 2016) and elsewhere against gau rakshaks—cow protectors thrashing Dalits on the pretext of the mistreatment of cows. In the Gujarati city of Una, for example, laborers were merely carrying out the task of skinning a dead cow, a job their extended family had been expected to do for generations. After these four youths were beaten, some protested by creating a pile of dead cows in front of government offices; some attempted suicide; others refused to skin cows found dead, declaring "those people can clean up their own filth." By August, thousands declared they would no longer help to skin cows while the government failed to provide water, electricity, and other services to areas mainly occupied by Dalit villagers. While a group action will gain more attention on the world stage, Jilakaramma's own small act of protest is quite significant within her situation as an abandoned wife who has never before shown the least sign of resistance.

The plan likely would have worked if Jilakaramma had been sneakier: rather than blocking all of the toilets at once, which invited suspicion, she could have done one or two at a time. However, she and her mate do not have such calculating minds. Six men wait for her at the end of the day, and they hurl abuses at her, repeatedly kicking Jilakaramma in the stomach. Desperate to hold onto the fortune that will ensure her daughter's future, she does not remove the money tied close to her belly. The men strip her in imagery reminiscent of Draupadi and finally one particularly vengeful man physically beats her to near death. There is a break in time, and the story ends with the following words:

> She didn't get the month-wise wages promptly for the job she had rendered for twenty-five long years…Neither bonus nor increments….
>   There was a blockage, and Kotilaxmi's wedding did not take place.
>
> (Vinodini 2013: 17)

This is more than a heart-wrenchingly sad tale. Yes, Jilakaramma is a victim of casteism, economic inequality, governmental neglect, and human cruelty. Over and above this, however, the story questions the mind-body split, insisting on our existence as both spirit-carrying and embodied beings. Consider the scene in which the protagonist clears heaps of waste collecting in the blocked toilets. The reader is not spared: "The shit appeared as severely fermented dark flour, stinking unbearably. A hair was floating here and there. The white worms had bored in here and there and were swarming in groups" (11); eventually these worms make their way up Jilakaramma's legs. We come to feel she has paid for her deception already by having to become one with such objectionable matter. Returning to the tradition of Ramdas, recall that he proclaimed "all human bodies are our own; for, we as the all-pervading Atman or Spirit reside in all bodies" (Ramdas qtd. in Perry 1971: 598). The worms may be disgusting, but the point is not to horrify the reader without reason. As she scrapes both worms and shit away, Jilakaramma of "Block" is treating all bodies as her own; by being so steadfast about the soil, figuratively she is also wiping the infants' behinds and cleaning the air of any repugnant smell—she is caring for these people who would otherwise have stench-filled nostrils as they tended their beautiful front gardens and write the love verses described early on in the story. Living in such an economically precarious situation, she might be so bitter as to steal or to clean only superficially, but instead this woman is steadfast in her sacrifice despite the utter disgust shown her by the people she serves.

Meeting Jilakaramma, we move with a person of dignity and proficiency. Who before has written about people in this profession with such empathy? Perhaps this is best shown in the following passage, when we learn Jilakaramma possesses an unusual kind of understanding:

> Somebody like Jilakaramma could easily know it all—what exact kind of stench would waft—when eating *biryani* or pulses; what kind of colour the turds would be corresponding to the curries one might've eaten; how powerfully one would defecate having eaten curry with pickle or tamarind juice; whether the shit was due to a pill, or loose-motions; how the kids would defecate and how the ailing ones would; how the ones who frequently visit the toilet would defecate; how one would defecate on the fourth day after a spell of three days of constipation; how to recognize the shit of the ones who ate and drank to the extent of bursting their bellies... Jilakaramma could easily know it all.
>
> (3)

In such a passage, fluids are not mere waste, but carriers of knowledge.

Having read this story, we will stuff ourselves and sit to relieve ourselves again, but maybe not without thinking about this process, some remembrance that our body carries information as it purges itself. Spirit seems to exist in all the fluids, even our waste products. If service is part of dharma, attending to bodily processes cannot be an exception.

Another short story, "The Parable of the Lost Daughter," though less obviously focused on the body, still forcefully depicts it as a place of primal identity. Loosely referencing the tale of the prodigal son in the Gospel of Luke, this story depicts a college student, Suvarthavani, who is hell bent on erasing every trace of her Christian religion and caste background. She polices herself to gain a foothold in her close friend's Brahmin household, a household headed by a father who has written books decrying the caste system. Sharply criticizing her own family members' habits to their faces, she judges her happiness to depend on shunning customs she used to relish, such as eating steaming meat from the bone. She now piously pastes a bindi on her forehead and is quick to draw distinctions between clean and unclean physical spaces. The tension grows as this young woman's strenuous efforts are only partially accepted by the Brahmin family she cares so much to impress.

Near the end of the story, Suvarthavani is staying with her friend's family but her friend is away, and two unexpected events occur. Riding on the back of her friend's brother's motorcycle, this man suddenly insists she tell him what sexual act she is ready to perform. He says she must be ready for fun because as a Christian she obviously has no purity to protect. Suvarthavani angrily shakes off his humiliating suggestions and enters the house. A short while later she overhears the supposedly progressive father angrily cussing out his wife because of some carpenters who have been there. He yells, "What have you been doing all day…displaying your body to those low caste bastards? You rotten old whore…you mala bitch…you madiga bitch…You act just like those low-caste bitches" (Vinodini 2013: 766). Suddenly, the happiness she has imagined fades into a mirage. Hearing this hypocrisy, the microaggressions of the past months begin to haunt her.

We last see her throwing the bottu (bindi) packet into the dustbin and leaving her forehead clear as well as restoring her hidden Jesus pendant to her neck. As she departs the house forever, she is asked about her missing bottu. She states, "No, Mother. I haven't forgotten. I am a Christian girl. I am a Dalit girl," and steps outside without waiting for a reply. When Suvarthavani decides to not only accept herself and her family but also assert herself as a whole and not a part, she uses her outer body to convey her inner unity and integrity. One cannot transform one's spiritual self by leaving the body behind—matter and spirit are interdependent.

"Horror in the Bathroom," by Jupaka Subadra, who has published poems and stories in a number of Telugu serials, conveys a moment of crisis centered on the young female body. The story begins by describing the squalid conditions of the average college hostel available to unprivileged young women. The girls are herded like cattle into a cowshed where they have hole-like rooms and must fight for a mugful of water to wash in. Running inside and outside the place are dogs and pigs. The story goes on to explain how the girls in their hostel, which does supply water, are blackmailed into lying about the hostel's conditions. The Warden compels the girls to state they are fed well and pockets the government subsidy she has saved by providing no weekly meat and only an irregular supply of vegetables. The students, whether young, intermediate, or undergraduate, must bow to the Warden's will or she arbitrarily fabricates a reason to send them away for good.

One day, the students return from college to find the hostel at a stand-still. The workers have found a "thick spread of blood in the bathroom" and a grim search is on for the girl who miscarried or aborted an embryo. No girl is hiding, and no girl looks weak from blood loss. The staff wonders aloud about this "sin" asking where is the "whore" and "whose life is ruined?" The narrator states, "Although we had not done anything wrong, agitation and anxiety were seen on our faces as if we had done something" (2012: 184). Interrogations begin. The warden subjects many students to the third degree: "Although she insulted and battered our basic necessities, habits, poverty, hearts and castes more than the police [would have], it [the confession] did not come out" (185). Fearing for her reputation, the Warden calls them ungrateful parasites of the government, dogs who are attracted to filth. Every girl who has attained puberty is to be rounded up and brought to the hospital. There, an elder girl explains, "They will check the stomach, unclothe us and check between the legs with a tester." Desperately afraid, the girls silently get ready, fully aware that if they do not cooperate they might "have to take the dirty blame" for the blood in the bathroom (186). The narrator asks herself, "But how to shamelessly take off the clothes for the tests? Why was this abortion test decided for girls though the warden was a woman?" (186). Hierarchies based on class, caste, and age trump any potential gender solidarity. The absolute silence about a male is striking: clearly one specific gendered body remains clean and therefore free. A search for the impregnator is not even mentioned; it is expected that women are the sole guilty party in an act with a sexual nature. The story builds to a fever pitch as the speaker decides that although she could be turned out of the hostel and thereby lose her chance at a college degree, she will refuse the medical exam. When the girl defies authority, the Warden becomes an animal, barking like a dog "whose ears are severed...'I will see how you will stay in the hostel'" (191).

The tests do not reveal anyone who might be connected to the blood in the bathroom, and when the girls return "many people covered themselves without even having food as if they had lost something. Some people wept." Clearly the girls suffer from the physical invasiveness and humiliation of the physical exam forced on to them by the Warden's order. With no person identified and the girl's defiance still on the minds of the staff, the atmosphere is tense. The girl has an anxious, nearly sleepless night, and the story ends with her awakening to workers' screams. The reader's suspense is heightened by uncertainty, for we hear the workers saying, "To hell with this bitch. Drive her away so that she doesn't come again." "Probably this is the one who soiled the bathroom yesterday." "...Ayyo, how much suffering and weeping fell on the children! We didn't know about this dog" (189). The double meaning of bitch as a repellent woman makes the culprit seem to be human until we get to the actual word dog. The girl's last words may unsettle the reader: "Hearing all this, …I got up happily and ran downstairs thinking that the warden cannot do anything against me" (189). While the girl is a critic of a corrupt and casteist hostel system, she has not yet fully spread her wings of courage, for she has only just discovered she possesses them. As the story ends, the small personal voice shrinks ominously, for this girl's momentary courage surprises even herself; will this quality reappear in such an environment? It is uncertain. The event was a non-crime—or was it? The actual crime has become publicly challenging the warden, and the reader knows the warden now will be looking for any excuse to punish this girl. Further injustice is merely postponed for now.

As with "The Mud-Rice," the narrator uses an objective tone throughout the story and thereby avoids heavy-handedness. And, similar to the speaker of "The Mud-Rice," the speaking "I" in "Horror" perceives herself as an assemblage of potentials rather than presenting herself as a singular "I." Of greatest significance, however, is the way the story highlights discrimination against women's bodies for their irregularity or inherent dirtiness. From culture to culture, honoring the concept of mastery and autonomy creates a hierarchy that shuns any sign of dependence as a sign of inferiority. By this "logic," as Elizabeth Grosz (1994) has argued—drawing on a long line of theorists including Mary Douglas and Julia Kristeva—woman, who sheds blood monthly, is a seeper and contaminator, not a self-cleansing person. She threatens the social system by symbolizing that which is outside of mental control. By menstruating, a woman is uncontainable: she loses any association with mastery. This story demonstrates that the true horror is not blood in the bathroom but the rounding up of all nearby young women like cattle to have the private areas of their body invaded against their will. Rather than simply showing how a woman's life is scripted around her body, "Horror in the Bathroom" confirms that gender and a false definition of bodily purity may operate as a life sentence.[13]

Not content to merely tell a tragic story, women writers such as Vinodini and Subadra force us to acknowledge the symbiotic relationship between the body and mind, to group purusa together with prakriti. "The Parable of the Lost Daughter" urges us to wear our identity markers with pride and build bridges through our bodies. Even more strikingly, "Block" suggests all of us can be reduced to our bodily output, and yet that our behavior to others may render us lower than our waste itself. Stories such as "Block" and "Horror in the Bathroom" also bring to light stigmatized female experience such as gendered violence and the policing of women's sexuality by other women. Women, in cultures around the world, have been rigidly separated from men as having inferior or at least specially demarcated bodies. Whether being typed as sexual gatekeepers, femme fatales, baby makers, or physical weaklings, they are in a unique position to bring us closer to our bodily processes, liquids, and ways of knowing. Through these stories, for instance, readers become more inclined to value women such as Jilakaramma who take care of bodies, and to value the companionship of body and mind to the advantage of both.

Gail Omvedt declares that Dalit literature is in danger of stagnating, becoming too identified with only one perspective, a perspective she believes will likely narrow even more because of the social and political fragmentation surrounding Dalit communities (Ananthamurthy and Omvedt 2010). Omvedt's warning appears to forget how newly literate these writers are. For instance, although Vinodini's mother can read a bit of scripture, she cannot write, and Vinodini's siblings still live in thatched homes. Gowri had only three years of English instruction before she was married off at the age of thirteen, and her schooling stopped until decades later when she finally gained "the funds and the fight" to enroll in distance education at Dr. B.R. Ambedkar Open University. As Gowri describes, "Up to 1970 my family did not know...even alphabets of any language....Dalits, particularly Dalit women could not even dream about education" (personal interview 2012).

While not all of these writers would embrace the term "feminist" because of its frequent association with (and use by) Western educated, high caste, and upper-class people, these authors forcefully and memorably articulate the concerns of women in their community. While they are gaining some attention within literary and academic circles from the desire to enlarge the literary landscape and be more inclusive, their opportunities to publish are still very limited. Telugu magazines and Sunday newspaper supplements will at times publish stories of Dalit experience, but often these writers are relegated to the sidelines, waiting for small-circulation serials to accept a piece or two. After writing a sufficient number of stories to form a book, they frequently choose self-publishing (as both Gowri and Vinodini have done) in favor of receiving yet another rejection from a publishing industry which approximately 90% of the time publishes work only by authors who are already known or who write on more expected conventional literary themes. Yet, readers of all backgrounds need these stories, perhaps now more than ever. Over the past year, protestors against cow-related lynchings and threats have allied themselves with the agitation for the restoration of farm land, particularly the state government's promise to give two hectares of land to each Dalit family affected by this abuse or by former displacements stemming from governmentally supported dam projects, for instance. As one case in point, local media is revealing the many atrocities suffered by the extended Sarvaiya family in Una whose support of a cross-caste marriage, involvement in cow removal, and economic good fortune created heated resentment amongst local Koli (OBC) families (Mondal 2016). The January 2016 suicide of Dalit University of Hyderabad student Rohith Vemula following acute harassment by some administrators; and the arrest of JNU Student Union President Kanhaiya Kumar for sedition after speaking at an event to protest the 2013 hanging of Kashmiri separatist Mohammed Afzal Guru expose authorities' brutal constraints on freedom occurring at institutes of higher education. Under Prime Minister Modi and BJP leadership, India has experienced an increase of rape against Dalit women (by 7% in 2015) and a yearly rise in crimes against Dalit community members (by 19% in 2015). Powerful narratives from these sections of society will strengthen the country's unity in the long run.

Writers from newly literate communities may choose a restricted canvas on which to paint, but the painting is not thereby deficient. Not noble savages, distantly embodying some "ongoing human connection to the land," Dalit people's stories demonstrate the dignity of a people formerly classified as dirt. After one feels the entreaties of an empty stomach ("The Mud-rice") or the terror of seeing a man crushing one's screaming sister ("Maria") one cannot abandon these girls "to a space of historical amnesia" (Gilmore 2001: 15). Furthermore, in all of these stories, the authors are engaged in transforming the genre of autobiography. While Mohandas K Gandhi and Edidamu Satyavati[14] chose to narrate their life chronologically and give the account of an individualized speaker, such an authoritative, formal, and literary tone is more likely to emerge from a culture that is allowed to believe that life is "linear and plausible." Why should Dalit authors be expected to replicate what has come before? From the authors Jajula Gowri, Vinodini, and Jupaka Subadra, we learn that life is sometimes most accurately captured in a fragment told by a desubjectified or collective "I." The writers match form to content, deliberately using fragments to express life as a fragment, the whole speaking out from a hole. Above all, this wholeness helps us reflect on the close relationship of body and mind, the unreality of trauma and the enigmatic but strong nature of survival.

Acknowledgements

The author is grateful to Antoinette DeNapoli for her helpful suggestions and to the audiences at the University of Hyderabad and the South Asia Literary Association Conference in Vancouver who heard earlier versions of this manuscript.

Notes

1 This Marathi group was founded by Namdeo Dhasal, Raja Dhale, and Arun Kamble in 1972. They chose the name Dalit Panthers in reference to the US civil rights group, the Black Panthers, to signal their similar demand for substantive improvements in the human rights of Dalit citizens. They organized marches and rallies, and created slogans stressing the need for direct action. See the Dalit Panther Manifesto in *The Exercise of Freedom: An Introduction to Dalit Writing*, edited by K. Satyanarayana and Susie Tharu (Delhi: Navayana Publishers, 2013).

2 In the first decades of the twentieth century, 50,000 people in two districts, Guntur and Kurnool, renamed themselves Adi-Andhras; at roughly the same time some Tamil groups adopted the name Adi-Dravida to call attention to their long and prominent history. Adi means first born, or original inhabitants, and thus the names countered scriptural authority and an ideology of class inferiority. The names reminded the public that the depressed classes or scheduled classes had been conquered by Aryan nomads rather than having less claim to the land. Self-respect refers to the social movement begun by Tamil leader EV Ramasamy (also known as Periyar) in 1925. He argued that freedom from discrimination began with the cultivation of individual self-respect. The reservation movement beginning in the 1980s (after the release of Parliament's Mandal Commission Report) called for the reservation of government jobs and university seats for the scheduled castes similar to the ones in the Lok Sabha and state legislative assemblies guaranteed in the Constitution of India.

3 The editor Gogu Shyamala has done a remarkable service by proving for the first time that low-caste writers such as Lingamma, Kalavva, Lakkamma, and Mallamma were creating texts in twelfth century A.D. See *Flowering from the Soil: Dalit Women's Writing from Telugu*, translated by K. Suneetha Rani, 201–5. (Hyderabad: Aneka Books, 2012): 4.

4 The Foreword explains how Christian missionaries helped women gain education and feel sufficiently encouraged to voice their stories in writing. Rani, *Flowering*, 5.

5 The Madiga are the very lowest caste group of the local hierarchy in Andhra Pradesh.

6 I am grateful to Afsar Mohammed for discussions about the triple marginalization of this group of women.

7 This was confirmed in personal interviews with Jajula Gowri and Vinodini as well.

8 Feminist critic Shari Benstock persuasively made the case for expanding the category of autobiography to include life writing, a term that would encompass women's memoirs, diaries, letters, and the bildungsroman. See Shari Benstock, *The Private Self: Theory and Practice of Women's Autobiographical Writings* (Chapel Hill: University of North Carolina Press, 1988).

9 This is carried out in the west as well. I quote at length from the Vancouver YinYoga.com site: "Consciousness resides only in purusha, or more properly, as purusha. Purusha, pure and distant, is beyond subject and object.... Purusha simply just is. But, because of the presence of prakriti, purusha gets attracted to nature in the way a man is attracted when he watches a beautiful woman dancing. He cannot help but try to get closer. And then the disaster occurs: purusha becomes trapped inside prakriti.... Purusha gets more and more entangled in prakriti. Soon purusha forgets that it was ever separate and ceases to struggle to regain its freedom."

10 Ramdas' lifelong practice was to view the world as various aspects of Ram; he also dismissed all caste markers.

11 See Ramdas Lamb, *Rapt in the Name: The Ramnamis, Ramnam, and Untouchable Religion in Central India* (Albany: SUNY Press, 2002).

12 See *Flowering from the Soil: Dalit Women's Writing from Telugu*, edited and translated by Suneetha Rani (Delhi: Prestige Books International, 2012) and *Steel Nibs are Sprouting: New Dalit Writing from South India Dossier II Kannada and Telugu*, edited by K. Satyarnarayana and Susie Tharu (Noida: HarperCollins, 2013). "Mariya" also appears in *That Man on the Road: Contemporary Telugu Short Fiction*, translated and edited by Ranga Rao (New Delhi: Penguin Books, 2006).

13 I am borrowing the idea of gender as a life sentence from Leigh Gilmore.
14 Edidamu Satyavati, the first woman to write an autobiography in Telugu, was a Brahmin widow; Vijayawada published her book *Atma Caritram* [My Story] in 1934.

Bibliography

Ananthamurthy, U. R. and Gail Omvedt. "Including the Excluded." *YouTube.* Silver Jubilee of IGNOU (Indira Gandhi National Open University), New Delhi, 20 August 2010. www.youtube.com/watch?v=34RiZ_MllU8 Accessed July 1, 2016.

Arnold, David and Stuart Blackburn. *Telling Lives in India: Biography, Autobiography and Life History.* Bloomington: Indiana University Press, 2004.

Gilmore, Leigh. *Autobiographics: A Feminist Theory of Women's Self-Representation.* Ithaca, NY: Cornell University Press, 1994.

Gilmore, Leigh. *The Limits of Autobiography: Trauma and Testimony.* Ithaca, NY: Cornell University Press, 2001.

Gowri, Jajuli. "The Mud-Rice." In Rani, *Flowering,* 201–5, 2012.

Gowri, Jajuli. Interview by Bonnie Zare. Personal interview. University of Hyderabad, January 4, 2012.

Grosz, Elizabeth. *Volatile Bodies: Toward a Corporeal Feminism.* Bloomington: Indiana University Press, 1994.

Hall, Stuart. "On Postmodernism and Articulation: An Interview with Stuart Hall." In *Stuart Hall: Critical Dialogues in Cultural Studies,* edited by David Morley and Kuan Hsing Chen, 131–50. London: Routledge, 1996.

Hawley, John, ed. *Songs of the Saints of India.* New York: Oxford University Press, 1988.

Kumar, Raj. *Dalit Personal Narratives: Reading Caste, Nation and Identity.* Hyderabad: Orient BlackSwan, 2010.

Leder, Drew. *The Absent Body.* Chicago, IL: University of Chicago Press, 1990.

Miller, Barbara Stoler. *Yoga Sutra: A Discipline of Freedom. The Yoga Sutra attributed to Patanjali.* Berkeley: University of California Press, 1996.

Mondal, Sudipto. "Una, Gujarat's Centre of Dalit Protests, Fears Backlash for Its Resistance." *Hindustan Times,* 18 August 2016. www.hindustantimes.com/india-news/una-gujarat-s-centre-of-dalit-protests-fears-backlash-for-its-resistance/story-5uX9goXn1Wj0IO1zSgh8MP.htmlNayar, 2016 Accessed September 10, 2016.

Nayar, Pramod K. "Bama's *Karukku*: Dalit Autobiography as Testimonio." *Journal of Commonwealth Literature,* 41(2): 83–100, 2006.

Perry, Whitall N. *A Treasury of Traditional Wisdom.* New York: Simon & Schuster, 1971.

Rani, Suneetha K., ed. *Flowering from the Soil: Dalit Women's Writing from Telugu.* Translated by Suneetha Rani. Hyderabad: Aneka Books, 2012.

Satyanarayana, K. and Susie Tharu, Eds. *Steel Nibs are Sprouting: New Dalit Writing from South India. Dossier II Kannada and Telugu.* Noida: HarperCollins, 2013.

Scholars without Borders. "Fables without Borders." *Scholars without Borders Blog,* 6 January 2012. http://swblogs.blogspot.com/ Accessed September 20, 2016.

Spelman, Elizabeth. "Woman as Body: Ancient and Contemporary Views." *Feminist Studies*, 8.1 (1982): 109–31.

Subadra, Jupaka. "Horror in the Bathroom." In Rani, *Flowering*, 182–7, 2012.

Vinodini, M. M. "Block." English Translation by K. Purushottam, 2013. Unpublished Manuscript (Under Review). Hindi Translation, "Avaroth" by Shanta Sundari, *Anyatha*, June, 2008.

Vinodini, M. M. "Maria." In Rani, *Flowering*, 258–69, 2012.

Vinodini, M. M. Interview by Bonnie Zare. Personal Interview, January 6. Kadapa, Andhra Pradesh, 2012.

Vinodini, M. M. "The Parable of the Lost Daughter: Luke 15: 11–32." In Satyanarayana and Tharu, *Steel Nibs are Sprouting*, 755–67, 2013.

Index

For Product Safety Concerns and Information please contact our EU
representative GPSR@taylorandfrancis.com
Taylor & Francis Verlag GmbH, Kaufingerstraße 24, 80331 München, Germany